Hermann Leberecht Strack

Hebrew Grammar With Reading Book, Exercises, Literature and Vocabularies

Translated from the German by R.S. Kennedy

Hermann Leberecht Strack

Hebrew Grammar With Reading Book, Exercises, Literature and Vocabularies
Translated from the German by R.S. Kennedy

ISBN/EAN: 9783337316488

Printed in Europe, USA, Canada, Australia, Japan

Cover: Foto ©Paul-Georg Meister /pixelio.de

More available books at **www.hansebooks.com**

HEBREW GRAMMAR

WITH

READING BOOK, EXERCISES,

LITERATURE AND VOCABULARIES

HERMANN L. STRACK.

TRANSLATED FROM THE GERMAN

BY

ARCH^D. R. S. KENNEDY, B. D.,
PROF. OF ORIENTAL LANGUAGES, UNIV. OF ABERDEEN.

SECOND ENLARGED EDITION.

BERLIN,
H. REUTHER'S VERLAGSBUCHHANDLUNG.

LONDON,
LLIAMS & NORGATE
, HENRIETTA STREET,
COVENT GARDEN.

NEW YORK,
B. WESTERMANN & Co
838, BROADWAY.

1889.

From the Preface to the first (German) Edition.

The superabundance of Hebrew grammars which perhaps already exists is not increased by the present work; it takes the place of the grammar of J. H. Petermann (1845 and —simply with new title—1864) which is now no longer in the market. It has been occasioned by a want which has been strongly felt by me for a considerable time. For the initiatory studies of the yearly increasing number of such as begin Hebrew at the university, the otherwise serviceable grammars at present in use are too extensive, besides being either too elementary or too difficult for beginners. Now since the whole of the accidence must, for obvious reasons, be gone over in at most one term, I found myself compelled to occupy the greater part of the time with dictating. Since, however, a new alphabet had to be learned at the same time, this method was attended with serious inconveniences, and the necessity of a printed compendium became every day more apparent. May the book which is now offered to the public as the result of many years' experience as a teacher prove useful to others besides my own students!

As already remarked, I have written in the first place for students wishing to prepare themselves in the shortest possible time for attendance on the easier exegetical lectures

VI

in the university and for the use of more extensive works on the Hebrew language. I feel justified, however, in hoping that my work [particularly since it has been materially enlarged in the second edition] will be found suitable for use in schools, since it discusses only the most important points, these, however, fully and clearly. Irregular forms not mentioned here may be explained by the teacher or looked up in the "Analytical Appendix" of the lexicons. That in a few places* more is offered than is found even in most of the larger grammars will not disturb the beginner, and will be welcomed by not a few other readers.

The present work differs more or less from the Hebrew grammars known to me in the following points:

The vocabulary, with the exception of the exercises in reading, is taken as far as possible from Genesis and Psalms.

All the Hebrew forms in the grammar and in the exercises really occur in the Bible; none have been constructed by the author.** Such hypothetical forms as are adduced simply to explain the genesis of existing forms, and formations that are warned against will in all cases be found transcribed in italics: only too easily does the learner retain precisely that form which he must not use when it is presented to him in Hebrew characters along with other forms.***

---

* §§ 7; 25 $f.g.h$; 28 o; 31 c; 60 k; 64; 65 i; 67; 70; 72; [84 d; 88; 90].

** The unavoidable exceptions are: the forms of קְטַל, certain forms of קוּם in § 71, the paradigms p. 40f., p. 2*ff. [and a few others which are pointed out as they occur].

*** לְחֲלִי, כְּאֲשֶׁר, בִּיהוּדָה, אֶל קְטַל, אֲחָיו, בַּכָּה, פְּרִי, חִרְיֹנִשְׁמֵר and similar monstrosities will be looked for in vain. How the genesis of לְחֲלִי, כְּאֲשֶׁר, בִּיהוּדָה is to be made clear to beginners with Hebrew types is shown in §11g.

The object of the arrangement adopted in the paradigms of the weak verbs, which differs from that usually followed, is to render a mechanical learning by rote impossible. It should also be borne in mind that all "complete paradigms" contain forms that can be justified by no certain analogy. [Should the teacher desire to complete any paradigm he may profitably allow this to be done by the students themselves.]

It is a matter of experience that for years the study of Hebrew is no pleasure to many from the fact that they have not, at the very outset, overcome the difficulties inherent in the reading of unfamiliar characters. To remove these difficulties is the aim of the carefully arranged exercises in reading.

In the exercises for translation so much matter has been condensed into a few pages that whoever has thoroughly mastered the whole is sufficiently prepared to read the easier sections of the Old Testament, and is no longer in need of a reading-book. [Cf. also p. VIII.]

I acknowledge with pleasure the assistance I have derived in my studies from the books cited on p. 11* ff. The following pages however are, directly or indirectly, almost exclusively the product of my own experience as an instructor.

Should they contribute in some degree to a better preparation for the study of the word of God, as contained in the Old Testament scriptures, I shall consider myself richly rewarded for the pains bestowed upon them.

Berlin W., May 6, 1883.

H. L. Strack.

VIII

Preface to the second (German) Edition.

The exceedingly kind reception which my book has met with on the part of both teachers and students*, has served as an incentive to bring it, so far as the shortness of the time permitted, nearer what it aims to be, viz: a short yet scientific grammar of the Hebrew language for beginners.

Apart from quite a number of minor additions and the short §§ 40 and 77, there has been added: first, almost the whole of the syntactical matter, that is not only §§ 81—91 but the bulk of the syntactical remarks in §§ 17—19. 21. 39. 41 f. 46 f. 63 f. The introduction of a part of the syntax into the chapter on the forms seemed to me to be justified by a regard for the practical work of instruction (§ 39 numerals!), and with reference to the space saved. Secondly, § 12 which treats of the syllable and in which the remarks on opened and loosely shut syllables should be carefully noted. Thirdly, the exercises for translation have been enlarged by the addition of a number of sentences, which I have preferred to take from Proverbs in order to give the student at least some acquaintance with the gnomic wisdom of the Old Testament. The wish to have connected pieces for reading and translation I have sought to comply with by adding for six extracts (I Sam. 9. 25; I Kings 3; Psalms 121. 127. 130) such explanatory notes as will enable the student to read

---

* An authorised translation appeared nine months ago in Danish under the title: *Hebraisk Grammatik. I. Hebraisk Formlære af H. L. Strack, oversat af H. Kissmeyer; II. Hebraisk Syntax af Fr. Buhl. Kjøbenhavn* 1885. *Gyldendal.*

them with the help of the appended vocabulary. In this connection it may be observed that the student who has mastered this little grammar, will be able, even without a dictionary, to read a considerable part of Genesis with but little assistance from the instructor.

I have to thank Professor S. R. Driver of Oxford (whose excellent work on the use of the tenses has been of special service to me for §§ 88 and 91) for detailed information on the recent literature in English.

For pages 2*—19* I have preferred Latin to English in order that the type may serve both for the German and for the English edition.

Berlin, August 15, 1885.

H. L. Strack.

PREFACE TO THE SECOND ENGLISH EDITION.

In compliance with requests made to me from various quarters I have prepared as a complement to my Hebrew Grammar Exercises for translation into the Hebrew language. In order to inspire the student with a greater interest in his work I have taken special pains to furnish him at as early a stage as possible with sentences for translation, in addition to the bare grammatical forms. These "Exercises", like the Grammar, are so arranged that the student may begin with the Noun or with the Verb, or may take them together, if he so choose. If he elects to follow the first of the three alternatives just given, he will take the exercises in order, passing over, meanwhile, those sentences in which verbal forms occur,—indicated by their position at the end and by two parallel bars. In the second case, the student, after finishing No. 4, may turn at once to the verbal forms in Nos. 24—30. In the third case he will have to master— before No. 5, the Perf. Qal (also the forms in No. 24), before No. 9, the whole of the Qal (cf. Nos. 25. 26), before No. 10, Niph'al, Pi'ēl, Pu'al (cf. Nos. 27. 28), before No. 21, Hiph'îl, Hoph'al, Hithpa'ēl (cf. Nos. 29. 30).

By far the greater number of the sentences are taken either *verbatim*, or with such modifications as the plan of the work required, from the Old Testament. Those who have had experience in such matters know that the making of such a selection is more difficult than to make up sentences for one's self—a task in which only too many have come to grief.

To render these exercises available also for those who use the well known grammars of Gesenius-Kautzsch (English edition by Dr. E. C. Mitchell 1880) and of Prof. A. B. Davidson I have added the corresponding sections of these grammars at the beginning of each exercise.

Since it is desirable that beginners should be furnished with a larger number of connected passages for translation than is, as yet, to be found in the chrestomathy at the end of the Grammar, I have added in the shape of an appendix such explanatory notes as seem to me necessary for the study of Gen. 1—3 and Psalms 1—3. With the help of these the student will be independent of larger works, as it will be sufficient for him to consult the vocabulary appended to the Grammar. Should a new edition of the latter be called for, the notes here given will be joined to those I have already given pp. 47*—50*.

May these pages likewise contribute to a better preparation for the study of the word of God, as contained in the Old Testament scriptures.

Gross-Lichterfelde near Berlin,
Pentecost, 1889.

H. L. Strack.

NB. $\hat{a}$, $\hat{e}$, $\hat{o}$ denote vowels long by nature or by contraction; $\bar{a}$, $\bar{e}$, $\bar{o}$ tone-long vowels; $\hat{\imath}$ and $\hat{u}$ stand for every long i and u.

The position of the tone is indicated by —́, e.g. מִזְבֵּ֫חַ; pausal forms by —̭.

Where no book is named, the quotation is from Genesis.

Forms occurring only once are accompanied by †; numbers in parentheses indicate how often a form occurs, e. g. § 17 e: בְּיָמִים (8).

"(2!)" and "(3!)" signify that a word may be explained in two or three ways.

'ה=הִי֫הֶ (§9b). ‖ G=Genesis. ‖ ψ=Psalm. ‖ 'פ=פְּלֹ֫נִי aliquis.

Page 13* line 15 read "566" in place of "500".

The Concordance of Schusslowicz gives the passages in full and is therefore more useful than Brecher's work.

ns.

Grammar.

I. Orthography and Phonology (§§ 1—14).

	Page
§ 1. Alphabet	1
§ 2. Pronunciation of the Consonants	3
§ 3. Classification of the Consonants	4
§ 4. Vowels	4
§ 5. Šᵉwâ and Chāṭēph	6
§ 6. Dāghēš, Mappîq, Raphè	8
§ 7. The Accents	9
§ 8. Mèthegh, Maqqēph, Pᵉsîq	13
§ 9. Qᵉrê and Kᵉthîbh	15
§ 10. Peculiarities of certain Consonants	16
§ 11. Changes of Vowels	19
§ 12. Of the Syllable	23
§ 13. Of the Tone	26
§ 14. Of the Pause	27

II. Morphology[1] (§§ 15—80).

A. *The Pronoun* (§§ 15—17).

§ 15. Personal Pronoun	29
§ 16. The remaining Pronouns	30
§ 17. The Article*	31

B. *The Noun* (§§ 18—39).

§ 18. Gender*	34
§ 19. Number*	35
§ 20. Case	35

---

[1] Sections in which syntactical matter is given are indicated by an asterisk (*).

		Page
§ 21.	The Construct State*	37
§ 22.	The Noun with unchangeable Vowels (Paradigms)	39
§ 23.	Masculines with changeable Vowel in the Penult	41
§ 24.	Masculines with changeable Vowel in last Syllable	42
§ 25.	Masculines with two changeable Vowels . .	43
§ 26.	Masculines of one Syllabe with the final Consonant doubled	45
§ 27.	Masculine Segholate Forms	46
§ 28.	A. Masculine Segholate Forms from strong Stems	47
§ 29.	B. Masculine Segholate Forms from ע״י and ע״ו .	50
§ 30.	C. Masculine Segholate Forms from ל״ה . .	51
§ 31.	Masculines from ל״ה with two Vowels . .	51
§ 32.	Feminines with unchangeable Vowels . . .	53
§ 33.	Feminines with one changeable Vowel . .	53
§ 34.	Feminines with two changeable Vowels . .	53
§ 35.	Feminines of Segholate Forms from strong Stems	54
§ 36.	Feminine Segholate Forms	55
§ 37.	Feminines in *ûth* and *îth*	57
§ 38.	Nouns of peculiar Formation	57
§ 39.	Numerals*	59

C. *Particles* (§§ 40—46).

§ 40.	Particles with Suffixes	63
§ 41.	Negative Particles*	63
§ 42.	Interrogative Particles*	64
§ 43.	Independent Prepositions	65
§ 44.	מִן	67
§ 45.	The Prefixes בְּ, כְּ, לְ	67
§ 46.	Wāw copulativum*	69

D. *The Verb* (§§ 47—80).

§ 47.	Tenses and Moods, how expressed* . . .	71
§ 48.	Origin of the Hebrew Verb	73
§ 49.	The Voices of the Verb (Conjugations, Genera verbi)	74
§ 50.	Laws of Vocalisation and Tone	77
§ 51.	Endings of the Perfect	77

	Page
§ 52. Endings of the Imperative	78
§ 53. Inflexion of the Imperfect	78
§ 54. Perfect Qal	79
§ 55. Infinitive Qal	80
§ 56. Imperative Qal	81
§ 57. Imperfect Qal	81
§ 58. Participle Qal	82
§ 59. Niph'al (Niqṭal)	83
§ 60. Pi'ēl and Pu'al (Qiṭṭēl and Quṭṭal)	84
§ 61. Hiph'îl and Hoph'al (Hiqṭîl and Hoqṭal)	85
§ 62. Hithpa'ēl (Hithqaṭṭēl)	86
§ 63. Infinitive Absolute*	87
§ 64. Wāw Consecutive*	89
§ 65. Guttural Verbs	93
§ 66. Verbs א״פ	97
§ 67. Verbs י״פ	98
§ 68. Verbs ו״פ (י״פ I. Class)	100
§ 69. Verbs ו״פ (י״פ II. Class)	102
§ 70. Verbs ו״פ (י״פ III. Class)	102
§ 71. Verbs ע״ו	103
§ 72. Verbs ע״י	108
§ 73. Verbs ע״ע	110
§ 74. Verbs ל״ה	113
§ 75. Verbs ל״א	117
§ 76. Doubly and trebly weak Verbs	119
§ 77. Defective Verbs	121
§ 78. The Verb with Suffixes. I. Infinitive and Participle	122
§ 79. The Verb with Suffixes. II. Perf., Imperf., Imptv.	123
§ 80. Nûn demonstrativum	126

III. Remarks on Syntax (§§ 81—91).

A. *Syntax of the individual Parts of Speech* (§§ 81—84).

§ 81. Pronoun	128
§ 82. Superlative and Comparative	129
§ 83. Verbs with the Accusative	129
§ 84. Union of two Verbs to express a single Idea	132

B. *The Sentence in General* (§§ 85. 86).

	Page
§ 85. Distinction between Nominal and Verbal Sentences	134
§ 86. Subject and Predicate	135

C. *Particular Kinds of Sentences* (§§ 87—91).

§ 87. Relative Sentences	137
§ 88. Conditional Sentences	141
§ 89. Optative Sentences	144
§ 90. Oaths	146
§ 91. Transition of the participial and infinitive Constructions into the Oratio finita	149

Paradigms.

Strong (regular) Verb	2*
Weak (irregular) Verb	4*

Literature.

I. Introductory. — II. Dictionaries. — III. Concordances. — IV. Grammars. — V. On special Points. — VI. For Beginners, Books of Exercises. — VII. Vocabularies . 11*

Chrestomathia.

I. Exercises in Reading	21*
II. Exercises for Translation from Hebrew (Words and Sentences)	25*
III. Explanatory Notes to the Connected Extracts: I Sam. 9. 25; I Kings 3; Psalm 121. 127. 130 . . .	47*
IV. Hebrew-English Vocabulary	51*
V. Exercises for Translation from English (Words and Sentences)	68*
VI. English-Hebrew Vocabulary	100*
VII. Appendix: Explanatory Notes to the Connected Extracts: Gen. 1—3; Psalm 1—3	112*

Corrigenda and Addenda.

Page 11, l. 8 from bottom, "first, when it is the".
16, l. 2 read: "except" for "only".
18, l. 7 read: "*huwrádh*".
22, l. 15 read: "appear" for "arise".
33, l. 8 read: "with proper names, when .. *e.g.* הַבַּעַל, תֵּירְדֵן, הַלְּבָנוֹן ..
76, l. 18 read: "with one another".
92, l. 5 read: "towards itself".
l. 8 read: "the penultimate syllable".
107, l. 9 read: "It is likely".
113, l. 4 read: "several times".
129, l. 16 add: "Cognate accusative".
147, l. 16, 17 read: "where follows".

Only in a part of the copies:

P. 7, l. 11 read: קְבֹר; l. 15 בְּרְכוּ; P. 11, 8: — [Sillûq]; P. 17, 5: בְּרָכִם; P. 32, 14: — [Páthach]; P. 43, 13: שִׁמְךָ; P. 48, 5: בְּכֹר; P. 48, 4 from bottom: שְׁנִי; P. 67, 17 בְּמוּ; P. 78, 13: אָהֳנָה; P. 81, 5 from bottom: רָדְפֵהוּ; P. 84, 2 from bottom: בְּסֹ; P. 88, 11: לָחֹם; P. 94, 9: לְשִׁחַת; l. 2 from bottom: שָׁבַח, שָׁבֵחַ; P. 133, 20: יָאֵץ; P. 141, 10: שְׁנִיר.

I. ORTHOGRAPHY AND PHONOLOGY.
(§§ 1—14).

§ 1. Alphabet. Hebrew is written from right to left. The alphabet consists entirely of consonants. Their form, names, transcription, pronunciation and numerical value are shown in the table on the following page.

§ 1.
a.

Since the fundamental idea of any stem in Hebrew, as in the Semitic languages generally, is almost always conveyed by the consonants, e. g. the three consonants קטל always express the idea of "killing" (whereas e. g. mtr in English may signify *metre, mitre, motor, mature, matter*), an alphabet that indicated the consonants only sufficed for the Hebrews. — In doubtful cases suitable consonants were employed as *matres lectionis*, i. e. to indicate the vowels, viz: י for *i* and *e*, ו for *o* and *u*, rarely א for long *a* (§ 30c note). Concerning ה at the end of a word see § 2b.

b.

Five characters have a different form at the end of a word (cf. Germ. ſ and ẞ): ך, ם, ן, ף, ץ. Vox memorialis כְּמַנְפֵּץ *kimnappēṣ*.

c.

I, § 1. ALPHABET.

Numerical value.	Form	Name	Transcription and pronunciation.
1	א	ʾĂlĕph	ʾ (spiritus lenis)
2	ב	Bêth	b (bh)
3	ג	Gîmĕl	g (gh)
4	ד	Dālĕth	d (dh)
5	ה	Hē	h (§ 2 b)
6	ו	Wāw	w
7	ז	Zájin	z (as in zeal).
8	ח	Chéth	ch (hard, as in Scotch loch).
9	ט	Ṭêth	ṭ (hard, against the back part of the palate).
10	י	Jôdh	j (German j = Engl. y).
20	כ, final ך	Kaph	k (kh)
30	ל	Lāmĕdh	l
40	מ, final ם	Mêm	m
50	נ, final ן	Nûn	n
60	ס	Sāmĕkh	s (hard)
70	ע	ʿAjin	ʿ (s. § 2 d)
80	פ, final ף	Pê	p (ph)
90	צ, final ץ	Ṣādê	ṣ ⎱ hard, against the back
100	ק	Qôph	q, k ⎰ part of the palate.
200	ר	Rēš	r
300 {	שׂ	Śin	ś (hard s)
	שׁ	Šin	š (sh)
400	ת	Tāw	t (th)

§ 2. Pronunciation of the Consonants.

When a vowel, a *Chāṭēph* (§5*d*), a *Sᵉwâ mobile* (§5*c*) or a loosely closed syllable (§12*q*) immediately precedes, the consonants have a softer pronunciation than when this is not the case. Six consonants have the harder pronunciation regularly indicated by a point (*Dāghēš lene*, §6*a*) inserted in the letter: בּ *b*, גּ *g*, דּ *d*, כּ *k*, פּ *p*, תּ *t*; but ב *bh* (almost *v*), ג *gh*, ד *dh*, כ *kh* (soft ch, as in ich)), פ *ph*, ת *th*, ϑ.

ה (otherwise הֿ, *v*. §6*c*) at the end of a word is usually only an (inaudible) sign, that the preceding consonant is followed by a vowel, *e. g.* that רבה is not to be pronounced *rábh*—but *rᵉbhê, robhė, rabbâ* &c. according to the context.

NOTE. This mater lectionis is especially employed when ה (§18*c*γ) or י (§31*b*. 74*c*) has been dropped in pronunciation and thereafter in writing.

י, when no vowel immediately follows, remains silent: 1) after *î* and *ê*, 2) in the middle of a word after ‒ֶ, *e. g.* יָדֶיךְ *jādhèkhā*, 3) at the end of a word in the ending יו *âw* (also written וְ), *e. g.* שָׁיר *nāšâw*; but גּוֹי *gôj*, יָדַי *jādháj* &c.

ע, a peculiar guttural, differently pronounced in different words, cf. Arabic ع and غ. The hardest pronunciation may be approximately reproduced by ʳ*g*.

§ 3. § 3. Classification of the Consonants:
1. Gutturals: א, ע, ה, ח. Vox mem. אֲהַחַע
2. Palatals: י, ג, כ, ק. V. m. גִּיכָק
3. Linguals: ל, נ and ד, ת, ט. V. m. דְּטַלְנֵת
4. Dentals or Sibilants: ז, ס, שׁ, צ. V. m. זְסְצַשׁ
5. Labials: ו, מ, ב, פ. V. m. בּוּמָף.

In regard to hardness of pronunciation (§ 62 *b* β) the following are identical: ק, ט and צ; כ, ת, פ and שׁ, ס; ג, ד, ב and ז. — ו and י are semi-vocalic consonants. ל, מ, נ and ר are liquids. — ר has several peculiarities of the gutturals, *v.* § 10 *b*.

§ 4. § 4. **Vowels.** After Hebrew had ceased to be
a. a living speech, a system of vocalisation was invented and elaborated, probably between the sixth and the eighth century A.D., in order to preserve the proper pronunciation of the sacred writings. The current enumeration of five long and five short vowels (as follows) was introduced by Joseph Qimchi (12th Cent.).

1. *Qāmeṣ* ‍ָ, *ā, â.* יָד *jādh*, שָׁב *šâbh*.
2. *Ṣērê* ‍ֵ, *ē, ê.* שֵׁם *šēm*, נֵר *nēr* (from *năwĭr*).
   ‍ֵי, *ê.* חֵיק *chêq*, עֵינֵי *'ênê.*
3. *Chîrĕq magnum* ‍ִי or ‍ִ, *î.* רִיב *rîbh*, דָּיִיך and דָּוִד *Dāwîdh.*
4. *Chōlĕm* וֹ and ‍ֹ, *ô, ō.* מוֹת *môth*, חֹק *chōq.* Often ‍ֹ for *ô, e. g.* קֹל alongside of קוֹל, more rarely וֹ for *ō.*
5. *Šûrĕq* וּ, *û.* אָרוּר *'ārûr*, הָיוּ *hājû.*

6. *Páthăch* —, *ă*. רַק *răq*.
7. *Sᵉghôl* —, *ĕ*. אֶגְדַּל *'ĕghdál*, אֶל *'ĕl*.
8. *Chírĕq parvum* —, *ĭ*. אִם *'ĭm*, עִם *'ĭm*.
9. *Qāmĕṣ-chāṭûph* —, *ŏ*. רָחְבּוֹ *rŏchbô*, כָּל־ *kŏl*.
10. *Qibbûṣ* —, *ŭ*. חֻלְדָּה *Chŭldā*, שֻׁלְחָן *šŭlchān*.

— ָ is also used to indicate the open *e*-sound *ệ* or *b.*
ä arising by vocalic modification (*Umlautung*) out
of *a*, *e. g.* זֶרַע *zéraʿ* (from *zarʿ*, §28*d*), רְאֶינָה *rᵉʾénā*
(§74*g*γ).

Whether — ָ is *Qāmĕṣ* or *Qāmĕṣ-chāṭûph* can fre- *c.*
quently be determined only by a knowledge of the
derivation of the form in question. For most cases
the following will suffice: — ָ is long *a* both in an
accented and in an (originally) open syllable. — ָ is
ŏ 1. in an unaccented closed syllable, *e. g.* חָכְמָה *chokh-*
mā; 2. before a guttural with — ֳ *e. g.* יַעֲמֹד for *joʿmádh*
(§5*e*), לָחֳלִי, פָּעֳלִי, הֶחֳלֵיתִי (§11*g*1) or with another *Qāmĕṣ-*
chāṭûph, *e. g.* פָּעֳלְךָ *poʿolkhā* (§5*f*); 3. in קָדָשִׁים *qŏdhāšîm*
and שָׁרָשָׁיו *šŏrāšâw*, pl. of קֹדֶשׁ and שֹׁרֶשׁ (§28*p*).

NOTE. An exception to No. 2 is the case where — ָ is the
vowel of the article, as in הָאֲנִיָּה, בָּאֲנִיָּה, *bāᵒnijjā*, from הָאֲנִיָּה + בְּ.

— ַ also indicates a short helping vowel, *Páthach* *d.*
furtivum, which is inserted before a hard final guttural
(ה, ח, ע) when preceded by a heterogeneous long vowel
(*i. e.* all long vowels except *a*). רוּחַ *rûᵃch*, זֹרֵעַ *zôrēᵃʿ*,
שִׂיחַ *síᵃch*, גָּבֹהַּ *gābhôᵃh*. See further §65*d*.

e. — appears frequently for וֹ, *e. g.* שֹׁב as well as שׁוֹב, קֹמוּ and קוּמוּ; very rarely ו for —, *e. g.* יֻלַּד *julládh*.

f. The employment in unpointed texts of the vowel letters (א,) ו and י as matres lectionis is called: scriptio plena, their non-employment: scriptio defectiva. רְקוּמוּ, סְבוֹת and דָּוִיד are written *plene,* יָקְמוּ, סְבֹת and דָּוִד *defective.*

g. When — and שׁ come together, the dot indicating Chōlĕm is, in printed texts, either placed over the left or right limb of the שׁ, (*e. g.* שֹׁמֵר *sômēr* for שֹׁמֵר, תְּפֹשׂ *táphōś* for תְּפֹשׂ) or, where it would coincide with the diacritical point of the שׁ, dropped altogether (*e. g.* שֹׂרֶק *sôrēq* for שׂוֹרֶק, מֹשֵׁל *môšēl* for מוֹשֵׁל).

§ 5. Sᵉwâ and Chāṭēph.

I. *Šᵉwâ quiescens (Š. q. simplex)*—, sign of the entire absence of a vowel, stands:

a. in the middle of a word under every audible consonant that closes a syllable, *e. g.* הִרְדִּלוּ, מַבְדִּיל (but מָצְאָה §10*c*β);

NOTE. For *Šᵉwâ* in a loosely shut syllable see §12*q.*

b. at the end of a word, 1) when the word ends in ךְ or in two consonants: אַתְּ, בָּרַדְתְּ, אָמַרְתְּ, בָּרוּךְ, לָךְ *att;* but with א final (§10*c*α): חֵטְא *chēt'*, וַיֵּרְא *wajjár';*
2) in old, especially Spanish, MSS. and in some printed texts, not uniformly however, in the 2. *sg. f. perf.* of verbs ל"ה and ל"א, *e. g.* Baer prints וְקָרָאתְ 16, 11 and thou *f.* callest, גִּלִּיתְ Isai. 57, 8, thou *f.* hast uncovered.

c. II. *Šᵉwâ mobile (Š. m. simplex),* vocal Š., —, the

shortest vowel, only, as it were, a slight vocalic glide, must be employed when the first consonant (except אהחע) of a syllable (of a word) has no longer a vowel of its own: פְּנֵי $p^e n\hat{e}$, עֲמָדָה ʻ$\bar{a}$-$m^e dh\bar{a}$, יַחְפְּרוּ $jach$-$p^e r\hat{u}$, מְאַלְּמִים $m^e all^e mim$.

III. *Chāṭēph.* In order to indicate distinctly the *d.* vocalic nature of Šᵉwâ mobile, it has uniformly added to it under gutturals, rarely with other consonants, the sign of one of the three short vowels $-$, $-$, $-$ (*Šᵉwâ compositum or Chāṭēph*). Especially common is *Chāṭēph-Páthăch*, $-$, cf. קבר and עֲבֹר, צְדָקָה and צְחָקָה; under other consonants particularly when a consonant is repeated in the middle of a word and the first is entitled to *Š. mobile:* אֲרָרָה, בְּוֹרְרַי, הַלְלוּ (for הַלְּלוּ, §6*f*); sometimes, too, under ר before the tone: בְּרְכוּ and after Wāw copulativum: וּזְהַב 2, 12.— Much less common are *Chāṭēph-Sᵉghôl* (esp. under א): אֱמֹר, אֱלֹהִים, and *Chāṭēph-Qāmeṣ:* אֳנִי, צֳרִי.

Chāṭēph serves besides in the middle of many *e.* words to facilitate the pronunciation of gutturals that would otherwise be quite vowelless: יֶחֱזַק, (17) יַחֲזֹק. See further §10*a*4.

Before Šᵉwâ we find instead of Chāṭēph the cor- *f.* responding vowel; (it is, however, only a helping vowel and does not form a syllable, cf. §12*p*) *e. g.* עֲמֹד, pl. וַעֲמָדוּ *jaʻamdhû;* יֶחֱזַק, pl. יַחֲזֹקוּ; מַעֲלֵי, עֲלָה.

§ 6.   § 6. Dāghēš, Mappîq, Raphè. *Dāghēš lene*,
a. a point placed in the bosom of a letter, is used with
the six letters ת פ כ ד ג ב (בְּגַדְכְּפַת) when these are not
immediately preceded by a vowel, a Šᵉwâ mobile, a
Chāṭēph or a loosely closed syllable (§12*q*), *e. g.*
בְּבָדָה, יִכְתֹּב, פְּתַבְתִּי; hence after a conjunctive accent
(§7*i*): פְּנֵי תְהוֹם; after a disjunctive accent, on the other
hand: כִּי אֹתוֹ 2, 3, כִּי אִשָּׁה 2, 23.

b.   NOTE. Many MSS place *D. l.*, according to §2*a*, in all other consonants as well. It is however indefensible on the part of Baer to place *D. l.*, apart from ב ג ד כ פ ת, only 1. after gutturals with Šᵉwâ quiescens, *e. g.* ψ 10, 1 תַּעְלִים for תַּעֲלִים; 2. when a word begins with the same consonant with which the immediately preceding word ends, *e. g.* Gen. 14, 23 אִם־מִחוּט, ψ 9, 2 בְּכָל־לִבִּי. And even in these cases Baer is not consistent. Cf. H. L. Strack, Theolog. Literaturzeitung 1879, No. 8, Col. 174.

c.   The point usually called *Mappîq*, which indicates
that ה at the end of a word is to be sounded as a consonant, is also a Dāghēš lene. דָּמָהּ pronounce *dāmā*;
דָּמָה *dāmâh*. — Mappîq is found four times in א, first
43, 26 וַיָּבִיאוּ.

d.] *Dāghēš forte*, in form the same as *D. l.*, is the sign
of the doubling of a consonant: יַמִּים *jammîm*. In ב ג
ד כ פ ת it serves also as a *D. l.*: יִפָּרֵד *jippārēdh* (out
of *j[ᵉh]inpārēdh*), יִתֵּן *jittēn* (out of *jintēn*).

e.   *D. f.* is α) either Dāghēš essential or *D. f. neces-
sarium*, when it is conditioned by the grammatical
derivation of the form, *i. e.* particularly when it

occurs in the second of two consonants originally found in the form: יַמִּים for *jammîm*, הִלֵּל for *hillēl*, הִשְׁבַּתִּי for *hišbath-tî*, נָתַתִּי for *nathan-tî;* β) or so-called *D. f. euphonicum, e. g.* when a single consonant has been doubled from considerations of euphony or when it is intended to indicate the vocalic nature of a Š^{e}wâ (*Š. mobile*). Exx. §25*c.i.*—On the different varieties of *D. f. euph.* cf. S. Baer (to be read with criticism), Liber Proverbiorum 1880, p. X—XIV. XV; König, I, 53—60.

NOTE. *D. f. nec.* is not written: 1. in a vowelless final consonant, *e. g.* גַּן (stem גנן). Concerning the lengthening which in such a case generally enters by way of compensation, see §11*e*. (Exceptions: אַתְּ *att*, נָתַתְּ *nāthatt*);—2. in gutturals; then often compensation lengthening §10*a*1.—3. frequently in a number of consonants with Š^{e}wâ mob. esp. ו, י; ל, מ, נ; ק and (particularly before gutturals) the sibilants. Examples: מוֹרִים, pl. of מוֹרֶה; חֲרֻבֹּשֵׂי § 17; יְחִי, יְגַל, always with י as prefix of the Impf. after Wāw cons. §64*f*; הַלְלוּ (§5*d*) for הַלְלוּ; לְבִצְעָךְ; וְהָנֵחוּ רְקָחוּ, בִּקְשׁוּ (§60*b*), from בְּאַב, רָסִיסֵי, רָאשֵׁי כִּלְאֹם for *mill*^{e}*ōm* 25, 23, מִשְׁבָּצֵי for *mišš*^{e}*mannê* 27, 28. 39, מִקְצֵה for *miqq*^{e}*ṣē* (קַצֵה) 8, 3. 47, 2.

f.

Raphè (רָפֶה, *i. e.* soft), a horizontal stroke over the letter, indicates its softer pronunciation. In printed editions of the scriptures Raphè is almost exclusively confined—not always consistently however—to cases whereit is meant to indicate that the absence of a Dāghēš or a Mappîq is intentional; in many MSS. also over בגדכפת, in all cases where these letters have no Dāghēš.

g.

§ 7. The Accents. In addition to the vowel signs, each word (except when joined to the follg. by

§ 7. *a.*

Maqqēph §8*b*) is furnished with one or two small signs which from their significance (now in more than one respect lost to us) for the chanting of the sacred text have been named Accents. We have here to treat of them *A.* as signs of the tone, *B.* as signs of interpunction.

b. *A.* As signs of the tone (§*b.c*). Most of the accents stand beside the syllable that has the main tone or stress, *e. g.* בָּרָא אֱלֹהִים and קָרָא לַיְלָה. Two are found at the beginning of the word without regard to the position of the tone (*accentus praepositivi*): *J^ethibh* כֶּ֚םָ 2, 23 and *T^elišā g^edôlā* הָאָ֕רֶץ 1, 30; four at the end (*accentus postpositivi*): *S^egholtā* הָרָקִ֕יעַ 1, 7, *Paštā* לָאוֹר֙ 1, 5, *Zarqā* וַיֹּ֘אמֶר 2, 23 and *T^elišā q^etannā* וַיִּ֩יצֶר 2, 7.

c. In words that do not have the tone on the last syllable, a second *Paštā* is placed over the tone syllable: תֹּ֙הוּ֙ 1, 2 *thôhû*, but 1, 5 לָא֑וֹר.

NOTE. Baer, without sufficient authority, also repeats *S^egholtā*, *Zarqā* and the two *T^elišā*'s, wherever these accents are otherwise not entitled to stand on the tone syllable: שָׁמַ֛יִם and אִשְׁתְּךָ 3, 11, הָאָרֶץ 1, 30, וַיֵּ֣לֶךְ 2, 22, instead of: שָׁמַיִם, אִשְׁתְּךָ, הָאָרֶץ and וַיֵּלֶךְ.

d. *B.* As signs of interpunction (§*d—o*). A distinction is made between disjunctive (*distinctivi*, masters) and conjunctive accents (*conjunctivi*, servants). The latter, indicating the close connexion of their word with the following one, have all equal value for the understanding of the sentence; it is only for the public cantillation of the sacred text that they have different values, one conjunctive demanding one height or modulation of the tone, another another.—If, on the other hand, a disjunctive is immediately repeated, the first has the greater disjunctive value (G. 21, 6. 22, 8); in the same way the first of two conjunctives standing together has the greater connecting power.

1. **Greatest Disjunctives.** *Sillûq* (—) under the tone syllable of the last word in every verse, always followed by *Sôph pāsûq* (:) the sign of the end of the verse.

— *'Athnâch,* divides the verse into two halves: אֱלֹהִים 1, 1. In short verses this is often done by certain other accents: 1, 13. 19. 23.

— *S^egholtā,* postpos., in longer verses the main divider before 'Athnâch. Always after Zarqā הָרְקִיעַ 1, 7. Also 1, 28. 2, 23 and often.

2. **Great Disjunctives.** — *Zāqēph qāṭōn.* We find instead — *Zāqēph gādhôl:* first, when the first accent in the verse (3, 10 וַיֹּאמֶר) or half-verse (2, 20 וּלְאָדָם), but וְהָאָדָם 4, 1; secondly, immediately after another Zāqēph (2, 9 הַגָּן וְעֵץ, cf. 1, 14 and oft.), but שְׁנֵיהֶם וַיֵּדְעוּ 3, 7.

— *R^ebhia'* often forms subdivisions in the Zāqēph-sections. אֱלֹהִים 1, 9. 14.

3. **Small Disjunctives.** — *Paštā,* postpos. לְאוֹר 1, 5; repeated when the word is not accented on the last syllable, יְהִי 1, 2.

For Pašṭā — J^{e}thîbh, prepos., when no conjunctive precedes and the tone rests on the first consonant: בִּצֵ֚ 2, 23, אַ֚ךְ 3, 1.

— Ṭiphchā, the disjunctive next before 'Athnâch and Sillûq: בְּרֵאשִׁ֖ית, הַשָּׁמַ֖יִם 1, 1.

— T^{e}bhîr אֱלֹהִ֛ים 1, 4.

— Zarqā, postpos., always before S^{e}gholtā. אֱלֹהִ֮ים 1, 7.

h. 4. Smallest Disjunctives. — Gèreš or 'Azlā הַשָּׁמַ֜יִם 1, 21. Instead double-Gèreš, when the last syllable is accented and the conjunctive Qadmā does not precede: פְּ֝רִי 1, 21.

— L^{e}gharmêh, always before R^{e}bhî^a·. בְּשֵׁ֓ם׀ 1, 29.

— Pāzēr וְהָֽאֱלֹהִ֡ים. Instead 16 times — Qarnê phārā, always after the conjunctive Galgal: בְּרִֽחֹקֵ֟ן יְ֟ירֻשְׁתָּם Jos. 19, 51.

— T^{e}lîšā g^{e}dhôlā, great-T., prepos. הֲ֠בֵא 1, 12.

i. 5. Conjunctive Accents. — Mêr^{e}khā. אֵ֥ת 1, 1. Instead 14 times double-Mêr^{e}khā: כָּל־יֶ֦רֶק 27, 25.

— Mûnāch. בָּרָ֣א 1, 1.

— Dargā, esp. before T^{e}bhîr. וַיַּ֧רְא 1, 4.

— Qadmā, esp. before Gèreš. יִקָּו֨וּ 1, 9.

— Mahpākh. בֵּ֤ין 1, 7.

— T^{e}lîšā q^{e}ṭannā, small-T., postpos. וַיֶּ֩רֶךְ׃ (paroxyt.) 2, 22.

k. 6. Rare accents are: — Šalšéleth (with following P^{e}sîq) e. g. וַיֹּאמֶר֓׀ 39, 8, one of the greatest disjunctives, only 7 times in the "twenty one books." Further the conjunctives — Galgal (16 times before Qarnê phārā) and — M^{e}ajlā (16 times before 'Athnâch or Sillûq, generally to indicate the secondary tone, יִֽצְאָה־נַ֖חַ 8, 18).

l. 7. Three of the "twenty four books" (i. e. of the O. T.), viz: Psalms, Job and Proverbs, have a different system of accentuation (generally called "the metrical accents"). In this there are 11 disjunctives (Ṣinnôr postpos., D^{e}chî prepos.), 8 conjunctives and one "underservant."

m. The disjunctives are besides Sillûq:

— ʽŌlè wᵉjôrēdh, halves larger verses. רְשָׁעִים ψ 1, 1.
— ʾAthnâch, halves smaller verses (ψ 1, 4) and in longer verses the part following ʽŌlè wᵉjôrēdh (ψ 1, 1).
— Great-Rᵉbhîaʽ. הָאִישׁ ψ 1, 1.
— Ṣinnôr, postpos. דַּרְכּוֹ ψ 1, 1.   n.
— Small-Rᵉbhîaʽ, immediately before ʽŌlè wᵉjôrēdh. תִּֽהְיֶה ψ 1, 2.
— Rᵉbhîaʽ mughrāš (i. c. R. with Gèreš, v. §h) before Sillûq. וַֽחֲטָאִים ψ 1, 5.
— Great-Šalšèleth. וַֽיְדַבֵּר־ ψ 7, 6.
— Dᵉchî, prepos. וְחַטָּאִים ψ 1, 1.
— Pāzēr. בְּקָרְאִ֡י ψ 4, 2.
Lᵉgharmêh. Either Mᵉhuppākh (Mahpākh) Lᵉgharmêh וְגַם׀ ψ 4, 2 or ʾAzlā Lᵉgharmêh וִֽיהִי׀ ψ 5, 9.
The conjunctives are: Mêrᵉkhā; Mûnāch; ʾIllûj יָדַ֥ע ψ 1, 3;   o.
Galgal; Tarchā יְדָ֖רְךְ ψ 1, 6 (under the accented syllable, hence easily to be distinguished from Dᵉchî); Mahpākh; ʾAzlā; Šalšèleth וַֽיְשַׁלַּ֓ח ψ 3, 3 (only 8 times).—In addition an "underservant", Ṣinnōrîth, in an open syllable before Mêrᵉkhā and Mahpākh הוֹצִֽ֤ ψ 1, 2, קִ֓ימָה 3, 8.

§ 8. Mèthegh, Maqqēph, Pᵉsîq. *Mèthegh* § 8. (bridle), a small perpendicular line beneath the letters   a. (thus same form as Sillûq), generally to the left of the accompanying vowel, indicates the **secondary tone**, esp. 1. in the second syllable before the tone when that syllable is open: הָֽאָדָם 2, 15, עֵֽינֵיכֶם 3, 5. If the syllable in question is closed, then *M.* stands in the third or even in the fourth syllable before the tone: וּמֵֽחֶלְבֵהֶן 4, 4, הָֽאַרְבָּעִים 18, 29.—2. With long vowels, when followed by Šᵉwâ mob. and by the tone: הָֽיְתָה,

רְשׁוּפָה, תּוֹלְדוֹת. Distinguish accordingly between חָכְמָה and חָבְמָה.—3. Before Ḫâṭēph in open or opened syllables: רַעֲלָה, הֶעֱלָה, מֶעֱמָד; צְעָקִים 4, 10; יְזָהָב 2, 12.— For וּ copulativum (§46) 1) and 2) do not hold good, hence וּרְבוּ; וּבְנוֹת, וּלְאָדָם 1, 22.

b. *Maqqēph,* a small horizontal stroke on a level with the top of the consonants, unites two to four words, connected in sense, more closely than is done by the servile accents, by making them one word as regards pronunciation and tone. Especially common with *M.* are: אֶל־ *to,* אֶת־ *with* or sign of the determinate Accus., כָּל־ *totality,* עַל־ *on,* פֶּן־ *lest* (cf. the Greek proclitics); מִן־ *from* has always *M.*—אֶת־כָּל־פְּנֵי 2, 6; כִּי־עֵירֹם 3, 10 (*Mèthegh* acc. to §8a1); וְאֶת־כָּל־אֲשֶׁר־לוֹ 12, 20.

c. *P*sîq or *Pāsēq* (stopper), a perpendicular line between two words, prevents two logically connected words from being pronounced too quickly in succession as if they formed but a single word. *P.* is chiefly found 1. when the first word ends with the same consonant with which the following begins: הָיְתָה ׀ הָרְמֵשֶׂת 1, 21; 2. when a word is repeated: יוֹם ׀ יוֹם 39, 10; 3. with the names of the Deity, to secure a consciously reverent pronunciation: אֱלֹהִים ׀ אֶת־ 1, 27 (to prevent the *M.* being carried over to the following *eth*, which would result in the word מֵת *dead* being heard), אֱלוֹהַּ ׀ רָשָׁע ψ 139, 19. After *P.* בגדכפת take Dāghēš even when preceded by a conjunctive accent, e. g. עָשׂוּ כָלָה 18, 21 (Mûnâch).

§ 9. Q⁵rê and K⁵thîbh. In not a few passages of the holy scriptures a reading different from that furnished by the consonantal text was (for various reasons) traditional. Attention is called to these differences in printed editions and in most MSS. by the consonants of the new reading, the $Q^e rê$ (קְרִי; usually, but falsely, $Q^e ri$), being placed in the margin while the vowels belonging thereto are added to the original reading in the text, the $K^e thibh$ (כְּתִיב), which remains unchanged, only the so-called *circellus massorethicus* being added as a mark of reference. 8, 17 we find in the text הַוְצִא, on the margin קרי הוצא, *i. e.* instead of the traditional consonants הוצא (which would have been pronounced הוֹצֵא) we have here to read הַיְצֵא.

In the case of a few words of frequent occurrence, the marginal note and the mark of reference have been dispensed with (so-called $Q^e rê$ *perpetuum*): הִוא (she), only in Pent., $Q^e rê$ הִיא, $K^e thibh$ הוּא.—יְרוּשָׁלַם, nom. prop., Q. יְרוּשָׁלַיִם, K. יְרוּשָׁלָם.— יִשָּׂשכָר, n. pr., Q. יִשָּׂכָר, K. doubtless יִשְׁשָׂכָר.—נַעֲרָ (maiden), only in Pent., Q. נַעֲרָה, K. נַעַר.—The numerical forms שְׁתַּיִם, שְׁתַּיִם (§39*e*3) are without doubt to be pronounced שְׁנֵי, שְׁתֵּי; K. then שְׁתַּיִם, שְׁנַיִם.—The divine name יהוה, the proper pronunciation of which seems to be *Jahwè*, owing to its utterance being considered unlawful, has the vowels of אֲדֹנָי, only Sʰwâ for Chāṭēph, hence יְהֹוָה; in the same way with מִן (§44) מֵיְהֹוָה (מֵאֲדֹנָי); but after the prefixes בְּ, כְּ, לְ, וְ, בֵּיהֹוָה, כַּיהֹוָה, לַיהֹוָה, וַיהֹוָה (בַּאדֹנָי &c., v. §10c4), read either *badhônáj* &c. or *bᵉjahwé* &c. Should אֲדֹנָי stand immediately beside יהוה, the latter receives the vowels of אֱלֹהִים, e. g. יֱהֹוִה אֲדֹנָי ψ 109, 21.

§ 10.
a.

§ 10. Peculiarities of certain Consonants.
I. The gutturals א ה ח ע.—1. Not Dāghēš forte, but either virtual doubling (Dāghēš f. implicitum), *i. e.* simply the omission of the D., or (§11e) lengthening by way of compensation (the former in decreasing, the latter in increasing frequency with ח, ה, ע, א). Article (§17): הָאוֹר, הָעִיר, הֶחָשֶׁךְ, הַיּוֹם. Verb: שִׁבֵּר, מִקְשָׁלָה, מֵאֲנָתֶם; but מְהַרְתֶּם, שֵׁבַרְתֶּם, מָאֲן; but מַהֵר, שִׁחַת, מְטֹהָרָה, but קָטַלְתְּ, רְחָצְתְּ. ‖ 2. Preference for the vowel *a* (§4*d*. 28*d*. 60*d*. 65); sometimes also *ĕ* for original *ĭ*, e. g. חֶפְצוֹ §28*l*. ‖ 3. No Sʰwâ mobile but Chāṭēph,— mostly Chāṭēph-Páthach, with א of the Qal before the tone syllable generally Chāṭēph-Sʰghôl: קָבְרָתֶם, אֲמַרְתֶּם, עֲבַרְתֶּם; but אֱמֹר, עֲבֹד, קְבֹר. ‖ 4. The pronunciation of the gutturals in a closed pretonic or antepretonic syllable is often lightened by insertion of the corresponding Chāṭēph (opening of the syllable, §12*o*). Noun: פָּעֳלוֹ, קָדְשׁוֹ; נַעֲרוֹ, מָלְכּוֹ. Verb (§65

(—m. p): וַיִּקְטֹל, יַעֲמֹד; יִקְטַל, יַעֲמִיד; יַקְטִיל, אֶעֱבֹר, אֶקְטֹל
וַיַּעֲבֹר, וַיֵּאָמֵן.

II. ר.—1. Not Dāghēš forte, but always lengthening by way of compensation. Article: הָרָקִיעַ, הַיּוֹם. Verb: מְבֹרָךְ, מְקֻטָּל; בָּרַךְ, קִטֵּל; בֵּרְכָם, קִטְּלָם.—2. Preference for *a*, esp. as preceding vowel, cf. §60*d*.—3. Chāṭēph-Páthach for Š^ewâ mobile, esp. in some verbs *med.* ר (§65*r*β).

III. א.—1. At the end of a syllable (and word) א completely loses its value as a consonant; hence α) without Š^ewâ: יָפֵת, וַיֵּרָא; בְּרֹךְ, חֵטְא, and β) the immediately preceding vowel is lengthened, because now standing in an open syllable: מָצָא, קָטָל; יִקְטֹל, מְצָא; מָצָאתָ, קְטַלְתְּ (§75*a*). ‖ 2. A preceding Š^ewâ mobile is often absorbed by the long vowel of א: מֵאָתַיִם 200 for *m^eāthájim*, רָאשִׁים (heads) for *r^eāšim.*—Note also: 3. *Inf.* אֱמֹר (say) with לְ becomes לֵאמֹר (to say, *dicendo*).— 4. אֱלֹהִים with the prefixes בְּ, כְּ, לְ, וְ becomes בֵּאלֹהִים &c. אֲדֹנָי retains after these prefixes the short vowel בַּאדֹנָי, בַּאדֹנָי &c. (Hence בַּיהוָֹה &c. §9*b*).

NOTE. In verbs *prim. gutt.* א at the end of a syllable has consonantal value, can, therefore, have Š^ewâ quiescens, *v.* §65*h.i.*

IV. ה.—ה is elided in certain cases after Š^ewâ mobile. The vowel of ה is then transferred to the preceding consonant: Article §17*e*, verb §§59*d.* 61*e.* 62*a.*

e. V. ו.—1. The soft semi-vocalic consonant ו is merged in the homogeneous vowels וּ or וֹ: α) in the middle of a syllable, especially before a homogeneous vowel, whether preceded by a vowel or a Šᵉwâ mobile: קוּם (arise *imp.*) for *qᵘwum*, קוֹם (to arise) for *qāwôm*; β) at the end of a syllable: הוּרַד, הָקְטַל for *howrádh*, and, under the influence of a preceding *a* (contraction): יוֹרִידוּ, יַקְטִילוּ for *jawrîdhû* (§68); γ) at the end of a word after another consonant: תֹּהוּ for *tohw*; δ) ו copulative *v.* § 46. ‖ 2. Original ו at the beginning of a word has in most cases passed into י: יָלַד (*peperit*) for *wáládh*; cf. §68*a*. ‖ 3. Transition of ו to י in the verbs ע"י (ע"ו) *v.* §72*a*. ‖ 4. Complete expulsion of ו in the verbs ע"ו, *v.* §71*f.g a.l.*

f. VI. י.—1. י is merged in a homogeneous long vowel: α) at the end of a syllable (and of a word) after *i* in *î*: יֵיטַב for *jijṭábh*, בִּיהוּדָה for *bijhûdhā*; after *a* often contraction to *ê*: יֵיטִיב, יַקְטִיל for *jajṭibh* §69*b*, סוּסֵי *st. c. pl.* §21*e*; but with suff. still sometimes *susaj* §22*f*; β) at the end of a word after another consonant, which has then to give up its vowel, in *î*: פְּרִי (fruit) for *parj* (§ 30), עֳנִי (misery) for ʿ*onj*; יְחִי and יְחִי *v.* §76*b.c.* ‖ 2. Compare besides §§ 31. 74.

g. VII. נ.—נ is assimilated to the following consonant, except when that consonant is a guttural or ר

(§a1.b1): a) in the verbs פ״נ: יִקְטֹל, יִפֹּל for *jinpōl*, הִקְטִיל, הִפִּיל, *v*. §67a.—β) also the final נ in the verb נָתַן (give), *e. g.* קָטַלְתְּ, נָתַתְּ; קְטַלְתֶּם, נְתַתֶּם; וּקְטַלְתֶּם, נְתַתֶּם.—γ) often, in prose almost without exception, in מִן, *c. g.* מִקֶּדֶם for מִן + קֶדֶם.—δ) In those nouns of the forms *qaṭl, qiṭl, quṭl,* whose second radical is נ, see §26a.b.

§ 11. Changes of Vowels. I. Vowels are unchangeable 1. when they are long either by nature or (as ô in כּוֹכָב star, for *kawkābh* from *kabhkābh*) by contraction, as ־ֵי, וּ, in most cases וֹ, and also ־ִי; 2. in a doubly closed syllable (§12e), *e. g. i* in מִקְדָּשׁ sanctuary, מִקְדְּשֵׁי אֵל the sanctuaries of God, and in כְּבָר circuit, כִּכַּר הַיַּרְדֵּן ἡ περίχωρος τοῦ Ἰορδάνου; 3. in syllables with virtual doubling: מְחָרְתָם; 4. when lengthening by way of compensation has taken place before a guttural or ר: מֵאֵן, מֵאַנְתֶּם.

§ 11.
a.

NOTE. Exception to 2.: Accented Páthach is often in pause lengthened to Qāmeṣ, cf. §§60f.61d.

II. Changeable—*i. e.* may be shortened or in certain cases entirely dropped—are 1. vowels made long only by the tone (tone-long vowels), esp. *ā* and *ē* in nouns (§ 24: מִקְדָּשׁ; אֹיֵב enemy, *pl.* אֹיְבִים), *ē* and *ō* in verbs (קָטַל he has murdered, *pl.* קָטְלוּ; יִקְטֹל he will kill, *pl.* יִקְטְלוּ); 2. pretonic vowels, *i. e.* vowels originally short, which are lengthened (*v.* §h) owing to

b.

2*

their position in an open syllable before the tone (דָּבָר word, pl. דְּבָרִים; עֵנָב grape, pl. עֲנָבִים; קָטַל *necavit*, קְטַלְתֶּם *necavistis*).

c. **III. Dropping and Shortening of Vowels.**
A. In the noun, in an open syllable. 1. When the tone is thrown forward (by an afformative or *st. constr.*), the vowel that stood in the syllable before the tone is dropped: נָשִׂיא prince, נְשִׂיא הָאָרֶץ the p. of the land, pl. נְשִׂיאִים, נְשִׂיאֵיהֶם *principes eorum*; נָתִיב path, *f.* נְתִיבָה *do.* ‖ 2. If two vowels are changeable, that vowel is dropped which, when the tone is moved forward, would stand in the second syllable before the tone; the vowel preceding the one just referred to, because now in a (loosely) closed unaccented syllable (§12*q*), is shortened, *a* being often thinned to *i*. כָּנָף wing, כְּנָפוֹ his wing, כַּנְפֵיהֶם *alae eorum*; דָּבָר word, דְּבָרוֹ his word, דִּבְרֵיהֶם *verba eorum*. — For the treatment of changeable vowels in a shut syllable see the chapter on the forms (esp. §§24.25).

d. B. In the verb the vowel of the second radical is dropped before accented afformatives beginning with a vowel—*i. e.* the vowel of the syllable immediately before the tone:

Noun.	Verb.
חָכָם σοφός, חָכְמָה σοφή.	חָכַם he is wise, חָכְמָה she is w.
יָקָר precious *m.*, יְקָרָה *f.*	(יָקַר he is p.) יָקְרָה she is p.

Exceptions see §50a.—Before accented afformatives beginning with a consonant § c applies: קָטַל, קְטַלְתִּיךָ, קְטַלְתֶּם *necavi te*.

IV. Compensation - lengthening appears *e.* wherever a Dāghēš required by the grammatical form has been omitted, ă being lengthened to ā, ĭ to ē, ŭ to ō: 1. when virtual doubling has not taken place, always before gutturals and ר (examples §10a1.b1);—2. at the end of a word (§6f1); ă, however, remains in most cases unlengthened, *e. g.* אֵם for *'imm*, חֹק for *chuqq*, גַּן for *gann*, cf. §§26b. 73i. 74s.

V. Of the remaining vowel changes the most important are those affecting *Páthach*. 1. P. in an unaccented closed syllable very frequently becomes ĭ: in the strong verb regularly in הִקְטִיל, קְטָל־, יִקְטָל־, קְטָל־ ; in the noun cf. דִּבְרֵי יוֹסֵף, the words of Joseph, for *dabrê*, דִּבְרֵיהֶם from דָּבָר §25b; פִּתְּה from פַּת §26dγ; צִדְקִי from *ṣadq* §28a. ‖ 2. P. becomes Sᵉghôl before *chă* and *ch°* and before unaccented *hā* and *ʿā*, when the guttural is virtually doubled: אֶחַי my brothers, אֶחָי; לֶהָבוֹת (for *lahhābhôth*) flames, לֶהֲבוֹת אֵשׁ flames of fire. More exx. §17c.—Exception הָרָה, to the mountain, 14, 10 for *hárrā*.

VI. Rise of new vowels. 1. The prefixes בְּ, כְּ, *g.* לְ, וְ before a guttural with Chāṭēph receive the corresponding short vowel. בְּ + אֱדוֹם becomes בֶּאֱדוֹם, so

בְּ + אֱשֶׁר ; חֲלִי + לְ becomes לֶחֱלִי, וְחֲלִי; וַאֲדוֹם, לֶאֱדוֹם
Exceptions: וַאֲשֶׁר, לַאֲשֶׁר, כַּאֲשֶׁר, so בַּאֲשֶׁר, becomes
לֶאֱמֹר, בֵּאלֹהִים, בַּאדֹנָי (בֵּיהֹוָה), וַאדֹנָי &c., see §10c.

2. בְּ, כְּ, לְ (§ 45) before Sᵉwâ receive the vowel î:
דְּבַר ה' the word of Jahwe, בִּדְבַר, כִּדְבַר, לִדְבַר (syllable loosely closed, v. §12r).—A following י quiesces in i (§10fa): בְּ + יְהוּדָה becomes בִּיהוּדָה; so, too, after ו copul.: וִיהוּדָה.

3. ו copul. (וְ) before Sᵉwâ and the labials (בומ״ף) becomes וּ (û): וּדְבַר ה', וּבַיִת, וּמֶלֶךְ, וּפָעַל (§ 46).

NOTE. Before lip-sounds the Babylonian punctuation has ו̄ i. e. וִ.

h. 4. In the syllable before the tone not only are originally short vowels lengthened (§62), but even new vowels arise: *a*) under the prefixes בְּ, כְּ, and esp. לְ, v. § 45;—β) under ו cop. at the end of a sentence or part of a sentence, *i. e.* after a large disjunctive, and with words occurring in pairs: יוֹם וָלַיְלָה day and night, טוֹב וָרָע good and evil, לֶחֶם וָמַיִם bread and water. Cf. Gen. 8, 22.

i. 5. In two consonants end, except אַתְּ, thou *f.*, and the 2 *f. sg. perf.*, קָטַלְתְּ &c., only a few forms from weak verbs (§74o.t), a few words ending in א, as שָׁוְא, חֵטְא, and נֵרְדְּ nard, קֹשְׁטְ truth. In all other cases the pronunciation is facilitated by the insertion of a helping vowel (genly. Sᵉghôl, hence the expression "segholate forms"; in the case of gutturals mostly Páthach; after Jôdh î). For details see §§27—30. 36a. 65. 74.

§ 12. Of the Syllable.—Commencement of a syllable (*Silbenanlaut*) (§a.b). Every syllable, and hence every word, must begin with one consonant, *i.e.* neither with a vowel (for single exception *v.* §11*g*3) nor with two consonants. If the first consonant of a syllable (or a word) has no vowel of its own, it receives Sʲwâ mobile §5*c*, or (with אַהחְע) Chāṭeph §5*d*. 10*a*3.

Close of a syllable (*Silbenauslaut*) (§ *c*—*s*).— A distinction is made between:

I. open syllables, or those ending with a vowel: קוּמוּ, עָשִׂיתָ, אֹתוֹ, שָׁנָה (ה *v.* §2*b*). They have always a long vowel. (Exception: the verbal suffix *áni* §79*e*).—Syllables ending in א are regarded as open: קָטַל, מָצָא (cf. however §10*c* note.)

Unaccented syllables with a long vowel are open; the following Sʲwâ is Š. mobile: שֹׁמְרִים *šô-mᵉrîm*.

II. shut syllables, or those ending in a consonant: קָטַל (2nd syll.).—They are called doubly shut, when the consonant closing the syllable is immediately followed by another consonant in the same word: מִצְרָיה (1st syll.), קְטַלְתְּ (2nd syll.). If the two consonants are identical or have been made

§ 12.
a.

b.

c.

d.

e.

so (*i. e.* if the vowel is followed by a cons. with Dāghēš), the syllable may also ˌbe termed *sharpened:* הַשִּׁשִּׁי (sylls. 1 and 2).

f. Unaccented shut syllables have always a short vowel: מַבְדִּיל (1.), יֶלֶד (1.), וַיָּקָם (1. 3.), וַיֹּאמֶר (1. 3.).

g. Unaccented syllables with a short vowel are shut: חַסְדּוֹ (1.).

h. In an accented shut penultima we find only following vowels: α) the tone-long vowels *ā, ē, ō:* רָמָה, יֵרְדוּ (2.), hence neither *î* nor *û*, nor yet the essentially (*i. e.* by nature or by contraction) long vowels *â, ê, ô;* β) the short vowels *ă, ĕ:* קָטַלְתְּ, מִשְׁפּוּ.

i. In an accented shut ultima all long vowels may appear; of the short vowels *ă* and *ĕ*, sometimes even *ĭ*, esp. the two particles אִם (if), עִם (with), which, however, are often (as מִן always) made toneless by Maqqēph, and the form וַיֵּשֶׁב §74oα.

k. III. Opened syllables, *i. e.* syllables, whose originally double close has been removed by a helping vowel.—1. At the end of a word: genly. a helping vowel (cf. §11*i*), in most cases S°ghôl, though also (esp. when the last letter, or the last but one, is a guttural) Páthach. The accented vowel of the opened syllable is then in most cases lengthened, viz: *ŏ (ŭ)* to *ō:* קֹדֶשׁ, רֹחַב, אֹרַח; *ĭ* to *ē:* סֵפֶר, שֵׁמַע; *ă* to *ĕ:* מֶלֶךְ, זֶרַע, *v.* §28*c.d.*

If the last letter but one is a guttural, Páthach *l.* remains in the opened syllable unchanged: נַ֫עַר §28*e*, דַּ֫עַת ,תּוֹכַ֫חַת §36*a*, וַיַּ֫עַל §74*o*ε.

If the last letter but one is י, Chîrĕq is used as *m.* helping vowel. Páthach remains in an opened syllable: חַיִךְ §29*a*; also in the suffix-form ־֫יִךְ, *e. g.* אֱלֹהַ֫יִךְ, and in the dual ending ־ַ֫יִם *ájim*.

In the apocopated impf. of verbs ל״ה the length- *n.* ening of *ĭ* to *ē* is often dispensed with, *v.* §74*o*γ, *e. g.* יִ֫גֶל for *jigl*.

2. In the middle of a word the consonant clos- *o.* ing the syllable, if a guttural, frequently receives for ease of pronunciation the Chāṭēph corresponding to the preceding vowel, without this vowel being lengthened. Exx. §10*a*4. נַעֲרוֹ, in syllables *na'ă-rô*.

The vowel remains unlengthened even when, in- *p.* stead of the Chāṭēph owing to its being followed by a S⁽e⁾wâ, the corresponding short vowel is written, *v.* §5*f.* יֶחֱזַק, *pl.* יֶחֶזְקוּ, divide יֶחֶזְ־קוּ, יַחְלֹם, *pl.* יַחְלְמוּ (יַחְלְ־מוּ).

IV. Loosely shut syllables we call such sylla- *q.* bles as were originally followed by a vowel, which has been dropped in accordance with the general laws in §§11*c*2 and 11*d*. That a syllable is loosely closed may be recognized by the fact that בגדכפת retain their aspiration. The S⁽e⁾wâ is not vocal, is not S⁽e⁾wâ mobile. Exx. to §11*c*2: בְּנֵה, בְּנֵיהֶם *kan-phê-hèm* §25 *a*; מְלָכִים

for *malakhim*, מַלְכֵיהֶם §28*h*; חָרְבֹתַיִךְ *chor-bhô-thájikh* §35*a*.—To §11*d*: יַעֲמֹד, *pl.* יַעֲמְדוּ; יֶחֱרַד, *pl.* יֶחֶרְדוּ; נֶאֱסָף, *pl.* נֶאֶסְפוּ, *v.* §65*f.h.k.*

r.   To the class of loosely shut syllables belong also such syllables as arise from the addition of the prefixes בְּ, כְּ, לְ to words, whose first consonant is pointed with S⁶wâ: לִדְבַר §11*g*2.—Exception: לְ before infin. Qal §55*d*.

Very seldom do we find a loosely shut syllable
s. where no vowel has been dropped, *v.* §28*q*. Cf. also הַבַּיְתָה §29*a*.—Complete closure of the syllable contrary to the rule in: בִּרְכַּת §34*da*, חֶרְפּוֹת §35*c*; cf. also בְּשָׁפְכָה §55*d*.

§ 13.   § 13. Of the tone. The principal tone in Hebrew
a.   rests generally on the last syllable; on the penultima almost exclusively in the following cases:

1. when the last vowel is a helping vowel (§11*i*); hence in the dual, *e. g.* שְׁנָתַיִם *biennium*;

2. before ה— *locale* (§20*c*): אַשּׁוּרָה to Assyria;

3. before the suffix נוּ, *e. g.* מַלְכֵּנוּ our king, שְׁלָחָנוּ *misit nos*, and before a few other suffixes, *v.* §§22. 79*h*;

4. the verbal forms ending in תָּ, תִּי, נוּ (perf.), ־ָה (impf., iptv.); in the Hiph'îl also those in ־ָה, ־ִי, ־ִי־: קָטַלְתְּ, קָטְלוּ, הִקְטִילָה, הִקְטִילוּ, וַיַּקְטִיל;

5. in the verbs ע"ו and ע"י the endings ־ִי, וּ, ־ָה— even in the other conjugations, *e. g.* from קוּם: קָמָה she has risen, קָמוּ they have r., קוּמִי arise (iptv. *f.*);

6. in a number of forms of the impf. without afformatives when ו consecut. is prefixed (§64*g.k—n*);

7. several times in pause, see §14*g.h.i*;

8. frequently, also, to avoid the concurrence of two tone-syllables: in a word with open penultima and long open or short closed ultima, when immediately followed by a monosyllable or by a word with the accent on the first syllable, the tone is generally shifted back to the penultimate syllable: קָ֤רָא לַ֗יְלָה 1, 5; תֹּ֥אבַל לָ֫הֶם 3, 19; עָ֥מַד שָׁ֖ם 19, 27.

> NOTE 1. Thus retrogression of the tone does not take place *b*. with a closed penultima or from a long vowel in a closed ultima (with the occasional exception of Ṣērê): עָפָ֣ר אָ֑תָּה dust art thou 3, 19; nor yet when the first word ends with a heavy suffix, nor when the distinctness of pronunciation would be affected: שִׁלְשֹׁ֖ה אֶ֗לֶּה these three 9, 19, לֹ֥א יִקְרָ֖א שׁ֑וֹד 17, 5.—Ṣērê, when deprived of the tone in a closed ultima, either receives Mèthegh (בְּגַ֥ל צַ֖רְיךָ Isa. 40, 7. 8) or is shortened to Sᵉghôl (cf. §59*f*).
>
> NOTE 2. The tone never rests on the antepenultima. Isa. *c*. 40, 18. 50, 8. Job 12, 15 are only apparent exceptions, to be explained acc. to §§5*f*. 12*p* (against Delitzsch on Isa. 40, 18 and in the preface to Baer's edition of Job p. VI).

§ 14. Of the Pause. I. At the end of sentences § 14. and of the larger divisions of a sentence, many changes *a*. take place in the accentuation and the vocalisation, which are occasioned partly by general considerations of rhythm, partly by a special regard for the solemn recitation of the sacred text.

28   I, § 14. OF THE PAUSE.

b.   II. These changes appear uniformly with *Sillûq*, *Sᵉgholtā, Šalšéleth* and *'Athnâch*, often with *Zāqēph*; in the books of Psalms, Job, Prov. (§ 7*l*): always with *Sillûq*, *'Ôlè wᵉjôrēdh*, and, in smaller verses, with *'Athnâch*, often with *'Athnâch* after '*Ôlè wᵉjôrēdh*; rarely with other accents.

c.   III. The pausal effects are not the same for all accents; אַתָּה, thou *m.*, *e.g.* appears with Sillûq, 'Athnâch and 'Ôlè wᵉjôrēdh as אָתָּה, with Zāqēph and 'Athnâch after 'Ôlè wᵉjôrēdh as אָתְּ, cf. Gen. 3, 19. ψ 2, 7.

d.   1. Lengthening of the vowel. *a*) Esp. frequent is the change of Páthach to Qāmeṣ: מַיִם water, מָיִם; זָכַרְתִּי, שָׁמַרְתִּי, שְׁמַרְתִּי; יָצַר *finxit*, יָצָר. לַיְלָה night, לָיְלָה; זָכָרְתָּ; יְלָדְנוּ, יְלָדְנוּ. In segholate forms (§ 28*g*) : נַעַר boy, נָעַר; and in the same way אֶרֶץ (bec. ground-form *arṣ*) אָרֶץ; זֶרַע seed, זָרַע.—β) Páthach and Sᵉghôl in the ground-form of the perf. Pi'ēl become Ṣērê: מִלֵּט, מִלֵּט; דִּבֶּר he has spoken, דִּבֵּר (§ 60*d.e*).

e.   NOTE. Monosyllables with Páthach remain in most cases unchanged: בֵּן 30, 21, כַּד 49, 27.

f.   2. Vowel changes. *a*) Ṣērê sometimes becomes Páthach: הֵפֵר *fregit*, הֵפַר; יֵלֶד *ibit*, וַיֵּלַךְ; וַיִּגָּמֵל, רְקָטֵל and he was weaned.—β) Ṣērê becomes Qāmeṣ in the perf., iptv., impf. Hithp. (bec. here originally *ă*), § 62*d*γ.—γ) Chōlĕm sometimes becomes Qāmeṣ: כַּאֲשֶׁר שְׁכֻלְתִּי שָׁכֹלְתִּי 43, 14; עֹז 49, 3; טָרֹף 49, 27.

g.   3. Retrogression of the tone. אַתָּה I, אָנֹכִי; אָנֹכִי *v.* § *c*; עָרוּ lay bare ψ 137, 7.

4. Retrogression of the tone with lengthening of the vowel. עַתָּה now, עַתָּה: אַתָּה, אַתָּה. *h.*

5. Retrogression of the tone with restoration or (and) lengthening of a vowel that has been reduced to Sᵉwâ. *a)* Esp. frequent in the verb, cf. §11*d*: נָתַן he has given, *f.* נָתְנָה, נָתַתָּ; מָלֵא he is full, *pl.* מָלְאוּ, מָלֵאוּ; יִשְׁמֹר he will keep, *pl.* יִשְׁמְרוּ, יִשְׁמֹרוּ; שְׁמַע hear (iptv.), *pl.* שִׁמְעוּ, שְׁמָעוּ; יֻלַּד he was born, *pl.* יֻלְּדוּ, יֻלָּדוּ. *i.*
— β) In masc. segholate forms from ל״ה stems (§30*c*) e. g. פְּרִי fruit (orig. *parj*, §10/β), פֶּרִי; חֳלִי sickness, חֶלְיִ.— γ) Before the *suff.* ךָ (thy, thee *m.*): דְּבָרְךָ, דְּבָרֶךָ thy word, יִשְׁמָרְךָ, יִשְׁמֹר; יִשְׁמָרֶךָ he will keep thee.

6. Before the full endings of the impf. *ûn* and *în* the reduced vowel is restored in pause as a long vowel without retrogression of the tone: תִּדְבָּקִין, יִלְקֹטוּן. *k.*

7. In the impf. the accent, which a Wáw consec. has drawn to the penultimate syllable, is restored to the ultima, whereby certain vowel changes are occasioned, see §64*g. m.* *l.*

II. MORPHOLOGY (§§ 15—80).
A. THE PRONOUN (§§ 15—17).

§ 15. Personal Pronoun, esp. the pronomen separatum. § 15. *a.*

I   אֲנִי, אָנֹכִי   we   אֲנַחְנוּ, נַחְנוּ[β]
thou אַתָּה[α], *f.* אַתְּ[β]   you אַתֶּם, *f.* אַתֵּן[ε], אַתֵּנָה
he   הוּא, she הִיא[γ]   they הֵם, הֵמָּה, *f.* הֵנָּה[δ]

II, § 15.—§ 16. THE REMAINING PRONOUNS.

Forms in pause: אָנֹכִי, אֲנִי; אַתָּה, אָתָּה (§14c); אֲנַחְנוּ.
Arabic forms: sg. 1. ánā; 2. ánta, f. ánti; 3. húwă,
f. híjă. — pl. 1. náchnu; 2. ántum, f. antúnna; 3. hŭm,
f. húnna. — du. 2. ántumā, 3. húmā.

b. NOTE. α) Five times K°thîbh *defective* אֲנִ.—β) Seven times K°thîbh אַתְּ, read *attî*; originally with the ending *în*, cf. §51b. 53b.—γ) In the Pentat. often הוא K°thîb; Q°rê perpetuum §9b.— δ) Once K°thîbh אֱיֻ.—ε) Originally *u* in the second syllable, cf. §51b.—ζ) הֵן without demonstrative הָ— only after prefixes, *e. g.* בָּהֵן, see § 45.

c. The forms enumerated in §*a* express the nominative case only; the other cases are indicated in part by very much shortened modifications, which are attached to the word qualified and unite with it to form one whole (suffix pronouns, genly. for shortness suffixes). The suffixes attached to nouns denote the genitive, those joined to verbs the accusative. For details on the nominal suffix see § 22, on the verbal suffix §§ 78 ff., on the suff. to particles §§ 40 ff.

§ 16. a. § 16. The remaining Pronouns. The *demonstrative pronoun* is: זֶה this, f. זֹאת; *pl. comm.* אֵלֶּה.— Examples of its use (cf. §17h): הַיּוֹם הַזֶּה this day, זֶה הַיּוֹם this is the day; הַדְּבָרִים הָאֵלֶּה these words, אֵלֶּה בְּנֵי שֵׁם these are the sons of Shem.—Secondary forms in the Pentat.: הָאִישׁ הַלָּזֶה this man 24, 65; הֶעָרִים הָאֵל these towns 19, 25.

NOTE 1. זֶה also as adverb: 1) here; 2) now.   *b.*
NOTE 2. The separate pron. of 3. pers. is also used as *c.*
demonstrative pron.: הָאִישׁ הַהוּא that man.

The three forms of the *relative pronoun:* אֲשֶׁר, זוּ *d.*
(poet.) and שֶׁ׳ (esp. North-Israelitish and late) stand
for all numbers and genders. The very common אֲשֶׁר
serves in fact as *Nota relationis.* Hence it confers, in
the first place, relative signification to following
pronouns and adverbs, *e. g.*: בּוֹ in him, אֲשֶׁר...בּוֹ in
which; שָׁם there, אֲשֶׁר..שָׁם where (cf. §21*h*); secondly,
it is used in place of some conjunctions (that, because, when). Cf. § 87.

The *interrogative pronoun,* מִי who?, מָה what? is *e.*
sometimes used also for the *indef. pron. (quisquis, qui-
cunque).*

NOTE. מָה retains Qāmĕṣ with disjunctive accents; further *f.*
always before א and ר, generally before ה, when this letter has
not Qāmĕṣ. Before non-gutturals we write מַה followed by
Dāghēš and, usually, Maqqēph: מַה־בָּךְ, בַּה־לְּךָ. Before הָ, חָ, עָ,
sometimes also at the beginning of a sentence, the pointing is מֶה
(cf. §11/2): מֶה חָטָאתִי and מֶה עָשִׂיתָ 20, 9.—כִּי זֶה, בַּה־זֹּאת *v.* §42*g.*

§ 17. A. The Article in Hebrew (as also *e. g.* § 17.
in Greek) was originally a demonstr. pron., cf. הַיּוֹם this *a.*
day, to-day 4, 14, הַלַּיְלָה this night 19, 34, הַפַּעַם this
time=at last 2, 23; כָּעֵת מָחָר (§ *e*) to-morrow at
this time.

32   II, § 17. THE ARTICLE.

NOTE. This pronominal force also shows itself when the article is joined to the finite verb: הַבָּאָה 18, 21. 46, 27 (§76*h*), בְּנוֹ הַיּוּלַּד־לוֹ his son, that was born to him 21, 3. Cf. also הַשּׁוֹק וְהֶעָלֶיהָ the thigh and what was thereon (the fat) 1 Sam. 9, 24.

b. As shown by the examples just quoted, the article is usually written הַ followed by Dāghēš forte. The D. is dropped according to §6*f*, esp. when יְ or a part. Pi'ēl follows: הַמְרַגְּלִים, הַיְקוּם, הַיְבוּסִי.

c. When followed by a guttural (§10*a*1), the article takes *a*) — before unaccented *hā* and *'ā*, as also before *chā* and *ch°* (§11*f*2): הֶחֳרִים, הֶעָרִים, הֶעָוֹן; הֶחֳדָשִׁים, הֶחָכָם, הֶחָג; β) — before ע in the other cases, and always before א, ר, *e. g.*: הָעֲבָדִים, הָעֶבֶד, הָעָם; הָרָעָב, הָאוֹר; γ) — before ה and ח, in the other cases, *e. g.*: הַחֹדֶשׁ, הַחָכְמָה, הַחִכְמָה; הַחֵיכָל, הַהוּא.—Exceptions: to β) עִוֵּר, blind, takes הַ; to γ) הָהָר the mountain, הָהָרָה towards the mt., הָחַם and הָהֵמָּה those, הָחַי the living one 6, 19.

d. אֶרֶץ (earth, country) with the article becomes הָאָרֶץ.—On הַר (§*c*γ), פַּר, עַם see §26*c*ε.

e. After the prefixes בְּ, כְּ, לְ (§45) the ה of the article is elided together with the preceding Sʰwâ: הַמַּיִם the water, בַּמַּיִם in the w., לַמַּיִם to the w., כַּמַּיִם like the w., הָאוֹר the light, לָאוֹר to the l., הַחֹשֶׁךְ the darkness, לַחֹשֶׁךְ to the d.; הֶעָשָׁן the smoke, כֶּעָשָׁן like the s.—Exception: כְּהַיּוֹם (8) 39, 11 etc.

B. **Use of the Article.**—The article in Hebrew *f.* differs from the article in English in being found: 1. with well known material and class names: Abram was very rich בְּמִקְנֶה בַּכֶּסֶף וּבַזָּהָב in cattle, in silver and in gold 13,2; pitch it בַּזֶּפֶת with pitch 6, 14.— 2. with many abstract nouns, esp. with physical and moral defects: struck them בַּסַּנְוֵרִים with blindness 19, 11.—3. frequently with names of towns, when the recollection of the appellative signification was still preserved: הָעַי, הָרָמָה.—4. with the vocative of nouns otherwise qualified to receive it: הַמֶּלֶךְ O King!— 5. with comparisons, when the *tertium comparationis* is regarded as attribute of the class to which the object employed in the comparison belongs: he staggers כַּשִּׁכּוֹר [because all drunken men stagger] like a drunken man; Isa. 1,18: if your sins be red כַּשָּׁנִים like scarlet, they shall become white כַּשֶּׁלֶג as snow; if they be red כַּתּוֹלָע like crimson, they shall become כַּצֶּמֶר like wool.* The article is not employed, however, when the *tert. compar.* is affirmed of only a part of the class.

The article does not stand: 1. before substan- *g.* tives that are determined by a following genetive or suffix: דְּבַר ה' the word of Jahwe, דְּבָרִי ὁ λόγος μου.—

---

* Cf. Ed. Riehm on ψ 17, 12 (in: Herm. Hupfeld, Die Psalmen² I, 445. 446).

34   II, § 17.—18. GENDER.

2. often in poetry: לְ 2, 2 אֶרֶץ; but after בְּ, כְּ, לְ usually as in prose: בְּמִשְׁפָּט לְ 1, 5, בַּשָּׁמַיִם לְ 2, 4.

h.   The article with adjectives: הָעִיר הַגְּדֹלָה the great city.—So usu. with the demon. pron.: הָאִישׁ הַזֶּה this man, בַּלַּיְלָה הַהוּא on that night 19, 35; though also: בַּלַּיְלָה הוּא 19, 33 &c. (doubtless for reasons of euphony), מִשְּׁבֻעָתִי זֹאת from this my oath 24, 8.

B. THE NOUN (§§ 18—39).

§ 18.
a.   § 18. G e n d e r. The Hebrew language has no special forms for the neuter. Where other languages use the neuter, we find in Hebrew mostly the *fem. pl.*, and not unfrequently the *masc. pl.* or *fem. sg.*, e. g. בָּזֶה אֵדַע thereby shall I know 24, 14.

b.   NOTE. The masculine, as the superior gender, stands not unfrequently for the feminine, especially in the suffix pronouns: סָתְמוּם they stopped them (the wells הַבְּאֵרוֹת *f.*) 26, 15; אֲבִיכֶם your father (Leah and Rachel are addressed) 31, 9.

c.   The masc. sing. has no termination. The old termination ת of the fem. sing. is still preserved α) after *û* and *î*: גָּלוּת, עֵדוּת; מִצְרִית, בְּרִית; β) when a helping vowel (— or —, §36*a*) has been inserted after the immediately preceding cons.: מַאֲכֶלֶת knife, for *maᵃkhalt*; תּוֹכַחַת reproof, for *tôkhacht*; esp. in partcps. יֹלֶדֶת a woman in childbirth, for *jô-ladht*; γ) seldom as *áth*, in בָּרֶקֶת, emerald, and in proper names צָרְפַת, גִּבְעַת.—The ת of the old ending *áth* has been in almost all cases dropped, the ă, now standing in an open syllable, lengthened to ā, and, as an indication of this, ה, rendered superfluous however by the introduction of the vocalisation, added as mater lectionis (§2b): מִצְוָה commandment, for miṣwăth, cf. §21d.

§ 19. Number. Besides the sing. and the plur. there is also a *dual* in Hebrew, which is formed almost exclusively, however, from names of things that occur in pairs. The ending of the dual is בִֿיִם— *ájim*: רַגְלַיִם feet, אַלְפַּיִם 2000.

§ 19. a.

The masculine plural ending is ־ִים, also *defective* ־ִם, the feminine וֹת, also *defective* ת: עֵד witness, עֵדִים; גּוֹי people, גּוֹיִם (pron. *gōjim*); צַדִּיק righteous, צַדִּיקִים, צַדִּקִים and צַדִּיקָם; סֻכָּה booth, סֻכּוֹת and סֻכֹּת.

§ 19. b.

NOTE 1. Many words with the termination of the fem. sing. have ־ִים— in the *pl.*, *e. g.* שָׁנָה year, שָׁנִים; *vice versâ:* אָב father, אָבוֹת; חֲלוֹם, חֲלֹמוֹת.

NOTE 2. The plural in Hebrew not only denotes a numerical plurality, but also serves to indicate other relations, especially in the case of abstract nouns. Note further the "internally multiplying" plural, *e. g.* אָדוֹן lord, אֲדֹנִים lords and lord, אֲדֹנֵינוּ our lord (cf. Germ. "unsere Herrschaft") 1 Sam. 25, 14.

§ 20. Case. Hebrew had originally three case-endings. Cf. in Arabic:

§ 20. a.

	the book	a book	the man	the b. of the man.
N.	al-kitâbu	kitâbun	ar-raǵulu	kitâbu 'r-raǵuli
G.	al-kitâbi	kitâbin	ar-raǵuli	
Ac.	al-kitâba	kitâban	ar-raǵula	

b.   NOTE. If the genet. is determined (*i. e.* is a proper name or has the article), the *nomen regens* is regarded in Hebr. as in Arabic as likewise determined.

c.   In biblical Hebrew these endings are preserved only in ה– *locale* and as meaningless affix-syllables (for the most part as archaisms and in poetry): α) *ā*, ה– of direction [cf. our suffix *-ward*], almost always unaccented: מִצְרַיִם, Egypt, מִצְרַיְמָה to E.; בַּיִת, הַבַּיְתָה to the house; אֶרֶץ, אַרְצָה כְּנַעַן to the land of C.*, הַחוּצָה, הָהָרָה, הַשָּׁמַיְמָה, הַנֶּגְבָּה. Entirely meaningless is the ending ה– *e. g.* in לַיְלָה night, mod. Gk. ἡ νύχθα.— β) *ō* and *i*, esp. in the *stat. constr.* (*v.* §21*a*): וְחַיְתוֹ אֶרֶץ 1, 24; בְּנוֹ בְעוֹר Num. 24, 3; גְּנֻבְתִי G. 31, 39; בְּנִי and אֹסְרִי 49, 11; מַלְכִּי־צֶדֶק 14, 18.

d.   Hence in many cases (*e. g.* always in *m. sg.,* of nouns with unchangeable vowels) the gen. and acc. are quite the same as the nom. Exx.: α) Gen.: שֵׁן ivory, כִּסֵּא שֵׁן a throne of ivory, כִּסֵּא דָוִד the throne (§*b*) of David; יוֹצֵר potter, כְּלִי יוֹצֵר a potter's vessel; הַנַּעַר the boy, קוֹל הַנַּעַר the boy's voice.—β) Acc.: מָצָא עֵזֶר he found help, אִישׁ הָרַגְתִּי a man have I slain; וַיְכַל מְלַאכְתּוֹ and he finished his work; נָסַכְתִּי מַלְכִּי I have appointed my king.

e.   The determined acc. is often, esp. in prose, indicated by prefixing אֶת־ or אֵת: In the beginning God

---

* בְּנַעַן has Dāghēš forte conjunctivum, §6*e*β.

created אֶת־הַשָּׁמַיִם וְאֵת הָאָרֶץ; and she bare אֶת־קַיִן Cain; thou hast scattered אֶת־כָּל־אֹיְבָי all my foes.

§ 21. A. The Construct State. In expressions such as "the voice of the boy", "a vessel of a potter", the second subst., the genetive, as the subject to which something is assigned, has the main tone or stress. The first word, the nominative, is pronounced more rapidly, with less stress. This explains the fact that in Hebr. the first subst. is, if possible, shortened, especially in regard to its vocalisation. §21. a.

The rule §11c is here applied as if the nom. were unaccented and the second word a monosyllable or had the accent on the first syllable. נָגִיד prince, נְגִיד צֹר the prince of Tyre. Further exx. v. §e. b.

The first member of such a connexion, indeed every noun (the *nomen regens*) closely connected with the following word, stands in the *status constructus* (construct state). *Status absolutus* (absolute state) is the name used to designate the unshortened form of the noun, when not intimately connected with the following word. c.

In consequence of the intimate relation of the first word to the gen., the old ending *áth* (§18cγ) has maintained itself in the *st. con.* of the *f. sg.* in place of the later ־ָה : מִצְוָה, מִצְוַת ה' the commandment of Jahwe. d.

e. The *st. con.* of the *m. pl.* ends in ◌ֵי־ (formerly *aj*, *v.* §10*f*a): גְּבוֹר, גִּבּוֹרֵי מוֹאָב the heroes of Moab; כּוֹכָב, *pl.* כּוֹכָבִים, *c.* כּוֹכְבֵי הַשָּׁמַיִם the stars of heaven; חָכָם, *pl.* חֲכָמִים, *c.* חַכְמֵי פַרְעֹה Pharaoh's wise men*. The ending of the *st. con.* of the dual is the same: עֵינֵי ה', עֵינַיִם the eyes of J.; רַגְלֵי הָאִישׁ, רַגְלַיִם the feet of the man. In the *fem. pl.* the ending of the *st. con.* is the same as that of the *st. abs.*: מִצְוָה, הַמִּצְוֹת the commandments, מִצְוֹת ה' the commandments of J.

f. B. Use of the Construct State. The *st. con.* serves to indicate not only the subjective but also the objective genetive: יִרְאַת ה' the fear of (one feels towards) Jahwe, זַעֲקַת סְדֹם the cry regarding (of) Sodom 18, 20. Before suffixes (§22*b*): חֲמָסוֹ his wrong ψ 7, 17, חֲמָסִי the wrong towards me G. 16, 5.

g. The *st. con.* can likewise stand 1. before prepositions: אַחַד מִמֶּנּוּ one of us 3, 22; שִׂמְחַת בַּקָּצִיר the joy in the harvest; esp. after a participle: יוֹשְׁבֵי בָהּ ψ 24, 1; מַשְׁכִּימֵי בַבֹּקֶר Isa. 5, 11; מְשִׁתָּאֵה לָהּ G. 24, 21.

h. 2. before relative clauses (that stand virtually in the gen.): מְקוֹם אֲשֶׁר יוֹסֵף אָסוּר שָׁם the place where J. was bound 40, 3; esp. with such as are not introduced by אֲשֶׁר, *e. g.* בְּיוֹם הִצִּיל ה' אוֹתוֹ on the day in which J.

---

* פַּרְעֹה is regarded as tone-syllable acc. to §*b*; ־ֵ syll. before the tone; ־ֵ loses its vowel acc. to §11*c*2; finally, the vowel of ח must be short, because now standing in a shut unaccented syllable.

had saved him ψ 18, 1; קִרְיַת חָנָה דָוִד the city where D. had encamped, Isa. 29, 1. More in §87h.m.

§ 22. The Noun with unchangeable vowels (Paradigm on p. 40 f.). § 22.

a. The derivation of the *suffixa nominis* from the *pron. absolutum* is particularly well seen in the 1. *pl.* With עָדֵנוּ and עָדֵינוּ comp. אֲנִי. This example shows at the same time that the pronoun on being affixed is mutilated at the beginning, cf. πατήρ μου with πατὴρ ἐμοῦ.—With the change of ה to כ in the 2. pers. (אַתָּה, ךָ; אַתֶּם, כֶּם) comp. the reverse change in the inflexion of the verb §51c.

b. The nominal suffixes denote the gen. and are attached to the *st. con.* (§21*f*). Forms like מִקְדָּשֵׁךְ §24a, מַלְכֵּנוּ §28g are only apparent exceptions.

c. A distinction is made between light and heavy suffixes. The heavy suff. are: כֶם, כֶן, הֶם, הֶן.

d. Between the singular noun ending in a consonant, and such suffixes as begin with a consonant, there is generally inserted a "union-vowel" (*Bindevocal*, cf. §79e). This vowel is:

ē with *suff.* 2. *f. sg.*: עָרֵךְ and 1. *pl.*: עָרֵנוּ,

a with *suff.* 3. pers.: עָדוֹ (î from *ahû*), עָדָהּ, עָדָם (ם — from *ahèm*), עָדְךָ; and 2. *m. sg.* in pause: עָדֶךָ (§14*iγ*, *ekhā* half lengthening for *ákhā*).

Šᵉwâ mob. with *suff.* 2. *m. sg.*: עָרְךָ, hence מִצְוָתְךָ with Qāmēṣ.

The union-vowel has often been completely dropped before the heavy suffixes: מִצְוָתְכֶם, מִצְוָתְכֶן.—In עַבְדְּכֶם Šᵉwâ mobile, because the vowel of the stem is unchangeable.

NOTE. כֶם, כֶן retain their aspirated pronunciation even after a shut syllable (contrary to §6a): חֲלַבְכֶם (cf. Germ. *Papachen* alongside of *machen*).

e. Forms without union-vowel [*sg.* 2. *f.* ךְ, 3. *m.* הוּ and וֹ, 3. *f.* הָ; *pl.* 1. נוּ, 3. *m.* הֶם, 3. *f.* הֶן] are appended to אָב, אָח, חָם, פֶּה, whose *st. con.* ends in a vowel, §38; likewise in part, for the same reason, to nouns from ל״ה-stems, §§30*c*. 31; finally, always to the *st. con.* of the *m. pl.*

II, § 22. THE NOUN WITH UNCHANGEABLE VOWELS.

f. In appending suffixes to masculine plurals the old form of the *st. con. aj* is taken as the ground-form (עֵדָיו, עֲדָיִךְ, עֵדַי). Before the 2. *m. sg.* and the 3. *f. sg.* it becomes ־ֶי־ (עֵדֶיהָ, עֵדֶיךָ), before the suffixes of the *pl.* ־ֵי־ (עֵדֵימוֹ &c.).

g. In appending suffixes to plurals in וֹת a twofold indication of the plural is found almost without exception, viz: a masculine in addition to the feminine ending: מִצְוֹתַי instead of *miṣwôth + î*, αἱ ἐντολαί μου. Only the *suff.* 3. *pl.* (ב־ֶ־, ־ָ־ן) are attached quite as frequently to the simple plural ending וֹת. We find always עַצְמוֹתָב, הֹורוֹתָם, שְׁמוֹתָן; mostly אֲבוֹתָם *patres eorum* (*suos*), not till later אֲבֹתֵיהֶם.

h. Only the follg. have a special form in pause: 1. *sg.* and 2. *f. sg.* in the *pl.* and *du.*: עֵדָי, עֵדֶיךָ, עֵדַיִךְ, עֵדָיהָ; as also 2. *m. sg.* (§*d*): קוֹלֶךָ, קוֹלְךָ.

i. Rare forms of *suff.* in the *sg.*: α) 2. *m. sg.* כָה for ךָ, acc. to §2*b*, יָדְכָה thy hand, cf. לְכָה, בְּאָכָה §76*h*.—β) 3. *m. sg.* חוּ, esp. לְמִינֵהוּ (14) for לְמִינוֹ (4) after its kind [union-vowel *ē*]. רֵעֲהוּ his neighbour, bec. רֵעַ is a contraction from רֵעֶה.—ה, etymological spelling for וֹ [*v.*§*d*], *e. g.* אָהֳלֹה (4) his tent.—γ) 3. *f. sg.* sometimes ־ֹה for ־ָּה. ∥ δ) 1. *pl.* ־ָנוּ, thus always כֻּלָּנוּ 42, 11 and elsewhere, cf. לָנוּ §45*b*.— ε) 3. *m. pl.* poet.: חֶלְבָּמוֹ their fat, פִּרְיָמוֹ their fruit, פִּימוֹ their mouth. Cf. לָמוֹ §45*c*, יְכַחֲלֻבוֹ §79*c*.—ζ) 3. *f. pl.* קִרְבָּנָה their inward part 41, 21, לְיַחְמֵנָה (Inf. Pi.) 30, 41. כֻּלָּנָה it all (lit. *summa earum, fem.=ntr.* §18*a*). לְבָנֶנָה 21, 29. לְבָהֶן 21, 28.

k. Rare forms of *suff.* in the *plur.*: α) 3. *m. pl.* מְבַחֲרִימוֹ, מוֹסְרוֹתֵימוֹ ψ 2, 3.—β) Written *defective*, *i. e.* with omission of the י, *e. g.* דְּבָרְךָ thy words for דְּבָרֶיךָ, often not to be distinguished from דְּבָרְךָ thy word, pause form of דְּבָרֶךָ. לְמִינֵהֶן 1, 21, וּמֵחֶלְבֵהֶן 4, 4.

Singular.

עֵד witness	מִצְוָה commandment
עֵד שֶׁקֶר a lying witness*	מִצְוַת ה' the com. of Jahwe
עֵדִי 1. *sg.* my w.	מִצְוָתִי 1. *sg.* my c.
עֵדְךָ 2. *m. sg.* thy w.	מִצְוָתְךָ 2. *m. sg.* thy c.
עֵדֵךְ 2. *f. sg.* thy w.	מִצְוָתֵךְ 2. *f. g.* thy c.

---

* Literally: *testis mendacii, i. e. testis mendax.*

Singular.

עֵדוֹ	3. m. sg. his w.		מִצְוָתוֹ	3. m. sg. his c.
עֵדָהּ	3. f. sg. her w.		מִצְוָתָהּ	3. f. sg. her c.
עֵדֵנוּ	1. pl. our w.		מִצְוָתֵנוּ	1. pl. our c.
עֵדְכֶם	2. m. pl. your w.		מִצְוַתְכֶם	2. m. pl. your c.
עֵדְכֶן	2. f. pl. your w.		מִצְוַתְכֶן	2. f. pl. your c.
עֵדָם	3. m. pl. their w.		מִצְוָתָם	3. m. pl. their c.
עֵדָן	3. f. pl. their w.		מִצְוָתָן	3. f. pl. their c.

Plural.

עֵדִים	witnesses		מִצְוֹת	commandments
עֵדֵי שֶׁקֶר	lying w.		מִצְוֹת ה׳	the c. of Jahwe
עֵדַי	1. sg. my w.		מִצְוֹתַי	1. sg. my c.
עֵדֶיךָ	2. m. sg. thy w.		מִצְוֹתֶיךָ	2. m. sg. thy c.
עֵדַיִךְ	2. f. sg. thy w.		מִצְוֹתַיִךְ	2. f. sg. thy c.
עֵדָיו	3. m. sg. his w.		מִצְוֹתָיו	3. m. sg. his c.
עֵדֶיהָ	3. f. sg. her w.		מִצְוֹתֶיהָ	3. f. sg. her c.
עֵדֵינוּ	1. pl. our w.		מִצְוֹתֵינוּ	1. pl. our c.
עֵדֵיכֶם	2. m. pl. your w.		מִצְוֹתֵיכֶם	2. m. pl. your c.
עֵדֵיכֶן	2. f. pl. your w.		מִצְוֹתֵיכֶן	2. f. pl. your c.
עֵדֵיהֶם	3. m. pl. their w.		מִצְוֹתָם	3. m. pl. their c.
עֵדֵיהֶן	3. f. pl. their w.		מִצְוֹתָן	3. f. pl. their c.

§ 23. **Masculines with changeable Vowel in the Penult.** Cf. the phonetic law §11c1.—נָשִׂיא, נְשִׂיא הָאָרֶץ the prince of the land, נְשִׂיאֵי יִשְׂרָאֵל, נְשִׂיאִים, נְשִׂיאָיהּ.

- b. With final guttural: a) *Páthach furtivum*: הַמָּשִׁיחַ, מְשִׁיחִי, but מְשִׁיחִי הֹ &c.; with final א: נָבִיא;—β) before הֹ, בֶם, כֶן *Cháṭēph-Páthach*: בְּרִיאֲכֶם.

c. If the word begins with a guttural, §10a3 takes effect: עָוֺן, הָאֲמֹרִי, עֲוֺנִי, עֲוֺנֺת *pl.*, עֲוֺנֹתַי.

d. In nouns of the formation קְדָרוֹן the *Dāghēš* is in most cases dropped with the —ָ. זְכָרוֹן, זִכְרוֹנָהּ; but עַצְבוֹן, עַצְבוֹנָהּ.

§ 24.
a.   § 24. Masculines with changeable Vowel in last Syllable. I. *Qāmēṣ* remains in an open syllable before the tone (also before הֹ, §22d), becomes Páthach in an unaccented closed syllable (*st. c. sg.* and before כֶּם, כֶּן) and disappears entirely, acc. to §11c1, when the tone is moved two places forward (*st. con. pl.* and before —ְיהֶן, —ְיהֶם, —ְיכֶן, —ְיכֶם). מִקְדָּשׁ, מִקְדַּשׁ ה', מִקְדָּשׁוֹ, מִקְדָּשִׁי, מִקְדָּשׁוֹת, מִקְדָּשִׁים, מִקְדְּשֵׁי; מִסְפָּר, מִסְפַּרְכֶם, מִסְפַּר־אֵל.

b. With a guttural: מוֹרָא, מַלְאָךְ; מַלְאֲכֵי דָוִד, מַלְאָכִים, מוֹרַאֲכֶם.

c. Monosyllables. יָד, יַד הָאָדָם, יָדְךָ, יֶדְכֶם!, *du.* יָדַיִם, יָדָיו, דָּמִים, הִמְּכֶם! (§11/1), דָּמָהּ, דַּם הָרָשָׁע, דָּם—יְדֵיהֶם, יְדֵי עֵשָׂו, דְּמֵיהֶם. (Shortened from *dámẹ, jádhẹ*, from ה"ל.)

d. II. *Ṣērê* remains in *st. con. sg.* unchanged: יֵצֶר הָאָרֶץ. It is found shortened to *Seghôl* only before Maqqēph; almost (§38) without exception in בֵּן, *e. g.* בֶּן־הָרָן the son of Haran, sometimes in שֵׁם, *e. g.* שֶׁם־

שֵׁמֵר.—On the other hand Ṣērê disappears even in the open syllable before the tone: אֹיְבִים, אֹיְבִי, אֹיֵב. Before הּ, כֶם, כָן it is shortened to ĕ or even to original ĭ. אֹיְבָה, אֹיֵב; לְגֵרָהּ, לְגֵרִי, לֵצֵר.—To this group belong all participles with ē in the last syllable and not a few adjectives, such as אִלֵּם dumb, חֵרֵשׁ deaf, עִוֵּר blind, pl. עִוְרִים, חֵרְשִׁים, אִלְּמִים (וְ) v. §6f).

With a guttural: גָּאֵל, גְּאָלִי, גְּאָלָה; בִּרְאָכֶם; מוֹעֵד, e. וּבְמוֹעֲדֵיכֶם, מוֹעֲדִים.—The forms מִזְבַּח, st. con. of מִזְבֵּחַ and מַעֲשַׂר or מַעֲשֵׂר, st. c. of מַעֲשֵׂר, are to be explained by the fondness of their final consonants for a. Cf. however מִסְפֵּד lamentation, con. מִסְפַּד and זָקֵן §25d.

Monosyllables. בֵּן see §38.—שֵׁם, שְׁמוֹ, שִׁמְךָ, שְׁמָהּ, f. עֵצְךָ, עֵצִים, עֵצָה, עֵץ הַחַיִּים, עֵץ.—שְׁמוֹת הַגִּבּוֹרִים, שֵׁמוֹת, עֲצֵי עֹלָה.

§ 25. **Masculines with two changeable Vowels.** Phonetic law §11c2.—I. Vowels ā and ă. §25. a.

כְּנָפָיו, כְּנָפַיִם, du. כְּנֵי הַכְּרוּב, כְּנָפוֹ, כָּנָף; but, since the tone is thrown forward two places, כַּנְפֵיהֶם and כַּנְפֵי רוּחַ. So זָנָב tail, זְנָבוֹת, con. זַנְבוֹת. Syllable loosely closed (§12q), hence פ and ב aspirated.

In the third syllable before the tone ă is reduced b. by thinning to ĭ (§11f1), except when one of the first two consonants is a guttural (two other exceptions §a): זְבִיחֶם. דִּבְרֵי ה׳, דִּבְרֵיכֶם, דְּבָרַי, דְּבָרִים, דָּבָר. But (cf. also §10a3) חַכְמֵי, חֲכָמִים, חֲכַם לֵב חָכָם,

נֶהָרוֹת פַּרְעֹה and נָהָר, נְהָרִים, כּוֹשׁ הָרֵי, fem. pl. נְהָרוֹת, נַהֲרוֹת בָּבֶל.

c. II. Vowels ē and ā. לֵבָב ·לִבְבִי, לְבָבִי, לְבַב פַּרְעֹה, לֵבָב, עִנְּבֵי רוֹשׁ, הָעֲנָבִים poisonous grapes (Dāghēš v. §6eβ).

d. III. Vowels ā and ē. 1. Substantives. Ṣērê is shortened in the st. c. to Páthach, remains, however, in an open syllable before the tone (differently with אֹיֵב &c. §24d): זָקֵן, זְקַן בֵּיתוֹ the eldest of his house, זְקֵנִים, חָצֵר, חֲצַר הַפְּחָנִים, זִקְנֵיכֶם. With a guttural: חָצֵר, זִקְנֵי יִשְׂרָאֵל .—Examples with כֶּם, כֶּן: חַצְרֵי בֵית הָאֱלֹהִים, חֲצֵרֶיהָ, חֲצֵרוֹ in the sg. do not occur.

e. In the st. con. the following resemble segholates גֶּדֶר wall, גֶּדֶר ; יַרְכַיִם, יַרְכֵי, יֶרֶךְ אַבְרָהָם, loin, יָרֵךְ (§28): כְּתֵפִי .suff ,כְּתַף humerus, latus, st. c. כָּתֵף ; גְּדֵרוֹ, הֶחָצֵר, cf. עָרֵל &c. §h.

f. . 2. Verbal adjectives (§58b). Several retain Ṣērê in the pl. st. con.: שְׂמֵחִי, שְׂמֵחִים, רָשַׁן, וְשֵׁנָה, pl. c. יְשֵׁנֵי; אֱלֹהִים, חָפֵץ, חֲפֵצִים, חֲפֵצֵי רָעָתִי ψ 40, 15; אָבֵל, אֲבֵל־אֵם! שְׂמֵחִים, שְׂמֵחָה, שָׂמֵחַ—·אֲבֵלָיו, אֲבֵלֵי צִיּוֹן, אֲבֵלִים ψ 35, 14, שְׂמֵחַי רָעָתִי at my misfortune ψ 35, 26 and שְׂמֵחַ־לֵב Isa. 24, 7. ‖ The pl. con. is wanting in: שָׁכֵן neighbour, inhabitant, שָׁלֵם integer, שָׁכֵן שֹׁמְרוֹן ,שְׁכֵנוֹ ,שְׁכֵנֵינוּ; שְׁלֵמִים; חָסֵר, c. חֲסַר לֵב: קָרֵב approaching, קְרֵבִים; יְבֵשָׁה, יָבֵשׁ dry. רְעֵבִים, רָעֵב; שָׂבֵעַ ,שְׂבֵעָה, c. שְׂבַע, עָמֵל, עֲמֵלִים; חָדֵל c. חֲדַל־. With rejection of Ṣērê: חָנֵף profane, חֲנֵפִים, חַנְפֵי לֵב.

g. Verbal adjectives ending in א retain Ṣērê in the

II, § 25.—26. MASC. OF ONE SYLL. WITH DOUBLE FINAL CONSONANT. 45

con. sg.: מְלֵא, יְרֵאִי; יְרֵאֵי ח׳, יְרֵאֶיךָ, יְרֵאִים, יְרֵא אֱלֹהִים, יְרָא, טְמֵאַת הַשֵּׁם, טְמֵא שְׂפָתַיִם, טְמֵאָה, טָמֵא; מְלֵאִים, מְלֵא יָמִים *impura quoad nomen;* צְמֵא, צְמֵאָה.

h. עָרְלֵי, עֲרֵלִים, *pl.* עֲרַל שְׂפָתַיִם, (§*e*) and עֲרֵל לֵב *c.* עָרֵל,
כְּבָדֵי לָשׁוֹן, כְּבֵדִים, כְּבַד לָשׁוֹן and כְּבַד עָוֹן *c.* כָּבֵד; בָּשָׂר;
(אֲרַךְ *long, only in st. c.*:) אֶרֶךְ אַפַּיִם *longsuffering.*

i. Anomalous: צֵלָע *side, rib, c.* צֶלַע and צֵלָע, *suff.*
צַלְעִי, *pl.* צְלָעוֹת, צַלְעֹתָיו.—עָקֵב *heel,* עֲקֵב עֵשָׂו, עֲקֵבוֹ,
עֲקֵבַי, עִקְּבֵי־סוּס (*hoofs, Dāg.* §6*e*β).

§ 26. **Masculines of one Syllable with the final Consonant doubled.** In those nouns of the forms *qaṭl, qiṭl, quṭl* in which the second letter of the stem is either identical with the third or is the letter נ, which assimilates with ease (§10*g*), the last two consonants coalesce and form one double consonant. From the stem חצץ we have, formed after *qiṭl,* חִצִּי my arrow, חִצִּים arrows; so from עזז: עִזִּים (for *ʿinzîm*), goats, עִזֵּךְ thy goats.

§ 26.
a.

In all forms with formative additions (esp. *suff.* *b.* and *pl.*) the vowel of the stem, because standing in a closed syllable, is unchangeable. In the sing. on the contrary, when without afformatives, compensation lengthening (§11*e*) takes place, since the last letter of a word cannot have *Dāg. forte.* *ŭ* becomes *ō, ĭ* becomes *ē; ă* alone usually remains unchanged, except when coinciding with a logical pause (Stade §193*b*). (See, however, §cε). Thus "arrow" is not *chiṣṣ* but חֵץ; "goat" not *ʿizz* but עֵז; "timbrel" not *tupp* but תֹּף; but from עַם, עֲמָם people. — The long vowel resulting from the compensation lengthening is shortened only before Maqqēph, e: g. רֹב abundance, רָב־אֹכֶל, but רָב הָגָן.

c. Anomalous. α) ŏ beside ŭ. עֹז strength, עֻזִּי beside עָזִּי, עֻזָּה beside עָזָּה. — β) Dāghēš is sometimes omitted before ה and כ (§6/3): חֹק, חָקָה, חָקְכֶם. — γ) In a few words ă is thinned to ĭ in a syllable with Dāghēš: פַּח, צַד, צִדָּה; פִּתָּה; *chăth* fear (חַת), חִתְּכֶם. — δ) When the consonant to be doubled is a guttural or ר, ă is always lengthened in the *plur*.: הָר, הָרְכֶם, הָרֵי שֹׁמְרוֹן; צָר, צָרֵי, צָרֵיהֶם. — ε) הָר, פַּר, עַם with the article are always written הָעָם, הַפָּר, הָהָר.

d. In some words the third radical is doubled without any etymological reason. Hence their inflexion resembles that of the nouns treated of in this §. Examples: לְאֹם nation, לְאֻמִּי, לְאֻמִּים; חֵירֹם and עֵירֹם naked, גְּמַלֵּיהֶם, עֵירֻמִּים, עֲרֻמִּים (written *plene*); גָּמָל, גְּמַלִּים, עֲרֻמִּים; קְטַנָּה, קָטֹן.

§ 27. § 27. Masculine Segholate Forms. General remarks. Nouns of the forms *qaṭl*, *qiṭl*, *quṭl* (*qoṭl*) not belonging to § 26 are called segholate nouns. They are so called because the helping vowel employed, acc. to §11*i*, in the formation of the uninflected *sing*. is most frequently Sᵉghôl.

We classify segholate forms as follows: A. from strong stems (to these belong also the stems with gutturals), which have a helping vowel in the *sg.* and *pl.*, §28; B. from stems ע״י and ע״ו, with a helping vowel in most cases only in the *sg.*, §29; C. from stems ל״ה with a helping vowel in the *pl.* and *du.*, §30.

§ 28. A. Masculine Segholate Forms from strong Stems. The monosyllabic ground-form remains in the singular before all afformatives, because by these the second consonant is drawn to the following syllable, and a helping vowel may accordingly be dispensed with: *malk* מַלְכּוֹ his king, *siphr* סִפְרִי my book, *arṣ* אַרְצָה כְּנַעַן to the land of Canaan.—Instead of the original *ŭ*, however, there is found (almost, *v.* §*n*) always *ŏ*: *qudš* קָדְשׁוֹ his holiness. Original *ă* is, acc. to §11/1, often thinned to *ĭ*: *ṣadq* צִדְקִי my righteousness.

§ 28. a.

The dual is likewise formed usually from the ground- b. form: אָזְנַיִם, רַגְלַיִם, קַרְנַיִם, אַלְפַּיִם. But אַלְפֵי יְהוּדָה is *pl*.

In the uninflected singular (*stat. abs.* and *con.*) c. the doubly closed syllable of the ground-form is opened by an (of course, toneless) helping vowel, mostly ֶ , being placed under the last consonant but one (§12*k*). In consequence of this

    ă becomes *ė*   *malk* מֶלֶךְ king
    ĭ becomes *ē*   *siphr* סֵפֶר book
    (*ŭ*) *ŏ* becomes *ō*   *qodš* קֹדֶשׁ holiness.

d.   If the third or the second radical is a guttural, Páthach is usually the helping vowel employed: זֶ֫רַע, תֹּ֫אַר‎, רֹ֫חַב‎, נֹ֫גַהּ‎; but with final א, S⁰ghôl: פֶּ֫רֶא wild ass, דֶּ֫שֶׁא young grass. (Exceptions: חֵטְא sin, גֵּיא §29a, שָׁוְא §29c).—The final consonant in בְּכָה (usually בְּכִי acc. to §30) and הֶ֫גֶה is, acc. to §2b, no guttural.

e.   When the second consonant of the stem is a guttural, an a under the first remains in most cases unchanged (§12l): נַ֫עַר‎, שַׁ֫חַר‎, לַ֫הַט‎. But לֶ֫חֶם‎, bread, and usually רֶ֫חֶם (4 times רַ֫חַם).

f.   The st. con. generally remains unchanged. But תְּמַע and שְׁבַע (§ 39) always תְּשַׁע and שֶׁ֫בַע; also occasional forms like זְרַע‎, נְטַע &c. along with the usual זֶ֫רַע &c.

g.   In pause (§14dα) — and — of the tone-syllable are in most cases changed to —: דָּ֫רֶךְ‎, כָּ֫סֶף‎, נָ֫עַר (unchanged remain esp. מֶ֫לֶךְ‎, צֶ֫דֶק); this seldom occurs with —: שֵׁ֫בֶט‎, שָׁ֫בֶט.

h.   In the plural a helping Qāmĕṣ* is inserted, the retention and omission of which are regulated acc. to §11c. מְלָכִים for malakhîm, so with light suff.: מְלָכֵ֫ינוּ, מְלָכֶ֫יהָ; with tone thrown forward: מַלְכֵי מָדָ֫ן‎, מַלְכֵיהֶם‎. So חֹדֶשׁ‎, חָדְשֵׁיכֶם‎. Syllable loosely closed, as §25a.

i.   If the last consonant but one is a guttural,

---

* De Lagarde (Mittheilungen 1884, p. 226) derives the plural from another ground-form (malak).

for greater ease in pronunciation Sᵉwâ is generally replaced by Chāṭeph (§ 10a 4): נַעֲרָה, פָּעֳלוּ, נַעֲרוֹ, נַעֲרֵי; then, acc. to §5f: נַעֲרָה, פָּעֳלָה.—Complete close of syllable generally with ח; e. g. לֶחֶם, always לַחְמִי, רֶחֶם, &c.; always רַחֲמָה. Less frequently with ע, e. g. זֶעַם, זַעֲמִי.

נֶגֶב south country, נֶגֶד opposite, נֶכֶד posterity, *k.* retain ֶ before afformatives in the sing.: נֶגְדִּי, הַנֶּגְבָּה, וּלְנֶכְדִּי.

Nouns beginning with חָ and עָ receive before *l.* Sᵉwâ almost uniformly Sᵉghôl, e. g. עֵגֶל calf, עֶגְלְךָ, עֶגְלֵי זָהָב, עֲגָלִים.

In the opened syllable of the stem some words *m.* have sometimes ֶ, sometimes ֵ, esp. רֶשַׁע and רֵשַׁע, נֶצַח and נֵצַח (in לָנֶצַח always ֶ), גֶּדֶר and גֵּדֶר. With suffixes: קָדְרוֹ, יִשְׁעֵנוּ.

Nouns of the form *quṭl.*—1. *ŭ* has been preserved only *n.* in גָּדְלוֹ ψ 150,2, but 5 times גָּדְלוֹ &c., קָמְצוֹ his handful (3), רֹב אִישׁ plottings of men ψ 31, 21.

2. Somewhat more frequent is the change of *ŭ (ŏ)* *o.* to *i*, e.g. חֹצֶן bosom, חִצְנוֹ alongside of חָצְנִי; נֹכַח opposite, נִכְחוֹ; בֹּסֶר unripe grapes, בִּסְרוֹ; אֹמֶר word, אִמְרוֹ, אֲמָרַי ה׳, אֲמָרִים. ('*ēmĕr* and similar forms in the lexicons are accordingly to be cancelled).

3. Short *o* for Sᵉwâ: גֹּרֶן, הַגֳּרָנוֹת, further קָדָשִׁים, *p.* קָדָשַׁי and שָׁרָשָׁיו, שָׁרָשֶׁיהָ (for the first sign under ק׳ and שׁ׳ cannot be *ā*, Jewish grammarians notwithstanding; cf. §4c3).

q. 4. The *pl.* of אֹהֶל is אֹהָלִים, so with light suffixes: לְאֹהָלָיו; but with בְּ *pl. st. abs.* בָּאֳהָלִים (4).

r. In the *sing.* the syllable is loosely closed, contrary to the rule, in בִּגְדִי, בִּגְדוֹ from בֶּגֶד (garment), in the *plur.* completely closed, contrary to the rule, in כַּסְפֵּיהֶם (2) from כֶּסֶף, as also in נְסָכֵיהֶם (19), יִסְבְּרֵכֶם:.

29. § 29. B. **Masculine Segholate Forms from**
a. ע״י and ע״ו. When in nouns of the form *qaṭl* the second radical is a weak Jôdh, the full-toned ground-form *(st. abs.)* of the *sg.* adopts *i* as its helping vowel, while in the *st. c.* and, in general, whenever the tone is thrown forward *aj* is contracted to *ê*: זַיִת olive, שֶׁמֶן זַיִת, זֵיתָהּ, זֵיתִים, זֵיתֵיכֶם; but: הַבַּיְתָה. With א as final consonant no helping vowel: גַּיְא valley, גֵּיא הִנֹּם the valley of Hinnom.

b. With a helping vowel in the *pl.* only: תַּיִשׁ he-goat, תְּיָשִׁים; עַיִר young ass, עֲיָרִים. (32, 16 with ו copul. וַעֲיָרִם; 49, 11 *sg.* with suff. 3. *m. sg.* עִירֹה.)

c. Wāw is found as second consonant of the stem in three words with helping vowel: מָוֶת death, מוֹת שַׁלְמֹה, מוֹתוֹ; אָוֶן mischief, אוֹנָם; תָּוֶךְ middle, בְּתוֹךְ הָעִיר, בְּתוֹכְכֶם, בְּתוֹכֵנוּ. Cf. also שָׁוְא falsehood, vanity.—More frequently *aw* has been contracted to *ô* even in the *st. abs.*: שׁוֹר, שׁוֹט, קוֹץ.

d. *Plur.* with helping vowel is rare (1 Sam. 13, 6. Hos. 12, 12); genly. קוֹצִים &c.

§ 30. C. **Masculine Segholate Forms from** § 30.
ל״ה (cf. §74a). When the third letter of the stem is *a.*
י or ו, it passes in the uninflected *sing.* into *î* or *û*.
i draws the tone to itself, and thus thrusts out the
preceding vowel (*parj* becomes פְּרִי, §10/β).

Nouns in *î* retain the helping vowel *ā* of the *pl.* *b.*
and *du.* even when the tone advances: גְּדִי kid, *pl.*
גְּדָיִים, *c.* גְּדָיֵי עִזִּים; לְחִי jaw, cheek, *du.* לְחָיַיִם, *c.* לְחָיֵי.

In the *sg.*, before afformatives and in pause, the *c.*
first consonant of the stem receives back its vowel
§14*i*β: *jophj,* יְפִי beauty, לְפִי, יָפְיוֹ; חֶלְיִי, חָלְיוֹ.—
An original *ă*, however, is thinned to *ĭ* (§11/1), but
in pause to *ĕ*; before ה, sometimes also before כֶם and
כֶן, to *ĕ*: פְּרִי, פֶּרְיִי, פִּרְיִי, פֶּרְיָךְ, פִּרְיָם (5), פִּרְיוֹן;
along with these without union-vowel (§22*e*) שְׂבִיכֶם,
פִּרְיְהֶם, פִּרְיְהוֹן.

NOTE. In צְבָאִים alongside of צְבָיִים and in פְּאָיִם א serves
simply as mater lectionis (§1*b*). (Another reading צְבָאִים, פְּאָיִם.)

Nouns in *ū*: תֹּהוּ for *tohw,* בֹּהוּ, שָׂחוּ. Forms with *d.*
afformatives belonging here: שַׁלְוִי my rest ψ 30, 7; קַצְוֵי אֶרֶץ the
ends of the earth; חַגְוֵי הַסֶּלַע the clefts of the rock.

§ 31. **Masculines from** ל״ה **with two Vowels.** § 31.
A. Original *ij* (form קָטִיא §23) at the end of the word *a.*
(*Auslaut*) becomes *î*, *e. g.* עָנִי *afflictus,* suffering, נָקִי
innocent, נְקִי כַפַּיִם; with afformatives עֲנִיָּה, עֲנִיִּים.

B. Original *aj* in *Auslaut* (שָׂדַי often in poetry *b.*
= שָׂדֶה, *e. g.* ψ 8, 8) is modified in the *st. abs.* after

52   II, § 31. MASCULINES WITH TWO VOWELS FROM ל״ה.

rejection of the *j* to *é* (ה ֶ◌) (cf. מֶלֶךְ); in the *st. c. aj* is contracted (§10*f*α) to *ê* (ה ֵ◌). Before suffixes and in the *plur.* this vowel is rejected (and with it, of course, the ה by which it is marked in the consonantal text, §2*b*): רֹעֶה herdsman, רֹעִים, רֹעִי, רֹעֵה צֹאנוֹ, רֹעֵי יִצְחָק, רֹעִי, רֵעֵיהֶם,רֵעֶיךָ, and with the first vowel changeable: פָּנִים (only *pl.*), שָׂדַי מוֹאָב; שָׂדֵינוּ, שָׂדֶךָ, שְׂדֵה עֶפְרוֹן, שָׂדֶה, פָּנָיו, פְּנֵי הַמַּיִם, פְּנֵיהֶם.

NOTE. With כֶּם probably *śadkhèm* with short *a*-sound (Luzzatto § 884), cf. דְּמְכֶם, יֶדְכֶם §24*c*.

c.   Before suffixes in the *sing.* the final sound of the stem (*Stammauslaut*) has often preserved itself in various shapes. Such forms look for the most part like plural forms, especially when the י is written. That these, however, are no real plural forms is evident from the fact that some of the words in question are not found in the plural, either in the absolute or in the construct state. From מִקְנֶה possessions in cattle, *e. g.* are found the follg. forms: מִקְנֵה אַבְרָם, מִקְנֵה, מִקְנֶי,מִקְנֵה and מִקְנֵיהוּ,מִקְנֵיָה, מִקְנֵנוּ, מִקְנֵכֶם and מִקְנֵיכֶם, מִקְנֵיהֶם and מִקְנֵיהֶם (but not: *miqnîm* or: *miqnê* with י—). So with מִשְׁתֶּה banquet, drinking, מִשְׁתֵּה הַמֶּלֶךְ, מִשְׁתָּיו, מַרְאֶה appearance, מַרְאֵה הַיְלָדִים, מַרְאֶיךָ,מִשְׁתֵּיהֶם; מַרְאֵיהוּ,מַרְאֶהָ, מַרְאֵינוּ, מַרְאֵיהֶן; probably also עָלֶה, leaf, *coll.* leaves, עָלֶה, עָלֵהוּ, עֲלַהְוָת (עֲלֵי־זָיִת Neh. 8, 15, only another orthography of עָלֶה?).

Suffixes in the *sing.*: 3. *m*. almost always (not ֹו, but) הוּ ֵ, *e. g.* מַעֲשֵׂהוּ; but 3. *f.* usu. הָ ֶ, *e. g.* שָׂדֶהָ.

§ 32. Feminines with unchangeable Vowels. Paradigm see § 22.—Here belong also the feminines of masculines with a changeable vowel in the penultimate syllable § 23 (נְתִיבָה from נָתִיב), since this vowel is always dropped acc. to §11*c*1; further the feminines from monosyllabic nouns with the final consonant doubled § 26 (חֻקָּה from חֹק).

§ 33. Feminines with one changeable Vowel.* Phonetic law §11*c*1.—שָׂפָה (ground-form *śaphath*) lip, edge, שְׂפַת הַיָּם, שְׂפָתָהּ, שִׂפְתֵי *du.* שְׂפָתַיִם, שְׂפָתֶיהָ, מִתְנוֹתֵיכֶם, מַתְּנֹת, מַתְּנַת יָדוֹ, שִׂפְתֹתֵיהֶם; מַתָּנָה, שִׂפְתֵי שֶׁקֶר. שֵׁנָה— sleep, שְׁנַת עוֹלָם, שְׁנָתוֹ; עֵדָה assembly, עֲדַת יִשְׂרָאֵל, עֲדָתָם.

In several nouns, esp. those with prefixed מ, the *st. c. sg.* is not *áth*, but with a helping vowel ־ֶת, or ־ַת, *e.g.* מִשְׁפַּחַת אֲבִימֶלֶךְ, מִשְׁפָּחָה; מַמְלֶכֶת כֹּהֲנִים, מַמְלָכָה. With *suff*. מַמְלַכְתּוֹ, מִשְׁפַּחְתּוֹ (cf. מַלְכִּי, זַעֲמוֹ). Cf. § 36, esp. *h*.

§ 34. Feminines with two changeable Vowels. In the *st. abs.* of the *sg.* and *pl.* on account

---

* The feminine ending here causes the tone to be moved forward one syllable, so that the vocalisation coincides with that of דָּבָר &c.

of the tone, which acc. to §11c1 rests on the ending, the first of the two vowels has disappeared: ṣadaqa(th) צְדָקָה*, צְדָקוֹת, but appears again, usually, however, thinned to ĭ, when the tone advances one syllable further: צִדְקוֹתֵינוּ, צִדְקוֹת ה׳, צִדְקָתְךָ, צִדְקַת הַצַּדִּיקִים *v.* §11c2.

b. If the word begins with א or ה, the original ă remains when the tone advances (cf. §25b); ח and ע receive generally Sᵉghôl. אֲדָמָה land, אַדְמַת הַכֹּהֲנִים, אַדְמַתְכֶם, אַדְמָתֵנוּ, *pl.* אֲדָמוֹת lands; עֲגָלָה cart, עֶגְלָתוֹ, עֶגְלֹת, *c.* עֶגְלוֹת.

c. Even when only the second radical is a guttural, ă has maintained itself under the first letter of the stem, cf. נַהֲרֵי and נַהֲרוֹת §25b, *e. g.* סְעָרָה storm, סַעֲרֹת, סַעֲרֹת תֵּימָן, סַעֲרַת ה׳.

d. Miscellaneous. a) Complete close of syllable as exception in *st. c.* of בְּרָכָה blessing, *e. g.* בִּרְכַּת ה׳, but בִּרְכָתִי. Further: חֲרָדָה trembling, fear, *c.* חֶרְדַּת. — β) בְּהֵמָה cattle, בְּהֶמְתְּכֶם, בְּהֶמְתֵּנוּ, בְּהֶמְתּוֹ, בֶּהֱמַת הַלְוִיִּם, בַּהֲמוֹת יַעַר, בְּהֵמוֹת.

35.
a. § 35. Feminines of Segholate Forms from strong Stems. Cf. § 28.—Since the two consonants closing the stem of the noun are always followed by an afformative—the feminine ending (*malk*, מַלְכָּה

---

* Vocalisation coincides with that of הֲבָרִים &c.

queen), the vowel of the stem remains unchanged in the *sing*. In the Plural a helping Qāmĕṣ, the retention or omission of which, as with the masc. segholate forms, is determined by §11c: מְלָכוֹת for *malakhôth*, cf. מְלָכִים. The *st. c.* and forms with *suff.* are not found in the *plur.* of this word; they must have been pronounced, with loose close of syllable: מַלְכוֹת, מַלְכוֹתַי, מַלְכוֹתֵיכֶם.—Cf. חָרְבָּה destruction, *pl.* חָרְבוֹתֵיהֶם, חָרְבֹתַיִךְ, חָרְבוֹת יְרוּשָׁלַם, ruins, חֳרָבוֹת.

An original *ă* appears in an unaccented shut *b.* syllable sometimes as *ĭ;* cf. כִּבְשָׂה *agna* with כִּבְשָׂה, כִּבְשׂת הַצֹּאן, כִּבְשֹׂת, כִּבְשַׂת הָאִישׁ 21, 28.—ח and ע in the same position at the beginning of the word receive instead of *ă* or *ĭ* usually *ĕ:* חֶרְפָּה, חֶלְקַת לָשׁוֹן, עֶגְלָה, (עֵגֶל) עֶגְלָתִי. Cf. §28*l*.

Syllable completely closed, as exception: חֶרְפָּה *c.* reproach, חֲרָפֶיךָ, חֲרָפוֹת.

§ 36. Feminine Segholate Forms we call § 36. such nouns as have the feminine ending ת affixed not *a.* by means of a full vowel, but only of a helping vowel (— or —): *mišmart* מִשְׁמֶרֶת, *tôkhacht* תּוֹכַחַת. (Cf. §18*c*β.γ).

Their inflexion coincides in the singular with that *b.* of masc. segholate forms from strong stems, § 28: מִשְׁמַרְתִּי, מִשְׁמַרְתְּךָ, תּוֹכַחְתִּי; *ō*, however, when suffixes are added, becomes more frequently *ŭ*, *e. g.* נְחֻשְׁתּ,

brass, נְחֻשְׁתָּם, du. נְחֻשְׁתַּיִם double chains, beside גֻּלְגֹּלֶת, גֻּלְגָּלְתּוֹ.—Examples of the thinning of ă to ĭ: גְּבִרְתָּהּ mistress, גְּבִרְתֵּךְ, גְּבִרְתָּהּ; the inff. שֶׁבֶת from יָשַׁב, לֶדֶת from יָלַד, רֶדֶת from יָרַד (§68f), גֶּשֶׁת from נָגַשׁ: שִׁבְתִּי, גִּשְׁתָּם, רִדְתּוֹ, לְדִתָּהּ.—S°ghôl (cf. §28k) is found in the inf. of הָלַךְ, לֶכֶת, לְכָתָם (§68i).

c. In the plur. a is preserved, in the syllable before the tone, in most cases as ā, e. g. מַאֲכֶלֶת; מִשְׁמָרוֹת knife, מַאֲכָלוֹת; כֹּתֶרֶת capital (of a pillar), כֹּתָרוֹת; טַבַּעַת, טַבָּעֹת. But אִגֶּרֶת, letter, pl. abs. אִגְּרוֹת. When the tone advances: טַבְּעוֹת זָהָב, מִשְׁמְרוֹתָם.

d. In the feminines of nouns inflected like אֹיֵב, יֵצֶר (§24d)—including, therefore, the fem. of the partt. Qal, Pi., Hithp.—the vowel of the second radical is dropped in the plur., e. g. יֹלֵד gignens, יוֹלֶדֶת pariens, mother, מְדַבֶּרֶת, מְדַבְּרִים, מְדַבֵּר; הַיְלָדוֹת, יוֹלַדְתְּכֶם, יוֹלַדְתּוֹ, מְדַבְּרוֹת.

e. Examples with final א: חַטָּאת sin, sinoffering, הַטֹּאת (for חַטֹּאת §10c2), חַטָּאתְכֶם, חַטָּאתְךָ, יְהוּדָה; חַטֹּאתֵיכֶם; part. יֹצֵא, יֹצֵאת, יֹצְאוֹת.

f. Note: כֻּתֹּנֶת tunica, כְּתָנְתָּהּ, כְּתָנְתִּי, כְּתֹנֶת יוֹסֵף, pl. abs. כֻּתֳנוֹת, כָּתְנוֹת עוֹר, בְּכָתְנֹתָם.

g. Some nouns have besides the segholate forms a st. abs. in ־ָה, which is in some cases much more frequent than the other: עֲצֶרֶת, also עֲצָרָה, assembly, תִּפְאֶרֶת, also תִּפְאָרָה, ornament, beauty, עֲצֶרֶת בְּגָדִים;

II, § 36.—§ 37. FEMININES IN ÛTH AND ÎTH.—§ 36.

אַיָּלָה hind, אַיֶּלֶת and אַיָּלָה; תִּפְאַרְתְּכֶם, תִּפְאַרְתְּךָ, תִּפְאֶרֶת יִשְׂרָאֵל
(מִלְחֶמֶת†) war מִלְחָמָה; אַיְלוֹת הַשָּׂדֶה, אַיָּלוֹת, אַיֶּלֶת הַשַּׁחַר
(st. c. wanting), מִלְחֲמוֹתַי, מִלְחֲמוֹת ה', מִלְחָמוֹת, מִלְחֲמֹתָיו;
מְלָאכָה f. mal'ākhā (†מְלֶאכֶת) business, work, מְלֶאכֶת
מַלְאֲכוֹתָיו, מְלַאכְתּוֹ, הַשָּׂדֶה.

Several nouns have their *st. abs.* always in ◌ָה and *h.*
nevertheless form their *st. c.* after the analogy of the
segholate forms: עֲטָרָה crown, עֲטֶרֶת זָהָב, עֲטָרוֹת, see §33*b*.

§ 37. Feminines in *ûth* and *îth*. Nouns with § 37.
the ending *ûth* form their plur. in *ujjôth*; in the bible *a.*
only מַלְכוּת, מַלְכִיּוֹת, and הֲדָיוֹת the vault (*sg.* חָנוּת post-
biblical), post-bibl. גָּלִיּוֹת.—Exception: עֵדוּת ordinance,
law, עֵדוּת ה', עֵדְוֹתָיךְ.

Nouns with the ending *îth*, esp. the feminines of *b.*
adjs. in *î*, have in the plur. *ijjôth*, *e. g.* מַשְׂכִּית picture
(of the heart), imagination, thought, מַשְׂכִּתוֹ, מַשְׂכִּיּוֹת
עֲמָנִיּוֹת, חֲצַמָּנִית, הַעֲמֹנִים, הֲצַמוֹנִי; לֵבָב.

§ 38. Nouns of peculiar Formation.   § 38.
אָב father, אֲבִי כְנַעַן (*c.* אָב 17, 4. 5!); *suff.* אָבִי, אֲבִיהָ,
אָבִיו and אֲבִיהוּ, אֲבִיהֶם (§22*e*).—*pl.* אָבוֹת, אֲבוֹת
אֲבוֹתֶיךָ, אֲבוֹתֵיכֶם.

[חָם] father-in-law, חָמִיךָ, חָמִיהָ.
אָח brother, *suff.* אָחִי, אָחִיךָ, אָחִיו and אָחִיהוּ,
אֲחִיכֶם. — *pl.* אַחִים*, אֲחֵי יוֹסֵף, אַחַי, אֶחָי (§ 11/2),
אֶחָיו, אַחֵינוּ, אֲחֵיכֶם.

---

* In the *st. abs.* and before light suffixes the *pl.* has *Dag. f. implic.*

II, § 38. NOUNS OF PECULIAR FORMATION.

אָחוֹת, sister אֲחוֹת אַהֲרֹן, אֲחוֹתִי, אֲחוֹתְךָ, *pl.*—אֲחוֹתָהּ. [אֲחָיוֹת]
אֲחִיתָיו, אַחְיוֹתֵיהֶם; אֲחוֹתַיִךְ, וְלַאֲחוֹתֵיכֶם.

חָמוֹת mother-in-law, חֲמוֹתֵךְ, חֲמוֹתָהּ.

אִישׁ, man, *pl.*—אִישָׁהּ. and אִישִׁים אֲנָשִׁים (3), אַנְשֵׁי סְדֹם,
אֲנָשָׁיו, אַנְשֵׁיהֶן.

אִשָּׁה woman, אֵשֶׁת אַבְרָם, אִשְׁתּוֹ, אִשְׁתָּהּ, *pl.*—נָשִׁים, נְשֵׁי לֶמֶךְ.

אָמָה, maid, אֲמָתִי, אֲמָתָהּ, *pl.*—אֲמָהוֹת*, אַמְהוֹת עֲבָדָיו,
אַמְהוֹתַי, אַמְהוֹתֵיכֶם.

בַּיִת, house, בֵּית עֲבָדְכֶם, בֵּיתָהּ, *pl.*—בָּתִּים**, בָּתֵּי יְרוּשָׁלַיִם,
בָּתֵּיהּ, בָּתֵּיכֶם.

בֵּן, son, בֶּן־הָרָן (17, 17) בֶּן; בִּדְנוּן; §20c β; בְּנוֹ and בְּנִי),
בְּנִי, בִּנְךָ, בְּנֵהּ.—*pl.*—בָּנִים, בְּנֵי יִשְׂרָאֵל, בָּנֶיךָ, בְּנֵיהֶם.

בַּת, daughter, *pl.*—בַּת־הָרָן, בִּתִּי, בִּתְּכֶם. בָּנוֹת, בְּנוֹת־לוֹט,
בְּנֹתֶיהָ, בְּנֹתֵיכֶם.

יוֹם, day, הַיּוֹם to-day, יוֹם מוֹתִי, בְּיוֹמוֹ; יוֹמַיִם *biduum*.—
pl. יָמִים, פְּלִי־יְמֵי אָדָם, יָמָיו, יְמֵיכֶם.

כְּלִי, vessel, כֶּלִי, כְּלִי נְחֹשֶׁת, כֶּלְיָהּ (§30c).—*pl.* כֵּלִים, כְּלֵי
זָהָב, כַּלַי, כְּלֵיהֶם.

מַיִם*** water, הַמַּיְמָה (§20ca), מֵי הַמַּבּוּל, מֵימֵי הַיַּרְדֵּן,
מֵימַי, מֵימֵיהֶם.

שָׁמַיִם*** heaven, הַשָּׁמַיִם וּשְׁמֵי הַשָּׁמַיִם, שָׁמָיו, שְׁמֵיכֶם.

עִיר *f.* town, עִירֹה.—*pl.* עָרִים, עָרֵי הַכִּכָּר, עָרֶיהָ, עָרֵיכֶם.

* Instances from Aramaic and Arabic of the insertion of *h* in the plur. are given by Nöldeke, Sitzungsberichte der Berl. Akad. der Wiss. 1882, p. 1178. 1179.

** Pronounce *bātîm*, *bātê* (exception to §6a).

*** Plural with ending stripped of the tone, not Dual.

רֹאשׁ* head, רֹאשֵׁי, רָאשִׁים, *pl.*—רָאשְׁכֶם, רָאשֵׁי הָעָם, רָאשֵׁיהֶן.

פֶּה mouth, פִּי ה', *suff.*; פִּי, פִּיו and פִּיהוּ, פִּיכֶם, פִּיהֶם.

§ 39. Numerals. אֶחָד 1, *st. c.* אַחַד; *f.* אַחַת, § 39. (אֶחָת §11/2) is an adj., *e. g.* מָקוֹם אֶחָד, בְּרָכָה אַחַת; rarely subst.: *st. c.* אַחַד הֶהָרִים, אַחַת הֶעָרִים. *a.*

שְׁנַיִם 2, *f.* שְׁתַּיִם**, is, properly speaking, an abstract subst.: the number *two*, couple. What is enumerated stands either in apposition: שְׁנַיִם פָּרִים, עָרִים שְׁתַּיִם, שְׁתַּיִם נָשִׁים, כְּרוּבִים שְׁנַיִם, or is subordinated in the genetive: שְׁתֵּי הַמִּשְׁפָּחוֹת, שְׁתֵּי נָשִׁים, שְׁנֵי בָנִים. *b.*

The numerals from 3 to 10 are likewise abstract *c.* nouns with forms for the masc. and fem.; notice, however, that the masculine form is employed when the word enumerated is of the feminine gender, and *vice versâ*.

Maculine form with fem. substs.:		Feminine form with masc. substs.:	
st. abs.	*st. cstr.*	*st. abs.*	*st. cstr.*
שָׁלֹשׁ 3	שְׁלֹשׁ	שְׁלֹשָׁה 3	שְׁלֹשֶׁת
אַרְבַּע 4	אַרְבַּע	אַרְבָּעָה 4	אַרְבַּעַת

---

* From *râš*, originally *ra'š;* hence plur. properly, acc. to § 28, *rᵉ'āšîm*, cf. §10c2.

** *Dāgheš lene* (contrary to §§5c.6a), because the punctuation presupposed the pronunciation *eštajim*, *ešté*.—Philippi, ZDMG. [Zeitschrift d. deutschen morgenländ. Gesellschaft] XXXII, 85 ff. and H. Strack, *ibid.* XXXIII, 301 f. may be compared.

Masculine form with fem. substs.:		Feminine form with masc. substs.:	
st. abs.	st. cstr.	st. abs.	st. cstr.
חָמֵשׁ 5	חֲמֵשׁ	חֲמִשָּׁה 5	חֲמֵשֶׁת
שֵׁשׁ 6	שֵׁשׁ	שִׁשָּׁה 6	שֵׁשֶׁת
שֶׁבַע 7	שְׁבַע	שִׁבְעָה 7	שִׁבְעַת
שְׁמֹנֶה 8		שְׁמֹנָה 8	שְׁמֹנַת
תֵּשַׁע 9	תְּשַׁע	תִּשְׁעָה 9	תִּשְׁעַת
עֶשֶׂר 10	עֶשֶׂר	עֲשָׂרָה 10	עֲשֶׂרֶת

שָׁלֹשׁ עָרִים; עָרִים שָׁלֹשׁ; שָׁלֹשׁ סְאִים; שָׁלֹשׁ מֵאוֹת; שְׁלֹשָׁה בָנִים; יָמִים שְׁלֹשָׁה; שְׁלֹשֶׁת בָּנָיו.

d.   In the composite numbers from 11 to 19, only the units from 3 to 9 come under the rule given in §c.

With masc. substs.:		With fem. substs.:
אַחַד עָשָׂר, עַשְׁתֵּי עָשָׂר	11	אַחַת עֶשְׂרֵה, עַשְׁתֵּי עֶשְׂרֵה
שְׁנַיִם עָשָׂר (82)	12	שְׁתַּיִם עֶשְׂרֵה (31)
שְׁלֹשָׁה עָשָׂר	13	שְׁלֹשׁ עֶשְׂרֵה
אַרְבָּעָה עָשָׂר	14	אַרְבַּע עֶשְׂרֵה
חֲמִשָּׁה עָשָׂר	15	חֲמֵשׁ עֶשְׂרֵה
שִׁשָּׁה עָשָׂר	16	שֵׁשׁ עֶשְׂרֵה
שִׁבְעָה עָשָׂר	17	שְׁבַע עֶשְׂרֵה
שְׁמֹנָה עָשָׂר	18	שְׁמֹנֶה עֶשְׂרֵה
תִּשְׁעָה עָשָׂר	19	תְּשַׁע עֶשְׂרֵה

e.   NOTE. 1. The formerly perplexing numeral עַשְׁתֵּי is found in Assyrian as *ištin*.—2. The units from 3 to 9 stand before עָשָׂר in the *st. abs.* of the fem., before עֶשְׂרֵה in the *st. c.* of the masc.—

3. The first unit stands in the *st. c.*; the second acc. to the $K^e th\hat{\imath}bh$ almost always in the *st. abs.*, since שְׁנַיִם עָשָׂר and עֶשְׂרֵה שְׁתֵּים are without a doubt $Q^e r\hat{e}$ *perpetuum* (§9*b*) for שְׁנֵי עָ׳ and שְׁתֵּי עָ׳, each of which is found only four times in the consonantal text.

אֶחָד עָשָׂר כּוֹכָבִים, שְׁנַיִם עָשָׂר אֲנָשִׁים, שֵׁשׁ עֶשְׂרֵה בָנוֹת.

Certain nouns frequently numbered (as אִישׁ, אֶלֶף *f.* 1000, אַמָּה cubit, בָּקָר cattle, יוֹם, נֶפֶשׁ, שָׁנָה, שֶׁקֶל) usually remain in the sing. after the numerals from 11 to 19, occasionally also after larger numbers (cf. Engl. "three pound ten", "five foot eight"), *e. g.* תִּשְׁעָה עָשָׂר חֲמֵשׁ עֶשְׂרֵה אַמָּה, אִישׁ.

20 עֶשְׂרִים (*pl.* of עֶשֶׂר); 30 שְׁלֹשִׁים, 40 אַרְבָּעִים, 50 *g.* חֲמִשִּׁים, 60 שִׁשִּׁים, 70 שִׁבְעִים, 80 שְׁמֹנִים, 90 תִּשְׁעִים (thus *pl.* of the corresponding units).

The noun numbered, when following the tens and undetermined, stands usu. in the sing.: שִׁשִּׁים עִיר, but שִׁבְעִים אָחִיו and שִׁשִּׁים עָרִים גְּדֹלוֹת, as also אִמּוֹת שִׁשִּׁים. —Rarely חֲמִשִּׁים צַדִּיקִם 18, 24 and such like.

In numbers containing both tens and units either *h.* the units are placed first (esp. in the earlier books) or the tens as is usually done in English, *e. g.* שְׁלֹשִׁים וְשָׁלֹשׁ 33, חָמֵשׁ וּשְׁלֹשִׁים 35. With a noun; שְׁתַּיִם שָׁנִים וְשִׁבְעִים שָׁנָה 12, 4. חָמֵשׁ שָׁנִים וְשִׁשִּׁים שָׁנָה 5, 20;

100 מֵאָה; 200 מָאתַיִם (§10*c*2); 300 שְׁלֹשׁ מֵאוֹת (and *i.* so on, as with עֶשְׂרָה).—1000 אֶלֶף; 2000 אַלְפַּיִם; 3000 שְׁלֹשֶׁת אֲלָפִים; 4000 אַרְבַּעַת אֲלָפִים (and so on acc. to §*c*, col. 4).—10000 רְבָבָה μυριάς.

מֵאָה אִישׁ, מֵאָה נְבִיאִים, מְאַת שָׁנָה; מָאתַיִם אִישׁ, מָאתַיִם דְּבֵלִים; אַרְבַּע מֵאוֹת שָׁנָה, שְׁבַע מֵאוֹת פָּרָשִׁים. ‖ אֶלֶף אַמָּה, אֶלֶף פָּרִים; אַלְפַּיִם אִישׁ, אַלְפַּיִם סוּסִים; שֵׁשֶׁת אֲלָפִים גְּמַלִּים, אַרְבָּעִים אֶלֶף פָּרָשִׁים. שְׁלֹשֶׁת אַלְפֵי אִישׁ, שְׁלֹשֶׁת גְּמַלִּים.

k. Many substantives denoting weight, measure, or time are dropped where the context leaves no doubt as to the meaning; Shekel: מֵאָה כֶסֶף, עֲשָׂרָה זָהָב; ephah: שֵׁשׁ שְׂעֹרִים; loaf: מָאתַיִם לֶחֶם.

l. Ordinal numbers: רִאשׁוֹן first, שֵׁנִי second, שְׁלִישִׁי third, רְבִיעִי fourth, (חֲמִשִּׁי) חֲמִישִׁי fifth, שִׁשִּׁי sixth, שְׁבִיעִי seventh, שְׁמִינִי eighth, תְּשִׁיעִי ninth, עֲשִׂירִי tenth.

m. The ordinals above 10 are wanting and in their stead the corresponding cardinal numbers are used: בְּאַרְבָּעִים שָׁנָה, בְּשִׁבְעָה־עָשָׂר יוֹם, בְּעַשְׁתֵּי עָשָׂר חֹדֶשׁ

n. NOTE. In counting years and the days of the month the first ten ordinal numbers are often indicated by the cardinals: בְּרִאשׁוֹן בְּאֶחָד לַחֹדֶשׁ in the first (month), on the first (day) of the month 8, 13.

o. To express fractional parts the feminines of the ordinal numbers above enumerated are most frequently employed: שְׁלִישִׁית third part, רְבִיעִית ¼, (חֲמִשִּׁית) חֲמִישִׁית ⅕, שִׁשִּׁית ⅙, שְׁבִיעִית ⅐, עֲשִׂירִית and עֲשִׂירִיָּה ⅒.— חֹמֶשׁ ⅕, רֹבַע ¼, and רֶבַע ¼, חֲצִי ½, חֵצִי ½.

p. Distributives: שְׁנַיִם שְׁנַיִם two each, שִׁבְעָה שִׁבְעָה seven each.

-fold is expressed by the feminine dual of the corresponding cardinal: שְׁבְעָתַיִם, אַרְבַּעְתַּיִם.

C. PARTICLES (§§ 40—46).

§ 40. **Particles with Suffixes.** The particles are joined to the suffixes of the noun.

Deviations with respect to the union-vowel. Frequently $ā$, where the noun has $S^ewâ$ or Ṣērê; even in pausal forms ךָ for ךְ.—הֶם, הֶן without a union-vowel when the stem ends in a consonant, v. §43*f*.— עִמָּהֶם v. §43*d*.

Verbal suffix (see §78*c*). See also אַיִן §41,2; אַיֵּה §42*f*; תַּחְתֶּנָּה §43*b*; כָּמוֹנִי §45*d*.

הֵן, הִנֵּה *ecce.*—הִנְנִי *ecce me,* הִנֵּנִי and (with Nûn demonstr. §80) הִנֶּנִּי; הִנֵּנוּ *ecce nos* along with הִנְנוּ, הִנֶּנִּי; 2. *p.* הִנָּךְ, *f.* הִנָּךְ, *pl.* הִנְּכֶם; 3. *p.* הִנּוֹ, הִנָּם.

יֵשׁ, רֶשׁ it is, was (converse of אַיִן).—יֶשְׁךָ thou art, יֶשְׁכֶם (הֲ יֶשְׁכֶם §42,1); יֶשְׁכֶם עֹשִׂים חֶסֶד ye show favour, יֶשְׁנוֹ (4) he is.

עוֹד still.—עוֹדֶנִּי הַיּוֹם חָזָק I am still vigorous; 2. *p.* עוֹדְךָ, *f.* עוֹדָךְ; 3. *p.* עוֹדֶנּוּ חַי he is still alive, *f.* עוֹדֶנָּה; עוֹדָם.—בְּעוֹדִי ψ 104, 33 and בְּעוֹדֶנִּי while I yet am (alive); בְּעוֹדֶנּוּ חַי G. 25,6; מֵעוֹדִי since I am (alive) =all my life long 48, 15.

§ 41. **Negative Particles.** 1. לֹא οὐ, negation of an action: *not;* without a verb: *no.*

2. אַיִן (proply. *subst.*, nothingness) negatives the being, existence of something or of somebody, hence joined not with verbs, but with nouns (participles): מַיִם אַיִן there is no water. Generally in the *st. c.* at the head of the phrase: אֵין לָהֶם וְאֵין מַיִם there is no bread and no water; but also: וּפֹתֵר אֵין אוֹתוֹ and there was no interpreter of it (the dream) 40, 8, cf. 19, 31.—With *suff.*: אֵינְךָ thou art not ... (אֵינְךָ יוֹדֵעַ thou knowest not), אֵינָם, אֵינְכֶם, אֵינֶךָ; with verbal suff.: אֵינֶנִּי I am not; אֵינֶנּוּ he is not, אֵינֶנָּה; אֵינֶנּוּ we are not.

3. אַל μή, *ne,* with the jussive (§47e), esp. with prohibitions and to express a wish that something may not happen: תַּשְׁחִית *perdes,* אַל־תַּשְׁחֵת *ne perdas.*

NOTE. אַל with Indicat. is rare: אַל־תַּבְדִּיל 19, 17, אַל־נָא רָשִׁים 1 Sam. 25, 25, cf. Jos. 1, 7. ψ 121, 3. Prov. 3, 30.

4. פֶּן (always with Maqqêph) μή, *ne,* esp. α) after expressions of fear, β)=that not, lest.

5. לְבִלְתִּי with the *inf.,* not to.

§ 42. § 42. Interrogative Particles. 1. הֲ, simple question, both when the answer is uncertain (הֲשָׁלוֹם לוֹ does it go well with him?), and esp. (like *num*) when a negative answer is expected (הֲשֹׁמֵר אָחִי אָנֹכִי) am I my brother's keeper?). Also in an indirect question: לִרְאוֹת הֲקַלּוּ הַמַּיִם to see if the waters had decreased 8, 8.—הֲלֹא *nonne.*

NOTE. ה interrogativum receives: α) before non-gutturals with a vowel always: Châṭēph-Páthach, הֲתַשְׁחִית wilt thou destroy? 18, 28; הֲתֵלְכִי wilt thou (f.) go? 24, 58.—β) before non-gutturals with S°wâ either: Páthach with follg. Dāḡ., הַבְצִבְּךָ 17, 17, הַבְצַעֲקָתָהּ 18, 21, הַבִתְּךָ בִּתְּךָ 37, 32, or: Páthach without follg. Dāḡ., הַמְבַשֵּׂר אֲנִי נֶאֱבְדָה do I hide from A.? 18, 17, הַיְדַעְתֶּם know ye? 29, 5, cf. 27, 38. 30, 15.—γ) before gutturals with Qāmeṣ: Sᵉghôl (cf. §11/2) הֶחָרֵשׁ 24, 5. הֶאָנֹכִי.—δ) otherwise before gutturals: Páthach (w. Dāḡ. forte implic.), הַעוֹד לָכֶם אָח have ye yet a brother?

2. אִם, if, whether, in an indirect question.   c.

3. הֲ...אִם, in a disjunctive question, direct (37, 8) d. and indirect (24, 21. 27, 21. 37, 32).

4. מִי, מָה see §16e.f.—לָמָה and לָמָּה §45e6. e.

5. aj where? only in composition: אַיּוֹ where is f. he? אַיָּם. אַיֶּכָּה where art thou? אַיֵּה where?—אֵי זֶה 1) where?, 2) which?; אֵי מִזֶּה whence?

זֶה, זֹאת, הוּא, אֵפוֹא not unfrequently to give ani- g. mation to the question: מִי זֶה quisnam?; מִי אֵפוֹא quis tandem? 27, 33; מַה־זֹּאת 3, 13. 12, 18.

Questions are sometimes found without an inter- h. rogative particle, esp. questions of surprise; אַתָּה זֶה בְּנִי עֵשָׂו thou here art my son Esau? 27, 24; cf. 18, 12. 1 Sam. 25, 11.

§ 43. Independent Prepositions. אֶל unto, §43. עַד till, עַל over, ended originally in aj, hence often a. in poetry: אֱלֵי, עֲדֵי, עֲלֵי. Before suffixes the fuller form is always employed; accordingly when joined with suff. these preps. look like plurals*: אֵלַי; אֵלֶיךָ, אֵלַיִךְ; אֵלָיו, אֵלֶיהָ; אֵלֵינוּ; אֲלֵיכֶם, אֲלֵיכֶן; אֲלֵיהֶם (defect. אֲלֵהֶם), poet. אֱלֵימוֹ (cf. §22ee), אֲלֵיהֶן.—עָדַי; עָדֶיךָ, עָדָיִו; עָדֶיהָ; עָדֵינוּ; עֲדֵיכֶם, עֲדֵיכֶן†; עֲדֵיהֶם—!עָלַי; עָלֶיךָ, עָלַיִךְ, עָלָיו, עָלֶיהָ; עָלֵינוּ; עֲלֵיכֶם; עֲלֵיהֶן, poet. עָלֵימוֹ.

b. The follg. really stand in the plural before suffixes: סָבִיב round about, אַחַר behind, תַּחַת under, instead of.— סְבִיבוֹתַי, סְבִיבוֹת; סְבִיבֶיךָ, סְבִיבָיו, סְבִיבֶיהָ. Oftener: סְבִיבוֹתַי round about me, &c.—More frequent than אַחַר is אַחֲרֵי. With suff. always: אַחֲרַי behind me, אַחֲרֶיךָ &c.—תַּחְתַּי; תַּחְתֶּיךָ; תַּחְתַּיִךְ, תַּחְתָּיו, תַּחְתֶּיהָ; תַּחְתֵּינוּ; תַּחְתֵּיכֶם; תַּחְתֵּיהֶם and תַּחְתָּם!, תַּחְתֵּיהֶן. With verbal suffix תַּחְתֶּנָּה 2, 21.

c. בֵּין between. בֵּינִי, בֵּינְךָ, בֵּינוֹ. The suff. of the plur., however, are attached to the plur.: בֵּינֵינוּ, בֵּינֵיכֶם, בֵּינֵיהֶם, to the fem. plur.: בֵּינוֹתֵינוּ, בֵּינוֹתָם.

d. עִם with. עִמִּי; עִמְּךָ, עִמָּךְ, עִמָּךְ f. עִמּוֹ; עִמָּהּ; עִמָּנוּ; עִמָּכֶם; עִמָּם (5), עִמָּהֶם†.— For עִמִּי oftener, esp. in the earlier period, עִמָּדִי (Böttcher §894, II).

e. אֶת, אֶת־ with: אִתִּי; אִתְּךָ, אִתָּךְ f. אִתּוֹ, אִתָּהּ; אִתָּנוּ; אִתְּכֶם; אִתָּם.

f. אֵת, אֶת־ (points out the determinate accus., §20e): אֹתִי me; אֹתְךָ, אֹתָךְ f. אֹתוֹ, אֹתָהּ; אֹתָנוּ; אֶתְכֶם; אֶתְהֶן, אֹתָם. Rarely אֶתְהֶם (2) and אֹתָן†.—Often written plene: אוֹתִי &c.

---

* P. de Lagarde, Symmicta II, 101—103, Mittheilungen 231f. pronounces the forms in question to be real plurals.

§ 44. מִן, from, has preserved its independence almost exclusively in the following cases: 1. often in poetry: מִן־קָמַי, מִן־אֹיְבִי; 2. in most cases before the article: מִן־הָעֵץ, מִן־הָאָרֶץ.—Elsewhere מִן coalesces with the following substantive to form one word: a) assimilation: מִן+יָם becomes מִיָּם, מִקֶּדֶם, מִבַּיִת. In letters with Š°wâ Dāghēš is sometimes omitted (§6f3), e. g. מִלְמַעְלָה from above; β) when the following word begins with י, contraction to מִי takes place; מִימִינֶךָ from thy right hand, מִידֵי רָשָׁע; γ) compensation lengthening before gutturals and ר, e. g. מֵאִישׁ, מֵחָרָן, מֵעַדַן, מֵרָחֹק, before the article מֵהָעוֹב; מֵיהוָה see §9b; δ) before ח and ה sometimes virtual doubling: מִחוּץ, מִחוּט 14, 23, מֵחִיוֹת.—Poetical bye-form מִנִּי.

With suffixes: מַהֶּנָּה, מֵהֶם, מִכֶּם. Elsewhere doubled: מִמֶּנִּי from me; מִמְּךָ, מִמֵּךְ, מִמֵּךְ /. מִמֶּנּוּ; מִמֶּנּוּ from him, מִמֶּנָּה from her; מִמֶּנּוּ from us.

§ 45. The Prefixes בְּ, כְּ, לְ. The prepositions בְּ (in), לְ (sign of the dative) and the particle of comparison כְּ (as), because short proclitics, are always fused with the following word into one whole. The fuller forms, forming an independent word, לְמוֹ, בְּמוֹ, כְּמוֹ (but v. § d) belong exclusively to poetry.

בְּ with suffixes: בִּי; בְּךָ /. בָּךְ, בּוֹ, בָּהּ; בָּנוּ; בָּכֶם; בָּהֶם and בָּם, בָּהֵן (15) and בָּהֶן (3).

לְ with suff.: לִי; לְךָ and לְכָה (cf. §22ia), לֵךְ /. לָךְ;

68   II, § 45. THE PREFIXES לְ, בְּ, כְּ.

לְהֶן, לָהֶם.—poet. לָכֶם (f. לָבְנָה Ez. 13, 18); לְוֵנוּ; לָה; לוֹ,
לָמוֹ (cf. §22ιε), e. g. 9, 27=לָהֶם; Isa. 44, 15. 53, 8=בּוֹ.

d.   כְּ with suff.: כָּכֶם, כָּהֶם. Otherwise always כָּמוֹנִי: כְּמוֹ
as I; 2. m. כָּמוֹךָ; כָּמוֹהוּ, כָּמוֹהָ; כָּמוֹנוּ; †כְּמוֹכֶם, כְּמוֹהֶם (3).

e.   With respect to the punctuation (cf. §11g.h) note
further:

1. before a vowel they have S°wâ: כִּדְוִד, לִמְלֹךְ, בְּבַיִת;

2. before a guttural with Chātēph the correspond-
ing short vowel: בֵּאלֹהִים, לֶאֱלִיעֶזֶר, לַחֲמֹרוֹ, but לֵאמֹר, בֶּאֱמֹר,
בַּאדֹנָי;

3. before S°wâ ĭ: לִשְׁלֹמֹה, but לִיהוּדָה;

4. before the article: לַמֶּלֶךְ, בָּהָר, see §17e.

5. before the tone-syllable is found sometimes ā:
often before זֶה, זֹאת and אֵלֶּה, e. g. בָּזֶה, כָּזֹאת, כָּאֵלֶּה.

6. before מה Páthach with Dāghēš: בַּמֶּה, in pause
and before א: בַּמָּה (see Delitzsch to Isa. 2, 22); כַּמָּה.—
לָמָה, לְמָה' for what purpose? why? Mostly לָמָּה, e. g.
לָמָּה תִשְׁקְלוּ wherefore will ye weigh?, לָמָּה לֹא הִגַּדְתָּ 12,18,
לָמָה חֲכַמְתִּי Cant. 2, 15, לָמָה־זֶּה wherefore then?; but
before א, ה, ע usu. לָמָה, e. g. לָמָה אָמַרְתָּ 12, 19, cf. 27, 45.

f.   ל before the tone-syllable receives, further, an ā:
α) before infinitives: לָלֶכֶת to go, לָלֶדֶת to bear, לָשֶׁבֶת,
לָרֶדֶת, לָבוֹא, לָגוּר, except when the inf. is closely connected with the following word, e. g. לְשֶׁבֶת אַבְרָם 16, 3;
β) in pause with pairs of words: בֵּין מַיִם לָמָיִם 1, 6;—

γ) note also: לְבֶ֫טַח in safety, לָעַד and לָנֶ֫צַח for ever, לָרֹב in abundance.

§ 46. Wāw copulativum (§11*g.h*). A. 1. Before a vowel ו takes Sᵉwâ: וְהָאָ֫רֶץ, וְהֹ֫שֶׁךְ, וְרוּחַ.—2. Before a guttural with Chāṭēph, the corresponding vowel: (וַיִהְוָה) וַאדֹנָי, וֵאלֹהִים; but וַחֲמֹרִים, וַעֲבָדִים.—3. Before Sᵉwâ and the labials ו is written: וּמֶ֫לֶךְ, וּבְקָר; וּשְׂפָחֹת, וּגְמַלִּים; so וּזְהָב 2, 12, because for וְ+זְהָב. For וְהָיִיתֶם, וְחָיָה &c. see §76*b.c.* וִיחִי (and may he live) out of וְ+יְחִי.—4. Before the tone-syllable often וָ, esp. *a*) in pairs of words: בָּבוֹד וָעֹז 8, 22, תֹּ֫הוּ וָבֹ֫הוּ, יוֹם וָלַ֫יְלָה, עָפָר וָאֵ֫פֶר; β) at the end of a sentence or part of a sentence. בְּהֵמָה וָרֶ֫מֶשׂ, לֶ֫חֶם וָמָ֫יִם

B. Use of Wāw copulativum. 1. In circumstantial clauses, to introduce the subject, *e. g.*: God appeared to Abraham וְהוּא יֹשֵׁב פֶּ֫תַח הָאֹ֫הֶל as he sat by the door of the tent 18, 1, cf. 19, 1. Also so as, at the same time, to bring out a contrast, *e. g.*: What wilt thou give me וְאָנֹכִי הוֹלֵךְ עֲרִירִי seeing I go hence childless? 15, 2, cf. וַאדֹנִי זָקֵן seeing my lord is old 18, 12; I have ventured to speak וְאָנֹכִי עָפָר וָאֵ֫פֶר although I am dust and ashes 18, 27.—Also in complex nominal sentences, *e. g.*: Wherefore wilt thou stand without וְאָנֹכִי פִּנִּ֫יתִי הַבַּ֫יִת seeing I have prepared the house? 24, 31. Why are ye come to me וְאַתֶּם שְׂנֵאתֶם אֹתִי seeing ye hate me 26, 27.

c.   2. To express the ground or reason, *e. g.*: Now I know that thou fearest God, וְלֹא חָשַׂכְתָּ since thou hast not withheld 22, 12; hinder me not וה' הִצְלִיחַ דַּרְכִּי since J. hath prospered my way 24, 56, cf. 20, 3. ψ 7, 10. 60, 13.

d.   3. To introduce final clauses (that, in order that), mostly after the imptv., but also after the jussive, Isa. 5, 19, and cohortative (§47*g*), Job 32, 20; occasionally, too, after the impf., 1 Kings 22, 20.

e.   The verb following ו stands a) in the cohortative (1. *pers.*) or β) in the jussive (2. and 3. *pers.*). Exx.: a) Give me a possession of a burying-place וְאֶקְבְּרָה that I may bury 23, 4; bring it to me וְאֹכֵלָה that I may eat 27, 4; bring them out וְנֵדְעָה אֹתָם that we may know them 19, 5, cf. 24, 56. 27, 25. 29, 21 &c. Isa. 5, 19; let down thy pitcher וְאֶשְׁתֶּה (§74*v*) 24, 14. — β) Serve him alone וְיַצֵּל אֶתְכֶם that he may deliver you 1 Sam. 7, 3; entreat Jahwè וְיָסֵר that he may take away the frogs from me Ex. 8, 4; wait on Jahwè וְיֹשַׁע לָךְ that he may help thee Prov. 20, 22; who will persuade Ahab וְיַעַל וְיִפֹּל that he may go up and then fall 1 Kings 22, 20. — The jussive is often not recognisable as such (cf. §47*e*): Bring her forth וְתִשָּׂרֵף that she may be burned 38, 24, cf. וְתֵלַד 30, 3; I will speak וְיִרְוַח־לִי that I may find relief Job 32, 20.

D. THE VERB (§§ 47—80).

§ 47. Tenses and Moods, how expressed. § 47.
The Hebrew verb has no special forms by which to *a.*
express the *time* of an action (present, past, future);
instead of this the action is represented only as
being *completed* or *uncompleted: Perfect* and *Imperfect*.

The perf. accordingly serves for the most part to *b.*
indicate the past; it is, besides, employed in prophecies particularly, and in asseverations, because in
these the action is regarded as certain, *i. e.* practically as completed.

The Hebrew impf. (often, but with less propriety, *c.*
termed future), as denoting the unfinished action, is
very often employed to express the future, then also
to express such actions as ought to happen ["thou wilt
not kill"="thou shalt not kill"], and such as are conceived as possible, permitted, becoming (Potential).

Both moods (this appellation is according to the *d.*
foregoing more suitable than the misleading "tenses")
may be used to give expression to general truths
known by experience, which are rendered in English
by the present, according as the event in question
is regarded as one that has regularly taken place
in the past, or as one continually recurring and

therefore belonging also to the future; *e. g.* ψ 10, 3 "for the wicked boasteth (הִלֵּל perf.) of his heart's desire" and Prov. 1, 16 "for the feet of the wicked run (יָרֻצוּ impf.) to evil and make haste (וִימַהֲרוּ impf.) to shed blood."

As varieties (sub-moods) of the imperfect are to be noted:

e. 1. The *Jussive*, to express a command, wish or (after אַל §41,3) prohibition, only in 2. and 3. *pers.* In Hebrew it has external marks of recognition only in the uninflected sing. (hence not in 2. *f.*) viz: α) the shortening of the vowel of the last syllable in all impff. in which this vowel is *î* (*i. e.* mostly in the Hiph'îl), and in the impf. Qal of verbs ע"י, *e. g.* יַכְרִית, *juss.* יַכְרֵת; יָשִׁיב *j.* יָשֵׁב; יָשׁוּב, *j.* יָשֹׁב; β) the rejection of the ending ה— in the verbs ל"ה, see §74*n.o.*

f. NOTE. α) Jussive in final clauses, see §46*e.*—β) Jussive frequently in conditional clauses, in the protasis (ψ 45, 12), in the apodosis (G. 4, 12), in the protasis and apodosis (הָשֶׁת־חֹשֶׁךְ וִיהִי לָיְלָה if thou appointest darkness, then it will be night ψ 104, 20). Cf. §88*e*β.

g. 2. The *Cohortative* or *Voluntative* is formed by affixing ה— to the 1. person (*sing.*: I will, I should like to; *plur.*: we will, let us). Cf. the ה— of direction §20*c.*—The cohortative and the *Nûn demonstrativum* (§ 80), preserved only before suffixes, are the remains of an old *Modus Energicus*.

On perf. and imperf. with Wāw consecutive see §64. *h.*

The *participle* α) is for the most part to be rendered in English by the present indic.; it describes, in that case, a continuing, abiding act or an event just taking place.—β) It further serves to indicate the future, especially when the event is represented as just at hand and in promises, כִּי מַשְׁחִתִים אֲנַחְנוּ אֶת־הַמָּקוֹם הַזֶּה *nam deleturi sumus hunc locum* 19, 13, cf. 19, 14; הַמְכַסֶּה אֲנִי מֵאַבְרָהָם אֲשֶׁר אֲנִי עֹשֶׂה shall I hide from A. what I am now about to do? 18, 17; אֲבָל שָׂרָה אִשְׁתְּךָ יֹלֶדֶת לְךָ בֵּן verily Sarah shall ... 17, 19; esp. after הִנֵּה, *e. g.* 6, 17. Isa. 3, 1, הִנֵּה הָעַלְמָה הָרָה וְיֹלֶדֶת בֵּן behold! a virgin shall conceive and bear a son Isa. 7, 14.— γ) Finally, the participle indicates something that happened while some other event was taking place, in which case it is to be rendered by a past tense, *e. g.* 18, 1. 19, 1. 29, 9. *i.*

For the infinitive absolute see §63. *k.*

§ 48. Origin of the Hebrew Verb. The Hebrew (Semitic) verb had its origin in the combination of a noun with the personal pronoun treated of in §15*a*. § 48. *a.*

The *perf.* is formed by a concrete (or participial) noun, *nomen agentis*, followed by the personal pronoun: קָטַלְתָּ a killer thou=killed hast thou=thou hast killed. *b.*

c. The *imperf.* is expressed by a (probably) abstract or infinitive noun, *nomen actionis*, preceded by the personal pronoun. תִּקְטֹל thou (to) kill = thou wilt kill.

d. The different position of the pron. is easily intelligible psychologically: in the completed action we are more particularly interested in the fact; in an action which is not yet completed, we take more interest in the person of the agent.

e. Owing partly to the origin of the verb as described, partly to the frequent use of the 3. person, we can understand how in the 3. person (of the perf. at least) all indication of the person came to be dispensed with, and the 3. *p. m. sg. perf. Qal* thereby to be the ground-form of the verb. Hence too the Hebrew verb is given in the lexicons under this form.*

§ 49.
a. § 49. The Voices of the Verb (Conjugations, Genera verbi). Just as in Greek we distinguish three genera verbi (active, passive, middle voice), so there are in Hebrew seven common and a few rare modifications of the verbal idea, for which the unsuitable name conjugations—unsuitable, because used in Latin in an entirely different sense—has become current, and for which we propose to substitute *voices*.

---

* In verbs whose second radical quiesces (ו״ע, י״ע, §§71. 72) this purpose is served by the infin. (construct).

They are usually named after the form they assume *b.* in the old paradigm פָּעַל (do)*. Only the first voice or the simple stem has a special name, קַל, *i. e.* light, because not burdened either by external or by internal afformative additions.—Recent authorities name these voices more appropriately after the form they present in the now usual paradigm קָטַל.

II. Niph'al, נִפְעַל (Niqtal, נִקְטַל), reflexive stem: *c.* 1. reflexive, *e. g.* נִשְׁמַר take care of one's self, נִסְתַּר hide one's self; 2. reciprocal, *e. g.* נִשְׁפַּט go to law with one another, נִלְחַם *proeliari*, יָעַץ counsel, נוֹעַץ take counsel together; 3. passive, *e. g.* קָבַר, נִקְבַּר and שָׂרַף, נִשְׂרַף.

III. Pi'ēl, פִּעֵל (Qittēl, קִטֵּל), active intensive stem, *d.* denotes the intensification of the idea, esp. 1. iterative: צָחַק laugh, Pi. joke, קָבַר bury, Pi. bury many; 2. causative: לָמַד learn, לִמַּד teach, יָלַד bear, Pi. assist in childbirth; hence also declarative: צָדַק be righteous, Pi. declare righteous; 3. sometimes (particularly in denominatives) privative: שֹׁרֶשׁ root, שֵׁרֵשׁ root out, extirpate.

---

* According to this paradigm also, the first letter of the stem is called its פ, the second its ע, the third its ל. Verbs פ"נ are thus verbs with נ as their first radical, ל"א those with א as last radical. By ע"ע (§ 73) are denoted those verbs whose third radical is the same consonant as the second.

IV. Pu‘al, קֻטַּל (Quṭṭal, קֻטֵּל), passive of III.

e. V. Hiph‘îl, הִפְעִיל (Hiqṭîl, הִקְטִיל), active causative stem, causative of I. 1. with personal object, indirectly causative: שָׁמַע hear, הִשְׁמִיעַ cause some one to hear; hence also declarative: הִצְדִּיק declare just; רָשַׁע be wicked, הִרְשִׁיעַ declare guilty; 2. so that the act or condition denoted by the Qal becomes the object, directly causative*: הִגְבִּיר exert one's strength, show one's self strong, הִזְקִין become old, הִשְׁרִישׁ (denom. from שֹׁרֶשׁ) put forth roots.—The same Hiph. has often both significations: זָכַר remember; הִזְכִּיר α) cause some one to remember, put one in mind of, β) exercise memory one's self in regard to=mention something.

VI. Hoph‘al, הָפְעַל (Hoqṭal, הָקְטַל), passive to V.

f. VII. Hithpa‘ēl, הִתְפַּעֵל (Hithqaṭṭēl, הִתְקַטֵּל), reflexive intensive stem: 1. reflexive: הִתְאַזֵּר gird one's self, הִתְקַדֵּשׁ sanctify one's self; 2. reciprocal: הִתְיָעֵץ take counsel with another; 3. medial (sibi): הָלַךְ go, הִתְהַלֵּךְ go about for one's self, ambulare; 4. show one's self as, feign to be something: הִתְעַשֵּׁר feign to be rich, הִתְרוֹשֵׁשׁ feign to be poor.

g. In addition to these, there are a few rarely occurring voices of which the most important, the Pô‘ēl,

---

* Others: "internally transitive" or "internally causative". The usual specifications "intrans." or "as the Qal" are incorrect.

Qôṭēl, may be specially mentioned. מֹצֵל, קֹטֵל, the stem expressing end or motive, is formed by the insertion of ô (originally â) after the first letter of the stem. Examples from strong verbs are few in number (Stade §158. König §26,1); more common from verbs ע״ע (§73c).

§ 50. **Laws of Vocalisation and Tone.** Phonetic laws. Cf. §11c.d. To the law regulating the inflexion of the verb, viz: that before accented afformatives beginning with a vowel* the vowel of the second radical, even when immediately preceding the tone, shall be reduced to Šᵉwâ, we must note the following exceptions: 1. frequently before suffixes, v. §79g; 2. in pause before the fuller, and hence always accented, endings ûn and în, e.g. תִּדְבָּקִין, יִלְקֹטוּן (cf.§14,6).

§ 50. a.

Accentual laws. a) Always accented are: the last syllable of the ground-form and the endings תֶּם, תֶּן (§51).—β) Also the verbal endings ־ָה, ־וּ, ־ִי (§§51. 52.53), except in: 1. the Hiph'îl, 2. the verbs ע״וּ, ע״י, ע״ע, 3. pausal forms, see §14ia.—γ) Unaccented are the endings תָּ, תִּי, נוּ; ־ָה, ־ְ.

b.

§ 51. **Endings of the Perfect.** 3. sg. m.— 3. sg. f. ־ָה. The older ־ַת always before suffixes,

§ 51. a.

---

* The so-called union-vowel treated of in §79e is here, on practical grounds, also regarded as beginning the afformative (suffix).

elsewhere rarely. ‖ 3. *pl.* ו, three times ון. Was it originally *ûna* (old plural ending of masc. nouns)?

b. 2. *sg. m.* תְּ, also תָּה (cf. אַתָּה). ‖ 2. *sg. f.* תְּ, sometimes in K°thibh תִי, before suff. always תְּ, תִי (cf. *atti* §15*b*β). | 2. *pl. m.* תֶּם, before suff. תוּ (אַתֶּם, Arabic *antum*). | 2. *pl. f.* תֶּן, no example with suffix.

c. 1. *sg.* תִי (אָנֹכִי, change of כ to ת *v.* §22*a*). 1. *pl.* נוּ (cf. אֲנוּ).

§ 52. § 52. Endings of the Imperative. 2. *sg. m.* —
a. 2. *sg. f.* ־ִי— (cf. *î* in *atti*).

b. 2. *pl. m.* וּ. | 2. *pl. f.* unaccented נָה, rarely ן (with this old ending of the *pl. f.* cf. the Aramaic ן־ָ, and the Hebr. הֵנָּה, אַתֵּנָה). Before suffixes, see §79*d*β.

c. NOTE. ה־ָ affixed to the ground-form often serves to strengthen it; not unfrequently, however, it seems to have no appreciable value.

§ 53. § 53. Inflexion of the Imperfect. 3. *sg. m.*
a. ***י. (Originally the preformative was in most cases *jă*, s. §57*d*). 3. *sg. f.* ***ת (ת sign of the *fem.*). 3. *pl. m.* ו***י; the older ending ון esp. in and immediately before the pause. 3. *pl. f.* ת***נָה, rarely ת***ן; thus with twofold indication of the gender. Before suffixes ת***וּ, cf. §79*d*β.

b. 2. *sg. m.* ת*** (cf. אַתָּה). ‖ 2. *sg. f.* ת***י; the older ending ין־ esp. in pause (cf. *attin* §15*b*β). ‖ 2. *pl. m.* ת***וּ, also ת***וּן see 3. *pl. m.* (ת, cf. אַתֶּם, to indicate

§ 54. PERFECT QAL.

the 2. person). 2. *pl. f.* תְּ***נָה, rarely תְּ***ןָ. Before suffixes תְּ***וּ.

1. *sg.* א*** (אֲנִי). 1. *pl.* נ*** (cf. אֲנַחְנוּ). *c.*

NOTE 1. Perhaps the analogy of the 2. *pl. f.* influenced the *d.* formation of the 3. *pl. f.*—2. The 1. *pl.* has no plural termination.—3. On א***ה, *pl.* נ***ה of the cohortative see §47*g*.

§ 54. Perfect Qal (§51). The following is the inflexion of the transitive perf. (cf. §11*c.d*):

§ 54. *a.*

Singul.			Plur.	
קָטַל *m.*	3.	קָטְלָה *f.*	קָטְלוּ	3.
קָטַלְתָּ *m.*	2.	קָטַלְתְּ *f.*	קְטַלְתֶּם *m.* קְטַלְתֶּן *f.*	2.
קָטַלְתִּי	1.		קָטַלְנוּ	1.

Forms in pause: קָטָלָה, קָטָלוּ acc. to §14*ia*. In the other forms accented ◌ָ is lengthened to ◌ָ (§14*da*), e. g. קָטַל, קָטַלְתָּ, קָטְלָה. קְטַלְתֶּם, קְטַלְתֶּן remain unchanged.

The perf. with simple intransitive vocalisation *b.* (termed *med. ē* from the vowel of the second radical) differs only in the 3. pers.,—in the 3. *f. sg.* and 3. *pl.* only in pause and before suffixes, e. g. כָּבֵד, כָּבְדָה, חָדְלוּ; אָהֵב to love, אָהֲבוּ *amaverunt*, אֲהֵבוּם *amaverunt eos*, but 1. *sg.* אָהַבְתִּי, אֲהַבְתִּי.

The perf. with strong intrans. vocalisation (*med. ō*) *c.* preserves the *o*-sound throughout (except where, acc. to §11*d*, it must be reduced to Š^ewâ),—in an accented syllable as *ō*, in an unaccented as *ŏ*: יָכֹל; יָכְלָה; יָכְלוּ, יִלְּלוּ.—יָגֹרְתָּ, יָגֹרְתִּי.—2. *pl.* is not found. On the analogy of יְכָלְתִּיו *superavi eum* it would doubtless be pronounced *jekholtèm*.

d.   NOTE 1. Many verbs have *ē* and *a* in the second syllable of the ground-form without any difference of meaning. In such cases *ē* alone is used in pause and before suffixes: אָהֵב and אָהַב, but always אָהֵב.—2. In many cases owing to the non-occurrence of the pausal ground-form the fact that a verb had originally an intransitive formation is now to be gathered only from the derived forms. Thus we have *e. g.* six times גָּבַר (not in pause), but גָּבֵרוּ.

§ 55. *a.*   § 55. Infinitive Qal. Usual form קְטֹל.—Rarer forms:

1. קְטַל, Arab. *qatl*. Only in verbs that have *a* in the imperf., *e. g.* שְׁכַב; esp. in verbs *med. gutt.* before suff. (cf. §*e*): וּלְסַעֲדָהּ and to support her, בְּזַעֲקֵךְ at thy (*f.*) calling out; without suff. זְעֹק.

b.   2. קְטָלָה (קְ), קָטְלָה (קָ), feminine nominal forms: אַהֲבָה to love, love (*subst.*); שִׂנְאָה to hate, hatred; יִרְאָה to fear, fear; חֶמְלָה spare 19, 16; אַחֲרֵי זִקְנָתָהּ after she was old 24, 36.—The fem. ending is more common with the weak verbs: פ"נ §67, פו"י §68 and, in all voices, ל"ה §74.

c.   Verbs *med. ē* form their inf. mostly in *ō:* חֲדֹל, יְשֹׁן, יְרֹא, שְׂנֹא.

d.   In composition with לְ we find complete close of the syllable: לִקְבֹּר, לִשְׁכַּב, only rarely with בְּ and כְּ, *e. g.* בִּשְׁכֹּן 35, 22. Thus usually: בִּנְפֹּל, בְּנָפְלוֹ.

e.   Before suffixes the characteristic vowel (*a* thinned to *i*) appears in most cases under the first letter of the stem (but אֲכָלְךָ 2, 17, אֲכָלְכֶם 3, 5, לְרָדְפְךָ 1 Sam. 25, 29),—the syllable being loosely closed before suffs. beginning with a vowel: בְּעָמְדוֹ at his standing 41, 46, לְהָרְגֵהּ 27, 42, בְּשָׁכְבָה 19, 33; but בְּשִׁפְטְךָ.—Exception: הָפְכִּי my overthrowing 19, 21.

§ 56. Imperative Qal (cf. §52).

§ 56. a.

Trans.: קִטְלִי m. sg. ‖ קִטְלִי f. קִטְלוּ m. pl. קָטְלָה f.
In pause: קָטְלִי קָטְלוּ
Intr.: שְׂמַח m. sg. שִׂמְחִי f. שִׂמְחוּ m. pl. שְׂמַעְנָה f.
In pause: שְׂמֵחִי שְׂמֵעוּ

Imptv. always in *a* where the impf. has *a*.   b.

Before the endings ־ָה, ־וּ, ־ִי, the characteristic c. vowel appears under the first radical. Loose close of syllable: כָּתְבָה (§ 52c) write, I pray. *ă* is always thinned to *ĭ*: לְבַשׁ, לִבְשִׁי, לִבְשׁוּ, שִׁכְבָה. So with *ŏ* almost always before ־ִי and ־וּ, e. g. שְׁפֹךְ, שִׁפְכִי, שִׁפְכוּ, כִּתְבוּ, but שָׁמְרָה, זָכְרָה.—Hence such forms as מָלְכִי, rule (f.), and מִכְרָה, sell 25, 31, are exceptions.

The ground-form of the imptv. in *o* has *ŏ* under d. the first radical also before suffixes: כָּתְבֵם write them, שָׁמְרֵנִי keep me, רָדְפֵהוּ persecute him.—But plur. עִזְבוּ, עִזְבוּהָ derelinquite eam.—For the imptv. in *a* before suffs. cf. §79g.

§ 57. Imperfect Qal (cf. §53). The transit. impf. is as follows:

§ 57. a.

Plur.	Singul.
תִּקְטֹלְנָה f. יִקְטְלוּ m. 3.	תִּקְטֹל f. יִקְטֹל m. 3.
תִּקְטֹלְנָה f. תִּקְטְלוּ m. 2.	תִּקְטְלִי f. תִּקְטֹל m. 2.
נִקְטֹל (נִקְטְלָה) 1.	אֶקְטֹל (אֶקְטְלָה) 1.

In pause: יִקְטְלוּ, תִּקְטְלוּ, אֶקְטְלָה, יִקְטְלוּ.

b. The intrans. impf. has ă (in pause ā) תִּלְבַּשׁ, יִלְבַּשׁ, תִּלְבַּשְׁנָה; יִלְבַּשׁ, תִּלְבְּשִׁי, יִלְבְּשׁוּ, תִּלְבְּשִׁי.—Imperfects with intransitive pronunciation are also formed from many verbs that have only *a* in the perf., e. g. שָׁכַב, שָׁכֵב, impf. only יִשְׁכַּב; but by no means from all verbs with intrans. signification, cf. e. g. מָלַךְ, יִמְלֹךְ.

c. *in* and *ûn*: תִּשְׁכָּבוּן, תִּשְׁכָּבוּן, יִלְקְטוּן, תִּשְׂרְפוּן; תִּדְבָּקִין.

d. In the preformatives the original ă (cf. Arab. *jaqtulu*) has been thinned to *ĭ* (§§11f. 65f. 71m. 73k); but in the 1. *sg.* to —, a result due to the preference of א for Sᵉghôl (cf. §5d).

§ 58.
a. § 58. Participle Qal. The part. in the active is written: קֹטֵל (קוֹטֵל), inflexion like יֵצֶר, אֹיֵב §24d; fem. for the most part קֹטֶלֶת, inflected like יֹלֶדֶת §36d; st. abs. also קוֹטְלָה. (ô of the first syllable has been obscured from â, Arab. *qâtĭl*; cf. קָם §71ga).—Pass. קָטוּל, קְטוּלָה, קְטוּלוֹת; קְטוּלִים, §§23. 32.

b. NOTE 1. Forms like כָּבֵד heavy, מָלֵא full, רָעֵב hungry (from verbs *med. ē*) are not so much real participles as rather verbal adjectives, to which in Arabic the adjectival formation *qătĭl* corresponds (W. Wright, Arabic Grammar §230 Rem. a, §232 No. 3). Inflexion *v.* §25f.g.h.

2. From verbs *med.* ō only יָגוֹר Jer. 22, 25. 39, 17 is found c..
used as a verbal adjective (participle).

§ 59. II. Niph‘al, (Niqtal). The characteristic § 59.
of this voice is נ prefixed to the stem. a.

The *i*-sound, which in the perf. and part. unites b.
this נ with the verbal stem to form נִקְטַל and נִקְטָל has
been thinned from original ă (cf. *prim. gutt.* §65*l.k*,
פו״ר § 68c β, ע״ו § 71m, ע״ע § 73k).

In the inf., imptv., and impf. the syllable *hin* [the c.
aspirate to render audible the *ĭ* that has been put
before *n*, cf. Arab. *VII 'inqátălă*] has been prefixed to
the stem, of which the נ is regularly assimilated to
the first radical: inf. הִקָּטֵל, imptv. הִקָּטֵל, impf. יִקָּטֵל
(with syncope of ה, §10*d*).

The 1. sg. impf., besides אֶקָּבֵר, אֶסָּתֵר, also appears d.
as אֶמָּלֵט, אִדָּרֵשׁ; voluntative always *i*: אֶמָּלְטָה, אִנָּקְמָה.
Cf. §68*h*.

2. and 3. fem. pl. (imptv. and) impf. have ־ֶ un- e.
der the second radical, notwithstanding that ־ֵ of
the ground-form has been lengthened from *ĭ* (Arab.
'inqătĭl and *janqắtĭlu*), e.g. תִּשָּׂרַפְנָה, תִּשָּׁבַרְנָה; so in pause:
תִּשָּׁגַלְנָה. Of the imptv. there happens to be no example
preserved.

NOTE. In the impf., inf., and imptv. *ē* is generally deprived f.
of the tone and shortened to *ĕ* when a syllable follows with the
tone: הִשָּׁרֶד נָא 13, 9, אַחֲרֵי הִפָּרֶד לוֹט מֵעִמּוֹ 13, 14.

§ 60.
a.
§ 60. III. Pi'ēl and IV. Pu'al (Qiṭṭēl and Quṭṭal). The characteristic of both, as also of the Hithpa'ēl, hence of the intensive stems (§49) in general, is the doubling of the second radical.

b. NOTE. When this letter has Sᵉwâ under it, the Dāghēs is sometimes, acc. to §6*f*, omitted: so always in the Pi'ēl of בקש (seek) with the exception of the imptv. (thus בְּקָשִׁי, רִבְקָשִׁי, דִּבְקִשְׁרִים; but בַּקְשִׁי). Other examples, in which the vocal nature of the Sᵉwâ is expressly indicated (by a Chāṭēph): הַלֲלוּ (§5*d*) for *hallᵉlû*, לְקֳחָה 2, 23.

c. A dark vowel serves, as in the causative stem (Hoph'al), to indicate the passive (Pu'al).

d. The perf. Pi'ēl had originally ă [Arab. II *qattălă*] in both syllables of the stem. The first ă has been in all cases thinned to ĭ (cf. however קוֹמֵם §71*b*). The second ă has maintained itself α) before afformatives beginning with a consonant קִטַּלְתָּ, קִטַּלְנוּ &c.; β) frequently in the ground-form when not in pause (cf. §14*d*β): אִבַּד, גִּדַּל, יִסַּד, לִמַּד, קִדַּשׁ, שִׁלַּם &c., esp. with an emphatic (ק"צט) final consonant: חִזַּק, מִלַּט, שִׁקֵּץ, and usually when the last radical, or the last but one, is ר or a guttural (§10*a*2.*b*2): שִׁבֵּר, בֵּרַךְ; רִחַם, שִׁלַּח. (Cf. also בִּלָּה §74*f*). Elsewhere this ă has become ē, perhaps influenced by the analogy of the vowel of the impf.: קִטֵּל, קִטְּלָה, קִטְּלוּ; further גִּדֵּל, גִּדְּלָה, שִׁלְּמוּ, שִׁבֵּר, שִׁלְּחוּ, בֵּרַךְ.

e. Note the following: כִּבֵּס, דִּבֵּר, כִּפֵּר; כִּבֶּס, דִּבֶּר.

f. In pause *a* remains unlengthened almost always

before תִי, and often before תָ, תְ, נוּ. E. g. always הִבְּרַתִי,
שְׁבַרְתָּ, שְׁבַרְתִּי; דִּבַּרְתָּ.

In the other moods *ă* of the first syllable of the *g.*
stem remains unchanged, while the original *ĭ* of the
second syllable has, through the influence of the tone,
been lengthened to *ē*: inf. קַטֵּל, imptv. קַטֵּל [Arab.
qattil], impf. יְקַטֵּל, part. מְקַטֵּל.

The preformative מ employed in the formation of *h.*
the participles of the Pi‘ēl and all following voices is
connected with the pronoun מִי (§16*e*).

Part. Pi‘ēl: מְקַטֵּל and מְקַטֶּלֶת (inflexion as in Qal).— *i.*
Part. Pu‘al: מְקֻטָּל, מְקֻטָּלִים; מְקֻטֶּלֶת, מְקֻטָּלוֹת.

The two purely passive conjugations have gener- *k.*
ally neither imptv. nor inf. The only exceptions are:
imptv. Hoph. Ez. 32, 19. Jer. 49, 8; inf. Pu. ψ 132, 1;
inf. Hoph. הֻלֶּדֶת (fr. יָלַד) §68*c*) G. 40, 20, also Lev. 26, 43.
Ez. 16, 4. 5.

§ 61. V. Hiph‘il and VI. Hoph‘al, (Hiqṭil and § 61.
Hoqṭal). The first radical, which is vowelless, is pre- *a.*
ceded by a vowel introduced by the aspirate ה.

In the Hiph‘il the verbal endings ־ָה, וּ, ־ִי do *b.*
not have the tone.

The perf. Hiph‘il had originally *ă* in both syl- *c.*
lables [Arab. *'aqtălă*]. The first *ă* has always been thinned to *ĭ* (but cf. §§65*k*. 68*c*β. 69*b*. 74*w*β, הִכְלַמְתּוּם 1 Sam.
25, 7). The second *ă* has maintained itself before end-

ings beginning with a consonant, e. g. הִקְטַלְתֶּם, הִקְטַלְתָּ, but elsewhere it has become i, perhaps influenced by the i of the impf. &c.: הִקְטִיל, הִקְטִילָה, הִקְטִילוּ. (But cf. הִשְׁקָה §74*f*).

d. In pause הִקְדָּשְׁנוּ &c.; sometimes, however, *a* remains unlengthened.

e. In the inf., impf., and part. the original ĭ of the second radical is lengthened to î (Arab. impf. *jaqtilu*, part. *muqtilun*), doubtless from analogy of the vowel in יָקִים (Hiph. ע"י §71*b*; cf. Stade §91, König I, 210): inf. הַקְטִיל; impf. יַקְטִיל and part. מַקְטִיל with syncope of the ה (§10*d*).

f. Normal lengthening to ē only: in the ground-form of the imptv. הַקְטֵל (Arab. *'aqtil*), in the jussive (§47*e*) יַקְטֵל and before the unaccented afformative נָה: imptv. הַקְטֵלְנָה (impf. תַּקְטֵלְנָה, as it happens, does not occur). The lengthened imptv., however, is written הַקְטִילָה.

g. ŭ is frequently found in the Hoph'al instead of ŏ; in the part. owing to the influence of the labial מ ŭ is, in fact, the usual vowel. E. g. הָשְׁלְכָה as well as הָשְׁלַכְתִּי; part. מֻשְׁלָךְ. Cf. פ"נ §67*g*.

h. Part. Hiph'îl: מַקְטִיל, מַקְטִילִים; מַקְטֶלֶת, מַקְטִילוֹת.— Part. Hoph'al: מָקְטָל (מְ), מָקְטָלִים; מָקְטֶלֶת, מָקְטָלוֹת.

§ 62. a. § 62. VII. Hithpa'ēl (Hithqaṭṭēl). Characteristics: Doubling of the second radical and the prefixing of the syllable הִתְ, the ה of which is syncopated in the impf. and part.

In prefixing the syllable הִתְ the following rules *b.* are to be borne in mind: a) If the first radical is a dental (T-*laut*) the ת is assimilated, *e. g.* הַמִּטַּהֵר *qui mundandus est,* מְדַבֵּר *colloquens.* Assimilation is also found in a few other cases, *e. g.* הִנַּבְּאוּ *prophetaverunt.* β) If the first radical is a sibilant, ת is inserted after this letter, and made like to it in respect of hardness (§3), *e. g.* שָׁמַר, אֶשְׁתַּמֵּר I shall take heed; סתר, מִסְתַּתֵּר hiding one's self; צָדַק, נִצְטַדָּק we shall justify ourselves.

NOTE. In the single example beginning with ז, the ה that is *c.* to be expected (cf. Dan. 2, 9) has been completely assimilated to the ז: הִזַּכּוּ purify yourselves (from זָכָה) Isa. 1, 16.

Inflexion as in the Pi'ēl.—But: a) Before הָ *d.* (imptv., impf.) the second radical seems to have had *a* more frequently than *ē*.—β) In the ground-form of the perf., imptv., and impf. *a* is frequently found instead of *ē, e. g.* הִתְחַזֵּק.—γ) In pause *ē* of the perf., imptv., and impf. becomes *ā* (§14/β); *e. g.* הִתְאַזָּר perf., הִתְקַדְּשׁוּ imptv., יִתְהַלָּךְ, יִתְקַדָּשׁ impf.

§ 63. **Infinitive Absolute.** In addition to the § 63. ordinary inf. or *inf. construct* there is in Hebrew an *a.* *infinitive absolute,* which derives its name from the circumstance that it is usually subordinated to another verbal form as absolute object, and can neither govern a genetive (suff.) nor be governed by a preposition.

b. The inf. absol. has *ô* in the second syllable of the stem in I, II, rarely in III, and in the single example of IV (גֻּב 40, 15); *ê* for the most part in III, always in V, VI, VII.—Thus: I קָטוֹל (קְטֹל). II הָקְטֵל, נִקְטֹל. III קַטֵּל, rarely קַטֹּל. IV קֻטֹּל. V הַקְטֵל. VI הָקְטֵל. VII הִתְקַטֵּל.

c. B. Use of the Infinitive Absolute.—With the finite verb: 1. It corresponds to the Latin gerund in *do, e. g.* Thus shall ye bless the children of Israel אָמוֹר לָהֶם *iis dicendo* Num. 6, 23; she sat down over against him הַרְחֵק כִּמְטַחֲוֵי קֶשֶׁת making distant like bowmen (§74*b*)=at the distance of a bowshot Gen. 21, 16; esp. הֵיטֵב *bene faciendo=bene,* הַרְבָּה (§74*wô*) *multum faciendo=multum* 41, 49.

d. 2. With verbs from the same stem: α) immediately before the finite verb (only the negation stands generally immediately after the inf., but see Gen. 3, 4. ψ 49, 8) it emphasizes, strengthens, *e. g.* מוֹת תָּמוּת thou shalt surely die 2, 17, רָאוֹ רָאִינוּ we have clearly seen 26, 28; esp. in adversative sentences, *e. g.* יַסֹּר יִסְּרַנִּי יָהּ וְלַמָּוֶת לֹא נְתָנָנִי (§80 note α) ψ 118, 18; אָסֹר נֶאֱסָרְךָ וְהָמֵת לֹא נְמִיתֶךָ we will bind thee, but kill thee we will not, Judges 15, 13.

e. β) immediately after the verb it indicates the continuance, or the lasting effect of the action, *e. g.*

אֹמְרִים אָמוֹר saying continually Jer. 23, 17; יִשְׁפֹּט שָׁפוֹט he will always play the judge G. 19, 9. Sometimes in such a way that another inf. is strengthened and a new idea added, *e. g.* וַיֵּצֵא יָצוֹא וָשׁוֹב it flew continually to and fro 8, 7; עָלוֹ עָלֹה וּבָכֹה they went up, weeping all the time 2 Sam. 15, 30. The new verb may also stand between the parts of the other verb: וַיָּשֻׁבוּ הַמַּיִם מֵעַל הָאָרֶץ הָלוֹךְ וָשׁוֹב and the waters subsided gradually from off the earth 8, 3; וַיִּסַּע אַבְרָם הָלוֹךְ וְנָסוֹעַ הַנֶּגְבָּה and A. moved gradually towards the south-land 12, 9.

With the derived voices we often find the inf. *f.* Qal, *e. g.* טָרֹף טָרָף 44, 28 and always מוֹת יוּמַת; but also גֻּנֹּב גֻּנַּבְתִּי 40, 15 &c.

§ 64. **Wāw Consecutive.** In the course of a statement the Hebrew very often pictures to himself an act, which by the beginning of the sentence (impf.; imptv.; part. with הִנֵּה §47*i*β; a statement of time and such like) has been assigned to the future, as **completed**; and in like manner, after an act has, by the beginning of the sentence (esp. perf.), been designated as completed or past, he very often transfers himself to the time of its occurrence, *i. e.* to the time when it was still uncompleted.—This change in the point of view is indicated, particularly in prose, by the particle *wă* (then), *Wāw consecutive.* The term *Wāw conversive* is less appropriate: since generally a perf.

with this Wāw must be rendered by a verbal form of the future, and an impf. by an expression of the past, it was supposed that this Wāw "converted" the signification of the perf. into that of the impf. and vice versâ.

b. NOTE. Specially noteworthy are וְהָיָה, the "prophetic formula", and וַיְהִי the "narrative formula".—a) וְהָיָה (properly "and it will come to pass", though often to be left untranslated), e. g. וְהָיָה כָל־מֹצְאִי יַהַרְגֵנִי and every one that findeth me will slay me 4, 14, cf. 12, 12; very common in prophetical speech, esp. before specifications of time: וְהָיָה בְּאַחֲרִית הַיָּמִים Isa. 2, 2 &c.—β) וַיְהִי (prop. "then it came to pass", likewise to be often left untranslated), e. g. וַיְהִי כְשָׁמְעוֹ . . יַעֲזֹב and when he heard, (then) he left 39, 15; וַיְהִי אַחַר הַדְּבָרִים הָאֵלֶּה וְהָאֱלֹהִים נִסָּה and (it came to pass) after these things (that) God tempted 22, 1.

c. I. Wāw consecutive of the perfect has been weakened to וְ, thus identical, as regards the vocalisation, with Wāw copulative. It is however clearly distinguished from the latter in many cases by the position of the tone in the following verbal form, the tone after Wāw consec. being thrown forward on the last syllable—which finds a natural explanation in the similar function of the *wa* which, so to say, throws the act forward into the future. This advance of the tone has no effect on the vocalisation of the verbal form (§11c1 does not come into operation). Examples: אֵצֵא וְעָמַדְתִּי לְיַד־אָבִי *steti*, עָמַדְתִּי I will go out and (then) stand by my father's side 1 Sam. 19, 3; עָמַדְתְּ *stetisti*,

צֵא וְעָמַדְתָּ בָהָר go out and (then) stand on the mountain 1 Kings 19, 11; מָחָר חֹדֶשׁ וְנִפְקַדְתָּ to-morrow is new moon, then wilt thou be missed 1 Sam. 20, 18, בְּיוֹם אֲכָלְכֶם וְנִפְקְחוּ עֵינֵיכֶם G. 3, 5.

The tone is not thrown forward: regularly α) in pause*: וְאָכַלְתָּ וְשָׂבָעְתָּ and thou shalt eat and be satisfied Deut. 8, 10; β) in the 1. pl.: we will go three days' journey into the wilderness and (then) sacrifice נֵלֵךְ בַּמִּדְבָּר וְזָבַחְנוּ Ex. 8, 23; γ) in the Hiph'il with the afformatives ־ָה and וּ: and it [the wild beast of the field] will destroy your cattle and make you few in number וְהִכְרִיתָה אֶת־בְּהֶמְתְּכֶם וְהִמְעִיטָה אֶתְכֶם Lev. 26, 22;—for the most part δ) when two tone-syllables would otherwise come together: when thou shalt come into the land and (then) shalt dwell therein וְיָשַׁבְתָּ בָּהּ Deut. 17, 14; ε) in the Qal of verbs ל"ה and ל"א: and I will blot out וּמָחִיתִי 7, 4, and thou shalt call his name וְקָרָאתָ אֶת־שְׁמוֹ 17, 19;—often ζ) with the endings ־ָה and וּ in the Qal and Niph'al of verbs ע"ו and ע"ע, e. g. וְסָרָה and she will retire Isa. 11, 13 (from סוּר), but also וְסָרוּ.

II. Wāw consecutive of the imperf. (§ e—n) is written: וַ (וַיִּקְטֹל); before א with compensation lengthening (וָאֶקְטֹל), e. g.: he died and they buried him וַיִּקְבְּרוּ

---

* Sometimes also with other disjunctive accents: ψ 28, 1 וְנִמְשַׁלְתִּי, 1 Sam. 29, 8 וְנִלְחַמְתִּי (other exx. in Driver 2nd ed. §104).

אֹתָהּ; and she watered the camels and I asked her וָאֶשְׁאַל אֹתָהּ 24, 47.

f. NOTE. The preformative י never receives Dāgheš (§6/3): וַיְהִי, וַיְהַדְבֵּר, וַיְקַדֵּשׁ, וַיְרָכְבוּ; but וַיְסַפֵּר, וַיֶּאֱסֹף.

g. The heavy prefix *wa* draws the tone to itself. This explains* the fact that the last syllable of the impf., when without afformatives, in many cases either loses the tone (of course only when the last syllable is an open one, cf. §13,9) or is at least shortened (hence the impf. with Wāw cons. is often orthographically identical with the jussive). In pause the tone returns to the ultima.

h. The 1. *sg.* retains the tone on the last syllable and likewise remains otherwise unchanged: וָאַשְׁמִיד, וָאֵשֵׁב and *defective* וָאַשְׁלִיךְ; but וַיַּשְׁלֵךְ, וַיַּשְׁמֵד; but וָאֵשֵׁב, from יָשַׁב (§68*f*); וָאָשׁוּב and וָאֵשֵׁב, but וַיֵּשֶׁב §71*x*; וָאָשִׂם, but וַיָּשֶׂם (§72*a.d*).—Exceptions: α) ל״ה often, §74*u*; β) from הָלַךְ: וָאֵלֵךְ together with וָאֵלְכָה (5, except in pause); וָאוֹלִךְ (4); from כּוּן: וָאָכֵן (2) and †וָאָכִיד; from שׁוּב: †וָאָשֵׁב and †וָאָשִׁיב.

i. Wāw cons. is frequently joined to the cohortative: *e. g.* 4 times in the Pent.: וָאֶשְׁלְחָה 32, 6, וָאֶחְלְמָה 41, 11, וָאֶפְתְּחָה 43, 21, וָאֶתְּנָה Num. 8, 19; in 5 ψψ: 3, 6. 7, 5. 69, 12. 90, 10. 119.

k. With strong verbs: *a)* Niph'al וַיִּקָּבֵר, וַיִּתְקַבֵּר; וַיִּמָּלֵט;

---

* Otherwise F. Prätorius, Ztschr. f. d. Alttest. Wiss. 1883, p. 24 f.

in pause וַיִּגָּמַל §14/a, retrogression of tone only in וַיִּצָּמֶד Num. 23, 5.— β) Hiph'il, *i* becomes *ē:* וַיַּקְרֵב, וַיַּשְׁבֵּן, וַיַּבְדֵּל.

With guttural verbs. As in §k, but α) in Niph'al *l.* sometimes retrogression of the tone, *e. g.* וַיִּלָּחֶם (always), וַתִּשָּׁחֵת, but וַיִּשָּׁאֶר 7, 23; (2) וַיֵּעָתֵר, וַיֵּאָסֵף and (4) וַיֵּאָסֶה, וַיֵּאָבֵק, וַיֵּחָלֵק; β) in the Pi'ēl of verbs *med.* ר retrogression: וַיְגָרֶשׁ, וַתְּגָרֶשׁ, וַיְשָׁרֵת; but וַיְמָאֵן.

With other weak verbs except those ל״ה. We are *m.* here concerned with the Qal and Hiph'il. In the latter we find retrogression of the tone wherever there is an open preformative syllable. In detail:

פ״א. וַיֹּאכַל, וַיֹּאכַל, יֹאכַל, אָכַל.

פ״י. וַיּוֹסֶף, יוֹסֵף, יוֹסִיף *Hiph.* וַיֵּשֶׁב, וַיֵּשֵׁב, יֵשֵׁב, יָשַׁב
| וַיִּירַשׁ, יִירַשׁ, יָרַשׁ!

פ״י. וַיֵּיטַב, יֵיטִיב, רטב! *Hiph.* וַיְיטַב, וַיִּיטַב.

ע״ו. וַיָּשֶׁב, יָשִׁיב *Hiph.* וַיָּשָׁב, וַיָּשׇׁב, שׁוּב.

ע״ע. וַיָּפֶר, יָפֵר *Hiph.* וַיָּסָב, יָסֹב, סָבַב.

With verbs ל״ה. Here the ending ה◌ָ is in most *n.* cases thrown off, the form thus becoming identical with the jussive (§74 *o*—*t*).

§ 65. Guttural Verbs are verbs in which one of the radicals is a guttural. Verbs ל״א § 75 and a few פ״א § 66 present several deviations and are therefore treated separately. In verbs ל״ה § 74 the ה is only mater lectionis. Here, on the other hand, belong

§ 65. *a.*

the verbs ל"ה, their ה being a firm consonant, *e. g.*
וַיִּתְמָהוּ, תָּמֲהוּ wonder (תָּמַהּ).—Phonetic laws §10*a*.

b.   I. Instead of Dāghēš forte either 1. lengthening by way of compensation: always in the inf., imptv., impf. Niph'al, *e. g.* יִקָּטֵל: רֵאָסֵר, הֵאָסְרוּ, בְּהֵאָבְקוֹ, אַל־תַּעֲצְבוּ, also before ר, *e. g.* בֵּרַךְ: קֹדָשׁ bless, רָאֲבָךְ, מְבָרֵךְ; often before א, *e. g.* פָּאֵר, וַיְמָאֵן beautify;—or 2. virtual doubling: almost always with ח, *e. g.* וְקִטֵּל, רְשִׁחַת, לְשַׁחַת, and ה, *e. g.* imptv. קַטֵּל: מַהֵר, *f.* וּמֵהַרְתָּם, מַהֲרִי; in most cases with ע, *e.g.* תִּבַעֵת *terrebit*, תַּעֲבוּנִי *abominati sunt me,* inf. יַתְעֵב; frequently with א, *e. g.* נָאֲפוּ *adulterati sunt,* נָאֵץ revile, וַיְנָאֵץ.

c.   NOTE. α) Only exception perf. Pi. אֵחַר delay, but מֵאֲחֲרֵי־. β) Exception נֵהֵלָה lead, but יְנַהֵל, בְּנַהֵל. ‖ γ) Part. and impf. Pi. from תעב fluctuate between Páthach and Qámeṣ. ‖ δ) נָאֵץ Pi. always with short vowel. ‖ ε) Numerous examples to §*b*—to be used, however, with criticism—are given by Arnheim p. 126—135.

d.   II. Preference for the vowel *a*. 1. Páthach furt. (§4*d*) after a heterogeneous long vowel, *e. g.* inf. קְטֹל: שָׁלֹחַ, שָׁלוֹחַ, וּשְׁלוֹחַ; part. מְשֻׁלָּח: מְשַׁלֵּחַ; Hiph. הִקְטִיל: מַשְׁמִיעַ, הִשְׁמִיעַ.

e.   2. *a* for other changeable vowels: α) for ō in imptv. and impf. Qal: שְׁלַח, יִשְׁלַח; also with verbs *med. gutt.:* בְּחַר choose out (2. sg. imptv.). יִבְחַר; β) for ē, which re-appears in pause, *e. g.* תִּקְּטֵל: תִּשְׁכַּח, תִּשְׁכָּח: קְטַל: שַׁלַּח (§60*d*β); inf. קַטֵּל: שַׁלַּח and שַׁלַּח, שַׁלֵּחַ; imptv. קַטֵּל: שַׁלַּח; impf. יִקְטֵל: יְשַׁלַּח, יְשַׁלֵּחַ: תִּקְטַלְנָה: תְּשַׁלַּחְנָה (α also in pause). In the part. usually שֹׁלֵחַ and always מְשֻׁלָּח.

NOTE. Exception: imptv. in ō: וּעֲבֹחַ 43, 16.

3. *a* frequently re-appears where it stood at an earlier period of the language, especially under the preformative of the impf. Qal (§57*d*). With complete close of syllable chiefly before ח, *e. g.* יַחְמֹל, יַחְמֹד, יַחְשֹׁב, וַיַּחְפֹּר, וַיַּחְתְּרוּ; rarely before ע and ה, *e. g.* יַעְזְרוּ, וַיַּעְזְרוּ. Very often Châṭeph acc. to §10*a*4: יַהֲרֹג, יַחֲלֹם, יַעֲזָר־לִי, יַעֲמֹד, יַעֲבֹר, יַעֲבֹד; then before Sʰwâ, acc. to §5*f*: וַיַּחַלְמוּ, וַיַּעַמְדוּ, וַיַּהַרְגוּ.

NOTE. Sᵉghôl remains in the 1 sg. impf. Qal: אֶחְמוֹל, אֶחְמוֹל, *g.* אֶהֱרֹג. The only exceptions are: וְאָחֲרִנָה 27, 41, אֶאֱחֳדָה Job 16, 6, אֵחַז Job 23, 9 and וָאֶצַּל, וָאֱצַו §740ε.

4. Instead of the original *a* frequently the cognate *h.* Sᵉghôl, esp. in the syllable before the tone: *a*) Impf. Qal. First, when the second radical has *a*, *e. g.* יֶחְדַּל, יֶאֱבַל, יֶחְסַר, יֶחְתָּר, יֶחְפָּץ, and with Châṭeph: יֶחֱזַק; יֶחֱרַד; יֶאֱנֶה, יֶאֱמָץ, וַיֶּאֱהַל, יֶאֱהַב; before Sʰwâ acc. to §5*f*: יֶחְרְדוּ. Secondly when the stem begins with א, *e. g.* תֶּאֱזוֹר, וַיֶּאֱסֹר, יֶאֱרֹב, יֶאֱסֹף and 42, 29 וַיֶּאֱסֹר (Baer ס, *v.* §6*b*1); seldom elsewhere: וַיֶּחְשֹׂךְ ψ 29, 9.

NOTE. The other verbs with א are: רֶאֱשַׁם, וַתֶּאֱרַבְנָה, יֶאֱלֶה, רֶאֱשֵׁר; *i.* יֶאֱרֹג, יֶאֱנַק (§66, 6), תֶּאֱחֹז, יֶאֱהוֹ; יֶאֱהֶה.

β) Niph. and Hiph.—Niph. perf. and part.: נֶהְפַּךְ, *k.* נֶהֶרְסָה, נֶעֱזַרְתִּי, נֶעֱזַב, נֶאֱחַז, נֶאֱסָף; נֶחֱמָד, נֶחְשָׁב; before

Šᵉwâ: אָסְפָה and אָסְפוּ. — Hiph.: הֶאֱמִיד, הֶעֱבִיר, הֶאֱמִין; וְהֶחֱרִישׁ, וְהֶחֱלִךְ.

l.   NOTE. The original *a* (§59*b*) under ־ָ of the Niph. is preserved in נַחְבֵּאתָ *occultavisti te* 31, 27; נַעֲרָץ *tremendus* ψ 89, 8 (alongside of נֶעֱרָץ) and often עָשָׂה make, do (§74): נַעֲשָׂה, plur. נַעֲשׂוּ, part. נַעֲשָׂה, נַעֲשִׂים, but 3. *f. sg. perf.* נֶעֶשְׂתָה and נֶעֶשְׂתָה.

m.   γ) When the tone advances for ־ָ and ־ֶ ־ָ often ־ֲ and ־ֲ ־ָ, *e. g.* impf. Qal יַחְסְרוּן, וַיֶּחְדְּלוּ, יֶאֶסְפֵנִי, וַיַּאַסְפוּ, וַיַּאַסְרֵהוּ, along with יֶחְדְּלוּן, נֶאֶסְרָה; — Perf. Hiph. with Wâw cons.: וְהַאֲכַלְתִּיךָ, הַאֲכַלְתִּי, וְהַאֲבַדְתִּי, הַאֲבַדְתִּיךָ, הַעֲבַרְתִּי, וְהַעֲבַרְתִּי, הַעֲמַדְתָּ, וְהַעֲמַדְתָּ, but הֶעֱמַדְתִּיךָ.

n.   III. Šᵉwâ. — 1. Instead of Šᵉwâ mob. generally Chāṭēph-Páthach. קְטַלְתֶּם: קְטַלְתֶּם; צְחַקְתְּ: צָחֲקָה; עֲמַדְתֶּם: עָמְדָה: וַיִּקְטְלוּ: וַיִּמְהֲרוּ: וַיִּקְטְלוּ; וַיִּשְׁאֲלוּ.

NOTE. *Chāṭēph-Sᵉghôl* (§10*a*3): אֱמֹר to speak, speak thou, (לֵאמֹר §10*c*3); אֱכֹל eat thou, לֶאֱכֹל to eat. With the tone thrown forward: אֲכָל־מִמֶּנּוּ to eat of it.

p.   Šᵉwâ quiescens α) remains in an accented penult, *e. g.* שָׁלַחְתִּי, also before תֶּם, תֶּן, *e. g.* שְׁלַחְתֶּם, יְדַעְתֶּן. — β) Elsewhere in an unaccented syllable the pronunciation is in most case lightened by means of Chāṭēph, cf. רַאֲשֶׁךָ, יַחְרֹם; אַעֲמִיד, אַהֲרֹג, אֶעֱבֹד; but also אֶחֱמוֹל, וַיֶּעְתַּק. Chāṭēph also in 1. plur. perf., when the position of the tone is changed by suffixes, *e. g.* יְדַעֲנוּךָ, יְדַעֲנוּ we know thee, שְׁמַעֲנוּךָ, שְׁכַחֲנוּךָ.

q.   Miscellaneous. 1. Position of the tone after Wâw cons. *v.* §64*l*.

2. Verbs *med. gutt.*: α) Imptv. Qal בְּחַר, *pl.* בַּחֲרוּ; *r.*
זְעַק, זַעֲקִי, זַעֲקוּ; β) In Pi. of ר בֵּרַךְ receives Châṭêph-Páthach instead of Sᵉwâ, when the vowel of the כ is accented, *e. g.* וְהִתְבָּרְכוּ, וַיְבָרְכוּ בוֹ, but ψ 72, 17 וְיִתְבָּרְכוּ בוֹ;
γ) In יִצְחָק־לִי 21, 6 Châṭêph serves to lighten the pronunciation.

3. Verbs *tert. gutt.*: α) In an accented ultima, *i. e.* *s*
esp. in the 2. *f. sg. perf.*, a helping-Páthach is inserted; the following ת, however, retains Dâghêš and Sᵉwâ,
e. g. קָטַלְתְּ : שָׁכַחַתְּ, לָקַחַתְּ, הִגַּעַתְּ (Hiph. of נָגַע). שָׁמַעַן
4, 23 for שְׁמַעְנָה.—β) In (those forms of) the imptv., juss., impf. with Wāw cons. of the Hiph'il (whose aformatives do not begin with a vowel) the second radical has *a* instead of *ē*, *e. g.* יַקְטֵל : יַבְטַח, תִּשְׁמַע;
הוֹדַע, הַצְלַח, וַיִּצְמַח, וַיֵּשְׁבַּע (from יָדַע §68). But in the 1. sing. impf. acc. to §64ℎ וְאַשְׁבִּיעַ.—γ) Part. fem. ־ַת,
e. g. קֹטֶלֶת, בֹּרַח, בֹּרַחַת מְצֹרָע leprous, מְצֹרַעַת.

§ 66. Verbs א״פ. Verbs beginning with א are § 66. verbs *prim. gutt.*, see §65, esp. *o.* We have here to do *a.* with the inflexion of the impf. Qal in a few of these verbs.—In the impf. Qal א quiesces in ô which has been obscured from â (*jaᵃkhâl* became *jâkhâl*, then *jôkhâl*).

always in: 1. אָבַד *perire,* יֹאבַד, יֹאבֵד, יֹאבְדוּ, תֹּאבַדְנָה.
2. אָכַל eat; אָכֹל, יֹאכַל. וַיֹּאכַל, יֵאָכֵל; יֹאכַל, וְאָכַל.

H. Strack, Hebr. Gramm.³ I.   7

3. אָמַר speak; וַיֹּאמֶר, יֹאמַר, יֹאמֶר,וַיֹּאמֶר [Job ch. 3—42, 1: וַיְּאֹמַר].אֹמֶר; וְאָמַר (also in pause); further two verbs that are also ל"ה (§74):

4. אָבָה be willing, יֹאבֶה. 5. אָפָה bake, 3. *m. pl.* יֹאפוּ; for the most part in: 6. אָחַז seize: יֹאחֵז, וַיֹּאחֶז; 1. *sg.* וָאֹחֵז (17 times ô, 3 times acc. to §65*i*);

rarely in: 7. אָסַף gather, carry off (44 times as *prim. gutt.*; 3 times ô: תֹּסֶף ψ 104, 29, אֹסְפָה, וַיֹּסֶף, cf. König I, 382 f.). [וַיֹּסֶף from יָסַף belongs to §68].

b. אָהֵב (§54*d*), love, has in the 1. *sg.* אֹהַב (4) and † אֱהַב, in the other forms always יֶאֱהַב &c. (§65*h*).

אָחַר, 1. *sg.* וָאֵחַר and I stayed 32, 5 (elsewhere *Pi.*, §65*c*).

c. א of the stem is always dropped in the 1. *sing. impf. Qal* (אֹמַר, אֹכַל), seldom in the other persons, cf. אסף above and תְּאֹמְרוּ 2 Sam. 19, 14 for תֹּאמְרוּ.

§ 67.
a. § 67. Verbs פ"נ. In verbs פ"נ the נ, when pointed with Sᵉwâ quiescens, is assimilated (§10*g*) to the second radical, *e. g.* יִקְטֹל, but from נָפַל (fall) יִפֹּל; הִקְטִיל, הִפִּיל.—But קְטֹל, inf. and imptv., נְפֹל and hence inf. with ל לִנְפֹּל (§55*d*).

b. NOTE. The assimilation is not unfrequently dispensed with in pause, *e. g.* יִנְצְרוּ, but יִנְצְרוּ (4); יִנְקֹפוּ and תִּנְגֹּשׂוּ.

c. Verbs פ"נ *med. gutt.* retain the נ, *e. g.* יִנְאַף, יִנְאַץ, יִנְהַג. One impf. in ō (contrary to §65*ea*): יִנְהֹם (growl, roar).—Exceptions: α) Niph'al, נִחַת. יֵחַת *descendit*; β) impf. Qal יֵחַת together with תִּנְחַת.

d. The following (in addition to those *med. gutt.* §*c*) have the impf. in *a*: יִגַּשׁ approach, יִשַּׁק kiss, יִזַּל flow

[and the rare verbs, יִתֵּן, יִתַּר, יִשָּׁל]. — ō and a are found
in: יִשָּׁךְ, †רְשָׁךְ (2) bite; יִדֹּר and וַתִּדֹּר (11), יִדֹּר (3) vow;
†יִדוֹד and †יִדְדוּן, וַתִּדַּד wander, flee.

Inf. Qal. נגשׁ and נפח (blow) reject the נ and *e.*
receive as compensation the ending ת (cf. §§68*f.* 74*k*):
גֶּשֶׁת (9), suff. גִּשְׁתָּם (§36*b*); †פַּחַת blow. Note in addition: גַּעַת (2), touch, as well as נְגֹעַ (6) and †טַעַת, plant,
as well as נְטֹעַ (4). — נתן *v.* §*i*, נָשָׂא §76*e.*

In the imptv. Qal the same two verbs, as also נְגַע, *f.*
and נְסַע (remove), נָשָׁל *exuere,* נָשַׁק (kiss), reject the נ.
The forms that occur are: גַּשׁ, גְּשָׁה־הָלְאָה 19, 9, גְּשׁוּ,
also גְּשִׁי. — גַּשּׁוּ. —†פְּחִי. — גַּע (3); סְעוּ (4); שַׁל (2) put off,
וּרְנִטְעוּ, נְתַג, נְפֹלוּ, דִּרְכוּ — But נָתַן §*i*, נָשָׂא §76*e.* — 27, 26.וּשְׁקָה

The vowel of the Hoph‘al denoting the passive is *g.*
always — (§61*g*), *e. g.* מֻגָּשׁ, הֻגְּשׁוּ, הֻגַּד.

לָקַח, take, follows, except in the Niph‘al (נִלְקַח), *h.*
the analogy of verbs פ"נ (נפח): imptv. קַח; inf. קַחַת,
with ל: לְקַחְתִּי) לָקַחַת §65*sa*); impf. יִקַּח, *pl.* יִקְחוּ (without Dāghēš, *v.* §6/3); Hoph. impf. יֻקַּח.

נָתַן, give, assimilates its last radical to the follow- *i.*
ing ת (§10*g*), *e. g.* נְתַתֶּם; 2. *masc. sg.* generally *plene*
נָתַתָּה; 1. *pl.* נָתַנּוּ; inf. תֵּת (for *tint*), suff. תִּתִּי; imptv.
תֵּן, תְּנָה, תְּנִי, תֵּנוּ; impf. יִתֵּן; Niph. נִתַּן; Hoph. only
impf. יֻתַּן.

Concerning doubly weak verbs like נָשָׂא, נָשָׁא; נָשָׂה, *k.*
נשׁה: נקה, נסה, נכה cf. §76.

7*

§ 68.
a.
§ 68. Verbs פ״י (פ״י I. class, originally פ״ו). Verbs פ״י are those verbs whose first radical was originally ו (וָלַד, Arab. *walădă*; cf. יָלָד child 11, 30). This ו (cf. §10e) has passed into י in I, III, IV, and VII in part, but has maintained itself, protected by the preformative of the voice, in II, V, VI, and VII in part, viz:

b. 1. at the beginning of a syllable as a consonant: α) always in Niph‘al: וִיָּלֵד, הִוָּלְדוֹ יוֹם the day of his being born; β) sometimes in Hithp.: הִתְוַדָּה confess, בְּהִתְוַדַּע 45, 1 when he made himself known, יִתְוַכַּח he will reason.—יָלַד, יחש, יָעַץ retain י in the Hithp.

c. 2. at the end of a syllable as a vowel: α) fusion with the homogeneous vowel in the Hoph‘al: הָקְטַל, תּוּרַד, הוּרַד; β) contraction with the original ă to ô in Niph‘al (§59b): נוֹלַד *natus est*, נוֹלָד *natus*, and in the Hiph‘il (§61c) הוֹלִיד *genuit*, וַיּוֹלֶד, יוֹלִיד, מוֹלִיד.

NOTE. Inf. Hoph. of יָלַד with assimilation of the י (cf. §70) הֻלֶּדֶת (§60k).

In the Qal we find two modes of inflexion:

d. 1. Impf. with the vowels *i ă*: יָשֵׁן sleep, inf. (with לֹ) לִישׁוֹן, impf. אִישַׁן, יִישַׁן, וַיִּישַׁן. יָרַשׁ take possession of, possess (*med. ē*, cf. וִירֻשָּׁהּ), inf. רֶשֶׁת (49; Judges 14, 15 לְיָרְשֵׁנִי), imptv. רֵשׁ (2), רָשׁ and †יְרָשָׁהּ; impf. יִירַשׁ, וַיִּירַשׁ. יָרֵא fear, imptv. יְרָא, impf. יִירָא v. §76g.—In the same way are formed the impfs. of: יעף (*med. ē*), יגע,

יָצַע, יָצַר. (Inf. and imptv. are wanting). ‖ —From יָסַד, found, inf. (with לְ) לִיסֹד. (Impf. and imptv. wanting).

NOTE. יקר be precious, impf. יִיקַר and יֵקַר, יֵקַר.—יקד burn, e. impf. תִּיקַד and יֵקַד.

2. Impf. with the vowels ê é,* or ê á, (7 verbs): יָשַׁב, f. sit, dwell; inf. שֶׁבֶת, suff. שִׁבְתִּי; imptv. שֵׁב, שְׁבָה, שְׁבִי, שֵׁבִי; impf. יֵשֵׁב, וַיֵּשֶׁב, וַיֵּשְׁבוּ, אֵשֵׁב §64h.—So: יָלַד, peperit, genuit, impf. תֵּלֵד, וַתֵּלֶד (not in pause), תֵּלַדְנָה; also יָרַד, descendit, imptv. רֵד, רְדָה, רְדִי; impf. יֵרֵד, וַיֵּרֶד; for יָצָא v. §76g.—And 3 verbs tert. or med. gutt.: יָדַע, know, דַּעַת, imptv. דַּע; impf. יֵדַע, וַיֵּדַע, וַתֵּדַע; יקע be sprained, impf. וַתֵּקַע 32, 26; יחד be united, impf. תֵּחַד 49, 6.

NOTE. 1. Inf. sometimes in ־ָה (cf. §55b): הֱיֵה (often), לֵדָה (4), g. מֶרְדָּה. ‖ 2. Inf. abs., where it occurs, regularly: יָדֹעַ, הָלוֹךְ. ‖ 3. יָכֹל be able, inf. יְכֹלֶת, inf. abs. יָכוֹל, impf. יוּכַל. ‖ 4. יהב give; only imptv. הַב; go to! הָבָה (even when several persons are addressed, 11, 3. 4) and הָבוּ.

Niph., 1. sing. impf. has always î: אִוָּרֵשׁ, וָאִוָּדַע. Cf. h. §59d.!

הָלַךְ, go, in the inf., imptv., and impf. Qal and in i. the Hiph'îl follows the analogy of יָרַד: inf. לֶכֶת (but with suffixes לֶכְתִּי); imptv. לֵךְ, לְכָה, לְכִי, לְכוּ, לֵכְנָה; impf. יֵלֵךְ, וַיֵּלֶךְ, תֵּלַכְנָה; Hiph. הוֹלִיךְ.—But הִתְהַלַּכְתִּי, הִתְהַלֵּךְ.—Exceptions e. g. יַהֲלֹךְ &c., תַּהֲלֹךְ.

---

* é in the second syllable from original ĭ; cf. Arab. wălădă, impf. jălĭdu. Cf. also יֵחַן יֵחַר §67i.

k.   NOTE. לְכָה *age,* come! even when a female 19, 32 and several persons 31, 44 are addressed.

§ 69.   § 69.   Verbs פ״י (פ״י II. class, originally פ״י).

a.   Qal. The imptv. is not found, inf. only יְבֹשׁ Isa. 27, 11.—יטב be good, וַיִּיטַב and יָטַב, וַיִּיטֶב; יָנַק suck, וַיִּינֶק. ‖ יקץ awake, הָאִיקֶץ, וַיִּיקֶץ, but 9, 24 וַיִּיקֶץ ׀ יָבֵשׁ (Arab. *jābisă*) be dry, inf. יְבֹשׁ and 8, 7 יְבֹשֶׁת, impf. יִיבַשׁ, וַיִּיבָשׁ ;וַיִּיבֶשׁ; Hiph. הוֹבִישׁ after the analogy of verbs פו״ר.

b.   Hiph'îl. Original *aj* (cf. §61c) is contracted to *ê*: וַיֵּיטִב, מֵיטִיב, הֵיטִיב &c.

c.   NOTE. Uncontracted forms: יַיְשִׁרוּ Prov. 4, 25, הַיְשַׁר make plain, imptv. ψ 5, 9 Q°rê (הוֹשֵׁר K°thîbh). Cf. also G. 8, 17 הַיְצֵא Q. (הוֹצֵא K°thîbh).

d.   Sometimes double forms: וַיְטִיב, יְיֵלִיל &c.

§ 70.   § 70.   Verbs פ״צ (פ״י III. classe). In a few verbs פו״י, esp. those whose second radical is צ, the first letter of the stem, when pointed with Šᵉwâ quiescens, is assimilated to the second, as in verbs פ״נ. Manifold variations appear in the inflexion, as is shown by the following summary:

יָצַק, pour, inf. צֶקֶת; imptv. יְצֹק and צֹק; impf. יִצֹּק and (*e. g.* 28, 18. 35, 14) יִצֹק (intr. וַיִּצֶק). Hiph. הִצִּיק set, place; Hoph. הוּצַק be poured, מוּצָק, יוּצַק.

יָצַר form, impf. יִצְרֵהוּ and וַיִּצֶר, וַיִּיצֶר. Niph. נוֹצַר; Hoph. יוּצָר.

יצת burn, impf. תִּצַּתְנָה. Niph. יִצַּת be set on fire; Hiph. הִצִּית.

(יצג), Hiph. הִצִּיג place, אַצִּיגָה, מַצִּיג. Hoph. impf. יֻצַּג.

(יצע), Hiph. spread out. יַצִּיעַ; יֻצַּע impf. Hoph. or perf. Pual.

(יצב), Hithp. הִתְיַצֵּב (take one's stand) seems not to belong here; for the Niph. נִצַּבְתָּ, Hiph. הִצִּיב, Hoph. מֻצָּב are rather to be taken from נצב (פ"נ).

§ 71. Verbs ע"ו*. In consequence of its semi-vocalic nature (cf. §10d) ו, when second radical, is thrown out or loses its value as a consonant: in all verbs that are weak in no other respect (e. g. קוּם arise, רוּם be high, שׁוּב return), and in the majority of verbs with a guttural (e. g. נוּחַ rest). Verbs of this class are given in the lexicons under their respective infinitives (§48e).

§ 71. a.

NOTE. ו remains as a consonant in all verbs ל"ה and in a few with a guttural (c. g. גָּוַע expire).

I. Formation of the intensive Stems. The doubling of the ו or of the י that has taken its place to lighten the pronunciation is rare (note esp. קַיַּם from קוּם); the same is true of the Pilpēl formation (תְּשַׂגְשֵׂגִי from [שׂוּג]), thou wilt hedge round Isa. 17, 11): generally, in order to preserve the intensive character,

b.

---

* According to A. Müller, Stade, Nöldeke, Hommel and others, verbs ע"ו, ע"י and verbs ע"ע were originally biliteral stems, at a later period lengthened and sharpened respectively. We feel bound however, for the present at least, to adhere to the view hitherto generally accepted.

the third radical has been doubled: קָטֵל, קוֹמֵם (from *qavmēm*, cf. §60*d*); קָטַל, קוֹמַם; הִתְקַטֵּל, הִתְקוֹמֵם.—With reference to the change of the first vowel occasioned by the weakness of the Wāw these voices (conjugations) are named Pôlēl, Pôlal, Hithpôlēl.

c. The active Pôlēl and the passive Pôlal are distinguished from each other (apart from the plur. part., cf. §60*i* מְקַטְּלִים, מְקֻטָּלִים) only in the follg. forms:

Act. קוֹמֵם *f.* קוֹמְמָה, קוֹמֵמָה. קוֹמֵם. יְקוֹמֵם. תְּקוֹמֵמְנָה. מְקוֹמֵם.
Pass. קוֹמַם *f.* קוֹמְמָה, קוֹמֲמָה. קוֹמַם. יְקוֹמַם. תְּקוֹמַמְנָה. [מְקוֹמָם].

d. II. The remaining Voices.—Rule for the tone. The endings ־ָה, וּ, ־ִי are not accented (§50*b*β) from a desire to give more weight to the shortened verbal stem.

e. NOTE. α) For the accentuation of the perf. with ־ָה and וּ after Wāw cons. see §64*d*ζ. ‖ β) The lengthened imptv. has the tone for the most part on the ending ־ָה before an immediately following א—hence also before יהוה (=אֲדֹנָי), *e. g.* ψ 3, 7 קוּמָה ה׳, Isa. 44, 22 שׁוּבָה אֵלַי.

f. Transitive Qal. (§ *f.g.h*).—1. In the perf. the vowel sound *a*, characteristic of the second radical, has completely thrust out the ו together with the preceding vowel: קַמְתָּ, קַמְתֶּם. The length of the vowel in the 3. *m. sg.* קָם is to be explained in the same way as the accentuation of the stem-syllable in 3. *f. sg.* קָמָה and 3. *pl.* קָמוּ.

2. Participles. a) The act. part. קָם is to be explained from the ground-form of the participle (cf. §58a, Arab. qâtŭl.—qâwĭm, [qâĭm], qâm); fem. קָמָה.—β) In the pass. part. קוּם the obscure vowel of the passive (ŭ) predominated.

3. In the other moods qwum became qûm: קוּם inf. and imptv., יָקוּם impf. (But inf. abs. קוֹם: קָטוֹל).

Intransitive Qal (med. ē and ō).—מַת die, f. מֵתָה, 2. מַתָּה, 1. מַתִּי, pl. מֵתוּ, מַתְנוּ; part. מֵת mortuus, f. מֵתָה mortua; inf. מוּת (abs. מוֹת); imptv. מֻת (written defective); impf. יָמוּת. ‖ בּוֹשׁ be ashamed, בּוֹשָׁה, 2. f. בֹּשְׁתְּ, 1. בֹּשְׁתִּי; pl. בּוֹשׁוּ, 1. בֹּשְׁנוּ (2. pl. had probably short o); part. pl. בּוֹשִׁים; imptv. בֹּשִׁי, בּוֹשׁוּ; impf. יֵבוֹשׁ. אוֹר shine, אֹרוּ; imptv. f. אוֹרִי.

Niph'al.—The vowel of the stem, which has become monosyllabic, is ô in all the moods. Inf. and imptv. הִקּוֹם: הִקָּטֵל; impf. יָקוֹם: יִקָּטֵל.

Hiph'îl.—Here ו has been completely thrust out by the following heterogeneous vowel without being able to modify it, impf. יָקִים (Arab. juqîmu)*.

The vowel of the preformative syllable (§m—p).— 1. Owing to ו being dropped as a consonant we have for the most part an open preformative syllable.

---

* This î-sound (cf. also part. muqîmun) seems to have given rise to the î in יַקְטִיל, in הֵקִים and also in הִקְטִיל. Cf. §61c.e.

Accordingly when the latter is the syllable before the tone, it receives a long vowel: a) ă becomes ā. הַקְטִיל: הָקֵם, הַקְטֵל: יַקְטִיל; יָקִים: הָקִים, and that not only where a is still preserved in the strong verb, but also where it is now thinned to ĭ, as in Qal and Niph'al: impf. Qal יִקְטֹל (§57d): יָקוּם; perf. Niph. נִקְטַל (§59b): נָקוֹם. When the tone advances, acc. to §11c1: impf. Qal יָקוּמוּן; impf. Hiph. יְקִימוּן, תְּשִׁיבֵם (תָּשִׁיב) thou wilt lead them back; inf. Hiph. הֲרִימִי my raising.

n. β) In the Hiph'il ĭ becomes ē. הָקֵם: הִקְטִיל and so also, with abnormal lengthening: part. מֵקִים (מַקְטִיל); same lengthening in verbs ע״ע, §73k).—When the tone advances: מְקִימִים.

o. NOTE. The preformative ה is frequently found with ־ֲ for ־ְ: always in the 3. person, e. g. הֱפִיצָם he hath scattered them, הֱמִיתֻהוּ they have killed him; seldom in the 1. and 2. person, e. g. הֱשִׁיבֹנוּ [ō see §7] we have answered,—not after Wāw cons. or before suffixes, thus הֲפִצוֹתִיךָ I have scattered thee, &c. (Olshausen, §255i).

p. 2. The Hoph'al has û throughout. Owing to the weight of this vowel it was not necessary to lengthen the vowel of the stem-syllable. הָקְטַל: הוּקַם, הוּקְמָה, הוּקַמְתֶּם, יוּקַם. (הוּרַד §68c is orthographically identical).

q. The parting-vowel (§q—v).—To support the long (lengthened) vowel of the now monosyllabic stem, the stem-syllable is kept open before the afformatives ת and נ by a so-called parting-vowel, viz: by ō in the perf., by é (י–ֵ, –ֵ) in the impf. — This vowel, which receives the tone in those cases where the stem-syllable would otherwise be entitled to it, is always employed in the perf. Niph., never in the Hoph. and perf. Qal (§ p.f.), but for the most part elsewhere (i. e., since no relevant instance of the impf. Niph. occurs, in the perf. Niph. and Hiph., and in the impf. Qal and Hiph.). Exx.: הֲקִימוֹתִי, תְּקוֹמֶינָה; הֵקִים, יָקוּם.

NOTE. Is it likely that the parting-vowel is not, properly *r*. speaking, an inserted vowel, but the vocalic final sound of the stem, which has been preserved (König I, 322), and is, in so far, analogous to the "union-vowel" (§§22d. 79e). In Arab. the vowel of the stem is shortened: 'ăqâmă, 'ăqamtă.

In the perf. Niph., at least when the tone is *s*. drawn forward by the parting-vowel, ō of the stem-syllable becomes û: נָסוֹג he has retired, נְסוּגֹתִי. — In the 5 cases in which the tone advances two syllables (2. m. pl.) ō has maintained itself: נָפֹצוּ they are scattered, נְפֹצוֹתָם.

The parting-vowel is sometimes omitted. The *t*. following examples show the changes thereby produced in the vowel of the stem. Impf. Qal תָּשֹׁבְןָ, תִּשְׁבְּרֶינָה; perf. Hiph. הֲנִיפֹתִי I have swung, הֵנַפְתָּ thou hast swung; impf. Hiph. f. pl. תְּבִיאֶינָה they will bring, תְּשֵׁבְןָ they will bring back.

NOTE. The parting-vowel is always omitted in the Hiph. of *u*. בוּת, e. g. הֲמִתָּה interfecisti, הֲמִתִּי, with the tone thrown forward וַהֲמִתִּיהָ et interficiam eam, הֲמִתֶּם; often in בּוֹא § 76h.

108

v. In the perf. Hiph. the stem-syllable has sometimes ē for î notwithstanding the parting-vowel, esp. after Wāw consec., *e. g.* הֶקְרִישִׁי, but יַהֲקַמְתָּ and thou wilt raise up.

w. Jussive.—Qal יָקֹם. Hiph. יָקֵם, *tert. gutt.* יָרַח (cf. §65sβ).

x. Wāw cons.—Qal וַיָּקָם, וַיָּקֹם; *tert. gutt.* or ר: וַיָּנַח, וַיָּסַר (exception וַיָּגֶר). Hiph. וַיָּקֶם; *tert. gutt.* or ר: וַיָּרַד, וַיָּסַר. ‖ But 1. *sg.* acc. to §64*h* הָקִים, הָקֵם, הָקוּם.

y. Miscellaneous: *a)* נוּחַ, rest, double Hiph'îl: הֵנִיחַ *quiescere fecit*, יָנִיחַ &c.; הִנִּיחַ lay, throw down, יַנִּיחַ, וַיַּנַּח. ‖ β) מוּל circumcise. Niph'al יִמּוֹל, *pl.* נִמֹּלוּ, part. *pl.* נִמֹּלִים.

§ 72.
a. § 72. V e r b s ע״י.—Not a few ע״ו stems allow their ו to pass more or less frequently into י (cf. §10*d*). Since the vowel of the stem-syllable adapts itself in such cases to the י, the result is a number of forms which resemble shortened Hiph'îl-forms and which are in fact by many regarded as such, *e. g.* בִּין he observed.—The stems referred to are: *bûn, gôªch, gûl, dûgh, dôn,* הוּשׁ, חוּל, חוּשׁ, לוּן, *nûr, rûbh,* שׂוּחַ, שׂוּם, שׁוּשׂ, *šûr,* שׁוּת.

b. Qal (§*b*—*e*).—Perf. and part. as in ע״ו, *e. g.* בִּנְתָּ, בָּנִים, רַבְתָּ, רַב, דָּנוּ, דָּן, גַּלְתִּי (part. *pl.*) &c. Part. pass. שִׂים 1 Sam. 9, 24.

c. Perf. with î only 4 times: בִּין, בִּינֹתִי (Dan.); רִיבוֹתָ (Job); וְדִיגוּם (Jer.).

d. In the other moods the follg. have in most cases *î*:

§ 72. VERBS ע״י.

impf. יָבִין, juss. יָבֵן, Wāw cons. וַיָּבֶן, inf. בִּין, imptv. בִּין,
יָשִׁישׁ‎ᵉ, יָשִׂים‎ᵟ, יָשִׂיחַ‎ᶻ, יָרִיב, יָלִין‎ᵝ, יָדִין‎ᵅ, יָגִיל, so: בִּינָה,
יָשִׁיר‎ᵋ. A preference for û is shown by: חוּל, impf.
תָּחִיל, imptv. וְחוּלִי‎ᶯ, and חוּשׁ‎ᶿ, impf. יָחוּשׁ, imptv. חוּשָׁה.

α) יָדוּן 6, 3 in another signf.—β) Inf. לָלוּן (6), לָלִינְךָ.—γ) Inf.
לָשׂוּחַ 24, 63 along with לָשִׂיחַ ψ 119, 148.—δ) Inf. almost always
שׂוֹם.—ε) Inf. only לָטוּשׁ.—ζ) לָשׁוּר† Kᵉthîbh, לָשִׁיר Qᵉrê.—η) also
חִילוּ.—ϑ) Inf. adverb. חִדֻשׁ ψ 90, 10.

NOTE. Impfs. of the form יָבִין are either not at all or only *e.*
by their signification to be distinguished from impfs. Hiph‘îl.—
2. The inf. in î is also used as inf. absol.; cf. however שִׂ״ה Isa. 22, 7,
רֹב Jud. 11, 25, שׂוֹם Neh. 8, 8, שׂוֹשׂ Isa. 61, 10.

Niph‘al, Hiph‘îl (Hoph‘al) as in verbs ע״ו: נָבוֹן be *f.*
intelligent; Hiph. inf. הָבִין, impf. יָבִין. Pôlēl &c. as in
ע״ו (§71b).

Only in a few verbs is י certainly the original *g.*
radical*: קָץ denominative perf. from קַיִץ summer (to
spend the summer) Isa. 18, 6.—Also the Pilpēl כִּלְכֵּל
(preserve, provide for): וַיְכַלְכֵּל, וְכִלְכַּלְתִּי, אֲכַלְכֵּל, the Pôlēl
קוֹנֵן (lament, moan) from qin, and perhaps זִיד (boil,
be proud), perf. זָדוּ, impf. יָזִיד; Hiph. הֵזִידוּ, וַיָּזֶד.

As regards the position of the tone, what has been *h.*
said under ע״ו §70d.e applies here also, e. g. שִׁיתָה ה׳
ψ 9, 21, שָׂמוּ אֹתִי בַּבּוֹר Gen. 40, 15. Also in certain other

---

* A comparison of Arab. and Ethiop. makes it probable that
י is also the original radical in several of the verbs cited in §a,
cf. Nöldeke ZDMG 1883, 525—540.

cases, esp. with a following guttural, the endings ה־ָ,
ִי, ־ֶ֫י receive the tone: רְבוּ 26, 22.

i. י as a firm consonant is rare, *e. g.* אוֹיֵב, אָיַ֫בְתִּי.

§ 73.
a.
§ 73. Verbs ע״ע. These are verbs that have the second and third radical alike.

b. I. The intensive Stems (§ *b—e*). — 1. Formation regular. Pi'ēl: הִלֵּל, חִלֵּל, מִלֵּל, קִלֵּל, impf. אָרֶנְךָ, יְמַשֵּׁשׁ, יְפַלֵּל; inf. with בְ and suff. בְּעַנְנִי 9, 14 (בְ §6/3) *med.* ר: אֲרָרָה, אָמָרַר. Pu'al: יְהֻלַּל, מְחֻלָּל. Hithp.: יִתְחַנֵּן, הִתְפַּלֵּל, תְּחָמֵּם ψ 18, 26.

c. 2. Insertion of an unchangeable ô after the first radical (cf. III Arab. *qâtălă* and §49*g*): Pô'ēl, Pô'al, Hithpô'ēl (orthographically identical with Pôlēl &c., and inflected in the same way, §71*b.c.*). Examples: יְהוֹלֵל he maketh fools of; מְהוֹלָל mad, יִתְהֹלָ֑לוּ they will be mad; תְּסוֹבֵב she will surround; וַיִּתְרֹצֲצוּ struggled 25, 22; לְהִתְגֹּלֵל 43, 18.

d. 3. Pilpēl: גלל, גִּלְגַּ֫לְתִּי, הִתְגַּלְגְּלוּ.

e. A few verbs form their intensive stems in more than one of the ways just enumerated, sometimes with a difference of meaning, as יְהַלֵּל he will praise, יְהוֹלֵל (§*c*); sometimes without, as רִצַּ֫צְתָּ thou hast destroyed, וַיְרֹצֲצוּ.

f. II. The other Voices. Main rule. The two identical consonants are contracted to one double consonant; the vowel of the second radical appears under the first. Owing to this shortening of the verbal stem, the endings ◌ָה, וּ, ◌ִי remain unaccented (cf. §71d): חתת be terrified: perf.: חַת, f. חָתָה, pl. חַתּוּ; סבב, inf. and imptv. סֹב.

g. The tone is thrown forward on the endings ◌ָה, וּ, ◌ִי often after Wāw consec. §64dε; frequently before a guttural, *e. g.* רַבּוּ עֲבָדִים 1 Sam. 25, 10; sometimes also elsewhere, esp. 3. *pl.* perf., *e. g.* ψ 3, 2. 55, 22. 104, 24.

h. Exceptions. In Qal the follg. are not contracted: α) the parts. and the inf. abs. in all cases: שָׁדוּד, שָׁדַד, סָבַב; שְׁדוֹד; β) the 3. perf. of transit. verbs in most cases, esp. before suffixes: סְבָבַ, סְבָבוּ, סְבָבוּנִי; but also סַבּוּנִי; γ) sometimes the inf. after ל, *e. g.* לִגְזֹז 31, 19, but also לָגֹז.

i. Lengthening of the vowel of the stem-syllable. If the word ends with the double consonant, Dāghēš is dropped. *ă* is not lengthened in such cases (§11e2). The stem-vowel of the Hiph'il appears as *ē* (*î* impossible before the double consonant), *e. g.* הָקֵל: הַקְטִיל, הָסֵב; often, esp. in the perf. 3. *pl.* and 3. *m. sg.*, as *d*: הַדַק, הֵסַבּוּ he has crushed.

k. Vowel of the preformative syllable. As in ע״ו (§71m—p). 1. α: Hiph. impf. יָפֵר, inf. and imptv. הָפֵר; Qal impf. יָסֹב, Niph. perf. נָסַב. ‖ 1. β: Hiph. perf. הֵפֵר, part. מֵפֵר (cf. מֵקִים §71n). ‖ 2.: Hoph'al הוּסַב, firm *û*.

l. Parting-vowel. (Cf. §71q—v). To secure the distinct pronunciation of the double consonant a parting-vowel is inserted before the afformatives ת and נ

in all four voices (thus also in the Hoph. and in the perf. Qal): ō in the perf., ē (י⸺, ⸺) in the impf. and * imptv.—ō and ē of the stem-syllable with Dāghēš are then shortened to ŭ and ĭ, since a long vowel cannot stand in an unaccented firmly closed syllable. ō: Qal סַבּוֹתִי, סַבֹּתֶם; Niph. נְקֻבֹּתִי; Hiph. הֲסִבֹּת. ē: Qal תְּסֻבֶּינָה, תְּסֻבִּינָה; Hiph. יָחֵלּוּ, תְּחִלֶּינָה.

NOTE. Examples of the Hoph. with a parting-vowel do not occur. The unchangeableness of the û in the preformatives is attested by the part. *f. pl.* מוּסַבּוֹת.

m. Doubling by way of compensation. Since in forms without afformatives the final letter is not orthographically recognizable as a double consonant, the first radical is sometimes doubled, as if by way of compensation: thus besides יִסֹּב we have יִסֹּב, וַיִּקֹּד, וַיִּתֹּם; Hiph. impf. יָסֵב and וַיָּסֵב. This doubling is seldom found in the plur.: וַיִּקְּדוּ (without Dāg. in the 2. radical), וַיִּסְּבוּ.—(In Aramaic this is the prevailing formation).

n. Omission of the doubling. From the fact that the double consonant at the end of the word is neither in the spoken nor in the written form recognizable as such, we can understand how now and then the doubling is even elsewhere dispensed with. Qal impf. 3. *pl.* יִזְמּוּ, יָסֹבּוּ they will devise 11, 6; 1. *pl.* נָסֹב, cohort. יָסֹבָּה [happens not to occur], נָבְלָה we will confound 11, 7;

---

* Probably; examples have not been preserved.

II. § 73.—§ 74. VERBS ל"ה.

Niph. perf. 3. *f. sg.* נִשָּׁמָה, נִפְצָה 9, 19; 2. *m. pl.* נְמַקֹּתָם (ye pine away, are wasted), וּנְמַלְתֶּם 17, 11.

Intransit. Qal. *a)* Perf. with *ō:* רֹבּוּ 49, 23, from *rābhōbh.*—β) Impf. serval times with the vowels *ē d* (cf. וַיִּכְבַּד), esp. יָמַר he is bitter, וָאֶקַל and I was despised, *pl.* יֵקַלּוּ; יֵחַת, יֵחַתּוּ; יֵרַע he will be wicked, וַיֵּרַע, but יֵתַקל 16, 4; יֵרַךְ he will be tender; וַיֵּצֶר, יֵצֶר and it was straitened [not to be derived from יצר]; תֵּשַׁם 47, 19 from שָׁמֵם.—γ) Inf. בְּשָׁגָּם in their erring 6, 3.

Wāw consec. וַיִּסֹב: יָסֹב; Hiph. וַיָּגֶל. *p.*

§ 74. Verbs ל"ה.—Verbs ל"ה are really ל"י. The § 74. י shows itself *a)* in the part. pass. Qal: שְׁבִיוֹת חֶרֶב, גָּלוּי *a.* *gladio captae* 31, 26; β) sometimes before the endings ־ָה, וּ, ־ִי, esp. in and before the pause: יִשְׁתָּיוּן *bibent,* הָסָיָה נַפְשִׁי my soul fleeth.

NOTE. That several verbs had originally ו as 3. radical is *b.* still to be seen in a few isolated forms. Note esp. שָׁלוּ *tranquillus,* שָׁלֵיתִי together with שָׁלַוְתִּי; also the Pi'lel formations: נָאֲוָה be becoming, lovely (from נאה), part. קֹשְׁתָיו, כִּמְשָׁחֲוֵי like bowmen 21, 16 (from שחה), and the frequently occurring הִשְׁתַּחֲוָיָה (§we).

In all other cases the third radical has lost its *c.* value as a consonant: either it coalesces with the preceding vowel or it is entirely dropped. In both cases ה stands at the end of the word to indicate the long vowel (§2*b*).—Cf. also §31*b*.

I. Coalescence of the י with the preceding vowel *d.* (§*d—e*).

1. *ê* in the ground-form of the imptv. Qal, *e. g.* רְאֵה, and, with orthographical retention of the י, before ת and נ of the passive perfects (Pu., Hoph. and mostly Niph.), *e. g.* צֻוֵּיתָה, נִגְלֵיתִי, נִבְנֵית *iussus es,* הָחֳלֵיתִי I am exhausted.

e. 2. *î* (almost always יִ—) before ת and נ of the perfect: α) always in that of the Qal: רָאִיתִי, רָאִיתָ, רָאִינוּ. β) for the most part in the perfects of the other active voices and the Hithp.: כָּסִיתִי, כָּסִינוּ, הִשְׁקִינוּ, הִתְגַּלֵּיתָ; sometimes *ê*, esp. in 1. sg.: קִוִּיתִי together with קִוֵּיתִי (8), וְהִרְבֵּיתִי, וְהִפְרֵיתִי, וְהִפְרֵיתִי. ‖ γ) always in the 1. pl. Niph.: נִגְלֵינוּ; only exceptionally in the sing. וְזָקִיתָ then art thou clean, free 24, 8.

f. II. Omission of the י, with retention—in certain cases lengthening or (and) modification *(Umlautung)*— of the preceding (original) vowel:

1. In the ground-form of all perfs., קָטַל: עָשָׂה, כָּלָה; צָיָה; צִוָּה; בָּלָה (§60dβ), so also הָגְלָה: הָקְטַל; נִרְאָה: נִקְטַל הָשְׁקָה (§61c); הִתְוַדָּה.

g. 2. With half lengthening *(Umlautung)* of *a* to *ê*: a) in all imperfs. without afformatives, *e. g.* יִרְאֶה, יִצַוֶּה, אַשְׁקֶה, יִשָּׁבֶה. ‖ β) In the ground-form of all participles, *e. g.* רֹאֶה, הַנִּרְאֶה, מַרְאֶה showing (part. pass. Qal §aα). ‖ γ) Before הָ in imptvs. and impfs. (י is generally retained in the written form), *e. g.* imptv. רְאֵיָה, impf. וַתִּרְאֶיָנָה, וַתִּכְהֶיןָ.—The perfect agreement of all the voices in this respect is probably owing in part to artificial assimilation.

3. In the ground-form of the imptvs. (except Qal), *h.*
e. g. קְטֹל, הַקְטֵל; צַוֵּה, הַקְרֵה.

4. In the inf. absolute: קָטֹל, רָאֹה, also רָאוֹ; קַטֵּל, *i.*
הַרְבָּה, הַקְטֵל (§*w*ô); קָנֹה.

5. In the inf. (constr.), which receives in all the *k.*
voices the ending ת (cf. §67*e*) preceded by ô: רְאוֹת,
לְהֵרָאוֹת.—As exceptions without ת: רְאֹה 48, 11. עֲשֹׂה 50, 20, עֲשׂוֹ 31, 28.

6. In the perf. the 3. fem. sing. with the old end- *l.*
ing *ath* was at first pronounced *galajath*, then *gālâth*,
e. g. עָשָׂת Lev. 25, 21; usually, however, with a double
feminine ending עָשָׂתָה, חָיְתָה, עֲנָתָה.

III. Omission of the י along with the preceding *m.*
vowel or S^ewâ mobile before the afformatives ־ִי, וּ
(־ְ ה cohort. see §*v*), *e. g.* קָטְלוּ and קְטָלוּ, רָבוּ; קָטְלוּ,
הִרְבּוּ, הִקְטִילוּ: וַתִּרְבִּי, וַתִּקְטְלִי; רְבוּ, and before suffixes,
e. g. רָאָם *vidit eos.*

IV. Apocope of י and the preceding vowel at the *n.*
end of a word (§*n—u*): *A.* seldom in the imptv. of the
Pi'ēl, Hiph. and Hithp.: צַוֵּה (3) and צַו (10) order; נַס
try; †הַרְבֵּה and הֶרֶב increase; הַרְפֵּה (2) and הֶרֶף (6);
הַעַל (3) lead up; הַטֵּה (7) and הַט from נָטָה, חֲבֵחֹד
and הַךְ (6) from נכה §76*d*.

B. In the jussive and after the impf. with Wâw *o.*

consec.:— 1. Qal: α) וַיֵּ֫שֶׁב; ‖ β) with the vowel lengthened וַיֵּ֫שְׁתְּ, וַיֵּ֫בְךְּ, וַיֵּ֫רֶד; juss. אַל־תֵּשְׁתְּ; ‖ γ) mostly with a helping vowel (§12n) וַיֵּ֫רֶד, וַיִּ֫פֶן, וַיִּ֫גֶל, וַיִּ֫בֶן, &c., juss. יִגֶל, יֶ֫רֶב &c.; med. gutt. וַיִּ֫שַׁע, וַיֵּ֫מַח 7, 23; ‖ δ) with a helping vowel and the principal vowel lengthened יֵרָא (41, 33 Baer תֵּרָא, juss. וַתֵּרֶא (γ!), וַתֵּרֶב (s. γ!) וַתֵּ֫פֶן); med. gutt. וַיִּ֫רָא!); וַתֵּתַע, וַתְּ֫כַח; ‖ ε) prim. gutt.: וַיַּ֫עַל, וַיַּ֫עַשׂ, וַתַּ֫הַר, וַיַּ֫חַץ, וַתַּ֫עַשׂ juss. יַ֫עַל.— 1. sg. וָאַ֫עַל, וָאֶ֫עֱשֶׂה (cf. §p and §65g); but with suffixes וָאֶעֶשְׂךָ 12, 2.

p. When the verb is at the same time prim. gutt., the impf. of the Qal (except in the 1. sing.) is identical with that of the Hiph.: יַעֲלֶה Qal (cf. יַעֲמֹד), he will go up; Hiph. (cf. יַקְבִּיל הַעֲלֶה) he will lead up.— 1. sg. Qal אֶעֱלֶה, Hiph. אַעֲלֶה; but after Wāw consec. both וָאַ֫עַל.

q. NOTE 1. Notwithstanding the guttural at the beginning we find וַיִּ֫חַר, וַיִּ֫חַן, but plur. יֶחֱנוּ.— 2. חיה חָיָה see §76b.c.— 3. The very common 3. m. sg. impf. Qal of ראה with Wāw cons. is וַיַּ֫רְא, the other apocopated forms of the impf. and the juss. acc. to §oδ.

r. 2. Niph‘al: תִּגָּל may she be uncovered; prim. gutt. וְנֵאָרָא, וַיִּ֫רָא, יֵרָא; med. gutt. וַיִּמָּח!

s. 3. Intensive stems. Without compensation lengthening (cf. §11e2) e. g. וַיִּתְגַּל, וַיְכַל, וַיְצַו; ă also with med. gutt.: וְתֵאַר, אֶל־תְּאַר (although impf. Pi. יְעָרֶה).

t. 4. Hiph‘il: α) וַיַּרְא, וַתַּשְׁק, וַיַּשְׁק (as in Qal), juss. יֶ֫פֶת. ‖ β) with helping vowel וַיֶּ֫פֶר, וַיִּ֫פֶן, וַיֶּ֫גֶל, juss. יֶ֫רֶב. γ) prim. gutt. וַיַּ֫עַל.

u. The apocope of the ־ֶה in the impf. is not unfrequently dispensed with: α) in the jussive, e. g. וְתֵרָאֶה

and let it appear 1, 9;—β) after Wāw cons., esp. in the 1. sing., e. g. וָאֶרְאֶה and וָאֵרָא, and, though not exclusively, in the later books, e. g. וַיִּשְׁתֶּה, וַתִּבְכֶּה, וַיִּשְׁתַּחֲוֶה &c.

The indicative is used instead of the cohort. which occurs only three times (ψ 77, 4. 119, 117. Isa. 41, 23): נַעֲשֶׂה אָדָם let us make; אֶעֱלֶה־נָּא I will go up now; לְכָה יָשְׁקָה (§68k) 19, 32.

Miscellaneous: a) In the forms without afformatives the impf. has sometimes הֶ— for הֶ—, esp. in pause or when followed by א or ע, from considerations of rhythm or euphony, e. g. תַּעֲשֶׂה עִמָּנוּ 26, 29.— β) Sometimes, particularly in the 3. m. sg., — appears as the vowel of the preformative in the perf. Hiph. (cf. §61c), e. g. הֶרְאָה (5), הֶגְלָה (12) and הִגְלְךָ; before suffixes הֶרְאָם (3), הֶרְאַנִי and הֶרְאַנִי (9). In the other persons only: הֶלְאֵתִיךָ I have wearied thee Micah 6, 3, הֶרְאִיתִיךָ Deut. 34, 4.—γ) Niph'al of עָשָׂה see §65l.— δ) הַרְבֵּה is used adverbially: "much" "abundantly"; the feminine form הַרְבָּה serves as inf. absolute.— ε) הִשְׁתַּחֲוָה, Hithpa'lel from שחה (§b) bow, fall down, 2. m. sg. הִשְׁתַּחֲוִיתָ; impf. יִשְׁתַּחֲוֶה, pl. יִשְׁתַּחֲווּ, with Wāw cons. sg. וַיִּשְׁתַּחוּ for wajjištáchw, וַיִּשְׁתָּחוּ, pl. וַיִּשְׁתַּחֲווּ.

§ 75. Verbs ל״א.—The weak consonant א (cf. §10c) can have neither a short vowel before it nor Sewâ (quiescens) under it. On the contrary א has

w.

§ 75.
a.

always a long vowel before it as if the syllable were an open one, *e. g.* קָטֵל: מָצָא find, יִקְטֹל: יִמְצָא; before ת and נ it is, in fact, entirely disregarded by the punctuation *e. g.* קְטַלְתְּ: מָצָאת, קְטַלְנוּ: מָצָאנוּ. Hence *ē* in the intransitive perfects even before ת and נ, *e. g.* חָפַצְתִּי: חָפַצְתָּ, יָרֵאת, יָרֵא: חָפֵץ.

b. א is a guttural. Hence 1. preference for the *a*-sound, in the imptv. and impf. Qal: מְצָא, יִמְצָא; 2. not Sᵉwâ mobile but Chāṭēph, מְצָאָה: יֶלְדָּה. Owing to the weakness of its guttural sound, however, א does not receive Páthach furtive: מֹצֵא, כָּלוּא, הַמְצִיא.

c. NOTE. The follg. phenomena are also explained by the weakness of the א-sound: α) א is sometimes dropped, *e. g.* בְּחֲטוֹ 20, 6 for מַחֲטוֹא; יָצְתִי, יָצָאתִי= Job 1, 21, בַּלֵּהִי Job 32, 18.—β) Sᵉwâ mob. is sometimes elided before א, and the vowel of א transferred to the foregoing consonant (cf. §10c2): רִאוּ (3), fear ye, from יָרֵא, and, with א also rejected orthographically: אֲחֶשְׁנָה 31, 39 for אַחֲשֶׁאנָה, cf. below §*e*.

d. Effects of the analogy of verbs ל"ה.—1. Before נָה א quiesces in Sᵉghôl, *e. g.* תִּקְרֶאנָה: תִּבְנֶינָה they will call, תִּמְצֶאנָה: תִּבְנֶינָה, imptv. מְצֶאןָ: רְאֶינָה find ye (*f.*).— 2. In all the perfs. from Niphʻal onward א quiesces before ת and נ in Ṣērê: נִגְלֵיתִי: מִמְצֵאתִי, מִלֵּאתִי, מִלֵּאנוּ.

NOTE to 2.: No example of the Puʻal occurs; of the Hophʻal only הֻבָאתָה Ezek. 40, 4. Nevertheless König I, 617 likewise defends the universality of the *ē*-sound.

e. Relationship of verbs ל"א and ל"ה. Forms from verbs ל"א are not unfrequently found inflected wholly

or partly after the analogy of verbs ל״ה: α) wholly,
e. g. יִכְלֶה 23, 6 from כָּלָא refuse, withhold; β) with the
vowels of ל״ה verbs, e. g. חֹטֵא, רְפָאתִי; γ) with the con‑
sonants, e. g. רָפָה heal ψ 60, 4, יְמַלֵּה he will fill.

On the other hand verbs ל״ה frequently follow the ƒ.
analogy of verbs ל״א, e.g. יִקְרָא 49, 1, יִקְרָאֻהוּ 42, 4, וּקְרָאֻהוּ
42, 38 from קָרָה meet.—תִּרְפֶּינָה Job 5, 18 they will
heal (from רָפָא), but Isa. 13, 7 they will be slack (from
רָפָה).

§ 76. Doubly and trebly weak Verbs. אבה, § 76.
אפה §66a; נוח 71ya; נתן §67i.   a.

הָיָה to be, הָיְתָה, חֱיִיתֶם; inf. absol. הָיוֹ and הָיֹה; b.
inf. constr. הֱיוֹת; imptv. הֱיֵה, הֱיִי, הֱיוּ; impf. יִהְיֶה, יְהִי,
Wāw cop. וַיְהִי (§ 11g2), וַיְהִי, וַיְהִי, תִּהְיֶינָה. When forms
beginning with a Chāteph have the prefixes בְּ, כְּ, לְ, וְ
attached to them, the latter receive the vowel i, and
the first radical S⁰wā quiescens: מִהְיוֹת, לִהְיוֹת, וִהְיִיתֶם,
וִיהִי, except וֶחְיֵה.

חָיָה live (after prefixes pointed like הָיָה), וִחְיִיתֶם, c.
חָיֹה and חָיוֹ, לִחְיוֹת; imptv. חֲיֵה, חֲיִי, חֱיוּ; impf. יִחְיֶה,
יְחִי, וַיְחִי, וַיְחִי, וַיְחִי; Pi. חִיָּה and Hiph. הֶחֱיָה let live,
revive, לְהַחֲיוֹת, הַחֲיִיתֶם, הֶחֱיִיתָנוּ, הֶחֱיִיתִי. ‖ The verb חִי—
perf. חַי, with Wāw consec. וָחָי 3, 22—which belongs
to the verbs ע״ע is to be distinguished from the above.

פ״נ and ל״ה.—נָטָה stretch out, bend, נָטִיתִי, נָטוּ, d.
יִטּוּ, נְטֵה; impf. יִטֶּה, וַיֵּט, אַל־תֵּט; Niph. נִטָּה, נְטוּיָה, נְטוּיָ;

Hiph. הִטָּה, הִטִּיתֶם, הִטִּיתֶם, מַטֶּה, לְהַטּוֹת; imptv. הַטֵּה and הַט (§74n), הַטִּי; impf. יַטֶּה, אַל־תַּט, וַיֵּט. ‖ נכה Hiph. strike, pass. Hoph. (Niph. and Pu. rare); Niph. נִכָּה, Pu. נֻכּוּ; Hiph. הִכָּה, הִכִּית, הִכִּיתִי, הִכּוּ, מַכֶּה, מַכִּים; impf. אַכֶּה, וַיַּךְ; נסה only Pi. try, נִסִּיתִי, תְּכוּ ‖. מַכֶּה, הֶכֵיתִי, הִכְּתָה, הָכָה, מְנַסֶּה. ‖ נקה Niph. be innocent, unpunished; Pi. let go unpunished, declare innocent. Niph. נִקָּה, נִקְּתָה, וְנִקִּיתָ 24, 8, נִקֵּיתִי; Pi. נִקֵּיתִי, יְנַקֶּה. ‖ נשׁה 1. forget, נָשִׁיתִי; Hiph. נַשַּׁנִי hath made me forget 41, 51*; 2. lend, נָשָׁה, נָשׁוּ.

e.   נ״פ and א״ל.—נבא, Niph. and Hithp. προφητεύειν, יִתְנַבֵּא; בְּהִנָּבְאוֹ, לְהִנָּבֵא, נִבֵּאתָ. Cf. also §62ba. ‖ נָשָׂא tollere (cf. §65e.f), שָׂאתִי; Inf. שְׂאֵת, also נְשֹׂא (4), with לָ: לָשֵׂאת; imptv. שָׂא, שְׂאִי, שְׂאוּ (Exceptions: נְשָׂא ψ 10, 12, קְחָה! ψ 4, 7); impf. יִשָּׂא, יִשְׂאוּ (always without Dāghēš, §6/3). Niph. נִשָּׂא, תִּנָּשֵׂאנָה. ‖ נשׁא Hiph. deceive, tempt, Niph. pass.; Ni. נִשְּׁאוּ, Hi. הִשִּׁיא, הִשֵּׁאתָ.

f.   פו״י and ל״ה.— ידה Hiph. praise, Hithp. confess. Hiph. perf. הוֹדוּ, הוֹדִינוּ, מוֹדֶה, לְהוֹדוֹת, imptv. הוֹדוּ, impf. אוֹדֶה; יוֹדוּ, הִתְוַדָּה (§68b), וַיִּתְוַדּוּ. יָרָה (Qal throw; Hiph. do., direct, esp. instruct, teach), inf. לִירוֹת; Hiph. יוֹרוּ, אוֹרֶה, Ipf. לְהוֹרוֹת, הוֹרַיְתִי.

g.   פו״י and ל״א.—יָרֵא (§68d), יְרֵאתִי, יְרֵאתֶם (§75a), inf. יְרֹא and יִרְאָה (§55b), imptv. יְרָא, יְראוּ (§75cβ);

---

* Pa'ēl for Pi'ēl for the sake of assonance with the name מְנַשֶּׁה.

impf. וַיִּרְאוּ, יִירָא, וַיִּרְאָ, תִּירְאִי, תִּירְאוּ and וַיִּרְאוּ (וַיִּרְאוּ) from רָאָה!); Niph. part. נוֹרָא, impf. תִּוָּרֵא. — יָצָא go out, יְצָאנוּ, יְצָאתֶם; part. יוֹצֵא, יֹצֵאת, יֹצְאוֹת, inf. abs. יָצֹא, inf. constr. צֵאת; imptv. צֵא, צְאוּ, צְאִינָה; impf. אֵצֵא, וַתֵּצֵא, וַיֵּצְאוּ, תֵּצֶאנָה; Hiph. הוֹצִיא, הוֹצֵאת, מוֹצִיא; inf. לְהוֹצִיא; imptv. הוֹצֵא (הַיְצֵא v. §69c), with ־ָה cohort. הוֹצִיאָה; impf. יוֹצִיא, juss. 3 f. sg. תּוֹצֵא, וַיּוֹצֵא (24, וַיֹּצֵא 4); Hoph. הוּצָאָה, part. מוּצָאת, מוּצָאוֹת.

ע"ו and א"ל.—בּוֹא come, Hiph. bring. *בָּא, בָּאָה, h. הַבָּאָה, בָּאָה, בָּא, part. ;בָּאתָם § 5b2), בָּאתְ בָּאת יָבֵאתָ, בָּאִים; inf. בּוֹא, בֹּאָה and בְּאָכָה (§ 22ia); imptv. בֹּא and בֹּאִי, בֹּאוּ; impf. יָבֹא, וַיָּבֹא, וְאָבוֹאָה, 3. f. pl. תְּבוֹאֶינָה and תָּבֹאןָ (12, תְּבֹאֶינָה 2, cf. §71t); Hiph. הֵבִיא, הֵבֵאתָ, הֲבֵאתִי, הֲבֵאתֶם (11, הֲבִיאֹתֶם 1, parting-vowel elsewhere in the perf. only before suffixes), part. מֵבִיא, מְבִיאִים, inf. לְהָבִיא, וְאָבִיא, הָבֵא, imptv. הָבִיאוּ, הָבִיאָה, impf. יָבִיא, וַיָּבֵא, מוּבָאִים, הוּבְאוּ, 32, 11 הֻבָאת 3.f. sg. הוּבָא, Hoph. ;תְּבִיאֶינָה יוּבָא.

§ 77. Defective Verbs. § 77.

בּוֹשׁ be ashamed, Qal §71i.—Hiph. הֵבִישׁ put to shame (הוֹבִישׁ be put to shame).

טוֹב be good, perf. Qal.—Impf. and Hiph. from יטב §69.

---

* הַבָּאָה (the woman) who has come, see §17a note.

יָגֹר fear. Perf. and part. (§58c) Qal.—Imptv. גּוּרוּ, impf. יָגוּרוּ (from gûr).

יָסַף add, Qal only perf. and part.—Impf. and inf. acc. to §68 from the Hiph. (which has a perf. and part. of its own: הֹסִיף, מוֹסִיפִים).

יקץ Qal only impf. §69a.—Perf. הֵקִיץ, inf. בְּהָקִיץ, imptv. הָקִיצָה, impf. also אָקִיץ, יָקִיצוּ (from qîṣ or qûṣ).

כָּשַׁל stumble. Qal: perf., part., inf. abs.—Niph.: impf., inf., also part.

נגשׁ approach. Qal: impf., inf., imptv. §67d.e.f.— Niph.: perf., part.

נָחָה lead. Qal: perf. (7), imptv. נְחֵה.—Hiph.: impf., inf., perf. (2).

שָׁתָה drink.—Hiph. הִשְׁקָה.

§ 78.
a.
§ 78. The Verb with Suffixes. I. Infinitive and Participle. The inf. and the part. being really nouns have usually appended to them the suffixes of the genetive or the nominal suffixes (§22). Since this genetive may also be a genetive of the object (§21f), the suffix of the inf. and part. often denotes the accus., e. g. יִרְאָה (§55b), יִרְאָתְךָ timor tuus Job 4, 6 and timor tui the being afraid of thee Deut. 2, 25; שַׁלְּחוֹ: his letting go Ex. 11, 1 and: to let him go Ex. 4, 23; דַּבְּרוֹ his speaking and, Gen. 37, 4, to speak to him.

b. Only the acc. of the 1. sing. is expressed by a special accusative form נִי, that is, by a verbal suffix:

always with the inf., with the part. only in the sing. and even then only in poetry. In f. בְּשָׁלְחִי at my sending, when I send Ezek. 5, 16, לְשַׁלְּחֵנִי in order to send me 2 Sam. 13, 16; so לְבַקְשֵׁנִי (ק without Dâg. §60*b*), הֲמִיתַ֫נִי.—Part. הַמְאַזְּרֵ֫נִי who girdeth me ψ 18, 33; עֹשֵׂ֫נִי who created me Job 31, 15. 32, 22, but also עֹשָׂ֫י (cf. §31*c*) my creator Job 35, 10; רֹאִ֫י he that seeth me (*ā* pausal for *ē*) Isa. 47, 10, but 3 times also רֹאִי. Much more frequently מְפַלְּטִי my deliverer ψ 18, 3, כָּל־מֹצְאִי every one that findeth me Gen. 4, 14, &c.

§ 79. The Verb with Suffixes.—II. Perfect, Imperfect and Imperative. The suffixes of the perf., impf. and imptv. denote (almost without exception, cf. צָמַ֫תְנִי §*da*) the accus. of the personal pronoun. This acc. may also be expressed by the particle אֵת (§43*f*): וַיִּשְׁמְרֵ֫נוּ and יִשְׁמֹר אֹתָ֫נוּ and he kept us. This is especially the case when it is necessary to indicate the pronoun of the 2. plur.: כֶן does not occur at all as a verbal suffix, כֶם only once with the perf. (בֵּרַכְנוּכֶם ψ 118, 26) and seven times with the impf. (Stade §635): the language avoided long forms; and in addition the affixing of כֶם and כֶן to the 3. *f. sg.* and 3. *pl.* would have produced forms inadmissible in Hebrew (König I, 219).

§ 79. *a.*

The acc. of the reflexive pronoun is not expressed by a suffix but by the reflexive stems (Niph. and Hithp.);

b.

thus יִרְאוּן can signify only *videbunt eas.*—For the dative of the reflex. pron. we often find לְ (§ 45) with suffixes: וַיִּקַּח־לוֹ לֶמֶךְ שְׁתֵּי נָשִׁים and L. took unto him two wives 4, 19, כָּל־אֲשֶׁר לָקְחוּ לָהֶם all that they had taken unto them 1 Sam. 30, 19.

c. As regards its consonants the suffix of the verb is identical with that of the noun, except that in the noun the suff. of the 1. sing. is *i*, in the verb *ni*: קוֹלִי, but רָאוּנִי *viderunt me*, יִרְאוּנִי *videbunt me.*— Suff. 3. *m. pl.* מוֹ often in poetry, *e. g.* שׁ 2, 5 יְבַהֲלֵמוֹ (§22 *is. k*α).

d. With suffixes appended the verbal forms assume in part another form older than that which they now present when standing alone (cf. §§51—53):

α) Perf. 3. *f. sg.* ת—: בָּאַתְנִי, הֶחֱזִקַתְנִי.

2. *f. sg.* תִּי, gen. *def.* תְּ: רְמִיתִנִי, נְתַתִּיהִי.

2. *pl.* תִּי: הֶעֱלִיתֻנוּ ye have brought us up Num. 20, 5. 21, 5, צַמְתֻּנִי ye have fasted unto me (from צוּם) Zech. 7, 5 seem to be the only examples:

β) impf. and imptv. *f. pl.* ן.—Impf.: תְּחַשְּׁבֻנִי Job 19, 15, תּוֹכִחֻךְ Jer. 2, 19 (3. *pl.*) and תִּרְאֻנִי Cant. 1, 6 (2. *pl.*) are the only examples. I know no example of the imptv. (Cant. 2, 5 is followed by other masculine forms.)

Between suffixes beginning with a consonant and *e.*
verbal forms that end with one there often* appears
a vowel (before ה, indeed, generally only as a vocalic
glide, Sᵉwâ mobile; in pause ה—), the so-called union
vowel, which has now got to be regarded as the remnant of a vocalic final sound that has more easily maintained itself in the middle of a word, that is, before
suffixes (cf. §22*d*. König I, 219 f.). This vowel appears
in the perf. as *a*, in the impf. and imptv.** as *ē*:

Perf.   ‏נְתָנָם‎   ‏נְתָנוּ‎   ‏*נְתָנוּ‎   ***‏שְׁמָרַנִי‎
Impf.   ‏יִתְּנֵם‎   ‏יִתְּנֵנוּ‎   ‏יִתְּנֵהוּ‎   ‏יִשְׁמְרֵנִי‎
Imptv. ‏תְּנֵם‎   ‏לַמְּדֵנִי‎   ‏תְּנֵהוּ‎   ‏שְׁמְרֵנִי‎

NOTE. 1. *ē* in the perf. always before the suff. of the 2. *f. f.*
sg. ךְ, *e. g.* ‏שְׁבָרֵךְ‎, ‏שְׁאֵלֵךְ‎, ‏שְׁאֵלָתֵךְ‎, ‏הֶחֱזִיקֵךְ‎ and, deprived of the tone,
‏אֲהֵבָתֵךְ‎ § *h*2. (ה— only twice, after רא and א־: Isa. 54, 6. 60, 9).
See Böttcher §881 γ.

2. *a* with the impf. and imptv. esp. before ה. Then often
contraction to ה— *e. g.* ‏וַיַּכִּירֶהָ‎ and he recognized her, ‏שְׂדֵהָ‎,
‏כְּבָהּ‎ *scribe eam*; but also half lengthening to *è*, *e. g.* ‏יִשְׂלֶחֶהָ‎,
‏תְּעַזְבֶהָ‎, ‏אֲהֵבֶהָ‎ *ama eam*. Seldom *a* before other suffixes: ‏יִדְבָּקֵם‎
19, 19, ‏יְאַהֲבֵם‎ 29, 32.

---

* Not in the 3. *f. sg.* of the perf. (*v.* §*h*2), nor yet with the
modus energicus of the impf. and imptv. (*v.* § 80).

** The ground-form of the imptv. has certainly had consonantal final sound from the first. Accordingly we must here assume
that the vocalisation has followed the analogy of the impf., see
Nöldeke ZDMG 1884, 408 end.

*** Páthach, *v.* §12*c*.

‡ Contracted from *ahû* (cf. ‏יְדוֹ‎ §22*d*), which form is sometimes found in pause, *e. g.* ‏יִשְׂמָחֵהוּ‎.

g. Phonetic law—§11d (cf. 50a1). יָרְדְּפֵם, ד vowelless as in יִרְדְּפִי—Exceptions: α) Hiph‘îl הִקְטִילָם, הִצִּילַנִי: β) perf. Qal מְכָרִי, מְכָרוֹ, מְכָרוּם; γ) impf. Qal in α: תִּשְׁמָעֵיהָ, וַיִּשְׁאָלֵהוּ; δ) imptv. Qal in α; שְׁמָעֵנִי, וְשִׁלָּחֵנִי, בְּחָנֵנִי.

h. Laws of the tone. 1. The suffixes: יִ, נִי, הוּ, הָ (and poet. מוֹ) are always unaccented: רְשֹׁטְמֵי, תִּרְפָּאֵנִי, וַיִּשְׁטְמֵהוּ, אֶקְבְּרָה.—2. The ending תְ— of the 3. f. sg. perf. (primarily to avoid non-Hebrew forms, cf. §a end) has always drawn the tone to itself: גְּנָבָתַם R. had stolen the Teraphim 31, 32, אֲכָלָתְךָ, אֲחָזָתַם, אֲהֵבְתָךְ. (Exception Cant. 8, 5).

i. Miscellaneous. α) The 3. f. sg. perf. with the suffix הוּ often appears as —תּוּ, with הָ always as —תָּה. Examples: גְּנָבַתּוּ, גְּמָלַתִּי and גְּמָלַתְהוּ, in pause always שָׂמַתְהוּ posuit eum, &c.; בַּעֲסָתָה, אֲחָזָתָה irritavit eam.—β) 2. m. sg. perf. Note the short vowel before נִי, due to the analogy of שְׁמָרַנִי &c., e. g. הוֹצֵאתָ, הוֹצֵאתַנִי, חִיִּיתַנִי; in pause שְׁלַחְתָּנִי &c.—γ) The verbal ending û is very often written defective before suffixes: וַיִּצָּאֻהוּ וַיַּנִּחֻהוּ 19, 16.

§ 80.
a. § 80. Nûn demonstrativum. Before the suffixes: נִי, הָ, הוּ, הָ, when appended to the impf. or to the ground-form of the imptv., we often find the syllable an, especially in pause and with a real cohortative (לְכוּ וְנִמְכְּרֶנּוּ go to, let us sell him 37, 27). This an, now for the most part meaningless, is the remnant

of a *modus energicus* (§47g), hence more appropriately termed Nûn demonstrativum than, as usually, Nûn epentheticum. The vowel *a* has maintained itself before ךָ, but has elsewhere passed into accented ◌ֶ.
נ assimilates itself to a following ךּ; whereas a following ה is usually assimilated to the נ. In this way, apart from a few exceptions, we derive the following forms:

נִי— me, תְּבָרֲכַנִּי, תְּבִעָתַנִּי.

ךָ— thee *m.*, יַעַזְרֶךָּ, אֶרְאֶךָּ, יֶאֱהָבֶךָּ, וִיבָרֶכְךָּ.

נּוּ— him, יְבָרֲכֶנְהוּ, יִצְּרֶנְהוּ—אֶדְרְשֶׁנּוּ.

נָּה— her, קְרָאֶנָּה; יִקָּחֶנָּה, תְּכַלֶּנָּה, תִּבְקָשֶׁנָּה, אֶשְׁמְרֶנָּה.

NOTE. α) Nûn demonstr. not found with the perf. The Dāghēš *b.* in דְּנַנִי 30, 6, שְׂדָנִי ψ 118, 18 is Dāg. euphonicum. The forms of the part. and the inf. that might be here adduced are questioned by Stade §355*b* note 3.—β) Nûn demonstr. not before the suff. כֶ, not even Hos. 12, 5 יִמְצָאֶנּוּ, ψ 12, 8 תִּצְּרֶנּוּ.—γ) Particles with verbal suffixes (also with Nûn demonstr.) see § 40.—δ) The old plural ending *ûn* (§51), which is also found at times before suffixes, is to be clearly distinguished from Nûn demonstr., *e. g.* Prov. 1, 28 יְשַׁחֲרֻנְנִי, יִמְצָאֻנְנִי, יִקְרָאֻנְנִי.

III. REMARKS ON SYNTAX (§§ 81—91).

A. SYNTAX OF THE INDIVIDUAL PARTS OF SPEECH (§§ 81—84).

§ 81. § 81. Pronoun. When a pronoun expressed by a suffix is to have special emphasis, the corresponding separate pronoun is in Hebrew employed for this purpose, and is generally placed after the suffix it is meant to emphasize, *e. g.* בָּרֲכֵנִי גַם־אָנִי bless *me* also 27, 34; אָבַד זִכְרָם הֵמָּה the memory of *them* ψ 9, 7; בְּנֵי אִם־חָכַם לִבֶּךָ יִשְׂמַח לִבִּי גַם־אָנִי *my* heart too will rejoice Prov. 23, 15.— יְהוּדָה אַתָּה יוֹדוּךָ אַחֶיךָ J., *thee* will thy brothers praise G. 49, 8.—In the same way also: וּלְשֵׁת גַּם־הוּא יֻלַּד־בֵּן and to Sêth too 4, 26, cf. 10, 21.

§ 82. § 82. Superlative and Comparative.—The
a. superlative is periphrastically expressed by the article placed before the adjective to be compared, or by a genetive after it, *e. g.* הַקָּטֹן the youngest (smallest) 42, 13; קְטֹן בָּנָיו the youngest of his sons.

b. The comparative is expressed in the same way by מִן; a) with adjectives, *e. g.* טוֹבָה חָכְמָה מִפְּנִינִים wisdom is better than pearls; טוֹב אֶרֶךְ אַפַּיִם מִגִּבּוֹר a man slow to anger is better than one that is mighty; גְּבַהּ מִכָּל־הָעָם 1 Sam. 9, 2.—גָּדוֹל עֲוֹנִי מִנְּשֹׂא my sin is too great for me to bear* Gen. 4, 13.— ‖ β) with verbs, e. g. צָדְקָה מִמֶּנִּי she is more righteous than I 38, 26; אָהַב אֶת־יוֹסֵף מִכָּל־בָּנָיו he loved Joseph more than all his other sons 37, 3, cf. 29, 30.—קָטֹנְתִּי מִכֹּל־הַחֲסָדִים I am too insignificant for all the mercies 32, 11.

When the adjective is not immediately followed c. by the object (or person) compared with מִן, the emphasis implied in the comparative is expressed by the article alone, e. g. הַמָּאוֹר הַגָּדֹל the greater light, 'הַמָּ הַקָּטֹן the lesser light 1, 16, בְּנָהּ הַגָּדֹל her elder son [because Rebecca had only two sons] 27, 15.

§ 83. Verbs with the Accusative. — Accu- § 83.
sativus etymologicus: וַיִּצְעַק שָׁם צְעָקָה אֶחָד ψ 14, 5; צְעָקָה גְדֹלָה וּמָרָה he wept loud and bitterly G. 27, 34; cf. νίκην μεγάλην νικᾶν &c.

The following are construed with the acc., differ- b. ing thereby from the English construction: 1) regularly verbs that express a state of being clothed, full and such like, or their contraries, e. g. הוֹד וְהָדָר לָבָשְׁתָּ with grandeur and glory art thou robed ψ 104, 1; יִמָּלֵא שְׂחוֹק פִּינוּ our mouth will be full of laughter; תְּשֹׂבְעוּ לֶחֶם

---
* Cf. Latin *maior sum quam cui possit fortuna nocere*.

ye shall be satisfied with bread Ex. 16, 12; לֹא חָסַרְתָּ דָּבָר thou hast not lacked anything Deut. 2, 7 cf. ψ 34, 11. G. 18, 28; לָמָה אֶשְׁכַּל גַּם־שְׁנֵיכֶם wherefore should I lose you both 27, 45.

c. 2) Frequently verbs of going or coming to a place. בּוֹא with בְּ or אֶל־, but also with ־ָה locale (§20), e. g. מִצְרַיְמָה to Egypt 12, 11, or with the simple acc., e. g. בָּאוּ שְׁעָרָיו to his gates ψ 100, 4; hence the part. with the gen.: בָּאֵי שַׁעַר־עִירוֹ that went in to the gate of his city G. 23, 10.—הָלַךְ, generally with אֶל־ or לְ; but also: חָרָנָה to Haran 28, 10, הַשָּׂדֶה to the field 27, 5.

d. 3) seldom verbs of dwelling (in, at a place). יָשַׁב, usually with בְּ 13, 12 and often; but also: יֹשֵׁב אֹהֶל וּמִקְנֶה in tents and with herds 4, 20, יוֹשֵׁב תְּהִלּוֹת יִשְׂרָאֵל enthroned upon the praises of Israel ψ 22, 4, cf. ψ 80, 2.—שָׁכַן usually with בְּ, e. g. וְיִשְׁכֹּן יֹשֵׁב הַכְּרֻבִים בְּאָהֳלֵי־שֵׁם 9, 27, cf. 14, 13; seldom יִשְׁכֹּן חֲצֵרֶיךָ ψ 65, 5.

e. 4) A few individual constructions may be noted: נָאַף commit adultery with, עָבַד serve, עָנָה answer &c.

f. Two accusatives may stand: 1) after the causative voices of all verbs that govern one accusative in the Qal, e. g. מַלֵּא קַרְנְךָ שֶׁמֶן fill thy horn with oil 1 Sam. 16, 1; וַיַּלְבֵּשׁ אֹתוֹ בִגְדֵי־שֵׁשׁ had him clothed in vestures of cotton G. 41, 42; וַיַּפְשִׁיטוּ אֶת־יוֹסֵף אֶת־כֻּתָּנְתּוֹ they stripped J. of his coat 37, 23; שְׁבָעָנוּ בַבֹּקֶר חַסְדֶּךָ

III, § 83. VERBS WITH THE ACCUSATIVE.

ψ 90, 14; אַשְׂבִּיעַ לֶחֶם אֶבְיוֹנֶיהָ ψ 132, 15; מִי יַאֲכִלֵנוּ בָשָׂר Num. 11, 18.—So too, of course, after those Pi'ēl and Hiph'îl formations with a like signification, of which no Qal occurs in a simple transitive sense, e. g. הִשְׁקָה water, give to drink (§77), וַתַּשְׁקֶיןָ אֶת־אֲבִיהֶן יָיִן 19, 32; וִיבָרֶכְךָ בִּרְכֹת שָׁמַיִם and may he bless thee with the blessings of heaven 49, 25.

2) sometimes after Qal formations with meanings *g.* corresponding to the above, e. g. דָּגָן וְתִירוֹשׁ סְמַכְתִּיו with corn and wine have I sustained him 27, 37, cf. ψ 51, 14; סָעַד Judg. 19, 5; זָבַד to present with G. 30, 20; דִּבְרֵי שִׂנְאָה סְבָבוּנִי ψ 45, 8; מְשָׁחַהּ שֶׁמֶן they have surrounded me with .. ψ 109, 3.—Generally after גָּמַל do something to some one, e. g. רָעָה גְמָלוּךְ evil have they done unto thee G. 50, 17, cf. v. 15. 1 Sam. 24, 18.

3) To make or appoint some person (or thing) to *h.* be something, e. g. קִנִּים תַּעֲשֶׂה [with] chambers shalt thou make it (the ark) 6, 14, v. 16. 27, 9; אַב־הֲמוֹן גּוֹיִם נְתַתִּיךָ 17, 5 (but cf. ל v. 5. 20); הֵן גּוֹיִם שֹׁמֵם תַּעֲשֶׂה לָךְ 27, 37.—Also the material out of which something is made frequently stands in the acc., sometimes even after the verb, e. g. and God formed man עָפָר of dust 2, 7.

4) The epexegetical accusative, e. g. הִכִּיתָ אֶת־כָּל־אֹיְבַי *i.* לֶחִי thou smotest them on the jaw (*i. e.* thou smotest their jaw) ψ 3, 8; לֹא נַכֶּנּוּ נָפֶשׁ we will not slay him G. 37, 21.

k. With passive verbs the logical object sometimes stands in the accusative (to be approximately rendered in English by the indefinite "they", Germ. *man*), *e. g.* וַיִּוָּלֵד לַחֲנוֹךְ אֶת־עִירָד and unto Enoch they bore Irad 4, 18; לֹא־יִקָּרֵא עוֹד אֶת־שִׁמְךָ אַבְרָם they shall not call thy name any more Abram 17, 5; cf. 21, 5. 8. 27, 42. 40, 20.

§ 84. *a.* § 84. Union of two Verbs to express a single Idea. In the Hebrew language which has comparatively few adjectives there is also but a small number of adverbs, and hence the notion expressed by a verb is often more precisely determined by an additional verb instead of by an adverb*. Note particularly: שׁוּב again; יָסַף, הוֹסִיף once more; מִהַר hurriedly; הֵיטִיב well; הִרְבָּה much. Examples in the sequel.

b. Verbs that express, whether by themselves or with other words, only the modality or nearer definition of an action are followed by the main idea 1) generally in the inf. with לְ: אָבָה, בִּקֵּשׁ, חָדַל, הֵחֵל (begin), חָפֵץ (desire, be inclined), יָכֹל, יָסַף and הוֹסִיף, כִּלָּה (finish), הִרְבָּה, מִהַר, מֵאֵן. Examples: לֹא תֹאבֶה לָלֶכֶת 24, 5; לִסְפֹּר 41, 49, cf. 11, 8; הֵחֵל הָאָדָם לָרֹב began to multiply 6, 1, cf. הוּחַל 4, 26; וַתֹּסֶף לָלֶדֶת she bare yet again 4, 2;

---

* Cf. French: *j'ai failli mourir* I had almost died; *vient de paraître* just out.

III, § 84. UNION OF TWO VERBS.   133

כַּאֲשֶׁר כִּלָּה לְדַבֵּר 18, 33; מִהַרְתְּ לִמְצֹא thou hast found quickly 27, 20, cf. 18, 7. 41, 32; הִרְבְּתָה לְהִתְפַּלֵּל she has prayed much 1 Sam. 1, 12, cf. ψ 78, 38; הַמַּגְבִּיהִי לָשֶׁבֶת הַמַּשְׁפִּילִי לִרְאוֹת who is throned on high but looketh deep down ψ 113, 5. 6 [— v. §20b].

2) Not unfrequently in the inf. without לְ. E. g.: c. מַדּוּעַ מִהַרְתֶּן בֹּא הַיּוֹם to magnify thee Jos. 3, 7; אָחֵל גַּדֶּלְךָ how are ye come so early to-day? Ex. 2, 18; וַיּוֹסִפוּ עוֹד שְׂנֹא אֹתוֹ then they hated him yet the more Gen. 37, 5.

NOTE. α) That the inf. occurs more frequently with than d. without לְ may be seen from the following data: אָבָה with לְ 29 times, simple inf. 9 times [Deut. 4, Sam. 1, Kg. 1, Isa. 2, Job 1]; בִּקֵּשׁ with לְ 19 times, inf. only הֲבִיאִי Ex. 4, 24. Jer. 26, 21; חָדַל with לְ 9, בֵּן 3 times, inf. only Isa. 1, 16; חָפֵץ usually with לְ, inf. without לְ only 3 times; יָכֹל with לְ 120, inf. 25; יָסַף with לְ 13, inf. 1; הוֹסִיף with לְ 63, inf. 24, Wāw and finite verb (v. §e) 12; בִּעָה with לְ 42, בֵּן 7, with simple inf. not at all; מֵאֵן with לְ 31, inf. 8.—β) In the case of some verbs both constructions are about equally common, e. g. אִישׁ יֹדֵעַ נַגֵּן לְנַגֵּן a man skilled in playing, נַגֵּן (imptv.) הֵיטִיבוּ play sweetly.

3) As a finite verb with Wāw. Particularly often e. after שׁוּב, e. g. וַיָּשָׁב וַיַּחְפֹּר and he digged again 26, 18; וַיָּשָׁב וַיִּשְׁלַח and he sent again 2 Kings 1, 13. Other examples: וַיֹּסֶף אַבְרָהָם וַיִּקַּח אִשָּׁה and Ab. took again a wife G. 25, 1; מַהֲרוּ וַעֲלוּ אֶל־אָבִי go up in haste to my father 45, 9, cf. v. 13. 24, 18. 20; וַתְּמַהֵר וַתֵּרֶד 1 Sam. 25, 23.

4) As a finite verb without Wāw. E. g. אָשׁוּבָה אֶרְעֶה צֹאנְךָ I will again feed thy sheep 30, 31; מַהֵר הִמָּלֵט

make haste to save thyself 19, 22; מַהֲרוּ שִׁכְחוּ מַעֲשָׂיו
ψ 106, 13; הֶרֶב כַּבְּסֵנִי מֵעֲוֹנִי purify me throughly
ψ 51, 4.

B. THE SENTENCE IN GENERAL. (§§ 85—86).

§ 85.   § 85. Distinction between Nominal and
 a.   Verbal Sentences.

I. A verbal sentence begins with a finite verb. Since the latter in Hebrew already contains its subject within itself (יִשְׁמֹר אֶת־נַפְשֶׁךָ he will ..), whatever follows to indicate the subject has really an appositional character, e. g. לֹא יָנוּם וְלֹא יִישָׁן שֹׁמֵר יִשְׂרָאֵל he slumbers not and sleeps not, (namely) Israel's keeper.

b.   Usual order: (negation), verb, (subject), object. מָלְאָה הָאָרֶץ חָמָס (cf. §83b) 6, 13.—Deviations of various sorts occur when special emphasis rests on any member of the sentence, e. g. precedence of the object: חַסְדְּךָ ה' מָלְאָה הָאָרֶץ of thy loving kindness, Jahwe, is the earth full.

c.   II. The nominal sentence. A. The simple nominal sentence consists of subject (subst. or pron.) and predicate (subst., adj. or part.). There is in Hebrew no special expression for the copula (am, art, is, &c.).*

---

* The separate pronoun of the 3. person frequently serves to give emphasis to the subject, in which case it seems to take

Usual order: Subject, predicate; e. g. מַלְכֵּנוּ ה' J. is our king, אֲנִי אֱלֹהֵיכֶם I am your God, ה' שֹׁמְרֶךָ. But, when it is meant to give special emphasis to the predicate: עָפָר אַתָּה dust art thou 3, 19.

An adjective in the predicate stands generally before the subj., e. g. חַנּוּן וְרַחוּם ה'. *d.*

B. A complex nominal sentence is one whose predicate is a sentence, which may be either α) a nominal sentence or β) a verbal sentence. Examples, to α): חֲסִידָה בְּרוֹשִׁים בֵּיתָהּ the stork, cypresses are her dwellingplace, i. e. cypresses are the stork's dwellingplace. To β): ה' יִשְׁמֹר צֵאתְךָ וּבוֹאֶךָ. *e.*

§ 86. Subject and Predicate. To the rule, which also holds good in Hebrew, that the predicate agrees in gender and number with the subject, the following exceptions are to be noted: §86. *a.*

1) Instead of in the dual (which is wanting) adjectives (participles) and verbs stand in the plural, e. g. עֵינֵי הָאָדָם לֹא תִשְׂבַּעְנָה Prov. 27, 20. *b.*

2) Constructio ad sensum. α) With singular subjs. that contain a collective notion the verb often appears *c.*

---

the place of the copula. Examples: הַנָּהָר הָרְבִיעִי הוּא פְרָת the fourth stream (it) is the Euphrates 2, 14, cf. 9, 18; אֱלֹחַ חַם בְּנֵי יִשְׂרָאֵל 25, 16; שְׁלֹשֶׁת הַשָּׂרִגִים שְׁלֹשֶׁת יָמִים הֵם the three branches, three days are they, i. e.: the three branches are three days 40, 12, cf. 40, 18. 41, 26. 34, 21.

in the plur., *e. g.* יִֽירְאוּ מה׳ כָּל־הָאָרֶץ all the world shall fear before Jahwe; וַיֹּאמְרוּ אִישׁ־יְהוּדָה Judg. 15, 10.— β) Sing. with nouns that have a plural form but denote only a unity (§ 19*d*). Always with אֲדֹנִים and בְּעָלִים, *e. g.* וַיִּקַּח אֲדֹנֵי יוֹסֵף אֹתוֹ 39, 20; גָּדוֹל אֲדֹנֵינוּ וְרַב־כֹּחַ ψ 147, 5; בְּעָלָיו יוּמָת Ex. 21, 29, almost without exception with אֱלֹהִים God 1, 1. 3. 4 (but see 20, 13).

d. 3) With plurals that designate animals, members of the body or lifeless objects, the verbal predicate is fond of appearing in the fem. sing.*, *e. g.* לֹא תִמְעַד אֲשָׁרָיו his steps are not unsteady ψ 37, 31; וְחַטֹּאותֵינוּ עָנְתָה בָּנוּ have testified against us Isa. 59, 12; בַּהֲמוֹת שָׂדֶה תַעֲרֹג the cattle of the field panteth Joel 1, 20.

e. NOTE. אֹרְרֶיךָ אָרוּר וּמְבָרֲכֶיךָ בָרוּךְ 27, 29. In this and similar expressions (especially when the plural subj. is a part.) the sing. of the pred. is to be explained as distributive (each of them, every one that).

f. 4) The verbal predicate when standing at the beginning of the sentence often remains in the masc. sing., *e. g.* יְהִי מְאֹרֹת let there be luminaries 1, 14; הַבְּרָכָה אֲשֶׁר הֵבִיא (for הֵבִיאָה) שִׁפְחָתְךָ 1 Sam. 25, 27. Cf. ψ 57, 2. 124, 5.

g. NOTE. It is found in a very few cases in the *masc. plur.* before the *fem. plur.*, *e. g.* וְרָבוּ עַצְּבוֹתָם ψ 16, 4.

---

* Feminine in a neuter sense; cf. §18*a*; Greek τὰ κακὰ γίγνεται, τὰ πρόβατα βαίνει.

III. § 86.—§ 87. RELATIVE SENTENCES.

5) If the subject consists of a noun with a follow- *h.* ing genetive the predicate frequently agrees with the gen. when the latter contains the main idea, *e. g.* קֶשֶׁת גִּבֹּרִים חַתִּים the bows of the heroes are broken 1 Sam. 2, 4.

6) If the predicate belongs to several subjects *i.* connected by ו "and", it stands in the plural when following them (*e. g.* 8, 22); when preceding them not unfrequently in the sing., *e. g.* וַיָּבֹא נֹחַ וּבָנָיו וְאִשְׁתּוֹ וּנְשֵׁי 9, 23; וַיִּקַּח שֵׁם וָיֶפֶת אֶת־הַשִּׂמְלָה 7, 7; בָּנָיו אִתּוֹ אֶל־הַתֵּבָה 33, 7 וַתִּגַּשׁ גַּם־לֵאָה וִילָדֶיהָ.

C. PARTICULAR KINDS OF SENTENCES.
(§§ 87—91).

§ 87. **Relative Sentences.** Chief characteristic: § 87. Relative sentences are introduced by the sign of rela- *a.* tion אֲשֶׁר (§ 16*d*).* Otherwise their construction is in the main that of independent sentences. Examples: הָאֲנָשִׁים אֲשֶׁר בָּאוּ אֵלֶיךָ 19, 5; בָּאוּ אֵלֶיךָ ,relat. הָאֲדָמָה אֲשֶׁר פָּצְתָה אֶת־פִּיהָ the earth which has opened its mouth 7, 2; הַבְּהֵמָה אֲשֶׁר לֹא טְהֹרָה הִיא 4,11; הוֹצֵאתִיךָ מֵאוּר כַּשְׂדִּים I have brought thee out of Ur Kaśdim. אֲנִי ה' אֲשֶׁר הוֹ־ צֵאתִי' כ' I am Jahwe, that brought thee out &c. 15, 7;

---

* In the language of the poets we find also זוּ (ψ 9,16. 142,4) and זֶה (ψ 74, 2. 78, 54. 108, 8) used to introduce relative sentences. Cf. Delitzsch on Isa. 43, 21.

אֲנִי יוֹסֵף אֲשֶׁר מ' אֹתִי, rel. מְכַרְתֶּם אֹתִי I am Joseph, whom ye sold 45, 4; הֶעָרִים אֲשֶׁר־יָשַׁב בָּהֵן לוֹט the towns in which Lot had dwelt 19, 29; אֲשֶׁר אָמַר (§9b) הַנַּעַר אֲשֶׁר דַּרְכִּי the maiden to whom I shall say 24, 14; אֲשֶׁר־אָנֹכִי הֹלֵךְ עָלֶיהָ my way, which I go 24, 42; הַמָּקוֹם אֲשֶׁר עָמַד שָׁם the place where he had stood 19, 27; הָאָרֶץ אֲשֶׁר־יָצָאתָ מִשָּׁם the land from which thou art gone out; הַמָּקוֹם אֲשֶׁר בֹּוא שָׁמָּה the place whither we shall come 20, 13; ה' אֲשֶׁר־הִתְהַלַּכְתִּי לְפָנָיו Jahwe, before whom (in whose sight) I have walked 24, 40, cf. 48, 15; אָחִיו אֲשֶׁר עַל־יָדוֹ הַשָּׁנִי his brother, on whose hand was the scarlet thread 38, 30; אָחִינוּ אֲשֶׁר רָאִינוּ צָרַת נַפְשׁוֹ our brother whose anguish of soul we saw 42, 21.

b. NOTE. The examples given above show that the word expressing the more precise reference of the relative particle is preferably separated from אֲשֶׁר. But cf. כָּל־הָעֵץ אֲשֶׁר־בּוֹ פְרִי־עֵץ every tree on which is the fruit of a tree 1, 29; the land of Hawila אֲשֶׁר־שָׁם הַזָּהָב 2, 11; עֲרֻלָּה אֲשֶׁר־לוֹ אִישׁ 34, 14.

c. The complement of the relative particle is omitted: a) always when it would be a pronoun in the nom. case. E. g. אִתּוֹ הֵם they (are) with him; הַמְּלָכִים אֲשֶׁר אִתּוֹ the kings that (are, were) with him 14, 5; הָעֵץ אֲשֶׁר בְּתוֹךְ הַגָּן 3, 3; הַמַּיִם אֲשֶׁר מֵעַל לָרָקִיעַ 1, 7; כֹּל אֲשֶׁר־בָּאָרֶץ יִגְוָע 6, 18.

d. NOTE. Exceptions sometimes in negative sentences: כָּל־בֶּן־נֵכָר אֲשֶׁר לֹא מִזַּרְעֲךָ הוּא every stranger, who is not of thy seed 17, 12, cf. 7, 2; very rarely in positive sentences: כָּל־רֶמֶשׂ אֲשֶׁר הוּא־חָי 9, 3 (חַי adj.). In these cases the pron. is to be explained acc. to §85c note. In a verbal sentence the complement is found only in 2 Kings 22, 13 (König I, 136).

β) In most cases, when it would be a pronoun *e.* in the accusative: הָאָדָם אֲשֶׁר יָצָר which he had formed 2, 8; חַיַּת הַשָּׂדֶה אֲשֶׁר עָשָׂה the beast of the field which he had made 3, 1; הָאָדָם אֲשֶׁר בָּרָאתִי which I have created 6, 7; הָאָרֶץ אֲשֶׁר אַרְאֶךָּ the land which I shall show thee 12, 1, cf. 15, 14. 17, 21. 19, 19. 20, 3. 25, 10 &c — Exceptions in the Gen. only: הַמּוֹעֵד אֲשֶׁר דִּבֶּר אִתּוֹ אֱלֹהִים the set time which God had announced 21, 2; לְבַדָּהּ (§22*i*ζ) 21, 29; רֵיחַ שָׂדֶה אֲשֶׁר בֵּרְכוֹ ה׳ the smell of the field which J. has blessed 27, 27 (otherwise *v.* 41!); אֲשֶׁר מְכַרְתֶּם אֹתִי 45, 4 (*v.* §*a*).

γ) In many cases where the complement would *f.* be a preposition with a suffix, a locative particle or such like. Examples: בַּמָּקוֹם אֲשֶׁר־דִּבֶּר אִתּוֹ in the place where he had spoken with him 35, 13. 14 (*v.* 15 הַמָּקוֹם עוֹד חָמֵשׁ שָׁנִים אֲשֶׁר אֵין־חָרִישׁ (אֲשֶׁר דִּבֶּר שָׁם אִתּוֹ אֱלֹהִים); וְקָצִיר yet five years in which there will be no ploughing and no harvesting 45, 6. Here, probably, belong also such passages as: הָעִיר אֲשֶׁר דִּבַּרְתָּ the city of which thou hast spoken 19, 21, אֲבִיכֶם אֲשֶׁר אֲמַרְתֶּם 43, 27.

אֲשֶׁר frequently stands for "he who", "that which". *g.* In this case the preposition that ought to have stood before the pronoun omitted is placed immediately before the relative particle. Examples: וַיֵּרַע בְּעֵינֵי ה׳

אֲשֶׁר עָשָׂה and that which he did was evil in the eyes of J. 38, 10; וַאֲשֶׁר תֹּאמְרוּ אֵלַי אֶתֵּן and that what ye shall say unto me I will give 34, 11, cf. 18, 17. 39, 23. 41, 55; אֵת אֲשֶׁר־עָשִׂיתָ לּוֹ שָׁכַח that, which thou hast done to him 27, 45, cf. 9, 24. 28, 15; לָקְחוּ .. וְאֵת אֲשֶׁר־בָּעִיר and that which was in the city they took away 34, 28; וַיֹּאמֶר לַאֲשֶׁר עַל־בֵּיתוֹ and he said to him who was (set) over his house, *i. e.* to his house-steward 43, 16, cf. 44, 4; וְלַאֲשֶׁר בְּבָתֵּיכֶם and for those that are in your houses 47, 24; hearken unto me לַאֲשֶׁר אֲנִי מְצַוְּךָ אֹתָךְ in regard to that which I command thee 27, 8; וּמֵאֲשֶׁר לְאָבִינוּ and he hath got all of that which was our father's 31, 1; make them chief herdsmen עַל־אֲשֶׁר־לִי over that (the cattle) which is mine 47, 6; אֲשֶׁר יִמָּצֵא אִתּוֹ יִהְיֶה־לִּי עָבֶד he with whom it (the cup) is found shall be my bondman 44, 10.

h. The construct state is found a few times before the sentence introduced by אֲשֶׁר (cf. §21*h*): מְקוֹם אֲשֶׁר the place where . . 39, 20. 40, 3.

i. אֲשֶׁר is omitted (sometimes in ordinary, frequently in poetical language): *a*) when followed by no complement, *e. g.* בְּאֶרֶץ לֹא לָהֶם in a land that is not theirs 15, 13; בִּנְיָמִין זְאֵב יִטְרָף Benjamin is a wolf that ravineth 49, 27; הַגֶּבֶר יֶחֱסֶה־בּוֹ the man that taketh refuge in him ψ 34, 9; תָּגֵלְנָה עֲצָמוֹת דִּכִּיתָ may the bones which thou hast broken rejoice ψ 51, 10.

III, § 87.—§ 88. CONDITIONAL SENTENCES. 141

β) When followed by the complement, e. g.: and *k.*
declare unto them אֶת־הַדֶּרֶךְ יֵלְכוּ בָהּ the way wherein
they ought to walk Ex. 18, 20.

γ) When אֲשֶׁר would be equivalent to "he that", *l.*
e. g. תּוֹעֵבָה יִבְחַר בָּכֶם an abomination is he that chooseth
you Isa. 41, 24.

In that case the substantive elucidated stands *m.*
not unfrequently in the constr. state, in particular:
α) when it is a noun denoting time or place, e. g. בְּיוֹם
אֶקְרָא in the day when I call ψ 56, 10; שְׁנוֹת רָאִינוּ רָעָה
the years wherein we have experienced misfortune
ψ 90, 15; כָּל־יְמֵי הִתְהַלַּכְנוּ אִתָּם all days of our intercourse with them 1 Sam. 25, 15; cf. also §21*h*.—β) always
when אֲשֶׁר would be equivalent to "of him who" &c.,
e. g. מְקוֹם לֹא־יָדַע אֵל the place [of him who] knew not
God Job 18, 21; כָּל־יֶשׁ־לוֹ all that belonged to him
(the whole [of that which] belonged to him) G. 39, 4;
שְׂפַת לֹא־יָדַעְתִּי the speech of one whom I knew not ψ 81, 6.

§ 88. Conditional Sentences. אִם denotes § 88.
pure condition and accordingly corresponds to the *a.*
Lat. *si*, and the Gk. εἰ.—לוּ stands when the condition
is really, or at least probably, not fulfilled in the
present or will not be fulfilled in the future.—כִּי as
conditional particle signifies "granted that", cf. Gk.
ἐάν. An instructive passage for the difference between
אִם and כִּי is Exod. 21, 2 ff.—לוּלֵי, לוּלֵא if not.

b.   α) The main clause (apodosis) is frequently introduced by ו consec. (33, 10), more rarely by ו copul. (וְאֵימִ֫נָה then I will go to the right 13, 9, cf. Jer. 15, 19). — β) To give special emphasis are employed: כִּי עַתָּה 31, 42. 43, 10 and כִּי אָז 2 Sam. 2, 7 (surely then, then indeed), rarely: כִּי Isa. 7, 9. — γ) The main clause often follows without an introductory particle: 20, 7. 24, 49. 43, 4, especially when it opens with a negation: 44, 23 and often.

c.   The main facts in regard to the tenses that are found in the conditional clauses (protases) may be learned from the following examples: אִם־לֹא יֵרֵד אֲחִיכֶם הַקָּטֹן אִתְּכֶם לֹא תֹסִפוּן לִרְאוֹת פָּנָי if your youngest brother come not down with you, ye shall not ... 43, 4; the perf. in the sense of the Latin future-perfect is rare: every one that remaineth in Jerusalem shall be called holy, אִם רָחַץ אֲדֹנָי if God shall have washed away Isa. 4, 4. The perf. is regularly used to express a condition which is regarded as already fulfilled: אִם־נָא מָצָ֫אתִי חֵן בְּעֵינֶ֫יךָ אַל־נָא תַעֲבֹר if I have found favour, as I trust I have, then ... 18, 3, cf. 33, 10. 47, 29. אִם־יֶשְׁךָ מְשַׁלֵּחַ אֶת־אָחִינוּ אִתָּ֫נוּ נֵרֵ֫דָה if thou (now) sendest our brother with us, then ... 43, 4, cf. 20, 7. 24, 49. — לוּ חָכְמוּ יַשְׂכִּילוּ זֹאת if they were (had become) wise, they would understand this Deut. 32, 29: לוּ חָפֵץ ה׳ לַהֲמִיתֵ֫נוּ לֹא לָקַח מִיָּדֵ֫נוּ עֹלָה if Jahwe had wished . . . .

III, § 88. CONDITIONAL SENTENCES.

Judg. 13, 23; לוּ חָפֵץ יְהוָֹה לַהֲמִיתֵנוּ לֹא לָקַח מִיָּדֵנוּ if my people were (now) obedient, I would humble their enemies ψ 81, 14. 15.— וְכִי יִשְׁמְעוּ הַשָּׂרִים ... וְאָמַרְתָּ אֲלֵיהֶם and if the princes will hear..., say unto them Jer. 38, 25; כִּי־תַכֶּנּוּ בַשֵּׁבֶט לֹא יָמוּת Prov. 23, 13.

לוּלֵא, לוּלֵי, if not, is almost always accompanied *d*. by the perfect (for it signifies: "if what really is were not"). Examples: לוּלֵי אֱלֹהֵי אָבִי .. הָיָה לִי כִּי עַתָּה רֵיקָם שִׁלַּחְתָּנִי if the God of my father had not been with me, verily thou hadst sent me away with empty hands 31, 42; לוּלֵא הִתְמַהְמָהְנוּ כִּי־עַתָּה שַׁבְנוּ זֶה פַעֲמָיִם if we had not delayed, we had certainly... 43, 10, cf. 1 Sam. 25, 34. Isa. 1, 9. ψ 27, 13.

Conditional Sentences without Condi- *e*. tional Particle. When the conditional particle is omitted in English, the verb is placed, as in interrogative sentences, before the subject, so that we at once perceive we have not to do with a fact. In Hebrew it is otherwise. Here the following combinations in particular, in accordance with their nature, readily adapt themselves to the signification of hypothetical sentences: α) two perfects with ו consec.; β) a double jussive; γ) an imptv. followed by another imptv. or by a jussive (cohortative). Examples. α) With me are young animals וּדְפָקוּם יוֹם (and they will overdrive them and they will die, *i. e.*) and if they

overdrive them, they will die 33, 13; וִּקְרָאָהוּ אָסוֹן
וְהוֹרַדְתֶּם .. and if injury befall him (§75e), then will
ye bring me down to the grave 42, 38; רְדֹף אַחֲרֵי הָאֲנָשִׁים
וְהִשַּׂגְתָּם וְאָמַרְתָּ אֲלֵהֶם follow hard after the men, and
when thou hast overtaken them, say unto them 44, 4,
cf. 44, 22.—β) תָּשֶׁת חֹשֶׁךְ וִיהִי לָיְלָה if thou makest darkness, then it is night ψ 104, 20 (cf. §47f).—γ) זֹאת עֲשׂוּ
וִחְיוּ do this and live, *i. e.* if ye do this, ye shall live
42, 18; דִּרְשׁוּ אֶתְ־ד' וִחְיוּ Am. 5, 6; שְׁמֹר מִצְוֺתַי וֶחְיֵה Prov.
4, 4; also without Wāw: פְּקַח־עֵינֶיךָ שְׂבַע־לָחֶם Prov. 20, 13;
הַרְבּוּ עָלַי מְאֹד מֹהַר וּמַתָּן וְאֶתֵּנָה even if ye ask much as the
price of the bride and as presents, I will give it G. 34, 12.

f.   NOTE. Many passages treated as final clauses under §46e may
equally well be explained as conditional sentences under §eγ; cf.
also Prov. 3, 9f. 4, 8. 20, 22. Note Am. 5, 14 דִּרְשׁוּ־טוֹב וְאַל־רָע לְמַעַן
תִּחְיוּ and Prov. 19, 20 קַבֵּל מוּסָר לְמַעַן תֶּחְכַּם accept instruction that
thou mayest become wise.

§ 89. § 89. Optative Sentences (sentences expres-
a. sing a wish or a request). The wish (request) is often
expressed 1. by the jussive (3. pers., 2. almost exclusively after אַל), *e. g.* יַפְתְּ אֱלֹהִים לְיֶפֶת God enlarge
Japheth 9, 27, cf. 31, 49; יְהִי שֵׁם ה' מְבֹרָךְ; יְהִי דַרְכָּם חֹשֶׁךְ
ψ 35, 6, cf. 7, 6; אַל־תַּסְתֵּר פָּנֶיךָ מִמֶּנִּי ψ 27, 9.—Often
with נָא, *e. g.* יִגְמָר־נָא רַע רְשָׁעִים O that ... might come
to an end! ψ 7, 10; תְּהִי נָא אָלָה G. 26, 28; יְדַבֶּר־נָא
עַבְדְּךָ O that thy servant might speak! 44, 18; אַל־נָא
יִחַר לַאדֹנָי may not Adonai be angry 18, 30.

2. by the cohortative, *e. g.* אֶשְׂבְּעָה I would fain be satisfied ψ 17, 15; אֵדְעָה I should like to know ψ 39, 5; אֶעֱלֶה־נָּא וְאֶקְבְּרָה ψ 25, 2.—Esp. with נָא, *e. g.* אֶעֱלֶה־נָּא אֶל־אֲבוֹשָׁה I would fain (let me, pray,) go up and . . . G. 50, 5.

The use of the particles אִם and לוּ (*si, o si!, utinam!*) is to be explained by an ellipsis, cf. אִם־תִּשָּׂא חַטָּאתָם וְאִם־אַיִן מְחֵנִי־נָא מִסִּפְרֶךָ forgive their sin (proply.: if thou wilt take away their sin I am satisfied); but if not . . Ex. 32, 32; יִשְׂרָאֵל אִם־תִּשְׁמַע לִי if thou wouldst but hearken unto me ψ 81, 9; אִם תִּקְטֹל אֱלוֹהַּ רָשָׁע ψ 139, 19.—לוּ with the impf. לוּ יִשְׁמָעֵאל יִחְיֶה לְפָנֶיךָ G. 17, 18, also with the juss. לוּ יְהִי כִדְבָרֶךָ 30, 34. But with the perf. לוּ מַתְנוּ O that we had died! Num. 14, 2; לוּ גָוַעְנוּ 20, 3, cf. Jos. 7, 7.

Optative sentences are not unfrequently expressed periphrastically by an interrogation, *e. g.* מִי יְשִׂמֵנִי שֹׁפֵט who will appoint me judge? *i. e.* would that I were appointed judge 2 Sam. 15, 4, cf. 23, 15; מִי יוֹבִלֵנִי ψ 60, 11; מִי־יִתֶּן־לִי אֵבֶר who will give me wings? *i. e.* if I but had wings ψ 55, 7; מִי יִתֵּן מִצִּיּוֹן יְשׁוּעַת יִשְׂרָאֵל ψ 14, 7; מִי־יִתֵּן עֶרֶב O that it were evening! Deut. 28, 67.—מִי יִתֵּן has then become simply an optative particle, *e. g.* מִי־יִתֵּן הַחֲרֵשׁ תַּחֲרִישׁוּן O that ye would be altogether silent Job 13, 5; מִי יִתֵּן בִּשְׁאוֹל תַּצְפִּנֵנִי O that thou wouldest hide me in Sh‘ol Job 14, 13.

The following expressions may be noted as optative sentences without a verb: שָׁלוֹם לָכֶם peace be with you, בָּרוּךְ אַבְרָם blessed be Abram 14, 19. Cf. 1 Sam. 25, 6.

§ 90. *a.* § 90. Oaths (assurances). Sentences containing an oath are generally expressly indicated as such by the verb וַיִּשָּׁבַע (but also simply וַיֹּאמֶר 14, 22 &c.). The content of the oath, which follows in "direct speech", is in most cases introduced by the particles: אִם "verily not", אִם־לֹא and כִּי "verily". Examples: נִשְׁבַּעְתִּי בְאַפִּי אִם־יְבֹאוּן אֶל־מְנוּחָתִי verily they shall not enter into my rest ψ 95, 11; כִּי יַעַן אֲשֶׁר עָשִׂיתָ אֶת־הַדָּבָר הַזֶּה . . . בָּרֵךְ אֲבָרֶכְךָ, verily, because thou hast done this, therefore will I bless thee G. 22, 16.

b. These particles are in most cases preceded by a formula of asseveration. Note esply.: α) חַי־ה' as sure as Jahwe liveth: חַי־ה' אִם־יוּמָת he shall not be put to death 1 Sam. 19, 16; חַי־ה' כִּי בְנֵי־מָוֶת אַתֶּם ye are children of death 1 Sam. 26, 16, cf. 2 Sam. 12, 5.—
β) חַי־אָנִי as sure as I live*: חַי־אָנִי נְאֻם אֲדֹנָי ה' אִם־אֶחְפֹּץ בְּמוֹת הָרָשָׁע as I live, saith the Almighty, I have no pleasure in the death of the wicked Ezek. 33, 11.—
γ) חַי־ה' וְחֵי** נַפְשְׁךָ as sure as Jahwe liveth and by thy life, *e. g.* 2 Kings 2, 2, where follows: אִם־אֶעֱזָבְךָ I will not leave thee.—δ) חַי** פַּרְעֹה אִם־תֵּצְאוּ מִזֶּה as

---

* אָנִי, so always in this formula.
** חֵי in these formulæ is not constr. state, but a bye-form of the adj. חַי (living) formed by the contraction of *aj* to *ê*.

sure as Pharaoh liveth, ye shall not go out hence G. 42, 15.—ε) הֲרִמֹ֫תִי יָדִ֫י אֶל־ה' 14, 22, where v. 23 follows with: אִם־אֶקַּח I will not take.—ζ) יִצֶף ה' בֵּינִי וּבֵינֶ֫ךָ the Lord watch between me and thee 31, 49, followed by v. 50: אִם־תְּעַנֶּה אֶת־בְּנֹתַי thou shalt not afflict my daughters.

The following have the same signification, i. e. *c.* they serve to strengthen the oath or assurance: η) the formula of protestation חָלִ֫ילָה לִּי far be it from me = God forbid!, certainly not, e. g. 2 Sam. 20, 20 where follows: אִם־אֲבַלַּע וְאִם־אַשְׁחִית I will not devastate and will not destroy;—and ϑ) the formula of cursing כֹּה יַעֲשֶׂה (לִי) אֱלֹהִים וְכֹה יוֹסִיף God do so and so to me, i. e. may God punish me (if I do not act up to my word,) e. g. 1 Sam. 14, 44 where follows: כִּי־מוֹת תָּמוּת יוֹנָתָן Jonathan, thou shalt surely die; 1 Kings 2, 23 which is followed by כִּי בְנַפְשׁוֹ דִּבֶּר אֲדֹנִיָּ֫הוּ אֶת־הַדָּבָר הַזֶּה verily at the expense of his life hath Adonijah spoken thus. Once before אִם־לֹא: 2 Sam. 19, 14 אִם־לֹא שַׂר־צָבָא תִהְיֶה לְפָנַי כָּל־הַיָּמִים verily thou shalt always be my captain of the host. Four times before אִם: 2 Kings 6, 31 אִם־יַעֲמֹד רֹאשׁ אֱלִישָׁע עָלָיו הַיּוֹם verily the head of Elisha shall not remain on him this day, cf. also 1 Sam. 3, 17. 25, 22. 1 Kings 20, 10.

The particles enumerated in §*a* are also frequently *d.* employed to give emphasis to the affirmation (assurance or denial). עַל־פְּנֵיכֶם אִם־אֲכַזֵּב to your face will I not lie Job 6, 28; אִם־לֹא עַל־פָּנֶיךָ יְבָרֲכֶךָּ verily to thy face will he renounce thee Job 1,.11, cf. 2, 5; זַעֲקַת סְדֹם וַעֲמֹרָה כִּי־רָבָּה the cry concerning Sodom and Gomorrah, it is indeed great, and their sin כִּי כָבְדָה מְאֹד, it is indeed very grievous G. 18, 20; כִּי אֲמִילַם yea, I will destroy them (Hiph. of מוּל; union-vowel *a* see §79*f*) ψ 118, 10. 11. 12; כִּי so especially in כִּי עַתָּה and כִּי אָז v. §88*b*β.

e.   כִּי, which in all the passages cited above signifies "it is the case that" and from this acquires an affirmative signification, is also used like the ὅτι *recitativum* to introduce the *oratio directa,* in which case it remains untranslated. Cf. 26, 9. 27, 20. 29, 33 &c. (In some of these passages it is possible that a remnant of the original meaning is still traceable.)

f.   NOTE. אִם as interrogative particle always expects an answer in the negative. Hence it has come to pass that אִם has assumed a negative signification; and from this again follows the use of אִם לֹא in a positive sense. The use of אִם and אִם לֹא in oaths is usually explained from the hypothetical אִם by assuming an ellipsis. But to fill up the expressions of cursing cited in §*c*ϑ in this way would produce nonsense in all the passages where God is mentioned as swearing, (cf. besides 2 Sam. 19, 8. 2 Kings 3, 14); moreover this formula is found in a few passages where it cannot be taken as the apodosis to the אִם-clause, which most scholars assume to have properly a hypothetical character (besides 1 Sam. 14, 44. 1 Kings 2, 23 cf. 1 Sam. 20, 13. 2 Sam. 3, 35).*

---

* Cf. P. Friedrich, Die hebr. Conditionalsätze pp. 98—101.

§ 91. Transition of the participial and infinitive Constructions into the Oratio finita.

§ 91.
a.

When a part. or an infin. is followed by other verbs, which, being logically coordinated, ought likewise to stand in the part. or the inf., Hebrew writers are fond of changing the construction and continuing the sentence with the finite verb. In such cases we must, in English, after the part. supply the corresponding relative, after the inf. the corresponding conjunction.

α) Where the partic. (or inf.) may be rendered by "whoever, whenever" (ὅς ἄν, ἐπειδάν) the perf. follows with ו consec. (but if this ו is separated from the verb, the impf.); β) where a concrete fact is spoken of, the impf. follows with ו consec. (but if this Wāw is separated from the verb, the perf.).

b.

Examples of the part.: α) Whoever remaineth in the city shall die, וְהַיּוֹצֵא וְנָפַל עַל־הַכַּשְׂדִּים but whoever goeth out and falleth away to the Chaldeans shall live Jer. 21, 9; if Wāw is separated from the verb, frequentative: Isa. 5, 23. Prov. 7, 8 (so also without Wāw, impf.: Isa. 5, 8. Prov. 2, 14). ‖ β) מִי־אֵפוֹא הוּא הַצָּד צַיִד וַיָּבֵא לִי τίς οὖν ὁ θηρεύσας μοι θήραν καὶ εἰσενέγκας μοι? 27, 33; לָאֵל הָעֹנֶה אֹתִי בְּיוֹם צָרָתִי וַיְהִי עִמָּדִי to the God who heard me and (who) was with me 35, 3, cf. ψ 18, 33; with Wāw separated from the verb: הַהֹלְכִים

c.

לָרֶדֶת מִצְרַיִם וּפִי לֹא שָׁאֵלוּ who go down to Egypt and have not asked of me Isa. 30, 2, cf. Prov. 2, 17.

d. Examples of the inf.: α) עַד־שׁוּב אַף־אָחִיךָ מִמְּךָ וְשָׁכַח till thy brother's anger turn away from thee and he forget 27, 45; wait seven days עַד־בּוֹאִי אֵלֶיךָ וְהוֹדַעְתִּי לְךָ till I come to thee and announce to thee 1 Sam. 10, 8; בְּשׁוּב צַדִּיק מִצִּדְקָתוֹ וְעָשָׂה עָוֶל if the righteous man turn away from his righteousness and do iniquity, he shall die Ezek. 18, 26; with Wāw separated from the verb, the impf.: I have determined לִשְׁבֹּר אַשּׁוּר בְּאַרְצִי וְעַל־הָרַי אֲבוּסֶנּוּ to break Asshur in pieces .. and to trample him under foot Isa. 14, 25. | β) וַיְהִי כַהֲרִימִי קוֹלִי וָאֶקְרָא and when I lifted up my voice and cried G. 39, 18; בַּעֲזָבְכֶם אֶת־מִצְוֺת ח' וַתֵּלֶךְ אַחֲרֵי הַבְּעָלִים in that ye forsook the commandments of Jahwe and thou wentest after the Baalim 1 Kings 18, 18, cf. ψ 50, 16. 92, 8. 105, 12f.; but the perf., when Wāw is separated from the verb: עַל־עָזְבָם אֶת־תּוֹרָתִי . . . וְלֹא שָׁמְעוּ בְקוֹלִי because they have forsaken my teaching and have not hearkened unto my voice Jer. 9, 12.

PARADIGMATA, LITTERATURA, CHRESTOMATHIA.

A

Paradigmata.

Verbum firmum (§ 51—64).

I. Perfectum.

I	קָטַ֫לְתִּי 1.	קָטַ֫לְתְּ f.	קָטַ֫לְתָּ 2.	קָטְלָה f.	קָטַל 3. sg.	*Qal*
	קָטַ֫לְנוּ	קְטַלְתֶּן	קְטַלְתֶּם	קָטְלוּ	pl.	
II	נִקְטַ֫לְתִּי s.	נִקְטַלְתְּ	נִקְטַ֫לְתָּ s.	נִקְטְלָה	נִקְטַל sg.	*Niph'al*
	נִקְטַ֫לְנוּ	נִקְטַלְתֶּן	נִקְטַלְתֶּם	נִקְטְלוּ	pl.	
III	קִטַּ֫לְתִּי s.	קִטַּלְתְּ	קִטַּ֫לְתָּ s.	קִטְּלָה	קִטֵּל sg.	*Pi'ēl*
	קִטַּ֫לְנוּ	קִטַּלְתֶּן	קִטַּלְתֶּם	קִטְּלוּ	pl.	
IV	קֻטַּ֫לְתִּי s.	קֻטַּלְתְּ	קֻטַּ֫לְתָּ s.	קֻטְּלָה	קֻטַּל sg.	*Pu'al*
	קֻטַּ֫לְנוּ	קֻטַּלְתֶּן	קֻטַּלְתֶּם	קֻטְּלוּ	pl.	
V	הִקְטַ֫לְתִּי s.	הִקְטַלְתְּ	הִקְטַ֫לְתָּ s.	הִקְטִ֫ילָה	הִקְטִיל sg.	*Hiph'il*
	הִקְטַ֫לְנוּ	הִקְטַלְתֶּן	הִקְטַלְתֶּם	הִקְטִ֫ילוּ	pl.	
VI	הָקְטַ֫לְתִּי s.	הָקְטַלְתְּ	הָקְטַ֫לְתָּ s.	הָקְטְלָה	הָקְטַל sg.	*Hoph'al*
	הָקְטַ֫לְנוּ	הָקְטַלְתֶּן	הָקְטַלְתֶּם	הָקְטְלוּ	pl.	
VII	הִתְקַטַּ֫לְתִּי s.	הִתְקַטַּלְתְּ	הִתְקַטַּ֫לְתָּ s.	הִתְקַטְּלָה	הִתְקַטֵּל sg.	*Hithp.*
	הִתְקַטַּ֫לְנוּ	הִתְקַטַּלְתֶּן	הִתְקַטַּלְתֶּם	הִתְקַטְּלוּ	pl.	

III. Imperativus.   II. Inf.

קְטֹ֫לְנָה f.	קִטְלוּ Pl.	קִטְלִי f.	קְטֹל Sg.	קָטֹל	*Qal*
[הִקָּטֵ֫לְנָה]	הִקָּטְלוּ	הִקָּטְלִי	הִקָּטֵל	הִקָּטֵל	*Niph.*
קַטֵּ֫לְנָה	קַטְּלוּ	קַטְּלִי	קַטֵּל	קַטֵּל	*Pi.*
הַקְטֵ֫לְנָה	הַקְטִ֫ילוּ	הַקְטִ֫ילִי	הַקְטֵל	הַקְטִיל	*Hiph.*
§ 62 d α	הִתְקַטְּלוּ	הִתְקַטְּלִי	הִתְקַטֵּל	הִתְקַטֵּל	*Hithp.*

Paradigmata. 3*

IV. *Imperfectum.*

Cohortat.							
אֶקְטְלָה	וָאֶקְטֹל 1.	תִּקְטְלִי f.	תִּקְטֹל 2.	תִּקְטֹל f.	יִקְטֹל	sg.
נִקְטְלָה	נִקְטֹל	תִּקְטֹלְנָה	תִּקְטְלוּ	תִּקְטֹלְנָה	יִקְטְלוּ	pl.
אֶקְטְלָה	אֶקָּטֵל	תִּקָּטְלִי	תִּקָּטֵל	תִּקָּטֵל	יִקָּטֵל	sg.
נִקְטְלָה	נִקָּטֵל	תִּקָּטַלְנָה	תִּקָּטְלוּ	תִּקָּטַלְנָה	יִקָּטְלוּ	pl.
אֲקַטְּלָה	אֲקַטֵּל	תְּקַטְּלִי	תְּקַטֵּל	תְּקַטֵּל	יְקַטֵּל	sg.
נְקַטְּלָה	נְקַטֵּל	תְּקַטֵּלְנָה	תְּקַטְּלוּ	תְּקַטֵּלְנָה	יְקַטְּלוּ	pl.
	אֲקֻטַּל	תְּקֻטְּלִי	תְּקֻטַּל	תְּקֻטַּל	יְקֻטַּל	sg.
	נְקֻטַּל	תְּקֻטַּלְנָה	תְּקֻטְּלוּ	תְּקֻטַּלְנָה	יְקֻטְּלוּ	pl.
אַקְטִילָה	אַקְטִיל	תַּקְטִילִי	תַּקְטִיל	תַּקְטִיל	יַקְטִיל	sg.
נַקְטִילָה	נַקְטִיל	תַּקְטֵלְנָה	תַּקְטִילוּ	תַּקְטֵלְנָה	יַקְטִילוּ	pl.
	אָקְטַל	תָּקְטְלִי	תָּקְטַל	תָּקְטַל	יָקְטַל	sg.
	נָקְטַל	תָּקְטַלְנָה	תָּקְטְלוּ	תָּקְטַלְנָה	יָקְטְלוּ	pl.
אֶתְקַטְּלָה	אֶתְקַטֵּל	תִּתְקַטְּלִי	תִּתְקַטֵּל	תִּתְקַטֵּל	יִתְקַטֵּל	sg.
נִתְקַטְּלָה	נִתְקַטֵּל	§62 da	תִּתְקַטְּלוּ	§62 da	יִתְקַטְּלוּ	pl.

V. *Participium.*

קְטֻלוֹת, (קְטֻלָה) קְטוּלָה et קֹטֶלֶת f.	קֹטֵל, קֹטְלִים; קָטוּל, קְטוּלִים;	} Qal
קְטוּלָה, קְטוּלוֹת		
(נִקְטֶלֶת) נִקְטָלָה, נִקְטָלוֹת	נִקְטָל, נִקְטָלִים;	Niph.
מְקַטֶּלֶת, (מְקַטְּלָה) מְקַטְּלוֹת	מְקַטֵּל, מְקַטְּלִים;	Pi'ēl
מְקֻטֶּלֶת, מְקֻטָּלָה et מְקֻטָּלוֹת	מְקֻטָּל, מְקֻטָּלִים;	Pu'al
מַקְטֶלֶת, (מַקְטִילָה) מַקְטִילוֹת	מַקְטִיל, מַקְטִילִים;	Hiph.
מָקְטֶלֶת, מָקְטָלוֹת	מָקְטָל, מָקְטָלִים;	Hoph.
מִתְקַטֶּלֶת (מִתְקַטְּלָה)	מִתְקַטֵּל, מִתְקַטְּלִים;	Hithp.

A*

Paradigmata.

Verba primae gutturalis (§ 65).

I *Perf.* עָמַד; .*pl* 2. עֲמַדְתֶּם" עֲמַדְתֶּן. — II נֶעֱמַד, נֶהְפַּךְ[k]
נֶעֶמְדָה, נֶעֱמַדְתָּ, *pl.* נֶעֶמְדוּ, נֶעֱמַדְתֶּם. — V הֶעֱמִיד[k] הֶעֱמִידָה,
הֶעֱמַדְתָּ. — VI הָעֳמַד[p3] הָעָמְדָה, הָעֳמַדְתָּ; *pl.* הָעָמְדוּ,
הָעֳמַדְתֶּם.

I *Inf.* עֲמֹד". — II הֵעָמֵד[b1]. — V הַעֲמִיד[p3].

I *Iptv.* עֲמֹד" עִמְדִי; עִמְדוּ עֲמֹדְנָה. — II הֵעָמֵד[b1]
הֵעָמְדִי. — V הַעֲמֵד[p3] הַעֲמִידִי.

I *Ipf.* יַעֲמֹד יַחְפֹּר[f] תַּעֲמֹד, תַּעֲמֹד תַּעַמְדִי, אֶעֱמַד;
pl. יַעַמְדוּ תַּעֲמֹדְנָה, תַּעֲמֹדְנָה, נַעֲמֹד. — II יֵעָמֵד[b1]
תֵּעָמֵד. — V יַעֲמִיד[p3] תַּעֲמִיד, תַּעֲמִידִי. — VI יָעֳמַד[p3]
תָּעֳמַד, תָּעֳמַד תָּעָמְדִי, אָעֳמַד; *pl.* יָעָמְדוּ תָּעֳמַדְנָה, תָּעָמְדוּ
תָּעֳמַדְנָה, נָעֳמַד.

I *Part.* אָסוּר, אֲסוּרִים. — II נֶעֱמָד[k]. — V מַעֲמִיד[p3]
— VI מָעֳמָד.

Verba mediae gutturalis (§ 65).

I *Perf.* שָׁחַט שָׁחֲטָה; *pl.* שָׁחֲטוּ". — II נִשְׁחַט נִשְׁחֲטָה;
pl. נִשְׁחֲטוּ. — III נִחַם[b2] נִחֲמָה[b2]; *pl.* נִחֲמוּ. בֵּרַךְ[b1] בֵּרְכָה;
pl. בֵּרְכוּ. — IV נֻחַם נֻחֲמָה; *pl.* נֻחֲמוּ. בֹּרַךְ בֹּרְכָה; *pl.* בֹּרְכוּ.
— VI הָשְׁחַט הָשְׁחֲטָה; *pl.* הָשְׁחֲתוּ. — VII הִתְנַחֵם הִתְנַחֲמָה;
pl. הִתְנַחֲמוּ. הִתְבָּרֵךְ הִתְבָּרְכָה; *pl.* הִתְבָּרְכוּ.

I *Itpv.* שְׁחַט" שַׁחֲטִי", שַׁחֲטוּ שְׁחַטְנָה. — II הִשָּׁחֵט
הִשָּׁחֲטִי" הִשָּׁחֲטוּ. — III נַחֵם[b2] נַחֲמִי; נַחֲמוּ [נַחֵמְנָה]. בָּרֵךְ[b1]
בָּרְכִי, בָּרְכוּ בָּרַכְנָה. — VII הִתְנַחֵם הִתְבָּרֵךְ (cf. III).

Paradigmata. 5*

I Ipf. יִשְׁחַט, 2. f., תִּשְׁחֲטִי‎ ; pl. יִשְׁחֲטוּ תִּשְׁחַטְנָה. —
II יִשָּׁחֵט, 2. f. תִּשָּׁחֲטִי, pl. יִשָּׁחֲטוּ תִּשָּׁחַטְנָה, תִּשָּׁחֲטוּ. —
III יְנַחֵם‎[b2], 2. f. תְּנַחֲמִי; pl. יְנַחֲמוּ תְּנַחֵמְנָה, תְּנַחֲמוּ. יְבָרֵךְ‎[b1],
2. f. תְּבָרְכִי; pl. יְבָרְכוּ. — IV יְנֻחַם, 2. f. תְּנֻחֲמִי; pl. יְנֻחֲמוּ.
יְבֹרַךְ, 2. f. תְּבֹרְכִי; pl. יְבֹרְכוּ. — VI יָשְׁחַט, 2. f. תָּשְׁחֲטִי‎:
pl. יָשְׁחֲטוּ. — VII יִתְנַחֵם יִתְבָּרֵךְ (cf. III).
I Part. שֹׁחֵט, שֹׁחֲטִים. — III מְנַחֵם, מְנַחֲמִים. מְבָרֵךְ,
מְבָרְכִים. — IV מְנֻחָם מְבֹרָךְ. — VII מִתְנַחֵם מִתְבָּרֵךְ (cf. III).

Verba tertiae gutturalis (§ 65).

I Perf. שָׁלַח, 2. f. שָׁלַחַתְּ‎[s]. — II נִשְׁלַח, 2. f. נִשְׁלַחַתְּ. —
III שִׁלַּח‎[d] שִׁלֵּחַ, 2. f. שִׁלַּחַתְּ. — IV שֻׁלַּח, 2. f. שֻׁלַּחַתְּ. —
V הִשְׁלִיחַ‎[d] הִשְׁלִיחָה, הִשְׁלַחַתְּ הִשְׁלַחַתְּ. — VI הָשְׁלַח, 2. f.
הָשְׁלַחַתְּ. — VII הִשְׁתַּלַּח, 2. f. הִשְׁתַּלַּחַתְּ. —
I Inf. שְׁלֹחַ‎[d]. — II הִשָּׁלֵחַ‎[e]. — III שַׁלֵּחַ (שַׁלַּח). —
V הַשְׁלִיחַ‎[d]. VII הִשְׁתַּלֵּחַ.
I Iptv. שְׁלַח‎[e] שִׁלְחִי, שִׁלְחוּ שְׁלַחְנָה. — II הִשָּׁלַח‎[e3]. —
III שַׁלַּח‎[e3] שַׁלְּחִי, שַׁלְּחוּ [שַׁלַּחְנָה]. — V הַשְׁלַח‎[e3] הַשְׁלִיחִי;
הַשְׁלִיחוּ הַשְׁלַחְנָה. — VII הִשְׁתַּלַּח.
I Ipf. יִשְׁלַח‎[e3] יִשְׁלָח; 2. f. pl. תִּשְׁלַחְנָה. — II יִשָּׁלַח‎[e3];
2. f. pl. תִּשָּׁלַחְנָה. — III יְשַׁלַּח וִישַׁלַּח; 2. f. pl. תְּשַׁלַּחְנָה‎[e3]. —
V יַשְׁלִיחַ (יַשְׁלַח)‎[s3] (juss.), 2. f., תַּשְׁלִיחִי; pl. יַשְׁלִיחוּ תַּשְׁלַחְנָה,
1 נַשְׁלִיחַ. — VII יִשְׁתַּלַּח (cf. III).
Part. שֹׁלֵחַ‎[d], שֹׁלְחִים; f. שֹׁלַחַת‎[s]. שָׁלוּחַ, שְׁלוּחִים. III
מְשַׁלֵּחַ. — V מַשְׁלִיחַ. — VII מִשְׁתַּלֵּחַ.
I Inf. abs. שָׁלֹחַ‎[d]. — II נִשְׁלֹחַ.

Verba פ"א (§ 66).

I *Ipf.* יֹאכַל‎ᵃ תֹּאכַל, תֹּאכַל תֹּאכְלִי, אֹכַל; .*pl* יֹאכְלוּ תֹּאכַלְנָה,
תֹּאכְלוּ תֹּאכַלְנָה, נֹאכַל. (*Wāw cons.* cf. § *a*).

Verba פ"נ § 67.

II *Perf.* נִגַּשׁ‎ᵃ נִגְּשָׁה, נִגַּשְׁתָּ. — V הִגִּישׁ‎ᵃ הִגִּישָׁה, הִגַּשְׁתָּ.
— VI הֻגַּשׁ‎ᵍ הֻגְּשָׁה, הֻגַּשְׁתָּ.

I *Inf.* נְפֹל. גֶּשֶׁת‎ᶠ. — V הַגִּישׁ‎ᵃ.

I *Iptv.* נְפֹל. גַּשׁ גְּשִׁי גְּשׁוּ [גַּשְׁנָה]. — V הַגֵּשׁ‎ᵃ הַגִּישִׁי;
הַגִּישׁוּ הַגֵּשְׁנָה.

I *Ipf.* יִפֹּל‎ᵃ תִּפֹּל, תִּפְּלִי תִּפְּלִי, אֶפֹּל; יִפְּלוּ תִּפֹּלְנָה. יִגַּשׁ
תִּגַּשׁ, 2. *f.* תִּגְּשִׁי; *pl.* יִגְּשׁוּ תִּגַּשְׁנָה. — V יַגִּישׁ, 2. *f.* תַּגִּישִׁי;
pl. יַגִּישׁוּ תַּגֵּשְׁנָה. — VI יֻגַּשׁ‎ᵍ, 2. *f.* תֻּגְּשִׁי; *pl.* יֻגְּשׁוּ תֻּגַּשְׁנָה.

II *Part.* נִגָּשׁ‎ᵃ. — V מַגִּישׁ‎ᵃ. — VI. מֻגָּשׁ.

Verba פו"י (פ"י I.) § 68.

II *Perf.* נוֹשַׁב‎ᶜ³ נוֹשְׁבָה, נוֹשַׁבְתָּ; .*pl* 2. נוֹשַׁבְתֶּם. —
V הוֹשִׁיב‎ᶜ³ הוֹשִׁיבָה, הוֹשַׁבְתָּ; *pl.* 2 הוֹשַׁבְתֶּם. — VI. הוּשַׁב‎ᶜ²
הוּשְׁבָה, הוּשַׁבְתָּ; *pl.* 2. הוּשַׁבְתֶּם.

I *Inf.* יְשׁוֹן‎ᵈ. שֶׁבֶת‎ᶠ. — II הִוָּשֵׁב‎ᵇ². — V הוֹשִׁיב‎ᶜ³.

I *Iptv.* יְרָא‎ᵈ. שֵׁב‎ᶠ שְׁבִי; שְׁבוּ שֵׁבְנָה. — II הִוָּשֵׁב‎ᵇ²
הִוָּשְׁבִי; הִוָּשְׁבוּ. — V הוֹשֵׁב‎ᶜ³ הוֹשִׁיבִי; הוֹשִׁיבוּ הוֹשֵׁבְנָה.

I *Ipf.* יִישַׁן‎ᵈ; *pl.* יִישְׁנוּ (יִישָׁנוּ). יֵשֵׁב‎ᶠ תֵּשֵׁב, תֵּשֵׁב תֵּשְׁבִי
אֵשֵׁב; *pl.* יֵשְׁבוּ תֵּשַׁבְנָה, תֵּשְׁבוּ תֵּשַׁבְנָה, נֵשֵׁב. — II יִוָּשֵׁב‎ᵇ².
V יוֹשִׁיב‎ᶜ³, 2. *f.* תּוֹשִׁיבִי; *pl.* יוֹשִׁיבוּ תּוֹשֵׁבְנָה. — VI יוּשַׁב,
2. *f.* תּוּשְׁבִי; *pl.* יוּשְׁבוּ תּוּשַׁבְנָה.

II *Part.* נוֹשָׁב. — V מוֹשִׁיב. — VI מוּשָׁב.

Paradigmata.

Verba פי"ו (ע"ו II.) § 69.

V *Perf.* הֵיטִיב, הֵיטִיבָה, הֵיטַבְתָּ, הֵיטַבְתְּ; *pl.* 2 הֵיטַבְתֶּם. —
I *Ipf.* יֵיטִיב, 2. *f.*, תֵּיטִיבִי; *pl.* יֵיטְבוּ (יִיטְבוּ). תִּיטַבְנָה. —
V יֵיטִיב, 2. *f.*, תֵּיטִיבִי.
I *Inf.* יְבֹשׁ V *Part.* מֵיטִיב.

Verba ע"ו § 71.

I *Perf.* קָם, קָמָה, קַמְתָּ, קַמְתְּ, קַמְתִּי; *pl.* קָמוּ, קַמְתֶּם, קַמְתֶּן, קַמְנוּ. — II נָקוֹם, נָקוֹמָה, נְקוּמוֹתָ, נְקוּמוֹת, נְקוּמוֹתִי; *pl.* נְקוּמוֹ, נְקוּמוֹתֶם, נְקוּמוֹתֶן, נְקוּמוֹנוּ. — III קוֹמֵם קוֹמֲמָה, קוֹמַמְתָּ, 2. *pl.* קוֹמַמְתֶּם. — IV קוֹמַם קוֹמֲמָה, קוֹמְמָה. —
V הֵקִים, הֵקִימָה, הֲקִימוֹתָ, הֲקִימוֹת, הֲקִימוֹתִי; *pl.* הֵקִימוּ, הֲקִימוֹתֶם הֲקִימוֹתֶן, הֲקִימוֹנוּ. — VI הוּקַם הוּקְמָה, הוּקַמְתָּ, 2. *pl.* הוּקַמְתֶּם. — VII הִתְקוֹמֵם (cf. III).

I *Inf.* קוּם. — II הֲקוֹם. — III קוֹמֵם. — V הָקִים.
I *Iptv.* קוּם, *f.* קוּמִי; קוּמוּ קֹמְנָה. — II הֲקוֹם הֲקוֹמִי; הָקוֹמוּ [הֲקוֹמְנָה]. — III קוֹמֵם קוֹמֲמִי; קוֹמְמוּ קוֹמַמְנָה.
V הָקֵם הָקִימִי; הָקִימוּ [הֲקֵמְנָה]. — VII הִתְקוֹמֵם (cf. III).
I *Ipf.* יָקוּם (יָקֹם) *juss.* (וַיָּקָם); תָּקוּם, תָּקוּם תָּקוּמִי, אָקוּם; יָקוּמוּ תְּקוּמֶינָה, תְּקוּמוּ תְּקוּמֶינָה, נָקוּם. — II יִקּוֹם, 2. *f.* יִקּוֹמִי *pl.* יִקּוֹמוּ אֶקּוֹם, — III תְּקֵמֶינָה [תְּקֵמֶינָה], 2. *f.* יְקוֹמֵם *pl.* יְקוֹמֲמוּ תְּקוֹמַמְנָה; — IV יְקוֹמַם, 2. *f.*, תְּקוֹמֲמִי; *pl.* יְקוֹמֲמוּ תְּקוֹמַמְנָה. — V יָקִים (יָקֵם) *juss.* (וַיָּקֶם); *pl.* תָּקִימִי, יָקִימוּ תְּקִימֶינָה u. תָּקֵמְנָה. — VI יוּקַם *pl.* 2. *f.*, תּוּקְמִי; יוּקְמוּ תּוּקַמְנָה. — VII יִתְקוֹמֵם (cf. III).
I *Inf. abs.* קוֹם. — II הֲקוֹם. — V הָקֵם.

Paradigmata.

I *Part.* קָם, *f.* קָמָה; *pass.* קוּם.⁹ — II נָקוֹם, "קוֹם", ‏קוֹמִים. — III מְקוֹמֵם. — IV [מְקוֹמָם]. — V מֵקִים, "מְקִים", מְקִימִים. — VI מוּקָם. — VII מִתְקוֹמֵם.

Verba ע״ע § 73.

I *Perf.* סָבַב‏ʰ³ סָבְבָה (קַל קָלָה) (*intr.*ᵇ סַבּוֹת‏ʰ סַבּוֹת, סַבּוֹתִי; *pl.* סָבֲבוּ (קַלּוּ) (*intr.* סַבּוֹתֶם סַבּוֹתֶן, סַבּוּנוּ. — II נָסַב‏ᵃ נָסַבָּה, נְסַבּוֹת‏ʲ נְסַבּוֹת, נְסַבּוֹתִי, נְסַבּוּנוּ. — *pl.* נָסַבּוּ, נְסַבּוֹתֶם נְסַבּוֹתֶן, נְסַבּוּנוּ. — III סוֹבֵב (cf. *Pi.*), הָלַל. — IV סוֹבֵב, הֻלַּל. — V הֵסֵב‏ᵏ’ⁱ הֵסַבָּה, הֲסִבּוֹת‏ʲ הֲסִבּוֹת, הֲסִבּוֹתִי; *pl.* הֲסִבּוּ (הָסֵבּוּ) הֲסִבּוֹתֶם הֲסִבּוֹתֶן, הֲסִבּוּנוּ. — VI הוּסַב‏ᵏ הוּסַבָּה, [הוּסַבּוֹתָ]; *pl.* הוּסַבּוּ, [הוּסַבּוֹתֶם]. — VII הִסְתּוֹבֵב, הִתְהַלֵּל.

Inf. I סֹב‏ᶠ. — II הֵסֵב. — III סוֹבֵב. הֻלַּל. — V הָסֵב.

Iptv. I סֹב סֹבִּי, סֹבּוּ [סֻבֶּינָה]. — II הִסַּב הִסַּבִּי; הִסַּבּוּ [הִסַּבֶּינָה]. — III סוֹבֵב סוֹבְבִי, הַלֵּל הַלֲלִי (§5*d*). — V הָסֵב הָסֵבִּי; הָסֵבּוּ [הֲסִבֶּינָה].

Ipf. I יָסֹב (וַיָּסָב) (*cons.*), 2. *f.* תָּסֹבִּי; *pl.* יָסֹבּוּ תְּסֻבֶּינָה, תָּסֹבּוּ תְּסֻבֶּינָה, יָסֹב (יִסֹב; יִסְבּוּ‎ᵐ). (נָקַל; יֵקַלּוּ). (*intr.*). — II יִסַּב, 1 [תִּסַּבֶּינָה], 2 *f.* תִּסַּבִּי; יִסַּבּוּ‏ — III יִסּוֹבֵב, יְהַלֵּל. — IV יְסוֹבֵב, יְהֻלַּל. — V יָסֵב, 2. *f.* תָּסֵב; *pl.* יָסֵבּוּ תְּסִבֶּינָה, תָּסֵבּוּ תְּסִבֶּינָה, נָסֵב. — VI יוּסַב; *pl.* יוּסַבּוּ [תּוּסַבֶּינָה].

Part. I סֹבֵב; *pass.* סָבוּב. — II נָסָב. — III מְסוֹבָב. — IV מְסוֹבָב. — V מֵסֵב. — VI מוּסָב, *f. pl.* מוּסַבּוֹת. —

Inf. abs. I סָבוֹב. — II הִסּוֹב.

Verba ל"ה § 74.

Perf. I גָּלָה, גָּלְתָה, גָּלִיתָ, גָּלִית (תְּ) (§ 5 b 2), גָּלִיתִי;
pl. גָּלוּ, גְּלִיתֶם גְּלִיתֶן, גָּלִינוּ. — II גִּלָּה גִּלְּתָה, גִּלִּיתָ
גִּלִּית, גִּלִּיתִי, *pl.* גִּלּוּ, גִּלִּיתֶם גִּלִּיתֶן, גִּלִּינוּ. — III גֻּלָּה
גֻּלְּתָה, גֻּלֵּיתָ; *pl.* גֻּלּוּ, גֻּלֵּיתֶם. — IV גָּלָה גָּלְתָה, גָּלֵיתָ;
pl. גָּלוּ, גָּלֵיתֶם. — V הִגְלָה (הֶגְלָה) הִגְלְתָה, הִגְלֵיתָ;
pl. הִגְלוּ, הִגְלֵיתֶם. — VI הָגְלָה הָגְלְתָה, הָגְלֵיתָ; *pl.* הָגְלוּ,
הָגְלֵיתֶם. — VII הִתְגַּלָּה הִתְגַּלְּתָה, הִתְגַּלִּיתָ; *pl.* הִתְגַּלּוּ,
הִתְגַּלִּיתֶם.

Iptv. I גְּלֵה, גְּלִי; גְּלוּ גְּלֶינָה. — II הִגָּלֵה הִגָּלִי;
הִגָּלוּ. — III גַּלֵּה גַּלִּי; גַּלּוּ גַּלֶּינָה. — V הַגְלֵה הַגְלִי;
הַגְלוּ הַגְלֶינָה. — VII הִתְגַּלֵּה (cf. III).

Ipf. I יִגְלֶה תִּגְלֶה, תִּגְלֶה תִּגְלִי, אֶגְלֶה, *pl.* יִגְלוּ תִּגְלֶינָה,
תִּגְלוּ תִּגְלֶינָה. — II יִגָּלֶה. 2. f. תִּגָּלִי; יִגָּלוּ תִּגָּלֶינָה;
— III יְגֻלֶּה. 2. f. תְּגֻלִּי; *pl.* יְגֻלּוּ תְּגֻלֶּינָה. — IV יְגֻלֶּה,
2. f. תְּגֻלִּי; *pl.* יְגֻלּוּ תְּגֻלֶּינָה. — V יַגְלֶה. 2. f. תַּגְלִי;
pl. יַגְלוּ תַּגְלֶינָה. — VI תָּגְלֶה 2. f. תָּגְלִי, *pl.* יָגְלוּ תָּגְלֶינָה.
— VII יִתְגַּלֶּה (cf. III). ‖ (*Ipf. apoc.* § o—t).

Part. I גֹּלֶה גֹּלִים; *pass.* גָּלוּי. — II נִגְלֶה. — III
מְגֻלֶּה. — IV מְגֻלֶּה. — V מַגְלֶה. — VI מָגְלֶה. — VII מִתְגַּלֶּה.

Inf. I גְּלוֹת. — II הִגָּלוֹת. — III גַּלּוֹת. — V הַגְלוֹת.
— VII הִתְגַּלּוֹת.

Paradigmata.

Verba ל"א § 75.

I *Perf.* מָצָא מָצְאָ֫"ה, מָצְאָ֫תָ"ᵃ מָצָ֫את (תָּ2 b 5 §), מְצָאתִי;
pl. מָצְאוּ, מְצָאתֶם מְצָאתֶ֫ן, מְצָאנוּ. (מָלֵא מָלְאָה, מָלֵ֫אתָᵃ. *intr.*)
— II נִמְצָאᵃ נִמְצְאָה, נִמְצֵאתᵈ², נִמְצֵ֫את, נִמְצֵ֫אתִי; *pl.* נִמְצְאוּ,
נִמְצֵאתֶם. — III מִצֵּא מִצְּאָה, מִצֵּאתᵈ²; *pl.* מִצְּאוּ, מִצֵּאתֶם,
— IV מֻצָּא מֻצְּאָה, [מֻצֵּאתᵈ²]. — V הִמְצִיא הִמְצִ֫יאָה,
pl. הִמְצִ֫יאוּ, הִמְצֵאתֶם; ᵈ²הִמְצֵ֫את. — VI הָמְצָא. — VII
הִתְמַצֵּא (cf. III).

I *Inf.* מְצֹא. — II הִמָּצֵא. — III מַצֵּא. — V הַמְצִיא.

I *Iptv.* ᵇמְצָאᵃ מְצָאִי; מִצְאוּ מְצֶ֫אנָהᵈ¹. — II הִמָּצֵא הִמָּצְאִי;
הִמָּצְאוּ הִמָּצֶ֫אנָהᵈ¹. — III מַצֵּא, *pl. f.* מַצֶּ֫אנָהᵈ¹. — V הַמְצֵא
הַמְצִיאִי; הַמְצִ֫יאוּ הַמְצֶ֫אנָהᵈ¹. — VII הִתְמַצֵּא (cf. III).

I *Ipf.* ᵇיִמְצָאᵈ¹, 2. *f.* תִּמְצְאִי, *pl.* יִמְצְאוּ תִּמְצֶ֫אנָהᵈ¹,
תִּמְצְאוּ תִּמְצֶ֫אנָהᵈ¹. — II יִמָּצֵא, נִמָּצֵא. *pl.* יִמָּצְאוּ תִּמָּצֶ֫אנָהᵈ¹.
— III יְמַצֵּא *pl.* יְמַצְּאוּ תְּמַצֶּ֫אנָה. — IV יְמֻצָּא; *pl.* יְמֻצְּאוּ
תְּמֻצֶּ֫אנָה. — V יַמְצִיא *pl.* יַמְצִ֫יאוּ תַּמְצֶ֫אנָה. — VI יָמְצָאᵃ;
pl. יָמְצְאוּ תָּמְצֶ֫אנָה. — VII יִתְמַצֵּא (cf. III).

I *Part.* ᵇמֹצֵא מֹצְאִים, מֹצְאָה *f.* מֹצֵאת (מָלֵא מְלֵאִים, *intr.* § 25*g*);
pass. מָצוּא. — II נִמְצָא, *f.* נִמְצֵאת. — III מְמַצֵּא. — IV מְמֻצָּא.
מְמֻצָּא. — V מַמְצִיא. — VI מָמְצָא. — VII מִתְמַצֵּא.

Litteratura.*

I.

M. Steinschneider, Bibliographisches Handbuch über die theoretische und praktische Literatur für hebräische Sprachkunde. Leipzig 1859, XXXVI, 160 p. [Addenda permulta et Corrigenda enumeravit J. Gildemeister, Zeitschrift der Deutschen Morgenländischen Gesellschaft XIV, p. 297 sqq.]

Wilh. Gesenius, Geschichte der hebräischen Sprache und Schrift. Eine philologisch-historische Einleitung in die Sprachlehren und Wörterbücher der hebräischen Sprache. Leipzig 1815. VIII, 231 p.

V. E. Loescher, De causis linguae Ebraeae. Francofurti et Lipsiae 1706. 496 p. 4.

S. D. Luzzatto, Prolegomeni ad una Grammatica ragionata della lingua Ebraica. Padua 1836. 234 p.

Franz Delitzsch, Jesurun sive Prolegomenon in Concordantias V^{is} T^i a Julio Fuerstio editas libri tres. Grimma 1838. XVI, 260 p.

W. Rob. Smith, Hebrew Language and Literature (Encyclopaedia Britannica⁹ XI [1880], 594b—602b).

B. Pick, The Study of the Hebrew Language among Jews and Christians, in: Bibliotheca Sacra 1884, p. 450—477. 1885, p. 470—495.

II.

**Wilh. Gesenius*, Thesaurus philologicus criticus linguae Hebraeae et Chaldaeae V^{is} T^i. Editio altera secundum radices digesta priore germanica longe auctior et emendatior. Lipsiae. Vol. I: 1835; vol. II: 1840; vol. III, 1 (ב—נפש): 1842; vol. III, 2: 1853 (composuit Aemil. Roediger); III, 3: 1858 (indices, additamenta et emendationes digessit et edidit Aem. Roed.). 1522+116 p. 4.

---

* Libros a Judaeis medii aevi conscriptos enumeravi in: Lehrbuch der neuhebräischen Sprache und Litteratur von H. L. Strack und C. Siegfried, Karlsruhe und Leipzig 1884, p. 107—116.

Wilh. Gesenius, Hebräisches und chaldäisches Handwörterbuch. Neunte Auflage neu bearbeitet von F. Mühlau und W. Volck. Leipzig 1883. XLVI, 978 p. [Dê hoc libro cf. C. Siegfried in: Theologische. Literaturzeitung 1883, Nr. 23; P. de Lagarde in: Göttingische Gelehrte Anzeigen 1884, Stück 7, p. 257—288, = Mittheilungen, Göttingen 1884, p. 208—239; Friedr. Delitzsch, Hebrew Language, praefat.; H. Strack in: Theol. Literaturblatt 1884, Nr. 22, col. 169. 170].

— —, Translationem Anglicam auctam et emendatam edituri sunt Charles A. Briggs et Francis Brown.

Jul. Fürst, Hebräisches und chaldäisches Handwörterbuch über das Alte Testament. Dritte verbesserte und vermehrte Auflage bearbeitet von Victor Ryssel. Leipzig 1876, 2 voll. XLVIII, 806+667 p.

Paul. Martin. Alberti, Porta linguae sanctae. Budissae 1704. 1259 p. 4.

[*B. Davidson*], The Analytical Hebrew and Chaldee Lexicon: consisting of an alphabetical arrangement of every word and inflection contained in the O. T. Scriptures, precisely as they occur in the sacred text, with a grammatical analysis of each word and lexicographical illustration of the meanings. London 1848. 90 [grammatica, paradigmata], 84 p. 4.

Samuel Lee, A Lexicon Hebrew Chaldee and English: compiled from the most approved sources, Oriental and European, Jewish and Christian. London 1840. XVI, 664 p.

**W. Gesenius*, Hebrew and Chaldee Lexicon to the O. T. Scriptures, translated with additions and corrections from the Author's Thesaurus and other works. By S. P. Tregelles. London 1859. XII, 884, 35 p. 4.

B. A. Davies, Hebrew and Chaldee Lexicon to the Old Testament with an English-Hebrew Index. 3d ed. revised by E. C. Mitchell. London 1880. 778 p.

Friedrich Delitzsch, The Hebrew Language viewed in the Light of Assyrian Research. London 1883. XII, 73 p.

W. Wright, The Book of Jonah in four Oriental Versions, namely Chaldee, Syriac, Æthiopic and Arabic, with Glossaries. London & Leipzig 1857. X, 148 p. [„Glossaries admirable, as introduction to comparative study of Semitic languages" Driver.]

III.

Isaak Nathan, מאיר נתיב. Venet. 1523. fol.

J. Buxtorfi Concordantiae Bibliorum Hebraicae . . . Accesserunt novae concordantiae Chaldaicae . . . cum praefatione . . . per J. Buxtorfium filium. Basileae 1632. fol.

J. Buxtorfi Concordantiae Bibliorum Hebraicae et Chaldaicae [auctae et emendatae ab] editore Bernh. Baer. Stettini 1867. 4.
J. Fuerst, Librorum sacrorum V^{is} T^i concordantiae Hebraicae atque Chaldaicae. Lips. 1840. fol.
*B. *Davidson*, A Concordance of the Hebrew and Chaldee Scriptures. Revised and corrected. London 1876. VI, 904 p.
The Englishman's Hebrew and Chaldee Concordance of the Old Testament. Being an attempt at a verbal connection between the Original and the English Translation with Indexes and a List of proper names and their occurrences. Second ed. revised. London 1860. XVI, 1682, 78 p.
W. Wilson, An English Hebrew and Chaldee Lexicon and Concordance to the more correct understanding of the English Translation of the O. T., by reference to the original Hebrew. Second ed. carefully revised. London 1866. XVI, 500 p. 4.
Robert Young, Analytical Concordance to the Bible on an entirely new plan, containing every word in alphabetical order, arranged under its Hebrew or Greek Original, with the literal meaning of each and its pronounciation. Edinburgh 1879. VIII, 1090 p. 4.
The Hebraist's Vade mecum; a first attempt at a complete verbal Index to the contents of the Hebrew and Chaldee Scriptures. Arranged according to Grammar ... the occurrences in full. London 1867. 582, 43 [proper names] p. — Subscriptio praefationis: G. V. Wigram.
Christian Nolde, Concordantiae particularum Ebraeo-chaldaicarum in quibus partium indeclinabilium ... natura et sensuum varietas ostenditur... Joh. Gottfr. Tympius ... recensuit et annotationes ... adiecit. Jenae 1734. 984, 24, 40 p. 4.
Concordantiae nominum propriorum quae in libris sacris continentur, a divo patre Gideone Brecher inchoata [!] ..., finita demum a filio Ad. Brecher. Francofurti ad M. 1876. 79 p. 4.
L. M. Schusslowicz, ספר איש המצה. Wilna 1878. 276 p. 4.
Die neubearbeitete hebräisch-chaldäische Bibel-Concordanz von Dr. *S. Mandelkern* in Leipzig. Leipzig 1884. 15 p.

IV.

Johannis Buxtorfi Thesaurus grammaticus linguae sanctae Hebraeae ... editio sexta. Recognita a J. Buxtorfio, Filio. Basileae 1663. 669, 33 p.
Wilh. Gesenius, Ausführliches grammatisch-kritisches Lehrgebäude der hebräischen Sprache mit Vergleichung der verwandten Dialekte. Leipz. 1817. 908 p.
— —, Hebräische Grammatik [Halle 1813]. 24. Aufl. Völlig umgearbeitet u. herausgeg. von *E. Kautzsch. Leipzig 1885. XII, 419 p.

Wilh. Gesenius, Hebrew Grammar. Translated by Benj. Davies from Rödiger's edition. Thoroughly revised ... by Edw. C. Mitchell. London 1880. XXXIII, 423 p.

Heinr. Ewald, Ausführliches Lehrbuch der hebräischen Sprache des Alten Bundes. 8. Ausgabe. Göttingen 1870. XV, 959 p. [1827: Kritische Gramm. der hebr. Sprache].

*Justus Olshausen, Lehrbuch der hebräischen Sprache. Buch I. Laut- und Schrift-Lehre. Buch II. Formen-Lehre. Braunschweig 1861. XVII, 676 p. [Olsh. † 28. Dec. 1882].

S. D. Luzzatto, Grammatica della lingua Ebraica. Padua 1853—69. 611 p.

Friedr. Böttcher, Ausführliches Lehrbuch der hebräischen Sprache. Herausgeg. u. mit ausführl. Registern versehen von Ferd. Mühlau. Leipzig 1866. 68. XII, 654, 699 p.

H. Arnheim, Grammatik der hebräischen Sprache. Berlin 1872. XVI, 331 p.

*Bernh. Stade, Lehrbuch der hebräischen Grammatik. Erster Theil. Schriftlehre. Lautlehre. Formenlehre. Leipz. 1879. XVIII, 425 p.

*Friedr. Ed. König, Historisch-kritisches Lehrgebäude der hebräischen Sprache. Erste Hälfte: Lehre von der Schrift, der Aussprache, dem Pronomen und dem Verbum. Leipzig 1881. X, 710 p. [Pars altera „Nomen und generelle Bildungslehre" anno 1886 in lucem prodibit.]

Samuel Lee, A Grammar of the Hebrew Language compiled from the best authorities and drawn principally from oriental sources. Second ed. London 1832. XXVIII, 388 p.

Isaac Nordheimer, A Critical Grammar of the Hebrew Language. London 1838. XXVIII, 280 p. [Editio altera Novi Eboraci a. 1842 (2 voll.) edita esse dicitur.]

Will. Henry Green, A Grammar of the Hebrew Language. Second ed. New York 1861. X, 400 p. 4th ed. 1883.

M. M. Kalisch, A Hebrew Grammar with Exercises in two Parts. I: The Outlines of the Language with Exercises being a practical introduction to the study of Hebrew. London 1862. XV, 374 p. (2nd ed. revised and corrected [?] 1875. XV, 374 p.). II: The Exceptional Forms and Constructions, preceded by an Essay on the History of Hebrew Grammar. London 1863. XVI, 324 p.— Key to the Exercises in Part I. London 1863. VI, 96 p.

Gust. Bickell, Outlines of Hebrew Grammar, revised by the Author and annotated by the Translator Samuel Ives Curtiss, Jr. Leipzig 1877, 140 p.

V.

C. Schlottmann, Schrift und Schriftzeichen (in: Riehm, Handwörterbuch des biblischen Altertums p. 1415—1431).

H. L. Strack, Schreibkunst und Schrift bei den Hebräern (in: Real-Encyklopädie für protestantische Theologie und Kirche ² XIII [Leipz. 1884], p. 689—696, quo loco libros huc pertinentes enumeravi).

Literarum figuras optime delineavit J. Euting in Bickell-Curtiss, Outlines (v. supra p. 14*) et in Chwolsonii Corpore Inscriptionum Hebraicarum.

De historia punctorum vocalium scripserunt: H. Strack in: Zeitschrift für die gesammte lutherische Theologie und Kirche 1875, p. 619—624; in: Theologische Studien und Kritiken 1875, p. 736—746 (cf. 1876, p. 554). M. Schwab, Des points-voyelles dans les langues sémitiques, Paris 1879, 48 p. J. Dérenbourg, Revue Critique 1879, 21. juin. H. Grätz, Die Anfänge der Vokalzeichen im Hebräischen, in: Monatsschrift für Geschichte und Wissenschaft des Judenthums 1881, p. 348—367. 395—405. Ad. Merx, Die Tschufutkale'schen Fragmente. Eine Studie zur Geschichte der Masora, in: Verhandlungen des internation. Orientalisten-Congresses (Berlin 1882) II, 1, p. 188—225.

De punctatione quae dicitur Babylonica legas praefationem meam in Prophetarum posteriorum codicis Babylonici editionem p. VII et: Zeitschrift für luther. Theologie 1877, p. 18—21.

Abrahamum Firkowitsch falsarium et defensorem eius, Danielem Chwolson, saepius impugnare coactus fui, cf.: A. Firkowitsch und seine Entdeckungen, Leipzig 1876, 44 p.; Zeitschrift der Deutsch. Morg. Ges. 1879, p. 301 sq., 1880, p. 163—168; Literar. Centralblatt 1883, Nr. 25, col. 878—880.

S. Baer und *H. L. Strack*, Die Dikduke ha-tᵉamim des Ahron ben Moscheh ben Ascher und andere alte grammatisch-massorethische Lehrstücke. Leipzig 1879. XLII, 95 p.

A. B. Davidson, Outlines of Hebrew Accentuation, prose and poetical. London and Edinburgh 1861. XXIV, 114 p.

De accentibus qui dicuntur prosaicis hebraice scripsit *W. Heidenheim*, טעמי אמת, Rödelheim 1808. 66 folia. De iisdem anno 1886 tractatum edet William Wickes.

S. Baer, Das Accentuationssystem der Psalmen, des Buches Job und der Sprüche, überlieferungsgemäss seinen Gesetzen nach dargestellt, in Franz Delitzsch, Commentar über den Psalter II (Leipzig 1860), p. 477—512.

— —, ספר תהלים, Rödelheim 1852. 71 p. [hebraice].

William Wickes, אמת טעמי. A Treatise on the Accentuation of the three so-called poetical Books of the Old Testament Psalms, Proverbs and Job. Oxford 1881. XI, 119 p.

S. Baer, Die Metheg-Setzung nach ihren überlieferten Gesetzen dargestellt, in: Archiv für wissenschaftl. Erforschung des Alten Testamentes I (1867—69), p. 55—67. 194—207.

Jos. Wijnkoop, Darche hannesigah sive leges de accentus Hebraicae linguae ascensione. Leiden 1881. 115 p.

Franz Delitzsch, Die Dagessierung der Tenues, in: Zeitschrift für die ges. luth. Theol. u. Kirche. 1878, p. 585—590.

S. Baer, De primarum vocabulorum literarum dagessatione, in: Liber Proverbiorum. Textum .. expressit .. illustravit .. S. Baer, praefatus est .. F. Delitzsch, Lipsiae 1880, p. VII—XV.

Franz Prätorius, Über den Ursprung des Dagesch forte conjunctivum, in: Zeitschr. für die alttestam. Wissenschaft. 1883, p. 17—31.

— —, Über den Einfluss des Accentes auf die Vocalentfaltung nach Gutturalen, ibid. p. 211—219.

Ed. König, Gedanke, Laut und Accent als die drei Factoren der Sprachbildung comparativ und physiologisch am Hebräischen dargestellt. Weimar 1874, 155 p.

F. Dietrich, Abhandlungen zur hebräischen Grammatik. Leipzig 1846.

F. W. M. Philippi, Wesen und Ursprung des status constructus im Hebräischen. Weimar 1871. 208 p.

— —, Der Grundstamm des starken Verbums im Semitischen und sein Verhältniss zur Wurzel (in: „Morgenländische Forschungen", Leipzig 1875, p. 69—106).

N. Porges, Über die Verbalstammbildung in den semitischen Sprachen. Wien 1875, 76 p.

Th. Nöldeke, Untersuchungen zur semitischen Grammatik. I. Die Verba ל״י im Hebräischen, in: Zeitschr. der Deutschen Morgenl. Gesellsch. 1883, p. 525—540. | II. Die Endungen des Perfects, ibid. 1884, p. 407—422.

F. Prätorius, Das Imperfectum יִקְטֹל, in: Zeitschr. f. d. alttest. Wiss. 1883, p. 52—55.

Adolf Koch, Der semitische Infinitiv. Eine sprachwissenschaftliche Untersuchung. Stuttgart 1874. 71 p.

A. G. Sperling, Die nota relationis im Hebräischen. Ein Beitrag zur hebr. Lexikographie und Grammatik. Jena 1876, 46 p.

Fritz Hommel, אֶת ursprüngl. Substantiv zu trennen von —ְּ (—ִּ) ursprüngl. Pronominalstamm, in: Zeitschr. der Deutsch. Morg. Ges. 1878, p. 708—715.

Geo. Wandel, de particulae Hebraicae בְּ indole, vi, usu. Jena 1875, 50 p.

E. Schwabe, כ nach seinem Wesen und Gebrauche im alttestam. Kanon gewürdigt. Inaugural-Dissertation. Halle 1883. 44 p.
F. Giesebrecht, Die hebräische Präposition Lamed. Halle 1876. 112 p.
M. Budie, Die hebräische Präposition ʻal (על). Halle 1882. 80 p.
P. de Jong, Over de met ab, ach enz. zamengestelde Hebreeuwsche Eigennamen. Amsterdam 1880. J. Müller. 15 p
*Heinr. Ewald, Syntax of the Hebrew Language of the Old Testament. Translated from the 8th German edition by James Kennedy. Edinburgh 1879. VIII, 323 p.
*Aug. Müller, Outlines of Hebrew Syntax. Translated and edited by James Robertson. Glasgow 1882. XIV, 143 p.
*S. R. Driver, A Treatise on the Use of the Tenses in Hebrew. 2nd ed. Oxford 1881. XVI, 320 p.
E. Trumpp, Über den Zustandsausdruck in den semitischen Sprachen, speciell im Arabischen. München 1876. 52 p.
Henry Ferguson, An Examination of the Use of the Tenses in Conditional Sentences in Hebrew (in: Journal of the Society of Biblical Literature and Exegesis .. for June and December 1882. Middletown, Conn. 1883. p. 40—94).
Paul Friedrich, Die hebräischen Conditionalsätze. Inaugural-Dissertation. Königsberg 1884. VIII, 109 p.
H. Mitchell, An Examination of some of the final Constructions of Biblical Hebrew. A Part of a Dissertation. Leipzig 1879. 38 p.
R. B. Girdlestone, Synonyms of the Old Testament; their bearing on Christian Faith and Practice. London 1871. XIV, 534 p.
Victor Ryssel, Die Synonyma des Wahren und Guten in den semitischen Sprachen. Leipzig 1872. 54 p.
Conr. v. Orelli, Die hebräischen Synonyma der Zeit und Ewigkeit genetisch und sprachvergleichend dargestellt. Leipz. 1871. 112 p.
Em. Kautzsch, Über die Derivate des Stammes צדק im alttestamentlichen Sprachgebrauch. Tübingen 1881. 59 p. 4.

VI.*

G. Brückner, Hebräisches Lesebuch für Anfänger und Geübtere. 3. Aufl. Leipzig 1863. 225 p.
Heinr. Ewald, Hebräische Sprachlehre für Anfänger. Vierte Ausgabe. Mit den Grundzügen des Biblisch-Aramäischen. Göttingen 1874. 235 p.

---

* Conf. „Hülfsmittel für den Unterricht im Hebräischen" in: Theolog. Literaturblatt (Leipz.) 1881, No. 20. 21, ei 1882, No. 33—35.

H. Strack, Hebr. Gramm.² II. B

P. Friedrichsen, Elementarbuch der hebr. Sprache. 2. Aufl. Mainz 1871. 199 p.

W. Hollenberg, Hebräisches Schulbuch. Bearbeitet von Joh. Hollenberg. 5. Aufl. Berlin 1884. 148 p.

E. Kautzsch, Übungsbuch zu Gesenius-Kautzsch' Hebräischer Grammatik. 2. Aufl. Leipzig 1884. 162 p.

K. L. F. Mezger, Hebräisches Übungsbuch für Anfänger. Ein Hilfsbuch zu den hebr. Sprachlehren von W. Gesenius und E. Nägelsbach. 4. Aufl. Leipzig 1883. 184 p.

Aug. Müller, Hebräische Schulgrammatik. Halle 1878. XII, 302 p. — Paradigmentafeln zur hebr. Sch. Ibid. 1879. 19 p.

K. W. E. Nägelsbach, Hebräische Grammatik als Leitfaden für den Gymnasial- und akademischen Unterricht. 4. verb. u. verm. Aufl. besorgt von Karl Nägelsbach. Leipz. 1880. XII, 310 p.

Aug. Herrm. Schick, Hebräisch-Deutsches und Deutsch-Hebräisches Übungsbuch. Im Anschluss an Nägelsbach's hebr. Grammatik. Leipzig. I. Theil. Die Formenlehre. Erste Hälfte. 2. verb. u. verm. Aufl. 1875. XII, 80 p. — Zweite Hälfte [„Hebräisches Übungsbuch"] 1862, 146 p. — II. Theil. Die Syntax. Erste Hälfte. Syntax des Nomen. 1876, 168 p.

G. H. Seffer, Elementarbuch der hebräischen Sprache. 7. Aufl. Leipzig 1883, 378 p.

G. Stier, Hebräisches Übungs- und Lesebuch. Leipz. 1880, 154 p.

— —, Kurzgefasste hebräische Grammatik für Gymnasien. Leipz. 1881. X, 122 p.

Friedr. Uhlemann, Anleitung zum Übersetzen aus dem Deutschen in das Hebräische für Gymnasien. Berlin. Erster Cursus. 1839. XII, 212 p. — Zweiter Cursus. 1841. VIII, 208 p.

*A. B. Davidson, An Introductory Hebrew Grammar, with progressive Exercises in Reading and Writing. 5th ed. Edinburgh 1882. VIII, 198 p.

C. J. Ball, The Merchant Taylor's Hebrew Grammar. London [1878]. X, 163 p.

— —, A Hebrew Primer adapted to the Merchant Taylor's Hebrew Grammar. London [1879]. 270 p. and Glossaries.

T. Bowman, A new easy and complete Hebrew Course: containing a Hebrew Grammar, with copious Hebrew aud English Exercises, strictly graduated; also a Hebrew-English and an English-Hebrew Lexicon. In two Parts. I: Regular verbs etc. II: Irregular verbs etc. Edinburgh 1879. 1882. XVI, 208 p. XVI, 423 p. [Syntaxis non habetur.]

VII.

Raph. Bendit, Hebräisches Vocabularium für jüdische Schulen. Frankfurt a. M. 1872. VIII, 144 p.

L. H. Kapff, Hebräisches Vocabularium in alfabetischer Ordnung, mit Zusammenstellung von Synonymen, gleich und ähnlich lautenden Wörtern und analogen Formen. Bearbeitet u. herausgeg. von L. Ableiter. Leipzig 1881. VII, 178 p.

G. Stier, Hebräisches Vocabularium. 2. Aufl. Leipzig. Erster oder grammatisch geordneter Teil. 1871. 135 p. — Zweiter oder sachlich geordneter Teil. 1871. 79 p.

Raehse, Grammatisch geordnetes hebr. Vocabularium. Halle 1883. 42 p.

William R. Harper, Hebrew Vocabularies. Second edition. Chicago, Ill. 1882. 125 p.

Chrestomathia.

I. Legendi exercitia.[1]

1. א ב ג ד ז ח י נ ע ר שׁ שׂ ת. רדבת אעשׁוג.
   $ā$— חָג יָד רָב שָׁב עָב עָשׁ עָב שָׁת שָׁשׁ גָע נָא אָח אָב אָז.

2. ל מ ס ק. $ĕ$— , —ִ , —ֵ , $ē$. זֵד חֵת[p] מֵת עֵט עֵד נֵר רֵק לֵב נֵס יֵשׁ אֵשׁ אֵל אֵד אֵת עֵז שֵׁת[p] שֵׁב. אִי מִי חִיק ‖ —ִי , i שִׁיר עִיר רִיב אִישׁ קִיר מִי לִי

3. ח ר ב צ. —ֹ , וֹ , $ō$. עוֹג[p] קוֹל לוֹב[p] אוֹת מוֹת טוֹב חוֹד חֹד הֹדִי אוֹר נוֹד[p] אוֹ לוֹ. קֹל לֹג לֹא קֹר צֹר[p] וּ , $ū$ סוּס מוּב חוּג חוּם הוּא צוּר לוֹ.

4.[2] מַס נַן צַץ כַּף[3] פַּף. כְּמִנְפָץ. יָם שָׁם שָׁם כֵּן אֵין חוֹן רָע קֵץ צִיץ לָךְ בֵּן אֵיךְ עוֹף סוּף הֵם חֵן עֵץ סוּף חֵן שָׁם קוּם אָן[p] יוֹם קָם קוֹץ אֵם.

5. נָחָר זָכַר זָהָב אָדָם שָׁמָן עָפָר וָלָד הָרָן[p] הָגָר[p] אָשָׁם רָעָב שָׁכָר לָבָן[p] חָמֵשׁ עָקֵב הָעֵץ לָכֵן אֲשֶׁר[p] רָחֵל[p] שָׁלֵם שְׁלֵו הָעִיר יָמִים שָׁנִים אָחִיו אָבִיו נָוִין אָשִׁית ‖ הָאוֹר מָקוֹם יָדוֹ אָכֹל לֵב

[1] p = nomen proprium. [2] §1c. [3] §5b1.

מָגוֹג נָחוֹרᵖ לָאוֹרᵖ בָּרָךְ שָׁפוֹט עָצַר אָרוּר הָיָה
עָשׂוּ כָּגוּר אָסוּר נָסוּ לָנוּ עֵינֵי חָדַל מֵעֵץ עָשׂוּᵖ
מֵאִישׁ חֲבִיא לֵוִיᵖ שְׁנֵיᵍ מֵאוֹת אַלּוֹן ׀ וִיהִי אִישָׁךְ
צִידֹךְᵖ קִיטֹרᵖ ׀ אֲהוֹ מַכֵּה אָדָם עוֹלָם מוֹאָבᵖ לֶמֶשׁ
חֹרֶשׁ חֹרֶג רָבַץ רוֹמֵשׂ יָצָא עָבַד יוֹסֵףᵖ קוֹלִי אָתָי ׀
סוּרוּ קוּמוּ עוּגָב רוּחִי רֵחוֹ ‖ אָחִיךָ עָשִׂיתָ תּוֹלִידוֹ[1]
יָדֵינוּ רְאִיתָ.

6.[2] בַּב גַּג דַּד כַּךְ פַּפ תַּת. בֵּן בֵּין בָּא בֹּא בּוֹ
בּוֹר. גֵּרᵖ גַּד גֵּו גּוּר גּוֹי. דָּןᵖ דּוֹר דָּם דִּין. כֹּל
כֵּן כּוּשׁᵖ כּוֹס כִּי. פּוּךְ פּוּר פִּי. חֵת הֹר ׀ תֹּסֶף תֹּפֵשׂ
פָּרוֹת גָּדוֹל בֶּגֶד כָּבֵד תֵּלֵךְ תָּמוֹת חֲטִיבֵי דָּבָר גָּלוּי
פִּיהָ וָאִירָא, כִּי עֵירֹם אָנֹכִי וָאֵחָבֵא:[3]

7.ᵃ⁻ עַל עַד נַם נֵן חַי רַק רַע קַח קַל אַל
אַף שַׂק בַּהּ פַּף ׀ שָׁבַת אָמַר אָכַל לָקַח יָלַד יָדַע
שָׁדַיᵖ אֵלַי אֹכַל אָמַר רֹעִי אוּלַי יוּכַל.

8.[4] דַּרְדַּר מַבְדִּיל יַחְדָּו נַפְתָּלִיᵖ שְׁמַעְתִּי חָרַגְתִּי.
אַנְשֵׁי אַבְרָםᵖ. אָכַלְתָּ כָּתַבְתָּ נָפַלְתְּ יָלַדְתְּ שָׁלַלְתִּי ׀
בָּךְ אָךְ בֵּרַךְ. זָכַרְתָּ מֵאֲנָה יָכַדְתָּ זָכַדְתְּ צָחֲקָה יָפָת
יָרַד חֵשֶׁת יוֹסֵף יָשֵׁם.

9.[5] צַדִּיק חַיַּת עַמּוֹן מַתָּן דִּבֶּר קִוּוּ צִוָּה. וַיְבַךְ
וַיֵּשְׁתְּ וַיְמָה. הַיּוֹם הַיָּם הַשָּׁם הַנָּחָשׁ. אַף ׀ גָּבַהּ
נֹגַהּ יִגְבַּהּ תִּרְמַהּ. עַמָּהּ כֹּחָהּ וְרָעָה אִישָׁהּ קוֹמָתָהּ.

---

[1] §8a 1. [2] §6a. [3] §7e. [4] §5a.b. [5] §6d.c.

Chrestomathia I.

¹10. יְהִי סְדֹם ᵖ פְּרִי שְׁמוֹ שְׁנֵי מְאֹד גְּבוּל שְׁלִישִׁי.
לְהַשְׂכִּיל בְּצַלְמֵנוּ לְהַשְׁקוֹת. פְּנֵי תְהוֹם ²אֲפָלוּ שָׂרָצוּ
מַלְכוּ עָבְדוּ חָרְפוּ בִּינֶךָ גָּחְנְךָ. חֲצָצֵי יַחְדְּלוּ
מַחְשֶׁבֶת מַמְלָכוֹת. דַּבְּרוּ תַגְבּוּל חַשְׁבֵּי מְרַגְּלִים.

—ʰ.11. אִם מָן עִם מִשְׁפָּט מְדַבֵּר אֲשִׁיבוֹ לַזֶּה
לִקְבֹּר יִשְׁפֹּט יִגְדַּל יְשָׁפְמִי וַיִּקְבְּרוּ וְנִפְקְחוּ וַיֵּשְׁבוּ.
גֶּבֶר שָׁשִׁים אָמוּ מֵעַל יָפְרַד יָקְוּוּ נֶגֶד וַיִּפַּח וַיֹּדַע
תְּשִׁישִׁי וַיִּקַּח. מִפְּנֵי מִפְּרִי מִבְּשָׂרִי | תַּמְבִּיר הֻשְׁחָתָה
יִקְרָא יְשַׁלַּח || —ᵘ יָד לָקַח יָקַם קָבֶר שְׁלָחַי גֹּלָב
גַּנְבָרָה. אֲמִנָם שְׁלָחָן.

³12. —ē, ě אֲגָדֵל אֶבֶן אֶסְתֵּר אֶשְׁמֹר נֶחְמָד
עֶשְׂרִים חֶבְרוֹן ᵖ. וַיּוֹלֶד וַיִּנָּחֵם | לָכֶם לֶחֶם לְחֵן
אָתֶם מְכֶרְכֶם שְׁעַרְתֶּם קַמְתֶּם וְדַעְתֶּן. דְּבַר כְּפַר
אָפֵס. בָּבֶל ᵖ שְׁכֶם ᵖ בַּרְזֶל גֹּרֶן חָתָג הֶעָרִים הֶחָתִים.
דַּרְכְּךָ שְׁמֶךָ כְּחִי יְחִי אֱחִי.

⁴13. —ŏ רְחָבוֹ רְחָבָה אַרְכּוֹ קָדְשְׁךָ אָנְכֶם
וַתְּכַלְמוּ הָכְרַת הָמְלַךְ הָפְקַד בָּאֳנוֹת אָכְלְכֶם חָדְשׁוֹ.
וַיָּקָם וַיֵּרֶד וַיֵּשֶׁב.

⁵14. ᵖ לָח תַּצְמִיחַ יֵדַע רָקַע מַגְבִּיהַּ נָגִיהַּ
מוֹרִיעַ. רֵיחַ הַנִּיחֹחַ.

⁶15. יָשׁוּבִי וַיֵּשְׁבוּ שׁוּב שָׁב תָּמוּן יְשׁוּבָן

---

¹ §5c. ² §8a2. ³ §4b. ⁴ §4c. ⁵ §4d. ⁶ §4e.f.

תֹּעָרְבִים יְנֻסוּ. צַדִּיקִם צַדִּיקָם שְׂמִי
וְאָשֹׁם עִירָם גּוֹיִם לֵוִים מְשׁוּעָתוֹ פּוֹעֵם (עָם).
16. יָשֵׁב (יֹשֵׁב) שֹׂנֵא שֹׁפֵנִי נָשָׂא לִלְבֹּשׁ שְׁמֵנִי
שֹׁד וְתִבֹּשֶׁשׁוּ שֹׁבְרִים קָשֶׁה.
17. שָׁנָה עָשָׂה שָׂח חָיָה אֵיבָה צִיָּה מִנְחָה
חֶרְבָּה חָכְמָה וְלָפָה חֶלְדָּה חָכְמָה אָכְלָה חָכְמָה
אָכְלָה הָיְתָה יְהוּדָה מִמֶּנָּה. הָמָּה חָנָה לָמָּה
לָמָה שָׁמָּה פָּרְעֹה כֹּה פֹּה גָּלֹה שָׂלְמָה חָנָּה
רָאֵה קָנֶה שָׂדֶה גָּלֹה אֵפֹה בָּנָה אָמְחָה יָבְנֶה
יְרֹאֶה מְקָנֶה שְׁמֹנֶה זֶה פֹּה שֵׁת. אָגָה.
18. פָּנֶיךָ אֵלֶיךָ חַיֶּיךָ גְּמַלַּיִךְ. תִּבְכֶּינָה תְּבֹאֶינָה
תִּסָּבֶינָה וַתַּחֲלִינָה ׀ פָּנָיו אָחָיו יָמָיו.
19. פָּארְךְ חָמָּאת יְצָאתָ. רֹאשׁ זֹאת צֹאן
תֹּאכַל וַיֹּאמֶר צֹאנוֹ. רֵאשִׁית מֵאתִי לֵאלֹהִים רִאשׁוֹן
וָאֹלִי. תִּצֶּאנָה תִּקְרֶאנָה תִּמְצֶאןָ גֵּיא שָׁוְא.
20. הִנּוֹ עֵדָה חָרְגוּ עָשֹׁה אֲשֶׁר עָמְרָה
אֹרֶחָה חָמֵשׁ אָכְלָה. וְרֵעַךְ גָּבְהוּ הַשְּׁאָבֹת בַּצֹּקִים
וַיֹּאחֲזוּ וְהִתְבָּרְכוּ תֵּאָכַלְנָה מֶרְכָּבֹת. וַיְחַלּוּ רֶגְנוּ
חֲלֻכְיָה חֲיוֹת אֱנוֹשׁ אֹכֶל חֳרִי שְׁבָלִים.
21. רָאֹה אַחֲרֵי הָאֹנִיָּה וְיַעֲקֹב הֶעָבִיד אֹהֶל
וְחָרַם הֶחֱרִיב מִמָּחֳרָת.

---

[1] §4g. [2] §2b. [3] §8a2. [4] §2c. [5] §10c. [6] §5d. [7] §5e.

¹22. אֱמֶת וֶאֱמֶת כֶּאֱמֶת אֲנִי וָאָנִי.
²23. מָלְאָם מִלְמַעְלָה תְּבַקְשׁוּ בַּלְאָמִּים.
³24. בֶּן־נֵכָר כָּל־עוֹף תִּמְשָׁל־בּוֹ.
⁴25. שֶׁרֶץ נֶפֶשׁ יָרֵק קֶדֶם דֶּרֶךְ חֶרְמֵשׁ שָׂדֶי
שֵׁבֶט בֹּקֶר גֹּפֶר כֹּפֶר ׀ עֶרֶב אֶרֶץ אֶבֶן חֶרֶב לֶחֶם
רֶחֶם דֶּשֶׁא. עֵדֶר עֵשֶׂב אֹרֶךְ חֹשֶׁךְ אֹהֶל אֹזֶן זֶרַע
פֶּסַח נֶגַע קֶמַח פֶּצַע צֶמַח צֹהַר שַׁחַם רַחַב אֹרַח
נַעַר פַּעַם לַחַם דַּעַת לֶחִי מָוֶת. לְחִי בְחִי. עַיִן
יַיִן קַיִץ תָּעִיב אַיִל וַיִת אַיִן בַּיִת.
⁵26. עֵינַיִם קַרְנַיִם אָזְנַיִם, רַגְלַיִם צָהֳרַיִם אַפַּיִם
נְתִיב שְׁנַיִם מָאתַיִם מַיִם שָׁמַיִם ⁶יְרוּשָׁלָיִם.

II. Exercitia transferendi ex Hebraeo.

A. Nomen (pag. 25*—34*).   B. Verbum (pag. 34*—47*).

I. מֵת מֵתִי מֵתָךְ מֵתוֹ מֵתִים מֵתֶיךָ. עִבְרִי
עִבְרִים הָעִבְרִים, עִבְרֵי יִשְׂרָאֵל⁷, עִבְרֵי הֲמוֹר אִמְרִי
חֲמוֹרִים הֶחֱלִיפוּ הֲמֹרֵיהֶם. גּוֹי גּוֹיִם, גּוֹיֵי הָאָרֶץ, הָאֱלֹהִים,
אֱלֹהֵי אַבְרָהָם⁸, אֱלֹהֵי אֱלֹהֵיכֶם אֱלֹהָיו אֱלֹהָהּ אֱלֹהֵיהֶם.
נְעוּרַי מְגוּרֵךָ מְגוּרֵיהֶם. חַיִּים, חַי לֹה, חַיֶּיךָ בְּחַיֶּיהֶם.
הֵיקֵר הִיקוּד הִיקְשָׁה צֹאנֵךָ צֹאנְכֶם צֹאנָם. כֹּה לָהֶּךְ. הָטוֹב
ה' וְצַדִּיק.

---

¹ §11*g*. ² §6*g*. ³ §8*b*. ⁴ §11*i*. ⁵ §13,1. ⁶ §38. ⁷ §9*b*. ⁸ §85*c.d*.

II. הִקָּה, הֲקַת עוֹלָם, הָקוֹת הָקֹתֶיךָ סִפָּתוֹ. אֲמִתָּם.
פִּתְּחָךָ כִּלּוֹתֵיכֶם. יָעָה, רָעַת הָאָדָם, רָעָתִי רְעַתְכֶם יָעָתְךָ
הָרָעוֹת. אֲחִיָּתְכֶם וַאֲחִיָּתְךָ, לַאֲחֻזַּת עוֹלָם. שֵׁי־בָתְךָ. הָעֲלָה,
עֲלַת הָעָם, וְעָלָתְךָ, עָלָתָם עֲלוֹת עֲלוֹתֵינוּ כְּלֻחֵיכֶם. תּוֹרַת
ה׳, וְתוֹרָתִי. נְתִיבָתִי, נְתִיבוֹת עוֹלָם. נְתִיבוֹתֶיהָ נְתִיבוֹתֵיהֶם
בְּעָרַי שָׁדָם[p], הַמְּעָרוֹת. הֲגַרַת בַּהֲגוֹרָתוֹ.

III. קוֹל בְּקֹלִי קָלְךָ קוֹלָן קֹלוֹת. חֲלוֹם חֲלֹמוֹ הֲחֲלֹמוֹת,
חֲלֹמוֹת שֶׁקֶר, הֲלֹמֹתֵינוּ. דּוֹר, לְדֹרֹת עוֹלָם, לְדֹרֹתֵיכֶם
לְדֹרֹתָם. בְּרֵיהוֹב. בְּאֵר, בְּאֵרוֹת הַמַּיִם. רָוּחַ רוּחִי רוּחֲךָ
יֻחֲךָ רוּחֲכֶם רוּחוֹת.

IV. יוֹנָה יוֹנָתִי יוֹנָתֵי יוֹנִים, c. יוֹנֵי. תְּאֵנָתִי תְּאֵנִים. סְאָה
סְאתַיִם. תְּחִלַּת הַחָכְמָה יִרְאַת ה׳.

§ 23. קָצִיר הַטִּים, קְצִירְךָ קְצִירְכֶם. הַפָּלִיט, פְּלִיטֵי
אֶפְרַיִם[p], פְּלֵיטְכֶם. פְּהָקָהּ. בְּעִיפָהּ. קְדוֹשִׁים. נְבִיאֵי נְבִיאֶיךָ
נְבִיאֶיהָ, הֶהָמוֹן, הֲמוֹן גּוֹיִם. הָאָדוֹן, אֲדֹנִי[1] יוֹסֵף[p],
אֲדוֹנֶיךָ אֲדֹנָי | מְקוֹם שְׁכֶם[p], הַמְּקוֹמוֹת בִּמְקוֹמֹתֵיכֶם. חֶצְיוֹן
עֶלְיוֹן. אֲחֻזַּת הָאָחוּזוֹת. הַמָּאוֹר מְאִירַת. לְשׁוֹן שֶׁקֶר,
לְשׁוֹנְךָ לְשֹׁנוֹת | בְּנִקְיוֹן, נְקִיוֹן שִׁנַּיִם. קָדוֹשׁ אֲנִי ה׳
אֱלֹהֵיכֶם.

§ 24. I. בַּמִּשְׁפָּט, מִשְׁפַּט הַיָּתוֹם, מִשְׁפָּטְךָ, בְּמִשְׁפָּטִים,
בְּמִשְׁפְּטֵי ה׳, מִשְׁפָּטָיו. מִגְדָּל חֲנַנְאֵל. מְגִלָּתָהּ. מִדְבַּר
קָדֵשׁ, מִדְבָּרָהּ. מִסְפַּר הָעִבְרִים. מִשְׁקַל הַזָּהָב, מִשְׁקָלָם.
בְּאָכְלוֹ פְּרִי־ה׳[p], וּבְאָכְלָהּ מַאֲכָלְכֶם. כּוֹכָב אֱלֹהֵיכֶם, לַכּוֹכָבִים,
כְּכֹבֵיהֶם. מַלְאַךְ ה׳. מַלְאָכוֹ לַמַּלְאָכִים, מַלְאֲכֵי דָוִד[p].

---

[1] § 19d.

וּבְהֵיכָלוֹ, הֵיכְלֵי שֵׁן | בְּיוֹשְׁבָם, לְמוֹשְׁבֹתָם מוֹשְׁבוֹתֵיהֶם | מוֹרָא.

II. הַשּׁוֹפֵט שֹׁפְטֵי שֹׁפְטֶיךָ שֹׁפְטֵיהֶם. וַיֵּשֶׁב, יֹשֵׁב הָאָרֶץ, וְיֹשְׁבֶיהָ. לָאֹרֵב הָאֹרְבִים, עָרְבֵי נַחַל. אֲבִי דָוִד, אָבִיו, סְבָכָה הֹחֵן הֹתֵן לְהִתְנוֹ נָתֵן גְּאַלְכֶם סְנֶאֲךָ, שֹׂנְאֵי צִיּוֹן, שֹׂנְאוּ שֹׂנְאֵיהֶם. לַכֹּהֲנִים, כֹּהֲנֵי ה', כֹּהֲנָיו. בְּמֹשְׁלוֹ. מוֹעֲדֵי ה'. | בַּמִּזְבֵּחַ, מִזְבַּח ה', מִזְבְּחֵי מִזְבְּחֹתֶיךָ הַמִּזְבְּחוֹת מִזְבְּחוֹתֶיךָ. מְעַשֵּׁר, מַעֲשַׂר (מַעְשַׂר) הַדָּגָן.

III. יָדְךָ בְּיֶדְכֶם יָדַיִם יָדֶיךָ יְדֵיכֶם. דַּם הָאָדָם, דָּמוֹ, דְּמֵי הֶהָבֶל, דְּמֵיכֶם דָּמֶיךָ. דָּגִים, דְּגֵי הַיָּם | שֵׁם הָעִיר, שֵׁם-אֲבִיכֶםp, שָׁנִים בִּשְׁמוֹתָם. הָעֵץ הָעֵצִים, עֲצֵי גֹפֶר, עֲצֵיךָ עֵצֶיךָ. | מָוֶת וְחַיִּים בְּיַד-לָשׁוֹן.

§ 25. דְּבַר ה', דְּבָרִי, דְּבָרְךָ, דְּבָרֶךָ, דְּבָרוֹ וּדְבָרֵנוּ וְדִבְרֵי דְבָרָיו דְּבָרֶיהָ וְדִבְרֵיהֶם דִּבְרֵיp יוֹסֵף. בְּטוּר אֵשׁ, בְּשַׂרְךָ שֹׁעַר שָׂעִיר, שְׂעָרֶךָ. זְקַן אַהֲרֹןp, זְקָנֶךָ זְקֵנְכֶם. שְׁלָלָה שְׁלַלְכֶם. נְחַשׁ נְחֹשֶׁת. לְרַעְבָּם. נְהַר מִצְרַיִםp, וַהֲרֹתֶיהָ. צְבָא הַשָּׁמַיִם, צְבָאֲךָ צְבָאָיו, אֱלֹהֵי הַצְּבָאוֹת, צִבְאוֹת ה', צִבְאוֹתֵינוּ. | בְּעָשְׁנוֹ, עֲשַׁן הָעִיר, עֲשָׁנָהּ. עֲפַר הָאָרֶץ. עֲפָרָיו. קְהַל הֲמִיסִים. הַלְּכָה. חֲכָמֶיהָ. הַלְלוּ ה', הַלְלֵל הַהֹלְלִים הֵמָּסוּ.

לְבָבָם. שַׁעַר רֹאשׁוֹ, שְׂעָרוֹ. | זַקְנְךָ חֲצֵרוֹת הַחֲצֵרוֹתָיו, בְּחַצְרוֹת אֱלֹהֵינוּ. יְרֵכָהּ. | יִשְׁנַיִם עֲלָה הַחֲלָלִים מְלֵאָה טְמֵאִים שְׁלָלָהּ טְבוּעִים יְבֵשׁוֹת רִבְקָה מְלֵאוֹת צְמֵאִים.

§ 26. [ע"ע] הִצַּו הִצְּךָ הִצַּיְו, הִצֵּי גִּבּוֹר. קֵן, קַן-צִפּוֹר. קוֹף קוֹפֵף קָדִים. קָצֵהוּ קָצוֹ קְצֵנוּ. צֵל עָם, בְּצֵל קוֹרָתִי.

שְׁפוֹ שְׁנַיִם שְׁנֵיהֶם, שְׁנֵי רְשָׁעִים. לְבְכֶם לְבוֹת. אָמָּה
אִמְקָן אִמְתָם אֲמִתֵּנוּ | כַּעֲנֻנֵּוּ בַעֲנִים, כָּעָף נְחֹשֶׁת. | כֹּל,
כָּל־יוֹם, כָּל־הַיּוֹם, פָּנָה כֻּלָנוּ¹, לְכֻלָּם. הָק־עוֹלָם, הֻקַּד
וְהָחֲזָקִים, הֻקֵּי הָאֱלֹהִים. בְּתָמִי. חַמּוֹ, בָּהֶם קָצִיר.
כְּרָבָם, וְרֹב דָּגָן. תְּפִים תָּפַיִךְ בְּעוֹ ה', עֻזְּכֶם עֻזָּה. |
עַם הָאָרֶץ, הָעָם עִמְּךָ הַשָּׁמַיִם, עַמֵּי הָאָרֶץ. שַׁקּוּ שַׁקֵּיהֶם.
בַּן־אֱדֶרֶךְ,ᵖ בְּנֵי בָנִים. כַּח פַּרְעֹה,ᵖ כַּפֶּךָ כַּפַּיִם בְּכַפֵּיהֶם,
כַּפֵּי אַהֲרֹן. שַׂר־צָבָא הַטּוּר שָׂרְכֶם וְשָׂרָיוּך, שָׂרֵי פַרְעֹה.
צָרֵינוּ, צָרֵי יְהוּדָה. הַדָּבָר הָרַע הַזֶּה, הַטּוֹב וְהָרַע,
רָעִים, רָעֵי גוֹיִם. הָדָר², הַר ה', הָהָדָה³ הָהָה⁴, הָרִים
הָרֵי, בַּהֲרָרָם⁵, הַרְרֵי צִיּוֹן. פָּרִים פָּרֶיהָ. יָם; יָם הַמֶּלַח,
יָם־כִּנֶּרֶתᵖ, יַם־סוּף, יָמָהּ יָמִים. פַּת־לָהֶם, פְּתִים.
צִדֵּי הַמִּשְׁכָּן. בְּצִדֵּיהֶם. | גְּמַלֶּיךָ, קְטַנִּים. עַם קָדוֹשׁ
אַתָּה לַה' אֱלֹהֶיךָ:

[ע"נ]. אַף ה', בְּאַפֶּךָ, אַפַּיִם, אַפֵּי דָוִד, אַפֶּיהָ,
גַּג הַמִּגְדָּל, לְגַגֵּךְ גַּגּוֹת. יְדְךָ יָדֶךָ. אַשּׁוּ אֶשְׁכֶם. לְעֵת
עֶרֶב, בְּעִתּוֹ, הָעִתִּים, עִתּוֹת.

§ 28. I. הִנֵּה דַרְכֵּךְ לְדַרְכְּכֶם הֶדְּרָכִים דַּרְכֵּי דְּבָרָיו דְּבָרוֹ⁶
דִּבְרֵי ה'. מֶלֶךְ בָּבֶלᵖ, מַלְכֵיהֶם. כָּלֵב כְּלָבִים כַּלְבֵּךְ,
כַּלְבֵּי צֹאנֶךָ. כַּרְמֶךָ כַּרְמְךָ וּכְרָמֵינוּ וְכַרְמְכֶם. יֶלֶד
הַיְלָדִים יַלְדֵי וִילָדֵיהֶן. לָחֶם לַהֲמְכֶם. רַחְמָה. נֶפֶשׁ
הָאָדָם, נַפְשֶׁךָ, נְפָשׁוֹת, נַפְשׁוֹת אֶבְיוֹנִים, לְנַפְשׁוֹתֵיכֶם. רַגְלָהּ
רַגְלֵיכֶם. קֶרֶן קַרְנֵךְ קַרְנְכֶם קַרְנַיִם. קַרְנֵי רְשָׁעִים, בְּקַרְנָיו
בְּקַרְנֵיהֶם; קְרָנוֹת, קַרְנוֹת הַמִּזְבֵּחַ. | עֶבֶד לַעֲבָדְךָ עֲבָדִים

---

¹ § 22iδ. ² § 17cγ. ³ § 20c. ⁴ § 11f. ⁵ § 5d. ⁶ § 22kβ.

עֲבָדֵיהֶם. חֶסֶד חַסְדּוֹ חֲסָדִים, חַסְדֵי ה'. הָעֲצָבִים.
אֵלֶּה, בְּאַלְפֵי יְהוּדָה, אֲלָפִים. אֶבֶן אַבְנוּ אַבְנֵיהֶם אֲבָנֶיךָ
בָּאֲבָנִים, אַבְנֵי זִכָּרוֹן. עַצְמְכֶם עַצְמֵי עֲצָמִים, עֲצָמוֹת,
עַצְמָתָם עַצְמֹתֵיהֶם. בְּחֶרֶב חַרְבְּכֶם חֲרָבוֹת, בְּחַרְבוֹת
צֻרִים. אֶרֶץ הָאָרֶץ בְּאַרְצוֹ הָאֲרָצוֹת בְּאַרְצֹתָם. | הַדֶּלֶת
בְּדַלְתּוֹ דְלָתַיִם דְּלָתֶיךָ, וְדַלְתֵי הַבַּיִת, דְּלָתוֹת, דַּלְתוֹת
נְחֹשֶׁת. קֶשֶׁת וּבְקַשְׁתִּי הַקְּשָׁתוֹת וְקַשְׁתוֹתָם¹ | צֶדֶק צִדְקֶךָ.
קֶבֶר קִבְרוֹ קְבָרִים קְבָרֵינוּ, קִבְרֵי מַלְכֵי יִשְׂרָאֵל. בְּקִרְבָּהּ
קִרְבִּי. שְׁקָרִים בְּשִׁקְרֵיהֶם. הַפְּגָרִים שֶׁקֶל שְׁקָלִים, שִׁקְלֵי
זָהָב. נִזְמָהּ, נִזְמֵי הַזָּהָב. בְּבִטְנָהּ בֶּטֶן. שְׁלֹשָׁה. בֶּתֶר
בְּתָרוֹ בְּתָרָיו. בִּרְכַּיִם, בִּרְכֵּי יוֹסֵף. בִּרְכֶּיהָ.

II. זַרְעֲךָ זְרָעָם. לְפִצְעֵי פְצָעַי. פֶּשַׁע. פִּשְׁעֵי
יִשְׂרָאֵל. נִגְעֲךָ נְגָעִים. פֶּתַח הַבַּיִת, הַפִּתְחָה הַפֶּתַח
פְּתָחוֹ פְּתָחִים פְּתָחֶיהָ, פִּתְחֵי עוֹלָם. | וְעָרָיו, נַעֲרֵי דָוִד.
בְּעֻלָה. בְּעָלִים בְּעָלֶיהָ לְבַעֲלֵיהֶן, בַּעֲלֵי הָעִיר. הַשַּׁעֲרָה
שְׁעָרֶיךָ. נַעַל נַעֲלֵי נַעֲלָהּ, נְעָלִים בַּנְּעָלִים וְנַעֲלֵיכֶם בְּרַגְלֵי
נַחֲלָה נַחֲלֵי מַיִם. פַּעֲמַיִם, מֵאָה פְעָמִים. זַעַם זַעֲמוֹ
זַעְמְךָ זַעֲמֶךָ.

III. בְּשִׁבְטֵךְ הַשְּׁבָטִים לְשִׁבְטֵיהֶם, שִׁבְטֵי יִשְׂרָאֵל.
עִמְקֵהּ הָעֲמָקִים עֲמָקֶךָ. עֲטָפָם. עָזְרֵנוּ. הַחֵלֶק חֵלֶק
חֲלָקִים חֶלְקֵיהֶם. חָפְצוּ הַחֲפָצִים הֲפָצֶיךָ חֶלְבּוֹ וּמֵחֶלְבֵּהֶן.²

IV. פָּרֶיךָ. תֻּשְׁעִי. הָאֵךְ לָאָרֶץ. בְּקָרִים. אֹזֶן
אָזְנְכֶם אָזְנַי אָזְנֵיךָ אָזְנֵיהֶם, בְּאָזְנֵי הָעָם. בַּחֹדֶשׁ הַשֵּׁנִי,
חָדְשׁוֹ הֶחֳדָשִׁים חֳדָשָׁיו, חָדְשֵׁי הַשָּׁנָה. רֹמַח יָמִים

¹ § 6eβ. ² § 22kβ.

רִמְחֵיהֶם. נְגָדָם. אֲדָמָה. תֵּבָה. אֲחֶיךָ אֲחָיוֹת, אֲחָיוֹת חַיִּים.
פָּעֳלְךָ פָּעֳלוֹ כְּפָעֳלוֹ פָּעֳלִים. בְּרֵנִי, בְּרֵנוֹת דָּגָן, בִּינָה.
קָדְשְׁךָ קָדְשֵׁיכֶם, קֹדֶשׁ הַקֳּדָשִׁים, קָדְשֵׁי דָוִד. אֹהֶל הָאֹהֱלָה
אָהֱלֹה[1] בְּאָהֳלְךָ אֹהָלִים בְּאָהֳלֶיךָ אֹהֳלֵיכֶם בְּאָהֳלֵי־שֵׁם.[p]
V. כֶּסֶף כַּסְפֶּךָ כַּסְפֵּיהֶם. בֶּגֶד בִּגְדוֹ, בִּגְדֵי עֵשָׂו.
הַצּוּר תָּמִים פָּעֳלוֹ[2] כִּי כָל־דְּרָכָיו מִשְׁפָּט: פַּלְגֵי־מַיִם
לֶב־מֶלֶךְ בְּיַד־ה'׃

§ 29. עֵין הָעַיִן, עֵין הַמָּיִם, עֵינַיִם, עֵינֵי ה', בְּעֵינֶיךָ
בְּעֵינֶיךָ עֵינֵיכֶם. יַיִן יֵינְךָ, יֵין הַלְּבָנוֹן. הָאַיִל, אֵיל
הָעֹלָה, אֵלִים. הָעַיִט, לְעֵיט הָרִים. צֵיד צַיִד. לַיִל
(לַיְלָה[3]), לֵילוֹת.

§ 30. שְׁבִי שִׁבְיָה שָׁבְיָךָ. בְּכִי בִּכְיִי. לִחְיָה, לֶחֱיוֹ, לְחֵיהֶם!
אֲרִי אֲרָיוֹת אֲרָיִים. חֲלָיִים חֳלָיֵינוּ. עֲנִי עַמִּי, עֲנִי עֲנָוֶךָ.

§ 31. A. לָעָנִי, עֲנָיֶיךָ, נְקִיִּים, עֲנִיֵּי עַמִּי. בַּעַל הַשּׁוֹר נָקִי׃
B. מַחֲזֵה שָׁוְא. מַשְׁקֵהוּ הַמַּשְׁקִים. מַעֲשֵׂנוּ, מַעֲשֵׂה ה',
מַעֲשִׂים מַעֲשֵׂי מַעֲשֶׂיךָ מַעֲשֵׂיכֶם, מַעֲשֵׂי יָדֶיךָ. מַחְסֶה
(מַחְסִי), מַחְסֵה כָזָב, מַחְסִי (מַחֲסִי), מַחְסֵהוּ. מַחֲנֵהוּ. הַחֹזֶה,
בַּד[p] חֹזֵה דָוִד, הַחֹזִים הוֹזֵי. מֹשֶׁה אַהֲרֹן, מֹשְׁךָ מַשּׂוּא
בֵּטוֹת מַטּוֹתָם. ‖ גְּדֹלִים[4] מַעֲשֵׂי ה'׃ עַל־אֱלֹהִים יִשְׁעִי
וּכְבוֹדִי צוּר־עֻזִּי מַחְסִי בֵּאלֹהִים[5]׃ טוֹב ה' לַכֹּל וְרַחֲמָיו
עַל־כָּל־מַעֲשָׂיו׃

שָׂדִי שָׂדֶיךָ; שְׂדוֹת שֹׂדְתֵיכֶם. קְנֵה הַמִּדָּה, קְנֵה
הַקָּנִים, קְנֵי מְנוֹרָה. נְוֵה צַדִּיקִים, נָוֵהוּ, פָּנֶיךָ, לִפְנֵי
מִזְבְּחֶךָ עַמֵּנוּ צָרֶיךָ בְּיֵיהֶם חֲלֻמֹּתָיו רֶגֶל הִרְבַּתָם

---

[1] § 22iβ. [2] § 85e. [3] § 20cα. [4] § 85d. [5] § 10cδ.

סַלְעֵי שְׁבָרִים הֶחָכָמִים אֲדֹנֵיכֶם חֲנִיָּה מְשָׁלוּ שַׁקִּים הַמֶּלֶךְ רָשׁוּתֵיהֶם זְהָבָם פָּפֶיךָ שְׁלָלְכֶם יֶשְׁבֶיהָ פֶּשַׁע הַגְּלֵה מְכַסֵּהוּ גְּבוּרֶיךָ קִלָּה לָהֶם שָׂרֵיהֶם אֱלֹהֵינוּ צֶלְצָלֵי בְּשַׁמֵּיהֶם יָרְבוּ מִגְדָּלִים טָבֶךָ סֶלַע עֲלֹתֶיךָ מַלְאָכָיו הִנֵּה תָּפֵךְ מַלְכְּכֶם הַבְּרִיתִי הֲבֵרֹתִי אָכְלֵךְ, יֵינֵךְ וְהָגְלָּתִים שְׁעָרֵיהֶם מֵחֲסוּ צַלְמֵיכֶם כְּהָקָתָם כַּלָּתֵךְ פַּדִּים הַלַּלַּיְלָה עִינֶיךָ שִׁבְטֶיךָ לַהֲיַךְ פִּתְחֵיהֶם מָגִנָּיו כְּהֶבְיָהֶם שָׂדִים בְּצַלְמֵנוּ שָׂרֵשֶׁךְ חָרְבֹתֵיהֶם גְּשָׁמִים תְּשׁוּקָתֵךְ לְפִשְׁעֲכֶם הָקֵךְ לְהֵיכָלָם. מֵתֵי מִלְחָמָה, בְּתָם־לְבָבִי, עַבְדִּי אַבְרָהָם[p], מִכְסֵה הַתֵּבָה, עַצְמוֹת יוֹסֵף, מִשְׁלֵי שְׁלֹמֹה, חַכְמֵי לֵב, חֲלַל חֶרֶב, וְאֵילֵי צֹאנֶךָ, שַׁעֲרֵי צִיּוֹן, שִׁיבַת צִדְקֵךְ, נְבִיאֵי ה', פֻּשְׁמֵי בְרָכָה, רַגְלֵי הַבְּהֵנִים, כּוֹכְבֵי הַשָּׁמַיִם, עַם אֶחָד.

§ 33. I. דְּגַת הַיָּם, וְגָתָם. בֶּן־מְאַת שָׁנָה[1]. שְׁנַת הָרָעָב, שְׁנָתוֹ, שְׁנָתַיִם, שָׁנִים שָׁנֵינוּ, שְׁנֵי חַיֵּי שָׂרָה[p], שְׁנוֹת חַיִּים, שִׂוֹתִי[p]. עֵצָה, עֲצַת הַזְּקֵנִים, עֵצוֹת. תּוֹעֲבַת מִצְרַיִם[p], תּוֹעֵבוֹת, תּוֹעֲבַת הַגּוֹיִם, תּוֹעֲבַתְךָ תּוֹעֲבֹתֵיהֶם.
II. מַמְלָכוֹת, בְּמַמְלְכוֹת הָאָרֶץ. לְמֶמְשֶׁלֶת הַיּוֹם. מַחֲשֶׁבֶת הָמָן[p], מַחֲשָׁבוֹת, מַחֲשָׁבוֹת לִבּוֹ, מַחְשְׁבֹתָם מַחְשְׁבוֹתֵיהֶם. מִשְׁפָּחוֹת, מִשְׁפְּחֹתָם. לְמִשְׁפְּחֹתֵיהֶם.

§ 34. נְקָמוֹת, נִקְמַת ה', נִקְמָתֵנוּ. רְבָבוֹת, רִבְבוֹת אֶפְרַיִם[p], בְּרִבְבֹתָיו. וְצוּחַת יְרוּשָׁלַם, צוֹחָתֶךָ. בִּרְכָתְךָ בְּרָכוֹת, בִּרְכוֹתֵיכֶם. נִבְלַת אִיזֶבֶל[p], נִבְלָתָם. | אֲחָתִי אֲחֹתַי. זַעֲקָתִי זַעֲקָתָם, זַעֲקַת סְדֹם[p]. צַעֲקָתוֹ[p].

---

[1] § 39i.

מַלְכַּת שְׁבָא[p]. עֲלָמוֹת. עַלְמַת רֶגֶךָ, עַלְמַת עַלְמָתוֹ וְעַלְמְבוֹת
עַלְמוֹתַיִךְ עַלְמֹתֵיכֶם. נְעָרוֹת, נַעֲרוֹת אֶסְתֵּר[p], וְנַעֲרֹתֶיהָ.
בִּקְעַת יְרִחוֹ[p], בְּקָעוֹת. שִׁפְחַת שָׂרָה, שִׁפְחָתְךָ הַשְּׁפָחוֹת
שִׁפְחֹתֵיכֶם. עֻמְלַת אִשָּׁה, טָבְלָתְךָ טָבְלַת טָבְלֹתֶיךָ.
שִׂמְחַת עוֹלָם, שִׂמְחָתִי שִׂמְחָתָם. מִנְחַת שָׁוְא, מִנְחָתֵךְ.
יִרְאַת אֱלֹהִים, בְּיִרְאָתֶךָ. אִמְרַת ה', אִמְרָתִי; אִמְרוֹת
ה' (אָבֵ' ψ 12, 7) אֲבָרוֹת טְהֹרוֹת | עֶגְלַת בָּקָר, עֶגְלוֹת
בֵּית אָוֶן[p]. חֶרְפַּת עַמּוֹ, חֶרְפָּתָם. | עָרְלַת לְבַבְכֶם, עָרְלַתְכֶם
הָעֲרֵלוֹת, עָרְלוֹת פְּלִשְׁתִּים[p], עָרְלֵיהֶם.

§ 36. I. מִשְׁפְּחֹתֵי מִשְׁפְּחוֹתֵיהֶם. מוֹלַדְתְּךָ, אֶרֶץ מוֹלַדְתּוֹ.
אַדֶּרֶת שֵׂעָר, אַדַּרְתּוֹ. | תוֹלָחוֹת. | טַבַּעַת הַמֶּלֶךְ, טַבַּעְתּוֹ
טַבְּעֹתֵיהֶם טַבְּעֹתָם. מִטְפַּחְתִּי. לְגֻלְגְּלֹתָם.

II. אֹגֶר אֲמָרִים אִגֶּרֶת הָאֲמָרוֹת. יוֹנַקְתּוֹ יוֹנְקוֹתָיו
יוֹנְקוֹתֶיהָ | הֲשִׁיאַתִי הַשֹּׁאתֵנוּ. | תִּפְאַרְתֵּנוּ.

§ 37. מַלְכוּת שָׁאוּל[p], מַלְכוּתְךָ. עֵלוּת יְהוּדָה, גָּלוּתֵנוּ.
מִצְרֵי מִצְרַיִם הַמִּצְרִית. תַּחְתִּים תַּחְתִּית תַּחְתִּיּוֹת.
הַפְּנִימִי הַפְּנִימִים הַפְּנִימִית הַפְּנִימִיּוֹת.

§ 38. I. בְּנֵי־אָחִיו אֲבוֹתֵינוּ בָּתֵּינוּ בְּתֵּנוּ אִשְׁתְּךָ אֲחוֹתֶךָ
בְּנוֹ בִנְתָם בְּנוֹתֵיהֶם אָבִיךְ אֲחִינוּ אָחִינוּ אִישֵׁךְ בָּנֶיךָ
אֲחוֹתֵנוּ אֲנִיָּתֶךָ בֵּיתוֹ אֲחִיךָ בְּנֵיכֶם וְאַמְהֹתָיו אָבִינוּ
בְּנֵה אָחִיךָ אָבִיךָ בְּנֹתֵינוּ לְאָחִיךָ, בֵּית אֲחִי אֲדֹנִי.

II. הֶעָרִים בְּפִיו כֻּלֹּךְ הַשָּׁמַיְמָה הָרָאשִׁים וְרֹאשׁוֹ
פִּיהָ מֵימֶיךָ. שְׁעָרֶיו־ירוֹ, רָאשֵׁי הֶהָרִים, עָרֵי הַגּוֹיִם,
מֵימֵי מִצְרַיִם, תַּחַת שְׁמֵי ה'.

Rep. I. תוֹעֲבֹתָם שִׁפְחָתְךָ נְטִיעֹתוֹ מִטְפְּחוֹתֶךָ שְׂמָחוֹת

Chrestomathia II A. § 39. § 44—46.

שְׁגִלְחֵיכֶם נִבְלָתְךָ עָלָתוֹ שִׂפְתוֹתָיו, צַעֲקַת הָעָם, בִּרְכוֹת טוֹב, נִשְׁבַּת הַיַּיִם, מִשְׁפְּחוֹת רְאוּבֵן.

II. עֲטֶרֶת זְקֵנִים בְּנֵי בָנִים וְתִפְאֶרֶת בָּנִים אֲבוֹתָם: אֲנִי עַבְדְּךָ בֶּן־אֲמָתֶךָ: תּוֹעֲבַת ה' שִׂפְתֵי שָׁקֶר: לֹא מַחְשְׁבוֹתַי מַחְשְׁבוֹתֵיכֶם וְלֹא דַרְכֵיכֶם דְּרָכַי נְאֻם ה':

§ 39. שִׁשָּׁה בָנִים, בָּנוֹת שֵׁשׁ, שֵׁשׁ שָׁנִים, שֵׁשֶׁת יָמִים. עֲשָׂרָה אֲנָשִׁים, פָּרִים עֲשָׂרָה, עֶשֶׂר שָׁנִים, עֲשֶׂרֶת יָמִים, עֲשֶׂרֶת הַדְּבָרִים. ‖ אַרְבָּעָה עָשָׂר כְּבָשִׂים, שְׁלֹשָׁה עָשָׂר פָּרִים, שְׁנַיִם עָשָׂר שִׁבְטֵי יִשְׂרָאֵל; שְׁתַּיִם עֶשְׂרֵה אֲבָנִים, שְׁלֹשׁ עֶשְׂרֵה עָרִים; עָרִים תְּשַׁע עֶשְׂרֵה. ‖ חֲמִשָּׁה עָשָׂר שֶׁקֶל, שְׁמֹנָה עָשָׂר אֶלֶף, אַרְבָּעָה עָשָׂר יוֹם, שְׁנֵים עָשָׂר אִישׁ, שְׁנֵי עָשָׂר בָּקָר; שְׁמֹנֶה עֶשְׂרֵה אַמָּה, שֵׁשׁ עֶשְׂרֵה נֶפֶשׁ, תְּשַׁע עֶשְׂרֵה שָׁנָה.

חָמֵשׁ שָׁנִים וְשִׁשִּׁים שָׁנָה, אַרְבָּעִים וְחָמֵשׁ שָׁנָה, שִׁבְעִים שָׁנָה וְחָמֵשׁ שָׁנִים. מֵאָה אִישׁ, מָאתַיִם שָׁנָה, עֶזְרִים מָאתַיִם, תְּשַׁע מֵאוֹת שָׁנָה, שְׁלֹשׁ מֵאוֹת שׁוּעָלִים. ‖ אֶלֶף אִישׁ, אֶלֶף פְּעָמִים, שִׁבְעַת אֲלָפִים פָּרָשִׁים, עֲשֶׂרֶת אֲלָפִים אִישׁ, מֵאָה אֶלֶף כָּרִים.

שְׁמֹנַת יָמִים, עֲשָׂרָה גְמַלִּים, שְׁתַּיִם עֶשְׂרֵה שָׁנָה, שֵׁשׁ מֵאוֹת כֶּסֶף. טוֹבִי־לִי תוֹרַת־פִּיךָ מֵאַלְפֵי זָהָב וָכָסֶף: בְּאַרְבָּעָה עָשָׂר לַחֹדֶשׁ. בְּאַרְבַּע עֶשְׂרֵה שָׁנָה לַמֶּלֶךְ חִזְקִיָּהוּ.[p] אֶלֶף כָּסֶף.

§ 44. 45. 46. I. בֵּאלֹהֶיךָ בַּחֲלוֹמִי בִּמְקוֹמֵנוּ לַעֲבָדָיו לִלְוֹתָם לִירֵאָיו כְּאָמְרָה[p] כִּירוּשָׁלַםִ מֵרָחֲבָה מֵהֶחָצֵר מֵעַמִּיָּה וֵאלֹהֶיךָ וְתַאֲוָתֵךְ וּבִגְדֵיכֶם וּמִשְׁפְּטֵי וִילָדִים

וַאדֹנָי וַחֲסָדָיו וּפְגָרֵיהֶם | מִתּוֹרָתֶךָ לְיָקְבוֹ מִשְׁפָּט
מְרַשְּׁעִים יְדָרֶכְךָ וּפִתְחֵיהֶם וְנָעֲלֵינוּ מִסְפְּרְךָ וּבוֹרְאֲכֶם
מְחַשֵּׁל מֵאַפְּכֶם לְרַעְבָם וַעֲצָבֶיךָ וּסְפָרִים מִצִּידִי מֵאָהֳלֶיךָ
מִקִּבְרֵיהֶם וּכְרָמֵינוּ מֵרַבְּכֶם וּבְגָדִים בְּבִטְחָם מִפְּנֵיהֶם
וְנִחֲלִים מִפִּרְיוֹ וּפְעָלְכֶם בִּנְעָרָיו כָּבֵדִים מִדַּרְכֵיכֶם בְּרֵחֶם
לִמְקֹמָתָם בְּשָׁמוֹתָם מִפָּדֶךָ מִפָּנֶיהָ וּפִגְרֵי מַלְכֵיהֶם,
בְּקָצֶה שָׁדֶחוּ, מִזְהַב אוֹפִיר^{p}, וְזָהָב^{1} הָאָרֶץ, בְּיַלְדֵי
הָעִבְרִים, וָחֵתָן הַמֶּלֶךְ, בְּצַד הַקֹּצְרִים, מִגְּמַלֵּי אֲדֹנָיו,
בִּרְקִיעַ הַשָּׁמַיִם, עֲצָם מֵעֲצָמַי, מִקְצֵה^{2} הַיַּרְדֵּן^{p}, מִקֶּרֶב עַמּוֹ,
בִּמְעָרוֹת צֻרִים. וּבְהִקָּתֵיהֶם וּלְשֹׁפְטִים וּכְנֹשְׂאֵי וְלִמְשָׁלִים
וּבִזְהַרְיָה וּבִלְשׁוֹנָם וְלָאֲלָפִים וּבְקַשְׁתִּי וּכְמִשְׁפָּטֵיהֶן
וּבַסְּלָעִים וְלָאֲלָלְכֶם וּמֵעֲוֹנוֹתֵיכֶם וּבְרִהְבָתָהּ וּמִבְּשָׂרֵי
וּלְאַלְפֵיהֶם וּמְעָרְךָ וּבְפָשְׁעָם וּכְמַדְבָּר וּבְלִבְכֶךָ | וּכְמוֹשַׁב
לֵצִים, וּלְיֹשְׁבֵי הָאָרֶץ, וּלְמִקְוֵה הַמַּיִם. נֵר לְרַגְלִי דְבָרֶךָ
וְאוֹר לִנְתִיבָתִי: אֵל גָּדוֹל ה' וּמֶלֶךְ גָּדוֹל עַל־כָּל־אֱלֹהִים:
הוּא צוּרִי וִישׁוּעָתִי: דָּמוֹ בְּרֹאשׁוֹ וַאֲחֵינוּ נְקִים:

II. וּכְמִשְׁלַחְךָ כְּדָמוּתוּ לַאֲנָשֶׁיךָ בַּעֲצָתְךָ וּשְׁנוֹתָם
וּשְׁנֵיהֶם וְאָתוֹ בִּכְלֵיהֶם וּמִנְחָתֵיכֶם וּמֵימֵיהֶם וּבְיָמֵיכֶם
וְלִבְךָ וּמִנְחָתִי וּבְמִשְׁפַּחְתּוֹ וְלִנְשֵׁיכֶם. | וּבְתֹכָחוֹת חֵמָה,
בִּימֵי אַדְרְכָּל^{p}, מִדִּבְרֵי שְׁלֹמֹה.

§ 54. כָּלַךְ מָלְכָה מָלְכוּ. שָׁמְרָה שָׁמַרְתִּי שְׁמַרְתֶּם שָׁמְרוּ
שָׁמַרְתִּי. מָכְרוּ מְכַרְתֶּם. זָכְרָה זָכַרְתְּ זָכַרְנוּ זָכְרִית זָכְרִית
כָּרַתְנוּ כָּרַתִּי כָּרֵת. שָׁכַב שָׁכַבְתָּ. סָגְרוּ סָגַרְתִּי רְדָפְתִי
רְדָפְתָּם. | שָׁלְחָה שְׁלַחְתֶּם שָׁלַחְתִּי. חָפְרוּ חָפְרוּ חָפַרְתִּי.

---

^{1} § 5d. 46a3. ^{2} § 6/3.

חָלַמְנוּ חֲלַמְתֶּם שְׁמַעְתֶּם שָׁמַעְתִּי שָׁמַעְנוּ שָׁמְעָה שָׁמַעְתְּ צָחַקְתִּי צָחַקְתְּ. יָדַעְנוּ יְדַעְתֶּן.
כָּבֵד כָּבְדָה כָּבְדוּ. קָרַב, קָרְבָה קָרַבְתִּי קָרַבְתָּ. זָקֵן זָקְנָה זָמַנְתִּי. חָפֵץ חָפְצָה חָפַצְנוּ. אָהֵב אָהֵב, אָהַב, אָהֲבָה, אָהַבְתְּ, אָהַבְתִּי ‖ יָכֹל יָכְלוּ יָכֹלְתִּי קָטֹנְתִּי. et

§ 55. 56. שְׁפֹט שְׁבוֹר לִשְׁפֹּט לִשְׁבֹּר לֶזְפֹּר לִלְבֹּשׁ מְקַבֵּר בְּשִׁפְךָ. | לִשְׁכַּב ‖ סְפֹר סִפְרוּ סִפְדוּ סְפַדְנָה קְבֹר קִבְרִי רְדֹף רִדְפוּ זְכֹר זִכְרוּ שְׁכַב שִׁכְבִי לְבַשׁ לִבְשִׁי חִדְלוּ | נָקְבָה שָׁפְטָה שָׁכְבָה שָׁכְנָה.

§ 57. אֶשְׁמֹר תִּשְׁמֹר נִשְׁמֹר יִשְׁמְרוּ תִּשְׁמְרוּ אֶשְׁמְרָה אֶשְׁמֹרָה. יִשְׁפֹּט יִשְׁפְּטוּ תִּשְׁפֹּךְ תִּשְׁפְּכִי תִּשְׁפְּכוּ יַקְבְּצוּ יִשְׁבַּתִּי תִּגְנְבוּ. | אֶגְדַּל יִגְדַּל יִשְׁכַּב יִשְׁכְּבוּ יִשְׁבְּבוּ לְשִׁכְבָה יִלְבְּשׁוּ יִקְרַב וְקָרַב נִקְרְבָה יִקְרְבוּ תִּקְרְבֶהָ תִשְׁאַל אִשְׁאַב תִּשְׁפַּחְנָה | יִשְׁכְּבוּן יִשְׁפְּכוּן תִּשְׁמְכוּן תִּשְׁמָעוּן.

§ 58. רֹבֵץ רֹבֶצֶת רֹבְצִים הָרֹמֵשׂ הָרֹמֶשֶׂת קֹבֵר קֹבְרִים קְבוּר קְבוּרִים הֹלֵךְ הַהֹלְכִים הֹלֶכֶת הֹלְכוֹת שָׁבוּר קְטוּרָה. שׂוֹנֵא אֹהֵב שְׁבוּרֵי לֵב. שֹׁמְרֵי הַבַּיִת. בָּרוּךְ ה'.

Rep. כְּשֶׁלֶף בָּאָרֶץ: הוֹי הָאֹמְרִים לָרַע טוֹב וְלַטּוֹב רָע: מַה־גָּדְלוּ מַעֲשֶׂיךָ ה' מְאֹד עָמְקוּ מַחְשְׁבֹתֶיךָ: זִכְרוּ תּוֹרַת מֹשֶׁה עַבְדִּי: מִי הָעָם וְיִשְׂמַח־אֵלֶה: הָעֹזְרִים בְּרָעָה יִקְצֹרוּ: כָּשְׁלוּ וְאֵין עֹזֵר: ה' אֱלֹהַי גָּדַלְתָּ מְאֹד הוֹד וְהָדָר לָבָשְׁתָּ: עִבְדוּ אֶת־ה' בְּיִרְאָה: הַשָּׁמַיִם שָׁמַיִם לה' וְהָאָרֶץ נָתַן לִבְנֵי־אָדָם:

§ 59. נִפְקְחוּ נִפְתְּחוּ נִשְׁמְעָה נִשְׁמַרְתֶּם לִשְׁפַּכְתִּי נִמְכַּרְנוּ נִסְתַּרְנוּ | לְהִמָּלֵט | הִמָּלֵט הִמָּלְטִי, הִקָּבְצוּ הִשָּׁמְרוּ הִשָּׁמְרִי
C*

יְפָרֵד יְפָרְדוּ אֶסְתֵּר נִסְתַּר תִּפָּקַחְנָה תִּשָּׁמֵר תִּשָּׁמְרוּ יִשָּׂרְפוּ
תִּשָּׁרֵף אֲבֻדָה אֹבְדָטָה נִשְׁפְּטָה ‖ הַנִּשְׁאָר הַנִּשְׁאֶרֶת
הַנִּשְׁאָרִים הַנִּשְׁאָרוֹת, נִסְתָּר נִסְתָּרִים נִסְתָּרוֹת.

§ 60. בַּקֵּשׁ בְּקַקְשְׁתִּי בְּקַשְׁתֶּם דַּבְּרוּ דִּבַּרְתָּ דִּבַּרְנוּ
דִּבַּרְתָּ דִּבְּרָה שָׁלַּמְתֶּם ‖ דִּבֶּר דִּבֶּר כִּבֵּס בִּקְשָׁה בִּקְשׁוּ ‖
לְדַבֵּר דַּבֵּר דַּבְּרִי דַּבְּרוּ לַמֶּדִינָה יְדַבֵּר תְּדַבֵּר נְדַבֵּר
תְּדַבְּרוּן תְּדַבֵּרְןָ תְּדַבֶּרְנָה נְבַקֵּשׁ תְּבַקְשׁוּ מְבַקְשֵׁי ה',
מְבַטֵּר מְבַשֶּׂרֶת מְבַשְּׂרוֹת, מְרַגְּלִים. מְקַדֵּשׁ מְקַדְּשְׁכֶם,
מְאַסֵּף, מְאַסֶּפְכֶם, מְאַסְּפַיִו הַמְדַבֵּר [1] קַבֵּר בְּנַבַּתִּי שִׁלְּחוּ
יִדַּבֵּר מִדַּבֵּר שִׁלְּחָה תְּלַקְטוּ לָקַט לַקְחָה יַלְּדָה יַלְּדוּ יְלָדְתֶם.

§ 61. הִמְטִיר הִבְדִּיל הִבְדִּילָה הִבְדִּילוּ הִבְדַּלְתָּ הִבְדַּלְתֶּם.
הִשְׁפִּים הִשְׁכַּמְתֶּם הִשְׁחִית הִשְׁחַתִּי הִשְׁחַתֶּם ‖ לְהַבְדִּיל
לְהַשְׁפִּיל הַשְׁלֵךְ הַשְׁלִיכִי הַשְׁלִיכוּ ‖ אַשְׁלִיךְ תַּשְׁלִיכִי יַשְׁלִיכוּ
נַשְׁלִיכָה אַשְׁחִית אַל־תַּשְׁחֵת יַשְׁלֵךְ יַבְדִּיל מַבְדִּילִים
מַשְׁחִיתִים מַקְרִיבֵי הַקְּטֹרֶת, מַזְפִּיר מַזְכֶּרֶת ‖ הָשְׁלְכָה
הָשְׁלְכוּ יֻשְׁלְכוּ מָשְׁעָב מֻשְׁלָךְ מֻשְׁלָכִים מֻשְׁלֶכֶת.

§ 62. הִתְהַלֵּךְ הִתְהַלְּכָה הִתְהַלְּכוּ הִתְהַלַּכְתְּ הִתְהַלַּכְנוּ
מִתְהַלֵּךְ מִתְהַלֶּכֶת מִתְהַלְּכִים אֶתְהַלְּכָה יִתְהַלֵּךְ תִּתְהַלַּכְנָה
יִתְהַלְּכוּן. הִתְאַפְּקוּ לְהִתְאַפֵּק אֶתְאַפֵּק תִּתְאַפֵּק, הַחֶרֶב
הַמִּתְהַפֶּכֶת.

§ 63. שָׁאוֹל שָׁאַל. עָצֹר עָצַר. הָמֵלךְ [2] תִּמְלֹךְ אִם־מָשׁוֹל
תִּמְשֹׁל בָּנוּ:

Rep. קָרוֹב ה' לְנִשְׁבְּרֵי־לֵב: דִּרְשׁוּ ה' בְּהִמָּצְאוֹ: נַפְשֵׁנוּ
כְּצִפּוֹר נִמְלְטָה מִפַּח יוֹקְשִׁים הַפַּח נִשְׁבָּר וַאֲנַחְנוּ נִמְלָטְנוּ:

---

[1] § 17b. [2] § 42,1.

נְצֹר לְשׁוֹנְךָ מֵרָע וּשְׂפָתֶיךָ מִדַּבֵּר מִרְמָה: בֶּן יְכַבֵּד
אָב וְעֶבֶד אֲדֹנָיו: ה' מַלְּטָה נַפְשִׁי: נְדָרַי לַה' אֲשַׁלֵּם:
אַל־תַּסְתֵּר פָּנֶיךָ מִמֶּנִּי: בֵּית וָהוֹן נַחֲלַת אָבוֹת וּמֵה'
אִשָּׁה מַשְׂכָּלֶת: עֵינֵי־כֹל אֵלֶיךָ יְשַׂבֵּרוּ וְאַתָּה נוֹתֵן לָהֶם
אֶת־אָכְלָם בְּעִתּוֹ:

§ 64. וְזָכַרְתִּי וְשָׁלַחְתִּי | וַיִּסְפֹּר וַיִּזְרֹק וַיִּמְכְּרוּ וַיִּקְבְּרוּ
וַיִּשְׁכַּב וַיִּגְדַּל וַתִּתְעַבְּנָה וַיִּגְדְּלוּ וְשָׁאַל וְאָזַר | וַתִּקְבֹּר
וַיִּפָּרְדוּ | וַיְדַבְּרוּ וַיְבַקֵּשׁ וַיִּלְקֹט | וַיִּבְהַל וַיִּשְׂרְפֵם וַתִּשְׁלַח
וַיַּשִּׂימוּ וַיִּשָּׁלוּ | וַיִּתְעַצֵּב וַיִּתְעַצְּבוּ.

§ 65. I. פָּרְשָׂה עָרַשׂ אֱגֹרֶשׁ יָבַרְךָ וַיְבָרֶךְ וּבֵרַכְתִּי יָהֲרֹג
תֶּהֱרַגְנָה יֵאָסְפוּ יַעַזְבוּ. טָרֹף¹ טֹרַף | מִצַּחֵק. בְּשַׂחֵת
מְרַחֶפֶת וַיְנַחֵם לְהִתְנַחֵם כֻּחַד וַתְּכַחֵשׁ וּמִמַּהֵר. נַחֵשׁ
יְנַחֵשׁ בּוֹ. מִהַרְתְּ וַתְּמַהֵר.

II. שֹׁמֵעַ מְשַׁלֵּחַ מַצְלִיחַ. לִבְרֹחַ כִּשְׁמֹעַ. וְהִצְלִיחַ.
תַּצְמִיחַ. אַטְבִּיעַ² ‖ שָׁמַע בְּיָחִידְךָ וַתִּבְרַח וַיִּזְרַע וַיִּפְתַּח
גָּאַל יִשְׁחַט | וַיִּבְקַע וַיִּפְתַּח וְגִלָּה וַיֵּשַׁע | תַּדְלַל
תַּחְמְלוּ. וַיִּחְבַּשׁ וּמַחְלְמָה³ וַיְיָרֵךְ וַיֶּהָבֹּהּ וַיַּחְפְּכוּ תַּצְבְּרוּ
וַתִּצְלַמְדְנָה וַיֵּעָזֹב וַיַּעֲזֹב תַּעַזְבִי תַּעֲזְבוּ תַּעַבְדוּן תַּעַבְדִין וַתַּעֲבֹד־
וַיֵּעָבְרוּ נֶהֱרָג | תֵּאָרֵב תֵּאָהֲבוּן תֵּאָנַס יֶחֱכָמוּ וַיֶּחֱרְדוּ.
נֶחְשַׁבְנוּ וְנֶאֶסְפוּ נֶהֶרְסוּ הֶעֱשִׁירוּ הֶאֱזִין הֶעֱבִירוּ
וְהֶעֱבַרְתָּם וַיַּחְסְרוּ וַיַּאַסְרוּהוּ. הֶחֱרִיד וְהָבַדְתִּי יֶחֱזָק.

III. עֲבַרְתָּם חָשַׁבְתֶּם אֲסוּרִים. צֹעֲקִים הַשּׂוֹאָבֹת
לַאֲכִים לַעֲזֹב בֶּהָפֹךְ לַעֲבֹד. צֳעֲדָה רָחֲצוּ. וַיִּשְׁחֲטוּ
יִרְחֲצוּ וְנִשְׁאֲלָה. נִבְהֲלוּ נִבְהֲלָה. וְיִבְחָנֵהוּ תִּבְחָנֵנִי

---

¹ § 63f. ² § 95d. ³ § 64i.

וְהִשֵּׁיגֻנוּ וַיֹּאחֲזוּ וְהָאָחֻזוּ. אַל־תֵּאָחֲרוּ אֹתִי. וְהִשְׁתַּהֲרוּ[1]
מָשַׁחְתָּ וַתְּפַקַּחְנָה וַתִּבְלַעְנָה וַתְּבַלְּעֻן, וּזְרַעְתָּם. וַיַּחֲזִיקוּ
וְהֶחֱזִיקִי נִתְהַלֵּךְ וְהֶחֱלִיפוּ הַאֲזִינוּ הַאֲזֵנָה וַאֲסֹד אָעֱבִיד ||
וַיִּשָּׁאֵר. וַתִּפְעֵם רוּחוֹ. וַיִּפָּחֵם (7), וַיִּפָּהֶם (2). רְחָצוּ
סֲעֲדוּ צִעֲקָה. בֹּרְכוּ וַאֲבָרֲכָה. טֹעֲמַת.

Rep. אָמַר עָצֵל אֲרִי בַחוּץ בְּתוֹךְ רְחֹבוֹת אֵרָצֵחַ: בְּרַכְיָ
נַפְשִׁי אֶתְ־הֲדֹ: מְהֲרוּ[2] שָׂכְחוּ מַעֲשָׂיו: יְבָרֵךְ יְרֵאֵי הֲ'
הַקְּטַנִּים עִם־הַגְּדֹלִים: || יוֹדֵעַ צַדִּיק נֶפֶשׁ בְּהֶמְתּוֹ: עֹבֵד
אַדְמָתוֹ יִשְׂבַּע־לָחֶם[3]: אוֹר־צַדִּיקִים יִשְׂמָח וְנֵר רְשָׁעִים
יִדְעָךְ: בֵּן חָכָם יְשַׂמַּח־אָב: עַד־מָתַי רְשָׁעִים תַּעֲלֹזוּ:
שֻׁבַּר לֻחוֹת נְחֹשֶׁת וּבְרִיחֵי בַרְזֶל גִּדֵּעַ: צַדִּיק אֹכֵל
לְשֹׂבַע נַפְשׁוֹ וּבֶטֶן רְשָׁעִים תֶּחְסָר: רָחוֹק הֲ' מֵרְשָׁעִים
וּתְפִלַּת צַדִּיקִים יִשְׁמָע: בָּרוּךְ הַגֶּבֶר אֲשֶׁר יִבְטַח בַּהֲ':
בְּרֹב דְּבָרִים לֹא יֶחְדַּל־פָּשַׁע וְחֹשֵׂךְ שְׂפָתָיו מַשְׂכִּיל: הֲ'
שָׁמְעָה תְפִלָּתִי: בְּטַח אֶל־הֲ' בְּכָל־לִבֶּךָ וְאֶל־בִּינָתְךָ
אַל־תִּשָּׁעֵן: || לֹא הִשְׁמִידוּ אֶת־הָעַמִּים אֲשֶׁר אָמַר הֲ'
לָהֶם. וַיִּתְעָרְבוּ בַגּוֹיִם וַיִּלְמְדוּ מַעֲשֵׂיהֶם. וַיַּעַבְדוּ אֶת־
עֲצַבֵּיהֶם וַיִּשְׁפְּכוּ דָם נָקִי דַּם־בְּנֵיהֶם וּבְנוֹתֵיהֶם אֲשֶׁר
זִבְּחוּ לַעֲצַבֵּי כְנָעַן: || שׁוֹמֵר הֲ' אֶת־כָּל־אֹהֲבָיו וְאֵת
כָּל־הָרְשָׁעִים יַשְׁמִיד:

§ 66. אָמַר וְאָמַרְתָּ יַאֲמִירְךָ תֹּאמַר תֹּאמְרוּ תֹּאמַר נֹאמַר וְאֹמְרָה
תֹּאמְרוּן וַיֹּאמֶר וַיֹּאמְרוּ וַתֹּאמֶר וַתֹּאמַרְנָה אֹמְרִים לֵאמֹר
אֱמֹר אִמְרִי יֹאמַר יֹאמַר | אָכַלְתָּ אָכַלְתִּי תֹּאכַל תֹּאכְלוּ
וְאֹכְלָה וְאֹכְלָה תֹּאכְלִי וַתֹּאכְלוּ וַתֹּאכַל וַתֹּאכַל וַתֹּאכַלְנָה אֱכֹלוּ

[1] Iptv. § 62b. [2] §84f. [3] § 83b.

לֶאֱכֹל יֹאבֵל אֹחֵז יְאָחֲזֶנּוּ. ‖ תִּקְוַת רְשָׁעִים תֹּאבֵד׃ לָמָּה
יֹאמְרוּ הַגּוֹיִם אַיֵּה נָא אֱלֹהֵיהֶם׃

§ 67. וַיִּפֹּל וַיִּפְּלוּ נָפְלָה וַיִּפֵּל וּלְהִתְנַפֵּל הַגֵּד הֻגַּד
וְאַגִּידָה וַיַּגֵּד וַיַּגִּדוּ הַגִּידִי הַגִּידוּ מַגִּיד, מַגִּידֵי קָתִידָה,
מַגֶּדֶת לְהַגִּיד הַצֵּל וַהַצֵּל וַתַּצֵּל הַטִּיבוּ תַּבִּיט וַיִּנָּשֵׁק
הָעֲבָדְהַדְעָא, הֻעֲשָׂה לִי, וַיִּתְחַבֵּר, וַיִּסַּךְ נֶסֶךְ, וַיֻּגַּד יָקָם
נִצָּב נִצָּבִים נִצָּבָה לִנְדֹּר לִנְגֹּהַּ, בְּנֹסַע לִנְשָׁק־לוֹ. יִתְאָם
וַיִּתְגַּב. וַתִּגַּשׁ וַיִּגְּשׁוּ וַתִּגַּשְׁןָ, וַיִּגַּשׁ אָדָם, גְּשָׁהדְרַנָא בְּשׁוּדרְנָא
עַד־גָּשְׁתוֹ וַיִּשָּׁקְ־לוֹ וַיִּפַּח וַיִּשַּׂע הַנֹּגֵעַ לִנְגֹּעַ תִּגְּעוּ מַגִּיעַ.
נָסְעוּ וַיִּסְעוּ וַיִּסָּעוּ, נָסְעָה, 12, 32, בְּנָסְעָם ‖ לָקַח וְלָקַחְתָּ
לְקַח לְקָחוֹ תִּקַּח קָחֵהוּ קָחוּ תִּקָּחֵהוּ קְחֶהָ וְלָקַחַת וְאֶקָּחָה
קְחָה וְתִקָּחָה לְקַח קַח וַיִּקָּחֵהוּ קַחְתְּךָ בְּקִחְתִּי׳ נָתְנָה נָתְנוּ
וְנָתַתִּי אֶתֵּן תִּתְּנוּ נָתוֹן נָתַן נֻתְּנָה (?!) וְאֶתְּנָה וְאֶקָּחָה
לָתֵת נְתָנוֹ נָתַן־זֶרַע וַיִּתֶּן־לוֹ תְּנִי־נָא וְאֶתֵּן תִּתִּי. ‖ כִּי
הוֹרַדְתִּי אֶל־תַּשְׁכֵּחַ וּמִצְוֹתַי יִצֹּר לִבֶּךָ׃ תְּנָה בְּנִי לִבְּךָ
לִי׃ צְדָקָה תַּצִּיל מִמָּוֶת׃ הַשָּׁמַיִם מְסַפְּרִים כְּבוֹד אֵל
וּמַעֲשֵׂה יָדָיו מַגִּיד הָרָקִיעַ׃

§ 68. וַיִּוָּלֵד וַיִּוָּלְדוּ וַיִּוָּתֵר פֶּן־תִּוָּרֵשׁ יִוָּדַע תִּוָּסְרוּ הוּסְרוּ
וְנִוְּעֲצָה וְיִתְיָעֲצוּ | הֹלַדְתָּ וַיּוֹרִדָהוּ וַתֵּלֶד לְהוֹרִיד וְהוֹרִדָם
הוֹדִיעַ וְהוֹרִידוּ (12!), הַנּוֹתֶרֶת, וַיֹּסֶף שֵׁבַח, וַתֹּסֶף לָלֶדֶת,
נוֹדַע, לֹא תְסָפוּן, הוֹיָדַעַתָּ, הוֹדַעְתָּ תֹּסֶף וַיּוֹסִפוּ הוֹשֵׁב מוֹשִׁיב
וְיוֹשֵׁב נוֹעֲצוּ הֹבִיאוּ וְהוֹכַח הֹכִיחַתָּ וַיּוֹלַח וְהוֹלִיכֻהוּ הוֹבֵשׁ
אוֹבִישׁ, הוֹאַלְתִּי לְדַבֵּר | יָשַׁנְתִּי וָיִּישָׁן אִישָׁן תִּירָשׁ יִירְשׁוּ
יָרְשׁוּ לְרִשְׁתְּךָ יֵעָפוּ יִישַׁן יָעֲצָה יָגֹאתִי וַיִּגַּשׁ
אֵלַד תֵּלְדִי וַיֵּלְדוּ וַתֵּלֶךְ, מִלֶּדֶת בְּלֶדְתָּהּ וַיֵּרֶד בְּיָדָהּ,

יָרֹד יָרַדְנוּ נֶגֶד אֶרְדָּה¹, רְדוּ־שָׁמָּה וְרֹדִים וַתֵּשֶׁב וְיָשְׁבוּ לָשֶׁבֶת שְׁבִי תֵּשֵׁבוּ, יָדַעְנוּ יְדַע אֵרַע אֶדְעָה וְנֵדְעָה דְּעוּ לָדַעַת יְדָעֶן וַיֵּרַד עִתִּי | וְהָלַכְתֶּם תֵּלֵךְ הָלֹךְ וְאָלְכָה וַתֵּלַכְנָה וְאֵלְכָה מִתְהַלֵּךְ לָלֶכֶת, לֶךְ־לְךָ, קָלוּ הֹלַכְתָּ, קְחוּ וָלֵכוּ, הוֹלַכְתִּי מוֹלִיךְ מוֹלִיכוֹת | תּוּכַל יוּכְלוּן וַתּוּכַל, לֹא נוּכַל דַּבֵּר, לֹא אוּכַל לְהִמָּלֵט. יְרֵאת ה' תּוֹסִיף יָמִים:

§ 69. יֵשֶׁב־לִי, וַיֵּיטְבוּ דִבְרֵיהֶם, אֵיטִיב עִמָּךְ, תֵּיטִיב וְאֵיטִיבָה מֵיטִיבִים לְהֵיטִיב וַתֵּשֶׁב הֵיטִיבָה (!2), וַיִּנַּקְתֶּם תִּינַקִי הֵינִיקָה מֵינֶקֶת מֵינַקְתּוֹ מֵינִיקוֹת מֵינִיקוֹתַיִךְ וְאִמֵּנָה. יָבֵשׁ יָבְשָׁה יָבֵשׁוּ וַיְבַקְשׁוּ הוֹבִישׁוּ אוֹבִישׁ. טוֹב אַתָּה וּמֵטִיב:

§ 71. אֲקוֹמֵם תְּקוֹמֵם יְקוֹמֵמוּ רוֹמַמְתִּי מְרוֹמַם יְרוֹמָם תְּרוֹמַמְנָה יְעֹרָף || קָמְעָה קָמוּ בָּר בְּרֵתָה גֵּרַתִּי נָסוּ נָסַתָם נַסּוּ לָגוּר לָנוּס לָמוּת קוּמוּ קוּמִי סוּרוּ שׁוּבָה לוּשִׁי וְצוּדָה יָסוֹר נָפִיץ וַיָּסִרוּ וַיָּנוּסוּ אֵמוּת וּנְקוּמָה אֲמוּתָה, מוֹת תְּמִיתוּן, וַיְמָלוּ, בְּהִמּוֹלוֹ, הִמּוֹל יִמּוֹל, נָכוֹן נָמוֹטוּ אָמוֹט יֵאָתוּ נָאוֹת אָקִים תָּמִיד וְהֵקַם וְהָכֵן חָסֵר חָסְרִי, חָדֵל חָדַל, לְהָתִים לְהָסִיר מֵקִים מְרִיקִים יוּמַת מוּבָת מְיוּמָתִים הֲמִתוֹ, נָע וָנָד, הֲקִמֹתִי וַהֲקִמֹתִי הֱשִׁיבֻנוּ הֲרִימוֹתִי הֲרִימֹתִי תְּבוּטִיעֶנָה | אַל־תָּהֵס יָמֹת וַיָּנַעַת וַיָּמָת וַיָּנָס וַתָּקָם וַיֵּרַע וַיָּחֵל וַתַּגֵּר וַיָּמֶת וַיָּפֶץ וַיֵּרֶק, וַתָּנַח הַתֵּבָה, וַיַּנַּח ה' אֶת־בְּרִית הַנִּיחֹה, וַיָּסַר (!2) | הֱנִיחוּ וַתַּנַח || הֵשִׁיב וַתָּשָׁב תָּשׁוּב תָּשִׁיב וַיָּשָׁב מֵשִׁיב

---

¹ alii אֱרֶדָה § 5d.

Chrestomathia II B. § 71—74.

טוּבִי שׁוּבִי, הָשֵׁב, הָשֵׁב אָטִיב, טוֹב אָשׁוּב, הוּשַׁב פִּסְפִּי, הֵקֶץ הַמּוּשָׁב, הֻשַּׁב. ‖ אַל־תָּסוּרוּ מֵאַחֲרֵי פְ׳. רַבּוֹת מַחֲשָׁבוֹת בְּלֶב־אִישׁ וַעֲצַת ה׳ הִיא תָקוּם:

§ 72. שַׂמְתִּי וְשַׂמְתִּי שָׁם, שִׂים־נָא יָדְךָ, שִׂימוּ, תָּשִׂים וְאָשִׂימָה וַיָּשִׂימוּ לָשׂוּם, שָׁת אָשִׁית יָשִׁית וַיָּשֶׁת, לוֹ, וְלֵיהּ, עָלָיו וַעֲלֵיהּ וַיָּרִיבוּ וַיָּרֶב, בָּן יָדִין, שָׁשׁ שַׂשְׂתִּי, שׂוֹשׂ אָשִׂישׂ, שִׂישׂוּ.

§ 73. לְקַלֵּל מְקַלְּלֶךָ וַיִּתְפַּלֵּל וַיִּתְפַּלֵּל מְשֻׁתָּף תְּהַלַּךְ וְנִמְשַׁט הֵלְלוּ וַיְהַלְלוּ מִתְשָׁתֵּעַ ‖ תַּם קַלּוּ יְבָהּ לָרֹב, לֹא צֹאנוֹ, כְּרֹם הַיּוֹם, חָנַן אֶת־עַבְדְּךָ, וְגִלּוּ אֶת־הָאֶבֶן, בָּלַל, אָרוּר אֲרוּרָה אֲרֵרֶיךָ, גָּזְזוּ צֹאנוֹ ‖ אָאֹר וַיָּשֹׁפּוּ וַיָּבֹזּוּ תָּחֹן הָחֵל הֵפֵר תָּחֵנוּ, עָנֵו לָךְ, הָרַעוּ, לְהָרַע לְהָרַע, הוּחַל ‖ תִּסְבִּינָה וַתִּחְלֶינָה הָרֵעֹתֶם הֲנֹתִי קַלֹּתִי בָּאוֹנוּ וָאָקֹד וָאֶסֹּב, וַתָּשֹׂם הַשָּׁנָה ‖ אַל־יֵרַע, וַיִּצֶר לוֹ.

§ 74. תִּסְפֶּה תִּסְפֶּה וְאֶרְאֶה נִרְאֹה (2!) יֵרָאֶה נִשְׁקָה אַרְבֶּה אֶבְכֶּה אַבְנֶה תַּעֲנֶה יַעֲשֶׂה בֹּנֶה עֹשָׂה, וַתִּכְלֶינָה וַתַּשְׁקֶיןָ ‖ יַעֲלֶה יַעֲנֶה יַעֲשֶׂה תַּעֲשֶׂה אֶעֱשֶׂה נַעֲשֶׂה אֶעֱלֶה אַצְלֶה וַתַּהֲרֶיןָ ‖ פָּרָה וּרְבֵה, שְׁתֵה הַקְרֵה־נָא עֲשֵׂה צֵלָה קְנֵה צַוִּתִי הָרְאֵיתָ ‖ קָנִיתִי עָשִׂיתִי עָשִׂינוּ עָלִיתָ עָלִינוּ עֲשִׂיתֶם הִשְׁקִית הִגְלִיתֶם קֹוִינוּ הֶגְלִית וְהֶגְלֵתֶם[1] II שָׁעָה קָנָה בָּכָה כִּלָּה נִשְׁבָּה הַקְרֵה הִשְׁקָה וְהֶעֱלָה רָאֹה עָלֹה ‖ לִבְנוֹת לִשְׁתּוֹת לְהַשְׁקוֹת מַרְאוֹת לְצַוּוֹת הִשָּׁנוֹת לְצַוּוֹת ‖ עָלְתָה עָנְתָה רָאֲתָה פָּסְתָה הֻשְׁקְתָה רֹאֲתָה נִרְאָתָה ‖ III רָאוּ רְאוּ יִרְאוּ יִרְאוּ יָקוּ וַיִּכְלוּ

---
[1] § 65h.

יְכַסּוּ וְהִשְׁקוּ וַשְׁקוּ הֶעֱלוּ תֵּרֵאי תִּכְבִּי תְּכַסִּי תַּרְבִּי תַּעֲשִׂי תֵּעָשׂוּ וַתַּעֲנוּ וַיַּעֲלוּ יַעֲשׂוּ, עֲשִׂי עֲלִי רְאִי הַעֲלִי הַתְעֵנִי עֲלוּ הַשְׁקוּ ‖ IV וַתֵּבְךְּ וָאֶשְׁתְּ וַיֵּבְךְּ וַיִּיקַץ יִקַץ וָאֵרֶא וַיִּרְא (2!), וַתֵּתַע, וַתְּמַלֵּא אֶרֶץ מִצְרַיִם, וַיִּשַׁן וַתֵּשַׁן תֵּעַל אַל־תַּעַשׂ וַתְּכַס וְאֶצְפֶּה (5), וָאָצֻר † וַתִּתְפָּשׂ, וַיַּעַל עֹלוֹת, וָאֹכַל (2!). נָקוּמָה וְנַעֲלֶה | הִשְׁתַּחֲוֵיתֶם וְאִשְׁתַּחֲוֶה וְיִשְׁתַּחֲווּ וַיִּשְׁתַּח וַתִּשְׁתַּחֲוֶיןָ מִשְׁתַּחֲוִים לְהִשְׁתַּחֲוֹת | הַרְבָּה אַרְבֶּה, וּשְׁכָרֵךְ הַרְבֵּה מְאֹד. ‖ בְּכָל־מָקוֹם עֵינֵי ה' צֹפוֹת רָעִים וְטוֹבִים: טוֹב לַחֲסוֹת בַּה' מִבְּטֹחַ[1] בָּאָדָם: אֶבֶן מָאֲסוּ[2] הַבּוֹנִים הָיְתָה לְרֹאשׁ פִּנָּה: פְּנֵה אֵלָי:

§ 75. בָּרָא בְּרֹא וַיִּבְרָא מָצְאָה אֶמְצָא לִמְצֹא וַיִּמְצְאוּ הִנְצְאַת נִמְצָא (3!) וַיִּמָּצֵא יִמָּצְאוּן מְצֹאוֹ תִּקְרָא יִקְרְאוּ וָאֶקְרָא וְקָרָאתָ(‎ת), מָלְאוּ וַיְמַלֵּא מִלֵּאוּ (2!) וַיִּמָּלְאוּ מָלֵא רַתְמַלֵּא שָׂנֹא שְׂנוּאָה וַיִּשְׂנְאוּ חָטָאתִי חָטָאוּ טָמֵא וָאֹהֲבָה אַל־תֶּחֱטָאוּ טְמֵאתֶם וַיִּקָּאוּ וְרָחֲצוּ תָבוֹאָן, מְלֵאָה מְלֵאתֶם קְנֹאתִי נְטַמֵּאתֶם נְקֵאתִי׃ | לֵב טָהוֹר בְּרָא לִי אֱלֹהִים׃

§ 76. נְשָׂאתֶם וַתִּשָּׂא וַיִּשְׂאוּ נְשׂוּאִים נְשׂוֹא תִּנָּשֶׂאנָה. תָּשֶׂה תֵּשֶׂה, זְרֹעוֹ הַנְּטוּיָה, וַיֵּט אָהֳלֹה, הַטִּי־נָא. וַיְפוּ הַבָּנוֹת הַקָּהֵל. תִּנָּקֶה. נִסָּה. יָרֵא יִרְאֶה אַל־תִּירָא אַל־תִּירְאִי אַל־תִּירְאוּ יָאִיר לִירְאָה. יָצֵאת יָצְאוּ יָצְאוּ יֵצְאוּ תֵּצְאוּ וַיֵּצֵא, יֹצְאֵי הַתֵּבָה, בְּצֵאתוֹ הוֹצִיא אוֹצִיאָה הוֹצִאתֶם הוֹצִיאוּ (!2) וַתּוֹצֵא, וַיְהִי כְהוֹצִיאָם. בָּאוּ בָּאנוּ אָבֹא אָבוֹא וַתָּבֹא וַתָּבֹאנָה וָאָבֹא הַבָּאִים הַבָּאת בְּבֹאוֹ בְּבֹאָן עַד־בֹּאֲ בֹּאֲנָה וּבֹאִי הֱבִיאוּ וַהֲבֵאתִי תָבִיא תָּבִיאוּ וַיָּבִיאוּ.

---

[1] § 82b. [2] § 87e3.

Rep. I. לֹא יָכְלוּ לָשֶׁבֶת יַחְדָּו: קַח נָא לֵךְ: לֹא יָסְפָה[1]
שׁוּב: אֶסְתֵּר וְהֲלִיתִי נָא וְגֹד: אֶרְדְּה־נָּא וְאֶרְאֶה: קוּם
הִתְהַלֵּךְ בָּאָרֶץ: אִם־יוּכַל אִישׁ לִמְנוֹת: לְנוּ וְנִהְצוּ
הֵבְלִים וְהִשְׁבַּעְתָּם וְהָלַכְתֶּם לְדַרְכְּכֶם: אַל־נָא יִחַר
לַאדֹנָי: וַיֹּסֶף לְדַבֵּר: לְכָה עַד־כֹּה וְהִשְׁתַּחֲוָה וְנָשׁוּבָה
אֲלֵיכֶם: אִם־לֹא תֹאבֶה הָאִשָּׁה לָלֶכֶת אַחֲרֶיךָ וְנִקִּיתָ
מִשְּׁבֻעָתִי: תֵּלֵךְ וְלָקְחָה אִשָּׁה: לְכָה נַשְׁקָה אֶת־אָבִינוּ
מַהֵר הִמָּלֵט: הִטִּי־נָא כַדֵּךְ וְאֶשְׁתֶּה: קוּם עֲלֵה[2] בֵּית־אֵל
וְשֶׁב־שָׁם וַעֲשֵׂה־שָׁם מִזְבֵּחַ: שְׁבָה וְאֵלְכָה: וַיֵּדַר לְיַעֲקֹב
וַיֵּרֶב בִּלְבָן וַיַּעַן: לְכָה נִכְרְתָה בְרִית: וְנָקִישָׁה וְנֵלֵכָה
יִקְהֶה וְלֹא נָמוּת: הֲיָדוֹעַ נֵדַע: מַהֲרוּ וַעֲלוּ: בָּנוּ(3!).
יָדוּ(2!). נָבִיא(2!). אוֹיֵב(2!).

II. הֵט שָׁכְךָ וְתֵרֵד גַּע בֶּהָרִים וְיֶעֱשָׁנוּ: אֱלֹחָתָה
חֲכַם בְּעֵינֶיךָ יְרָא אֶת־ה' וְסוּר מֵרָע: אַל־תֹּאמַר לְרֵעֶךָ
לֵךְ וָשׁוּב וּמָחָר אֶתֵּן: בְּלֶכְתְּךָ לֹא יֵצֵר צַעֲדֶךָ וְאִם
תָּרוּץ לֹא תִכָּשֵׁל: אַל־תֹּאמַר אֲשַׁלְּמָה־רָע קַוֵּה לַה'
וְיֹשַׁע[3] לָךְ: בִּנְפֹל אוֹיִבְךָ אַל־תִּשְׂמָח וּבִכָּשְׁלוֹ אַל־יָגֵל
לִבֶּךָ: פֶּן־יִרְאֶה ה' וְרַע[4] בְּעֵינָיו וְהֵשִׁיב מֵעָלָיו אַפּוֹ:
בְּנִי לִדְבָרַי הַקְשִׁיבָה לַאֲמָרַי הַט אָזְנֶךָ: גַּם כִּי אֵלֶּה
בְּגִיא צַלְמָוֶת לֹא אִירָא רָע: ה' נָתַן וה' לָקָח יְהִי שֵׁם
ה' מְבֹרָךְ: ה' לִי לֹא אִירָא מַה־יַּעֲשֶׂה־לִּי אָדָם: יִרְאוּ
אֹתְךָ וַעֲבָדְתָּם אֹתוֹ בֶּאֱמֶת בְּכָל־לְבַבְכֶם:

(Prov 6, 6—11) לֵךְ אֶל־נְמָלָה עָצֵל רְאֵה דְרָכֶיהָ
וַחֲכָם: אֲשֶׁר אֵין לָהּ קָצִין שֹׁטֵר וּמֹשֵׁל: תָּכִין בַּקַּיִץ

---

[1] § 84c. [2] § 83c. [3] § 46eβ. [4] § 64.

לָהֶמָה אָגוּרָה בַקָּצִיר מַאֲכָלָהּ: עַד־מָתַי עָצֵל תִּשְׁכָּב מָתַי
תָּקוּם מִשְּׁנָתֶךָ: מְעַט שֵׁנוֹת מְעַט תְּנוּמוֹת מְעַט חִבֻּק
יָדַיִם לִשְׁכָּב: וּבָא כִמְהַלֵּךְ רֵאשֶׁךָ וּמַחְסֹרְךָ כְּאִישׁ מָגֵן:

§ 78. I. לְהָרְגֵנִי לְגָרְשֵׁנִי לְהָבִיאֵנִי לַהֲמִיתֵנִי שׁוּבוֹ לַהֲשִׁיבוֹ
וְלִשְׁמֹעַ בְּעָמְדוֹ בְּשִׁכְבָהּ, לְעָבְדָהּ וּלְשָׁמְרָהּ, וְלִבְלָתָּה
בְּבָרְאֲךָ לְהָרְגֶךָ כְּהָרִיגִי לְשַׁלְּחָם בְּהִבָּרְאָם | שֹׁמְרֶךָ עֹזְרָיו
עֹזְרֶיהָ מֹשִׁיעַ מוֹשִׁיעֶךָ מוֹשִׁיעִי מוֹשִׁיעָךְ מוֹשִׁיעָם מְרוֹמֲמִי
מְבָרְכֶךָ.

§ 79. לְקָחַנִי אֲכָלָנִי שָׁמַעֲנִי הִשִּׁיאַנִי חִנַּנִי שְׁלָחַנִי עֲצָרַנִי נְחָנִי
הִגִּידַנִי הִפְצִיר וְהִפְצִי וּשְׁאָלְךָ וַהֲשִׁיבֶךָ הִשְׁבִּישְׁךָ הֲרָגוּ
אֲהֵבוּ בֵּרְכוּ צִוָּהוּ וְקָרָהוּ וְהִפָּהוּ יְדָעָהּ חֲשָׁבָהּ נְתָנָהּ
מְצָאָהּ שְׁלָחָנוּ הִצִּילָנוּ נְתָנָם צִוָּם רָאָם הוֹצִיאָם קִבְּצָן.

אֲכָלָתְנִי יְלָדַתְךָ אֲהֵבַתְהוֹן אֲכָלָתְהוּ הֶחֱזִיקַתְהוּ אֲכָלָתַם.
רְדָפוּנִי וַהֲרָגוּנִי אֲשׁוּרוּנִי וְהִפּוּנִי גְמָלוּךְ שְׁפָטוּךָ
הִבִּיאוּהוּ הוֹרִידוּהוּ וַעֲבָדוּם וּדְפָקוּם סְתָמוּם.

עֲבָדְתַּנִי וּקְבַרְתַּנִי לִמַּדְתַּנִי וְהִזְבַּרְתַּנִי שִׁלַּחְתַּנִי בֵּרַכְתַּנִי
נְשִׁיתַנִי רְמִיתַנִי וְהוֹצֵאתַנִי וּנְשָׂאתַנִי יְדַעְתּוֹ הֱבִיאתוֹ
מְצָאתָהּ בְּהַנַּחְתּוֹ צִוִּיתָנוּ וְהִטַּשְׁתָּם וְשַׂמְתָּם.
נְתַתִּיהוּ נְשָׂאתִים.

שְׁלַחְתִּיךָ שְׁמַעְתִּיךָ נְתַתִּיךָ עֲבַדְתִּיךָ וּבֵרַכְתִּיךָ צִוִּיתִיךָ
וְהִרְבִּיתִךָ הוֹצֵאתִיךָ וַהֲשִׁבוֹתִיךָ עֲזַבְתִּיךָ סְמַכְתִּיו נְתַתִּיו
יְדַעְתִּיו שַׂמְתִּיו הֲבִיאתִיו וְהִצַּגְתִּיו[1] נְתַתִּיהָ מְצָאתִיהָ
וּרְאִיתִיהָ וּבֵרַכְתִּיהָ עֲטִיתָם יְדַעְתִּין.

---

[1] § 70.

יְדָעֲנוּךְ נְגָעוּךְ עֲבַדְנָהּ מְצָאנָהּ מְצָאוּהָ בְּרַכְנוּכֶם יְדַעֲנוּם.

II. תְּקָפַנִי יְהַדְגַנִי וַיַּעַקְבֵנִי יְמַשֵּׁנִי וְיָשֵׁנִי תְּלַמְּדֵנִי וִיבָרֲכֵנִי וַיַּשְׂבִּעֵנִי אֲבָדְךָ אֱזָבְךָ וַאֲשַׁבְּךָ אֲשַׁלְּחֶךָּ וַאֲשַׁלְּחֶךָ תְּבָרְכָךְ וַאֲבָרְכָה וַאֲבָרְכָךְ יִתֶּנְךָ שׁוּפְךָ יְסוֹבְךָ אֲסִירְךָ יִפְדְּךָ וְיִרְבְּךָ וְאֶעֶשְׂךָ אַלְּךָ. אֲתָנוּךְ אֲהַבְנוּךְ וַתִּתְפְּשֵׂהוּ וְיִשְׁאָלֵהוּ וַיִּפְקְדֵהוּ וַיַּעֲמִדֵהוּ וְנִשְׁלָחֵהוּ וַיְבִיאָתֵהוּ וֶיֱבִיאָהוּ וְיִשִׁיתָהוּ וִיבָרַכֵהוּ וַיְחָרְגֵהוּ וְנִהַרְגֵהוּ וַיְמָשֵׁהוּ (וָאֶמְשָׁךְ¹ 27, 21) וַיִּקֳחֵהוּ וַיְצַוֵּהוּ וַיַּעֲלֵהוּ וַתִּשְׁקֵהוּ. אֲתָנָה תַּעַזְבָה וַתְּהַשֵּׁבָה וִירִשָׁה וַתִּקְרָאָה וַיְבִיאָה וַיִּרְאָה וַתַּעֲשָׂה וַיְעַנָּה. יִתְּנָה יְלַדָה יְלַמְּדָה יַפִּידָה. יִשְׁמָעֵנוּ יְדַחֵמֵנוּ וְיִשְׁלָחֵנוּ תְּאַכְּלֵם אֱלַמֶּדְכֶם. אֲתָנָם אֲחַזְקֵם וְיִשְׁלָחֵם וַאֲבָרְכֵם וַיִּלְבָּשֵׁם וַיַּעֲבִירֵם וַיַשִׁמֵם וַיַּכֵּרֵם וַיַּצִּלֵם וְאָפִיצֵם וַתַּשִּׂיגֵם וַיַּכֵּם, יְבַלְּעֵמוֹ.

יִדְּפוּנִי יְרָאוּנִי יַהַדְגֵנִי וַתְּשַׁלְּחֵהוּ יִשְׁפְּטוּךְ יַעַבְדוּךְ יוֹדוּךְ יַצִילוּךְ יַעַבְדוּהוּ וִימָהֲרוּהוּ וִירִישָׁהוּ וַיֹּצִאֲהוּ וַיִּנַחֵהוּ יִלְכְּדוּהָ יְעַנּוּנוּ תִּתְּנֵנוּם וִימַלְּאוּם וְיִסְתְּמוּם.

הָרְגֵנִי לַמְּדֵנִי שַׁלְּחֵנִי בָּרֲכֵנִי הַלְעִיטֵנִי, וְהַשִׁיבֵנִי דָבָר. רְדָפָהוּ עֲבָדָהוּ תְּנָהוּ וְהַעֲלֵהוּ לְבַדָּה לַמְּדָה הוֹצִיאָה. עֲזָרֵנוּ הַצִּילֵנוּ שְׂבָרֵם תְּנָם הוֹרִידֵם ‖ שַׁלְּחוּנִי שַׁלְּחוּהוּ הַשְׁקִינִי הַגְמִיאִינִי אָכְלֵהוּ וְכָבְשֻׁהָ הוֹצִיאוּהָ הַשְׁמִיעֻנוּ תְּפֶתְּחוּם הֲפוּם.

III. תְּשַׁלְּחֵנִי יִשָּׂאֵנִי יִירָשְׁךָ יִמְאָסְךָ אֲשַׁלֵּחֲךָ יִגְאָלֶךָ

---
¹ König I, 356.

אֲרָפֵאךְ וַיִשְׁפָּחֵהוּ יְקָרָאֵהוּ וַיִמְצָאֵהוּ וַיִשָּׁקֵהוּ וַיִקְרָאָה
וִיְאֵהָבָה וַיִקָּחֶהָ יְרָפֵאנוּ תְּשַׁלְּחֵנוּ וְנִשְׁאָלָם וַיִּקָּחֵם תִּשָּׂאֵם
אֲשַׁלְּחֵם תִּשְׁעֵמוֹ. יִשְׁאָלוּנִי יִרְאוּךָ תִּמְצָאֵהוּ וַיִּקְחֻדוּ
יִשָּׂאוּנוּ תִּירָאוּם יְשִׁיטוּם.

שְׁלָחַנִי קְרָאַנִי דְעֵהוּ שְׂאֵהוּ אֲהֵבָה שְׁמָעֵנוּ כִּלָּאָם
שְׁמָעוּנִי טָאוּנִי קְרָאֵהוּ וּסְדָרֵהוּ.

§ 80. תְּבָרְכֵנִי וַאֲבָרְכְךָ וְיַעֲזְרְךָ יֶאֱהָבְךָ אֶעֶזְרֶכָּה תְּבַקְשֵׁנוּ
אֲעַטְּרֵנוּ וְאֶרְאֵנוּ אֲשִׁימֵמוּ אֲבִיאֵמוּ נַשְׁקֶנוּ נָקְנוּ תְשׁוּפֶנּוּ
אִירָשֶׁנָּה אֶתְנֶנָּה תֹּאכֲלֶנָּה שְׁמָעֶנָּה תְּנֶהָ. ‖ אֵלֶי אַתָּה
וְאוֹדֶךָ אֱלֹהַי אֲרוֹמְמֶךָ׃

Rep. I. שִׁמְעוּ לִי יִרְאַתְ־ה' אֲלַמֶּדְכֶם: בַּקֵּשׁ שָׁלוֹם וְרָדְפֵהוּ:
מְקַלֶּלְךָ אָאֹר: נָחֵל לַהַשְׁקֹתוֹ: בֶּרֶךְ יִכְמָה לְבִיתוֹ:
הִרְחַבְתִּיךָ בַּמְּעִילִי יָשָׁר: אִם־רָעֵב שֹׂנַאֲךָ הַאֲכִילֵהוּ לָחֶם
וְאִם־צָמֵא הַשְׁקֵהוּ מָיִם[1]: הַשֵּׁה אֵלַי אָזְנְךָ בְּיוֹם אֶקְרָא[2]
מַהֵר עֲנֵנִי: קָרוֹב ה' לְכָל־קֹרְאָיו לְכֹל אֲשֶׁר יִקְרָאֻהוּ
בֶאֱמֶת: בָּרֵךְ אֲבָרֶכְךָ וְהַרְבָּה[3] אַרְבֶּה אֶת־זַרְעֶךָ: סַעֲדֵנִי
וְאִוָּשֵׁעָה[4]: וּסְקָר[5] רַגְלְךָ מִבֵּית רֵעֶךָ פֶּן־יִשְׂבָּעֲךָ[6] וּשְׂנֵאֶךָ[7]:
קְנֵה לְבָבָה, אַל־תַּעֲזֹבָהּ וְתִשְׁמְרֶךָּ אֱהָבֶהָ וְתִצְּרֶךָּ:
יְבָרֶכְךָ ה' וְיִשְׁמְרֶךָ: יָאֵר ה' פָּנָיו אֵלֶיךָ וִיחֻנֶּךָּ: יִשָּׂא
ה' פָּנָיו אֵלֶיךָ וְיָשֵׂם לְךָ שָׁלוֹם:

II.[8] תִּמְשָׁל־בּוֹ. יַעֲבָד־אִישׁ. לֶאֱכָל־לֶחֶם. וַיִפְתָּר־לָנוּ.
אֶת־הָאֱלֹהִים הִתְהַלֶּךְ־נֹחַ. הַבֶּט־נָא. הַפְרֵךְ. וַיְפַשְּׁט־לוֹ.

---

[1] § 83f. [2] § 87mα. [3] § 74w. [4] § 46. [5] § 65s. [6] § 83b
[7] § 64b. [8] § 9b. 13,9.

וַיְּגֶּד־לוֹ. וַיֵּצֶב־שָׁם מִזְבֵּחַ. וַיְדַבֶּר־נָא. לְדְ־נָא. לֶד־לְדָ.
אֶתֶּן־לְדָ. מַה־תִּתֶּן־לִי. תֵּן־לִי. וַיִּטַּ־שָׁם אָהֳלוֹ ׀ אָמַר־
לוֹ. יֶשְׁב־נָא. קָחֶם־נָא. ׀ יֵשֶׁב לְדָ. וַיָּבֹא נֹחַ. — וַיֵּצֵא
נֹחַ. הֹצֵּא־נָא. לְצַחֵק בָּנוּ (39, 14). הֵחֵל בִּי (31, 7).
לָתֵת לְדָ (15, 7). הִשָּׁמֶר לְדָ.

III. EXPLANATORY NOTES ON SOME SECTIONS OF THE OLD TESTAMENT.

a) 1 Sam. 9, 1—10, 1.

1. אִישׁ יְמִינִי a Benjamite, cf. v. 4 אֶרֶץ יְמִינִי the Benjamite country. חַיִל here: riches. **2.** מִכָּל־הָעָם § 82*b*. **3.** אֶחָד § 21*g*
4. שָׁלִשָׁה, שְׁעָלִים and v. 5 צוּף are proper names. **5.** . . . הֵמָּה בָאוּ
וּשְׁמוּאֵל אָמַר subordinated in English: after w. plupf. לְכָה § 68*k*.
וְדָאַג Wāw consec.

6. אִישׁ־אֱלֹהִים a man of God (contrary to §20*b*). בֹּא יָבֹא
§63*d*. שָׁמָּה=שָׁם . . אֲשֶׁר עָלִיהָ § 87*a*. **7.** אָזַל go away; fail, *deficere*.
תְּשׁוּרָה present, gift. **8.** וַיֹּסֶף §84*a.b.* **9.** לְפָנִים beforetime. בְּלֶכְתּוֹ
§68*i*. יִקְרָא Ipf. frequentative: they (one) used to call.

11. וְהֵמָּה בְּצֵאוּ . . הֵמָּה עֹלִים subordinated in English: as w.
ipf., cf. v. 14. 27. מַעֲלֶה rising ground. פָּרַח §45*e*5. הַיּוֹם §17*a*.
13. חָשִׁיר Acc. §83*c*. הַבָּמָתָה §20*c*. כְּהַיּוֹם §17*e*. **14.** לִקְרַאת (proply.
Inf. of קְרָה=קָרָא) to meet, *obviam*. **15.** גָּלָה אֹזֶן פ׳ uncover the
ear of some one, *i. e.* reveal, disclose something to some one.

16. כָּעֵת מָחָר to-morrow at this time. רָאִיתִי cf. Ex. 2, 25.
3, 7. **17.** אֲשֶׁר אָמַרְתִּי of whom I have spoken §87*f*. עָצַר hold
back, restrain; בְּ *coercere imperio*, rule over. **18.** וַיִּגַּשׁ here w. Acc.,
more frequently with אֶל־. אֵי זֶה §42*f*. **19.** עֲלֵה . . וַאֲכַלְתֶּם §64*c*.
20. וְלָאֲתֹנוֹת לְ: in regard to. טוּב לֵב *animum advertere*, לְ or אֶל־.

21. הַצְּעִירָה § 82*a*. The second שִׁבְטֵי denotes subdivisions
of the tribe (as Num. 4, 18. Jud. 20, 12), if the text is correct
(שִׁבְטֵי?). **22.** לִשְׁכָּה chamber (in which the sacrificial feast was
celebrated). אִישׁ § 39. **23.** תְּנָה § 67*i*. מָנָה part, share, portion.

24. שׂוֹק crus. ‖ וְהָעֲלֵיהָ §17a note. עָשִׂים §72b. ‖ לַמּוֹעֵד probably: for this (the) meeting. | לֵאמֹר as I said to the cook (the text seems to be corrupt here).
26. הַחוּצָה out of doors (on the street). ‖ 27. וְיָגָבֵּר that he .., cf. §46eβ. ‖ כַּיּוֹם now. ‖ Chap. 10, 1 פַּךְ viol. ‖ וַיִּצֹק §70.

b) 1 Sam. 25.

1. בְּרָבָח §17f3. Also מָאֹרָן, מָעוֹן, כַּרְמֶל are proper names, so v. 3 נָבָל (as appellative: fool [often=godless], see v. 25), אֲבִיגַיִל, v. 10 רֹשִׁי. ‖ 2. מַעֲשֶׂה here=possessions. ‖ בְּגִזוֹ §73hγ. ‖ כָּלִבִּי Qᵉrê: a Calebite, of the family of Caleb. ‖ 5. וּבָאתֶם . . . עָלוּ §64c.
6. לֶחָי (§17ca)=לַחָי (to the life), salve. ‖ וְאָתָה שָׁלוֹם §89e.
7. הַכַּלְבְּנוּם §61c. ‖ פָּקַד here and v. 15: miss. ‖ 8. וְיָגִירוּ . . שָׁאַל §46eβ. ‖ וְיִמְצְאוּ as an optative. ‖ בְנוֹ, translate acc. to the Qᵉrê בָּאנוּ. ‖ 9. וַיָּנוּחוּ Vulgata: siluerunt. ‖ 10. רַבּוּ §73g. ‖ פָּרַץ VII break away. ‖ אֲדֹנָיו, cf. אֲדֹנֵינוּ v. 14. 17. § 19d.
11. וְלָקַחְתִּי and should I take away? §42h. ‖ טִבְחָה meal of slaughtered meat. ‖ 12. הָפַךְ here intr.: turn, turn back. ‖ 14. עִיט (עוּט) attack (with words), scold, בְּ. ‖ 15. יְמֵי §87m.
17. מִדַּבֵּר (מִן away from . .) so that one cannot speak to him. ‖ 18. לֶחֶם §39h. ‖ עֲשׂוּוֹת Kᵉthîbh as ל״י, עֲשׂוּיָה Qᵉrê as ל״י (ל״ה) "prepared", i. e. slaughtered. ‖ קָלִי parched corn. ‖ צִמֻּקִים cakes of dried grapes. ‖ 20. סֵתֶר הָהָר hidden part of the mountain, i. e. depression.
21. לַשֶּׁקֶר for nothing, pro nihilo, frustra. ‖ 22. אִם §90a.c. ‖ שֶׁתַן V mingere. ‖ בָּשׁוּתְרִין בְּקִיר i. e. all persons of the male sex. ‖ 23. וַתְּמַהֵר וַתֵּרֶד §84a.e. ‖ מֵעַל (עַל + מִן) from off. ‖ אֶרֶץ acc. loci. ‖ 24. בִּי I pray! ‖ 25. אַל c. ind. §41,3.
26. חַי §90bγ. ‖ אֲשֶׁר like ὅτι recitativum (כִּי §90e) to introduce direct speech: utique. ‖ דָּמִים bloodguiltiness. ‖ וְהוֹשֵׁעַ, as in v. 33 inf. absol., dependent of מִן in מִבּוֹא; יָדְךָ and יָדִי are nominatives of the subject. English: that thou camest not (from coming) in bloodguiltiness and thy hand helped thee not (from helping thee). Cf. Ewald §351c. ‖ וְהִתְחַבַּקְשִׁים §17b. 60b. ‖ אֶל in regard to. ‖
27. וְנִתְּנָה Wāw cons. perf. ‖ 28. בָּא §76e. ‖ מִיָּמֶיךָ from the beginning of thy life on. ‖ 29. וַיָּקָם forms with וְהָיְתָה a conditional sen-

tence without a conditional particle: "and should anyone arise ..
then will", cf. §88e. ‖ לְרָדְּפָךְ cf. אֲבָלֶךָ G. 2, 17, v. §55e. ‖ צָרַר bind
together, tie up; צְרוֹר bundle. ‖ אֵת with, apud. ‖ קָלַע I. III sling;
קֶלַע a sling, בַּף הַקֶּלַע hollow of the sling. ‖ וְצִוָּךְ לְנָגִיד and appointed
thee (to be) a prince.

31. Apodosis to v. 30. מוּקֵשׁ and מִכְשׁוֹל offence. ‖ וְהֵטִיב... יָזַכֵּר
§88ea. ‖ 32. שָׁלְחָהּ §79f1. ‖ 33. בִּלְתִּי from בָּלָא v. §75e; Suff. §79da. ‖
34. מֵחֲרַד Inf. Hiph. of רָעַד. כִּי.. בְּ, the כִּי introducing the content of the asseveration (§90a) is here repeated before the main
clause of the oath. ‖ ותבאתי lvpsus calami for וַתָּבֹאִי, König I, 647 sq.

36. עֲלֵי thereat, at the feast. ‖ 37. בְּצֵאת §76g. ‖ 39. מֵיָי Deus
enim Davidis causam ita egerat, ut David a Nabal poenas haberet. ‖
וַיְדַבֵּר בְּ spoke concerning her=wooed her.

41. אַפַּיִם with her face. ‖ 43. גַּם־שְׁתֵּיהֶן both of them.

c) I Kings 3.

1. כַּלּוֹתוֹ with בְּ §84b. ‖ 3. לָלֶכֶת §45f. ‖ גִבְעוֹן proper name, ה ֽ
§20ca. ‖ יַעֲלֶה Impf. without Wâw consec. in historical connexion
and without frequentative signification almost exclusively poetical,
except after אָז (v. 16), בְּטֶרֶם, טֶרֶם.

6. כַּאֲשֶׁר according as, as. ‖ יִשְׁרַת לֵבָב uprightness of heart
(ת only st. constr.). ‖ כִּסְאוֹ §6f3. ‖ כַּיּוֹם הַזֶּה as is now the case. ‖
7. לֹא אֵדַע I know not (how to). ‖ 8. מֵרֹב, מִן for, by reason of. ‖
9. וְנָתַתָּ give therefore. ‖ כָּבֵד here: great in number.

11. מִשְׁפָּט here: cause (at law). ‖ 13. נָתַתִּי §47b. ‖ 14. וְהַאֲרַכְתִּי
§65m. ‖ 15. וַיִּיקַץ, another reading is וַיֵּקַץ §69a. ‖ שְׁלָמִים peace-offering (with accompanying sacrificial feast).

16. תְּבֹאנָה §76h. ‖ 17. בִּי I pray (thee). ‖ וָאֵלֵד §64h. ‖ 18. לְלִדְתִּי
§68f; לְ periphrasis of the Genetive. ‖ זוּלָתִי and זוּלָתֵנוּ save, except. ‖
19. לַיְלָה acc. temporis to the question: when? ‖ אֲשֶׁר because.

22. כִּי לֹא nay! but. ‖ הֲתִי §17c. ‖ 24. קְחוּ §67h. ‖ 25. גְּזֹרוּ cleave
asunder, divide. ‖ אֶחָת §39a.

26. אֲשֶׁר־בְּנָהּ whose son §87a. ‖ נִכְמְרוּ רַחֲמֶיהָ her love had
become too strong, she was overpowered (כמר of doubtful etymology, cf. Friedr. Delitzsch, The Hebrew Language p. 40—42).
וְהָמֵת §63d. ‖ 28. וַיִּירָאוּ §76g.

d) Psalm 121.

1. בְּעֲלָה the ascent, pilgrimage (to Jerusalem). מֵאַיִן whence. 2. מֵעִם the help is with J. and comes from him. ‖ אַל־יִתֵּן and אַל־יָנוּם. אַל c. *ipf.*, esp. in poetry often as strong subjective negation, as if: by no means. ‖ יָכָבָה §76e, Suff. §22iα. הִכָּה of the injurious effects of the sun, as in Isa. 49, 10. 8. יֵצֵר . . מִן from . . to (more frequently even than מִן . . עַד).

e) Psalm 127.

1. לִשְׁלֹמֹה belonging to Solomon. (According to most scholars also here the so-called לְ *auctoris*). ‖ שָׁוְא adverbial Acc.: in vain. 2. מְאַחֲרֵי־שֶׁבֶת (you) who sit up late. ‖ שֵׁנָא Aramaic spelling for שֵׁנָה (*acc. temporis*, v. to I Kings 3, 19). ‖ 3. בָּנִים and פְּרִי הַבֶּטֶן are subject. ‖ 5. יֵבשׁוּ §71i. ‖ כִּי §88a. ‖ בַּשַּׁעַר *i. e.* in court.

f) Psalm 130.

2. קַשֻּׁב prop. pricked up, (of the ear): attentive ‖ 6. נַפְשִׁי supply: waiteth. ‖ מִן, מִשֹּׁמְרִים §82b.

VOCABULARY.*

אָב 38.
אָבַד § 66 a.
אָבָה § 66 a.
אֶבְיוֹן poor.
אֵבֶל mourning §25f.
אָבֵל mourn §65h.
אֶבֶן stone *28.
אבק II wrestle §65b.
אֵבֶר pinion, wing.
אָגַר gather.
אִגֶּרֶת §36c.
אָדוֹן lord §19d. *23.
אָדָם man; genly. collect.
אֲדָמָה §34b.
אֲדֹנָי §10c4.
אַדֶּרֶת cloak *36.
אָחַב (ē) §66b.
אֹהֶל tent 28q.
אָהַל pitch one's tent.

אוּלַי perhaps.
וְאוּלָם, אוּלָם on the contrary, nevertheless.
אָוֶן § 29 c. [
אוֹר shine §71i. V.
אוֹר light.
אוֹת II agree, consent *71.
אֹזֶן ear *28.
אזן V give ear to *65.
אָזַר gird *65.
אָח, אָחוֹת 38.
אֶחָד one §39a.
אָחַז 66 a. *65.
אֲחֻזָּה possession *22.
אַחֵר § 66 b; III morari 65c.
אַחֲרֵי, אַחַר § 43 b.
אַחֲרִית end, last state.
אֹיֵב enemy 24d.
אַיֵּה, aj, § 42f.
אַיִל ram *29.

---

* The Arabic figures correspond to the numbers of the paragraphs; § refers only to the grammar,* only to the exercises; numbers in parentheses indicate the paragraph according to which the accompanying word is to be inflected. The Roman figures (I—VII) with verbs indicate the conjugations; V alone signifies: causative. Unpointed verbal forms are found in the *Qal* either not at all or very seldom.

D*

אַיָּלָה, אַיֶּלֶת §36g.
אֵיךְ §41,2.
אִישׁ 38.
אַךְ 1. in truth, surely; 2. only.
אָכַל 66a.
אֹכֶל food.
אֵל §43a.
אַל §41,3.
אָלָה oath (32).
אֱלֹהִים God *22.
אִלֵּם dumb §24d.
אֶלֶף thousand *28.
אִם if §88; optative particle §89c; interrogative part. §42c.d; אִם and אִם־לֹא with an oath §90.
אֵם mother *26.
אָמָה 38.
אַמָּה 39f.
אֻמָּה nation *22.
אָמַן V believe; II be lasting, sure.
אָמֵץ be strong §65.
אָמַר 66a.
אֹמֶר speaking *36.
אֵמֶר §28o.
אִמְרָה utterance *35.
אֲנָחָה sigh *34.
אָנַף be angry 65h.
אָסַף §66a. §64l.
אָסַר bind 65.
אַף anger; du. nose, face *26.
אָפָה §66a.
אֵפֹא §42g.
אָפַק VII refrain one's self.
אֵפֶר ashes.
אָרַב lie in wait §65.

אָרוֹן chest, ark; with art. הָאָרוֹן.
אֹרַח path *28.
אֲרִי lion *30.
אָרַךְ be, become long V.
אֶרֶךְ §25h.
אֹרֶךְ length *28.
אֶרֶץ earth, land §17d. *28.
אָרַר I. III curse 73.
אֵשׁ fire *26.
אִשָּׁה 38.
אַשְׁפָּה quiver.
אֲשֶׁר 1. relative particle §16d. §87; 2. that; 3. because.
אָשַׁר III call happy.
אַשְׁרֵי (only pl. st. con.) blessed-nesses of the..=blessed is the..
אֲשֻׁרִים steps.
אֵת, אֶת־ with §43e.
אֵת, אֶת־ (acc.) §43f.
אָתוֹן she-ass *23.

בְּ §45.
בְּאֵר well *22.
בָּאַשׁ stink; V.
בֶּגֶד garment 28r.
בָּדַל V part.
בָּהַל II be amazed; III causat.
בְּהֵמָה §34d.
בּוֹא 76h; V bring.
בּוּס tread on.
בּוֹשׁ §71i. §77.
בָּזָה despise *74.
בָּזַז plunder *73.
בָּחוּר youth, pl. בַּחוּרִים.
בָּחַן prove.
בָּחַר choose out.

VOCABULARY. 53*

בָּטַח trust (בְּ in); V.
בֶּטֶן womb, stomach *28.
בִּין discern, understand §72; VII consider, give heed; אֶל to.
בֵּין §43c; בֵּין..לְ between.. and.
בִּינָה understanding.
בַּיִת 38.
בָּכָה weep 74.
בְּכִי weeping *30.
בְּלִיַּעַל worthlessness.
בָּלַל confound §73n.
בָּלַע swallow.
בָּמָה high place (32), esp. as site of religious worship.
בָּמָה, בָּמָה §45e.g.
בֵּן 38.
בָּנָה build 72.
בֹּסֶר sour grapes §28o.
בַּעַל lord *28. בְּעָלִים §86c.
בצר III §65b.
בָּקַע I, III cleave.
בִּקְעָה valley *35.
בֹּקֶר morning.
בָּקָר (large) cattle.
בִּקֵּשׁ seek 60b.
בָּרָא create *75.
בֹּרֵא creator §24e.
בְּרוֹשׁ cypress.
בָּרַח flee 65.
בְּרִיחַ bar.
בְּרִית covenant.
בֶּרֶךְ knee *28.
בֵּרַךְ III bless 65b.r.
בְּרָכָה blessing 34d.
בָּשָׂר flesh *25.
בשׂר III bring good news.

בַּת 38.
בֶּתֶר piece cut off (from the sacrifice) *28.
גָּאַל redeem.
גֹּאֵל redeemer 24e.
גָּבַהּ (23).
גִּבּוֹר hero *22.
גְּבִיר lord.
גָּבַר (ē) be, become strong.
גֶּבֶר man (mostly poet.).
גְּבֶרֶת §36b.
גַּג roof *26.
גְּדִי §30b.
גָּדַל (ē) be great.
גָּדֵל greatness §28n.
גדע III break in pieces.
גֶּדֶר §25e.
גּוֹי (§19b) nation, people.
גָּוַע expire.
גּוּר sojourn (as stranger) 71x.
גָּזַז shear 73h.
גָּחוֹן belly *23.
גַּיְא valley §29a.
גִּיל rejoice §72d.
גֻּלְגֹּלֶת skull 36b.
גָּלָה a) reveal; III uncover; II. IV. pass.; VII uncover one's self.
—b) go into exile, V lead into exile 74.
גָּלוּת the captivity; the exiles 37a.
גלח III shave (the head).
גָּלַל roll 73.
גַּם also; גַּם..גַּם et..et.
גמא V give to drink.
גָּמַל a) wean; b) do, render §83g.

גָּמָל camel 26 d.
גָּמַר cease.
גַּן garden *26.
גָּנַב steal.
גֹּפֶר cypress. (?)
גֹּרֶן threshing-floor 28 p.
גָּרַשׁ usu. III, drive out 65.
גֶּשֶׁם heavy rain (28).

דָּאַג be anxious, distressed.
דְּבֵלָה, pl. ־ים, fig-cake.
דָּבַק (ē) cleave, hold fast to.
דָּבָר word 25 b.
דִּבֶּר speak 60 e.
דָּג fish *24.
דָּגָה fish collect. *33.
דָּגָן corn.
דּוֹר generation, γενεά *22.
דִּין judge 72.
דֶּלֶת f. door *28.
דָּם blood 24 c.
דְּמוּת likeness; image.
דִּמְעָה tear, also collect. (35).
דָּעַךְ extinguish.
דָּפַק overdrive (the cattle).
דֶּרֶךְ V make to walk, guide.
דֶּרֶךְ way *28.
דָּרַשׁ seek, search.
הֵ §42.
הָדָר majesty (25).
הוֹד splendour.
הוֹי woe! ah!
הוֹן goods, treasure.
הָיָה §76 b.
הֵיכָל palace *24.

הָלַךְ go 68 i. §64 h; VII walk *62 —
III Part. מִתְהַלֵּךְ advancing vigorously.
הָלַל Pō'ēl §73 c; Pi. praise 73.
הָמוֹן noise, tumult *23.
הִנֵּה, הֵן see §40 d.
הָפַךְ vertere 65.
הַר mountain *26 c s. הָרָה §11 f.
הָרְבָה §74 w δ.
הָרַג slay 65.
הָרָה conceive, be pregnant 74.
הָרַס pull down 65.

זְאֵב wolf.
זֶבֶד §83 g.
זֶבַח slaughter, sacrifice; III sacri-
זָבַח slaughter, sacrifice. [fice.
זֶה §16 a.b. §42 g.
זֶה, זוּ relat. §87ᵃ note.
זָהָב gold (25).
זִיד §72 g.
זַיִת §29 a.
זָכַר remember.
זֵכֶר memory, memorial (28).
זִכָּרוֹן memorial 23 d.
זָמַם purpose §73 n.
זָנָב §25 a.
זָנָה go a-whoring; Part. זוֹנָה
זַעַם anger *28 i. [harlot.
זָעַק cry out §65.
זָעֲקָה cry *34.
זָקֵן senex 25 d.
זָקֵן be old.
זָקָן beard (bearded chin) *25.
זָר strange (22).
זְרוֹעַ arm.

VOCABULARY. 55*

זֶרַע seed *28.
זָרַע sow.

חבא II hide one's self.
חִבֻּק folding of the hands (as sign of idleness).
חַבּוּרָה weal, scar.
חָבַשׁ bind, bind up 65.
חָגַר gird, gird on (sthg.).
חֲגוֹרָה girdle *22.
חָדַל (ē) cease, leave off §65h.
חָדֵל leaving off §25h.
חֹדֶשׁ month 28h.
חִיל (חוּל) be in labour, tremble
חוֹמָה wall. [§72d.
חוּס spare.
חוּץ 1. street, lane; 2. adv. outside.
חוּשׁ (חִישׁ) make haste §72d.
חֹזֶה seer *31.
חָזַק be firm, III make firm, fortify; V seize, usu. w. בְּ or acc.
חָזָק strong.
חָטָא sin 75.
חַטָּאת 36e.
חִטָּה, pl. יבּ. wheat.
חַי living §90b.
חִידָה riddle.
חָיָה (perf.) §76c.
חַיָּה beast, often collect.
חַיִּים life *22.
חַיִל, suff. חֵילוֹ 1. strength; [2. wealth.
חֵיק bosom *22.
חֵךְ palate *26.
חָכַם be wise 65h.
חָכָם wise §25b.

חָלָב milk *25.
חֵלֶב fat *28.
חֲלוֹם dream *22.
חֳלִי sickness 30c.
חֲלִילָה §90c.
חָלַל, III חֵלֵל profane, V begin 73.
חָלָל pierced *25.
חָלַם dream 65.
חָלַף pass by, V change, alter.
חָלַק part, divide.
חֵלֶק part *28.
חֹם, חָבוּה §38.
חֹם warmth, heat *26.
חָמַד desire §65.
חֶמְדָּה preciousness, precious
חֵמָה wrath, anger. [things.
חֲמוֹר ass *22.
חָמַל spare 65.
חָמַם be warm.
חָמָס violence, injustice *25.
חֲמִשׁ §39o.
חֵן favour, grace *26.
חָנָה encamp §74.
חַנּוּן merciful.
חִנָּם 1. gratis, 2. frustra.
חָנַן be merciful, pity; VII (pray for mercy) 73.
חָנֵף profligate §25f.
חֶסֶד mercy, kindness *28.
חָסָה take refuge §74.
חֲסִידָה stork.
חָסֵר want, be without 65h.
חָסֵר wanting §25f.
חָפֵץ take pleasure, desire, feel inclined.
חָפֵץ taking pleasure §25f.

חֵפֶץ pleasure; *pl.* pleasing, precious things *28.
חָפַר dig 65.
חֵץ 26.
חָצָה halve §74.
חֲצִי half §39o.
חֹצֶן bosom, *sinus* §28o.
חָצֵר court 25d.
חֹק statute 26c.
חָקָה do. *22.
חֶרֶב sword *28.
חָרְבָּה §35a.
חָרֵד tremble 65h. V
חֲרָדָה trembling, terror §34d.
חָרָה burn §74; חָ לוֹ it burned within him=he grew angry.
חָרִישׁ ploughing.
חרם V *devoveo* §65p.
חֶרְפָּה §35c.b.
חרשׁ V be dumb, silent.
חֵרֵשׁ deaf §24d.
חָשָׂה hold back §65.
חָשַׂף make bare §65h.
חָשַׁב *aestimare* 65.
חֹשֶׁךְ darkness *28.
חַת fear §26c.
חַת broken.
חתן VII ally one's self (in marriage).
חֹתֵן father-in-law*24. [riage).
חָתָן son-in-law *25; bridegroom.
חָתַת be terrified §73f.o.

טָבַח slaughter §65e.
טַבָּח 1. cook, 2. executioner.
טַבַּעַת signet-ring 36c.
טָהוֹר clean, pure.

טָהַר be clean, VII purify one's self §62b. *65 III.
טוֹב he is good §77.
טוֹב good.
טִחֵחַ Pi'lēl §74b.
טָמֵא be unclean, III defile, II defile one's self *75.
טָמֵא unclean 25g.
טַעַם taste, metaph. understand-
טֶרֶם notyet; בְּטֶרֶם before. [ing.
טָרָה flay, IV *pass.*

יאל V take in hand, wish, will
יבל V conduct (66). [*68.
יָבֵשׁ become dry 69a.
יָבֵשׁ dry 25f.
יָגֵעַ be weary 68d.
יָגֹר fear §54c. §77.
יָד f. hand 24c.
ידה V. VII. §76f.
יָדִיד lover, friend.
יָדַע 68f.
יָהַב §68g.
יְהוָה §9b.
יוֹלֶדֶת §36d.
יוֹם 38.
יוֹמָם by day.
יוֹנָה dove *22.
יוֹנֶקֶת sprout *36.
יָחַד §68f.
יַחְדָּו *unā.*
יָחַל, III חִיל and V הוֹחִיל wait,
יָעַב 69. [on לְ, אֶל.
יַיִן wine *29.
יבח V judge, rebuke *68.
יָכֹל 68g. §54c.

יֶלֶד 68 f. c. b.
יֶלֶד son, child *28.
יָלַל V howl §69d. – yell –
יָם sea *26.
יָמִן V turn to the right *69.
יָנַק 69a, V suck.
יָסַד §68d.
יָסַף I. V add *68. §77. §84.
יָסַר III punish, rebuke, II pass.
יָעַד appoint §68d. [*68.
יַעַן אֲשֶׁר for the reason that, because.
יָעַף become weary 68d.
יָעַץ advise; II. VII take counsel
יָפֶה beautiful (31). [sel 68d.
יְפִי §30c.
יָצָא 76g.
יצב VII §70.
יצג V §70.
יצע V §70.
יָצַק §70.
יָצַר fingere §70.
יֹצֵר figulus §24 d.
יָצַת §70.
יָקַד §68e.
יָקֵץ §68f.
יֶקֶב §69a. §77.
יָקַר §68e V.
יָקוֹשׁ fowler.
יָרֵא 76g. §68d.
יָרֵא timens §25g.
יִרְאָה §55. *35.
יָרַד 68f.
יָרָה I. V. §76f.
יָרֵחַ moon.
יָרֵךְ 25e.

יָרַשׁ (ē) 68 d.
יֵשׁ §40e.
יָשַׁב 68f.—c. acc. §83d.
יֹשֵׁב inhabitant *24.
יְשׁוּעָה help, safety.
יָשֵׁן sleep 68d.
יָשֵׁן sleeping 25f.
יָשַׁע V help, save (68).
יֵשַׁע, יְשׁוּעָה salvation §28m.
יֹשֶׁר uprightness.
יָתוֹם orphan.
יתר II remain over, V *68.

כְּ §45.
כָּאַב feel pain *65 III.
כָּבֵד be heavy; II be honoured;
כָּבֵד heavy §25h. [III honour.
כָּבַס wash 60e.
כֶּבֶשׂ lamb.
בַּכְּנֵשׂוֹחַ, כְּ' §35b.
כָּבַשׁ subdue.
כַּד pail (26).
כֹּה thus (w. ref. to what follows);
עַד־כֹּה hither.
כָּבָה go out (of a light) §74.
כֹּהֵן priest *24.
כּוֹכָב star *24.
כּוּן V set up, prepare; II pass.
כָּזַב lie 25b. [*71.
כֹּחַ strength *22.
כחד III dissemble *65 I.
כחשׁ III infitiari *65 I.
כִּי 1. for; 2. if, when, ἐάν §88; with oaths and affirmations §90, כִּי אָז and כִּי עַתָּה. §90.
כֹּל totality, all, whole *26.

VOCABULARY.

כָּלָא keep back *75.
כֶּלֶב dog *28.
כִּלְכֵּל, כִּיל §72g.
כָּלָה be finished, III finish, cease *74. §84.
כַּלָּה daughter-in-law *22.
כְּלִי 38.
כָּלַם V put to shame; dishonour, injure anyone; II be ashamed, be put to shame.
בָּמָה §45e.g.
כֵּן thus, so.
כָּנַע V bring down, abase.
כָּנָף wing §25a.
כסה III cover 74.
כֶּסֶף silver 28 r.
כַּף (hollow of the) hand *26.
כִּפֶּר atone 60e.
כֹּפֶר ransom *28.
כַּר lamb.
כְּרוּב cherub.
כֶּרֶם vineyard *28.
כָּרַת cut off, destroy; כ' בְּרִית make [a covenant.
כָּשַׁל §77.
כָּתַב write.
כְּתֹנֶת §36f.
כָּתֵף §25e.
כְּתָרֶת §36c.

לְ §45.
לֹא §41,1.
לָאָה become weary, V §74wβ.
לְאֹם §26d.
לֵב heart *26.
לֵבָב heart §25c.
לְבִלְתִּי §41,5.

לָבַשׁ (ē) put on (clothes) 57b.
לָהָה be exhausted *74.
לוּ §88. §89c.
לוּלֵי, לוּלֵא §88.
לוּשׁ knead *71.
לְחִי cheek, jaw 30b.
לחם II proeliari §64l.
לֶחֶם bread 28 i.
לַיִל night *29.
לַיְלָה §20c; הַלַּיְלָה §17a.
(לוּן) spend the night 72d.
לָכַד capere.
לָמַד learn, III teach.
לָמָה, לָמָּה §45e6.
לעט V give to eat.
לֵץ scoffer.
לָקַח take (away) 67h.
לָקַט I. III gather.
לָשׁוֹן tongue *23.

מְאֹד very.
מֵאָה hundred.
מְאוּמָה anything whatever.
מָאוֹר luminary *23.
מַאֲכָל food *24.
מַאֲכֶלֶת §36c.
מאן III refuse §65b.
מָאַס despise, reject.
מִגְדָּל tower *24.
מָגֵן shield *26.
מְגוּרִים wanderings *22.
מִדְבָּר desert *24.
מִדָּה the measure.
מַדּוּעַ why? (for what reason?).
מַה, מִי §16e.f. §45e.g.
מהר III make haste 65b. §84.

VOCABULARY. *59

מוּג stagger *71.
בּוּל 71y.
מוֹלֶדֶת birth, *concrete* family *36.
מוֹעֵד 1. point of time; 2. feast (feast-day); 3. meeting, as-sembly 24 e.
מוֹרָא fear 24 b.
מוֹשָׁב dwelling *24.
מוּת 71 i. u.
מְזִי §29 c.
מִזְבֵּחַ altar 24 e.
מָחָה blot out *74.
מַחֲזֶה vision *31.
מַחֲנֶה camp *31.
מַחֲסֶה refuge *31.
מַחְסוֹר want.
מָחָר to-morrow.
מַחֲשָׁבָה purpose *33 II.
מַטֶּה tribe, staff *31.
מטר V cause to rain.
מִי יִתֵּן, כִּי §89 d.
מַיִם 38.
מִין kind §22 i β. k.
מִכְסֶה covering (31).
מָכַר sell.
מָלֵא be full, *acc.* §83 b; III fill 75.
מָלֵא full 25 g.
מַלְאָךְ ἄγγελος 24 b.
מְלָאכָה §36 g.
מֶלַח salt.
מִלְחָמָה 36 g.
מלט III save, II *pass.* and *refl.*
מָלַךְ *regnare.* V.
מֶלֶךְ king 28 h.
מַלְכָּה queen 35 a.
מַלְכוּת *regnum* 37 a.
מלל II circumcise §73 n.

מִלֵּל speak.
מַמְלָכָה kingdom 33 b.
מֶמְשָׁלָה rule *33 II.
מִן §44. §82 b.—Often compounded with other prepositions: מֵאֵת, מֵעַל, מֵעַל לְ, מֵעִם above.
מָנָה count 74.
מְנוּחָה rest.
מְנוֹרָה candlestick.
מִנְחָה gift, mealoffering *35.
מָנַע hold back.
מִסְפֵּד §24 e.
מִסְפָּר number 24 a.
מַעְגָּל track.
מָעַד stagger, slip.
מְעַט little; כִּמְעַט nearly; soon,
מַעְלָה upwards. [speedily.
מַעֲלָלִים deeds, actions.
מַעֲמַקִּים depths.
מַעַן, לְמַעַן only: 1. for the sake of, on account of; 2. לַאֲשֶׁר and לְ with the intention of, in
מְעָרָה cave *22. [order to.
מַעֲשֶׂה deed *31.
מַעֲשֵׂר tithe 24 e.
מָצָא find 75.
מִצְוָה commandment §22.
מִצְרִי Egyptian *37.
מִצְרַיִם Egypt.
מִקְדָּשׁ sanctuary 24 a.
מִקְרָא assembly (31).
מָקוֹם place *23.
מִקְנֶה §31 b.
מקק II §73 n.
מַר sour.
מַרְאֶה §31 b.

מִרְמָה deceit.
מָרַר be bitter, *ipf.* §73o; III make
מַשְׂכִּרֶת §37b. [bitter.
מַשְׂכֹּרֶת hire, wages *36.
מָשַׁח anoint.
מָשִׁיחַ anointed one §23b.
מִשְׁכָּן dwelling, tabernacle.
מָשַׁל rule, בְּ over.
מָשָׁל proverb (25).
מִשְׁמֶרֶת *custodia* 36b.
מִשְׁפָּחָה family 33b.
מִשְׁפָּט justice, judgment *24.
מַשְׁקֶה drink, cupbearer *31.
מִשְׁקָל weight *24.
מָשַׁשׁ feel (like a blind man); III search thoroughly 73.
מִשְׁתֶּה §31c.
מֵת *mortuus* *22.
מָתַי when?
מַתָּנָה present §33a.

נָא pray!
נאה Pi´lēl §74b.
נְאֻם (only *st. c.*) utterance.
נָאַף I. III commit adultery 65b. §83e.
נָאַץ I. III mock, revile 65b.
נבא 76e.
נבט V look at *67.
נָבִיא prophet 23b.
נֵבֶל 1. water-bottle (of skin); 2. harp (28).
נָבָל fool, godless person.
נְבָלָה folly.
נְבֵלָה corpse *34.
נֶגֶב §28k.

נגד V show 67.
נֶגֶד §28k.
נֹגַהּ brightness *28.
נָגִיד prince (23).
נָגַע 67e.f.
נֶגַע blow, plague *28.
נָגַף smite, push (67).
נָגַשׂ press §67b.
נָגַשׁ 67d.e.f. §77.
נָדַד §67d.
נָדַר 67d.
נֶדֶר, נ׳ vow §28m.
נָהַג drive (cattle) 67.
נחל III §65c.
נָחַם *ipf.* §67c.
נָהָר river 25b.
נוד *vagari* *71.
נָוֶה pasture, dwellingplace *31.
נוּחַ 71x.y.
נום slumber (71).
נוס flee *71.
נוּעַ swing, wander around *71.
נוף V §71t.
נָזַל flow §67d.
נֶזֶם nosering, earring *28.
נָחָה I. V lead §77.
נַחַל brook *28.
נַחֲלָה inheritance.
נחם II repent, comfort one's self; III comfort; VII have pity on
נָחָשׁ serpent *25. [67.
נחשׁ III *augurari*.
נְחֹשֶׁת §36b.
נָחַת §67c.
נָטָה 76d.—נ׳ אֹהֶל pitch.
נָטַע 67e.f.

VOCABULARY.

נָטַשׁ throw down, leave (behind),
נֶּדֶר §28 k. [leave off.
נבה IV. V. VI. 76 d.
נָכַח opposite §28 o.
נכר V look steadily at, recognise; VII disguise one's self
נֵכָר foreign country. [*67.
נְמָלָה ant.
נסם III §76 d.
נֶסֶךְ drink-offering §28 r.
נסךְ V *libare* *67.
נָסַע 67 f.
נְעוּרִים youth *22.
נַעַל shoe *28.
נָעֵם be pleasant.
נַעַר 1. boy; 2. lad, (=Germ. *Bursche*) 28 i.
נַעֲרָה girl *35. §9 b.
נָפַח 67 e. f.
נָפַל 67.
נֶפֶשׁ f. soul *28.
נצב V place; II *pass.* *67. §70.
נֶצַח, נֵצַח duration (of time) §28 m.
נצל V save; II *pass.* 67.
נָצַר watch, guard 67 b.
נָקַב appoint; curse.
נקה II be innocent; III leave unpunished 76 d.
נָקִי innocent 31 a.
נִקָּיוֹן innocency *23.
נָקַם revenge; VI *pass.* 67.
נְקָמָה revenge *34.
נֵר lamp.
נָשָׂא §76 e; נָשָׂא ': פָּנִים πρόσωπον λαμβάνειν, לְ ': pardon some one.

נשׂג V reach, overtake *67.
נָשִׂיא §23 a.
נשׁא V §76 e.
נָשַׁח §76 d.
נָשַׁךְ bite §67 d.
נָשַׁל §67 f.
נְשָׁמָה breath (34).
נָשַׁק I. III kiss 67 d. f.
נְתִיבָה path *22.
נָתַן 67 i; make (=appoint) §83 g.

סְאָה Sea, a measure *22.
סָבַב turn, go around, surround
סָבִיב *suff.* §43 b. [73.
סָגַר shut.
סוג I. II turn back §71 s.
סוּס horse.
סוּף flags (=papyrus).
סוּר turn aside 71 x.
סֻכָּה booth *22.
סְלִיחָה forgiveness.
סֶלַע rock (28).
סָעַד uphold, support §83 g.
סַנְוֵרִים blindness.
סָעַד uphold, sustain §83 g.
סְעָרָה §34 c.
סָפַד complain, *plangere*.
סָפָה carry off *74.
סָפַר count; III relate.
סֵפֶר book §28.
סָתַם I. III stop (e. g. wells).
סתר V conceal; II *refl.*
סֵתֶר 1. what is hidden; 2. covering, shade, defence.

עָבַד 65, serve, *c. acc.* §83*e*; till (the ground).
עֶבֶד servant *28.
עָבַר *transire* 65.
עִבְרִי Hebrew.
עֵגֶל §28*l*.
עֶגְלָה *vitula* 35*b*.
עֲגָלָה §34*b*.
עַד §43*a*.
עַד §22.
עֶדְרָה §33*a*.
עֵדוּת §37*a*.
עוּד V protest, bear witness *71.
עוֹד §40*f*. [§64*h*.
עָוֶל unrighteousness.
עוֹלָם eternity.
עָוֹן sin 23*c*.
עוּף fly, עָפָה do. *71.
עִוֵּר blind §24*d*.
עֹז strength 26*c*.
עֵז goat §26*a.b*.
עָזַב leave, forsake 65.
עָזַר help *c. acc.* §65.
עָזַר help *28.
עֶזְרָה §36*h*.
עַיִט bird of prey, *coll.* *29.
עַיִן eye, spring *29.
עִיר 38.
עִיר §29*b*.
עָרִים §26*d*.
עַל §43*a*.
עָלָה go up 74.
עֹלָה burnt offering.
עָלָה §31*c*.
עָלַז rejoice, be merry.
עַלְמָה virgin *35.

עַם people 26*c*¢.
עִם with §43*d*.
עָמַד stand 65.
עַמּוֹנִי Ammonite §37*b*.
עָמַל exert one's self, labour, צ at.
עָמֵל labouring §25*f*.
עָמֹק be deep.
עֵמֶק valley *28 III.
עֵנָב grape §25*c*.
עָנָה answer 74, *c. acc.* §83*e*.
עָנָה be bowed down; III oppress, humble; VII humble one's
עֳנִי misery *30. [self 74.
עָנִי 31*a*.
עָנַן III bring clouds together
עָפָר dust *25. [§73*b*.
עֵץ tree 24*f*.
עֶצֶב pain, hard work *28.
עָצַב II. VII be grieved.
עִצָּבוֹן sorrow, toil §23*d*.
עֲצַבִּים idols.
עַצֶּבֶת pain.
עֵצָה counsel *33.
עָצֵל lazy.
עֶצֶם bone, *pl.* זה *28.
עָצַר hold back, shut up.
עֲצֶרֶת §36*g*.
עָקֵב §25*i*.
עָקַב take by the heel, cheat.
עָרַב VII mix (in), mix with, hold intercourse with.
עֶרֶב evening.
עֹרֵב raven *24.
עָרַג pant.
עָרָה III uncover, empty §74*s*.
עָרוֹם naked §26*d*.

VOCABULARY.

עָרַךְ arrange, prepare *65.
עָרֵל uncircumcised §25h.
עָרְלָה foreskin *35.
עֵשֶׂב herb *28.
עָשָׂה do 74. §65l.
עָשַׂר III tithe.
עָשַׁן to smoke.
עָשָׁן smoke *25.
עָשַׁר V enrich.
עֹשֶׁר riches (28).
עֵת time *26.
עַתָּה now.

עָתַק V strike one's tent, set forward *65.
עָתַר pray; II hear (prayer).

פָּאַר III §65b.
פֶּגֶר corpse *28.
פָּגַשׁ acc. to light on, meet any
פָּדָה redeem. [one.
פְּדוּת redemption.
פֶּה 38.
פּוּץ I. II scatter 71o. s. V.
פַּח snare.
פָּחַד shake, tremble.
פַּחַד fear, terror (28).
פֶּלֶג stream (28).
פָּלִיט one escaped.
פָּלַל judge; VII pray 73.
פָּנָה turn §74.
פִּנָּה corner, 'פ רֹאשׁ cornerstone.
פָּנִים face 31a; לִפְנֵי in the presence of, before; לִפְנֵי before me, before my face; מִפְּנֵי from
פְּנִימִי interior *37. [before &c.
פְּנִינִים pearls.

פֹּעַל work *28.
פַּעַם time *28; הַפַּעַם §17a.
פּוּם II be disquieted.
פָּצָה open (the mouth).
פֶּצַע wound *28.
פָּקַד visěre; V praeficere.
פָּקַח open.
פַּר young bullock 26cε.
פָּרַד II to part.
פָּרָה be fruitful 74.
פְּרִי fruit 30c.
פָּרַר V break 73k.
פָּרָשׁ horseman, pl. פָּרָשִׁים.
פָּשַׁט V strip τινά τι.
פֶּשַׁע transgression (28).
פַּת morsel 26c.
פָּתָה stand open; V make wide.
פָּתַח open.
פֶּתַח door *28.
פָּתַר expound.

צֹאן small cattle.
צָבָא host, army *25.
צְבִי gazelle §30c.
צַד side 26c.
צַדִּיק righteous, just.
צָדַק be righteous.
צֶדֶק righteousness 28.
צְדָקָה do. §34a.
צוּד hunt *71.
צִוָּה order, charge 74.
צְוָחָה cry *34.
צוּר rock 22.
צָחַק laugh, III joke 65.
צַיִד venison *29.
צֵל shadow *26.

צָלַח prosper; V make to prosper, bring to a prosperous issue
צֶלֶם image, idol (28). [65 s.
צַלְמָוֶת deep darkness.
צָלִי §25i.
צָמֵא thirsty 25g.
צָמַח sprout, V 65 s.
צָעַד pace, walk.
צַעַד pace.
צְעִיף veil, covering *23.
צְעִיר small (23).
צָעַק cry out.
צְעָקָה cry *34.
צָפָה spy, watch *74.
צִפּוֹר sparrow *22.
צָפַן I and V conceal.
צַר oppressor, enemy §26c.
צָרָה oppression, distress (32).
צָרַר be narrow 73o.

קָבַץ I. III gather.
קָבַר bury.
קֶבֶר grave *28.
קָדַד προσκυνεῖν 73m.
קָדוֹשׁ holy (23).
קָדַשׁ be holy; III sanctify.
קֹדֶשׁ sanctuary; pl. devout offerings 28p.
קָוָה II assemble; III wait 74, לְ
קוֹל voice *22, pl. ־וֹת. [on.
קוּם 71.
קוֹץ thorns §29c.d.
קוֹרָה beam.
קָטָן small 26d.
קָטֹן 1. be small; 2. small.
קָטַר III. V offer incense.

קְטֹרֶת incense.
קַיִץ summer.
קִיר wall.
קָלַל I. II be of no account, despised; קִלֵּל curse 73.
קָצִיץ §28n.
קֵן nest; pl. compartments of the ark *26.
קָנָא III be zealous *75.
קָנָה parare, comparare *74.
קָנֶה reed *31.
קֵץ end *26.
קָצֶה end (31).
קָצִין judge, leader (23).
קָצִיר harvest *23.
קָצַר reap.
קָרָא call *75.
קָרַב (ē) approach; V.
קָרֵב approaching §25f.
קֶרֶב the inside *28.
קָרָה meet; V 74.
קָרוֹב near (23).
קִרְיָה town (mostly poet.).
קֶרֶן horn *28.
קָשַׁב V attend, hearken, לְ to.
קָשֶׁה hard (31).
קָשַׁר bind.
קֶשֶׁת bow *28.

רָאָה see; V. 74.
רֹאשׁ 38.
רֵאשׁ poverty.
רַב much; רַב־כֹּחַ of great strength
רֹב multitude 26 b. [(26).
רָבַב be, become many 73.
רְבָבָה myriad *34.

VOCABULARY. 65*

רָבָה be, become many 74.
רָבַב, רֹבַב §39o.
רָבַץ lie (of quadrupeds).
רֶגֶל foot *28.
רָגַל III spy out.
רָדָה subjugate §74.
רָדַף pursue.
רוּחַ wind, spirit 22.
רוּחַ V smell 71.
רוּם 71; III. V raise.
רוּץ run *71.
רוּק V empty *71.
לֶחֶם bread *28.
רְחוֹב street, square *22.
רַחוּם merciful, compassionate.
רִחַם III show compassion *65.
רֶחֶם womb *28 i.
רַחֲמִים compassion.
רִחֵף III hover over sthg. *65.
רָחַץ wash *65.
רָחוֹק, רָחֹק distant.
רִיב strive 72, רִיב אֶת־רִיב דָּוִד
    plead D.'s cause.
רִיב strife, cause (at law).
רֵיחַ smell; ר׳ חַנִּיחֹתַי a sweet sa-
רָכַב ride, drive. [vour.
רֶכֶס §28n.
רָמָה throw; III deceive.
רֹמַח lance *28.
רָמַשׂ move (esp. of smaller crea-
רֶמֶשׂ small animals.   [tures.)
רָנַן shout for joy, exult §73.
רִנָּה shout of joy.
רֵעַ friend, neighbour.
רַע wicked, subst. wickedness *26.
רָעָב hunger *25.

רָעֵב hungry 25f.
רָעָה evil, wickedness, misfortune
רָעָה pascěre, pasci §74. [*22.
רֹעָה §31a.
רָעַע (רַע) be bad, evil 73 o.
רָפָא heal §75.
רָפָה be slack §74.
רָצַח murder.
רָצָץ III. VII. §73c.e.
רָקִיעַ firmament (23).
רָשָׁע wicked person *25.

שָׂבַע (ē) be sated, satisfied, acc.
    §83b; V §65.
שָׂבֵעַ satiated, full 25f.
שֹׂבַע satiety, one's fill.
שׂבר III wait, hope, אֶל on.
שָׂדֶה field 31a.
שׂוּחַ (שִׂיחַ) meditari §72d.
שׂוּם (שִׂים) set, lay 72.
שׂוּשׂ (שִׂישׂ) exult 72.
שְׂחוֹק laughter.
שָׂטַם show enmity to.
שֵׂיבָה canities *22.
שָׂכִיר hireling, day-labourer.
שָׂכַל V have understanding.
שֵׂכֶל, שֶׂ understanding (28).
שָׂכַר to hire.
שָׂכָר hire *25.
שַׂלְמָה garment *35.
שָׂמַח (ē) rejoice; III make glad.
שָׂמֵחַ rejoicing §25f.
שִׂמְחָה joy *35.
שִׂמְלָה garment *35.
שָׂנֵא hate 75.
שׂנֵא hater *24.

H. Strack, Hebr. Gramm.² I.   E

שֵׂעָר hair *25.
שְׂעֹרִים barley, κριθαί.
שָׂפָה §33a.
שַׂק sack *26.
שַׂר prince *26.
שְׂרִגִים vine-branches.
שָׂרַף burn.

שָׁאַב draw (water).
שָׁאַל (ē) ask, demand; לְשָׁלוֹם ask after the health, greet, with לְ of the person.
שָׁאַר II remain over; V.
שָׁבָה carry away captive §74.
שֵׁבֶט staff, tribe *28.
שְׁבִי captivitas, captivi *30.
שָׁבַע II swear; V. 65.
שְׁבֻעָה (שְׁבוּעָה) oath.
שָׁבַר break.
שָׁדַד lay waste §73g.
שָׁוְא §29c.
שׁוּב 71. §84e.
שׁוּעָל fox.
שׁוּק aim at, attack.
שׁוֹפֵט, שָׁפַט judge *24.
שׁוֹר bull, ox.
שׁחח VII προσκυνεῖν 74we.
שָׁחַט slaughter *65.
שַׁחַר dawn.
שׁחת III. V corrupt, destroy; II be corrupt 65.
שֹׁטֵר overseer (24).
שִׁיר sing §72d.
שִׁיר song.
שִׁית set, place 72d.
שָׁכַב lie down.

שִׁכּוֹר, שִׁכֹּר drunk.
שָׁכַח (ē) forget.
שָׁכֵחַ forgetful of §25f.
שָׁכַךְ sink *71.
שָׁכֹל become childless.
שְׁכֶם, suff. שִׁכְמוֹ, shoulder.
שׁכם V rise early.
שָׁכַן dwell c. acc. §83d; V.
שָׁכֵן §25f.
שָׁלַח send; III send away, προπέμπειν.
שׁלך V throw. VI §61g.
שָׁלָל booty (25).
שָׁלֵם make good.
שָׁלֵם integer 25f.
שֵׁם name 24f.
שָׁם there.
שׁמד V destroy.
שָׁמָּה thither.
שָׁמַיִם 38.
שָׁמֵם be desolate §73o.
שֶׁמֶן oil.
שָׁמַע hear.
שָׁמַר watch, keep; II take heed.
שֶׁמֶשׁ m., f. sun 28.
שֵׁן tooth, ivory; שִׁנַּיִם teeth *26.
שָׁנָה repeat; II pass. *74.
שָׁנָה year *33.
שָׁנָה (pl. Prov. 6,10) §33a.
שֵׁנִי second.
שָׁעָה look towards 74.
שׁעך II lean.
שַׁעַר gate *28.
שִׁפְחָה handmaid *35.
שָׁפַט judge.
שָׁפַךְ pour out.

שָׁקַד watch, be watchful.
שָׁקָה V give to drink 74. §77.
שֶׁקֶל shekel *28. §39f.
שָׁקַץ abhor.
שֶׁקֶר mendacium *28.
שֹׁרֶשׁ root 28p.
שָׁרַת serve.
שָׁתָה drink 74. §77.

תְּאֵנָה fig(tree) *22.
תֹּאַר form, shape (28).
תֵּבָה ark.
תְּהִלָּה song of praise, psalm.
תָּוֶךְ §29c.
תּוֹכַחַת reproof 36.
תּוֹעֵבָה abomination *33.
תּוֹרָה instruction *22.
תְּחִלָּה beginning *22.
תַּחֲנוּנִים requests, supplications.

תַּחַת under, instead of §43b.
תַּחְתִּי lower, lowermost *37.
תִּירוֹשׁ (unfermented) wine.
תַּיִשׁ §29b.
תָּלַל V disappoint, deceive (I).
תֹּם integritas (26).
תָּמַהּ wonder §65a.
תָּמִים integer (23).
תָּמַם be finished, complete 73m.
תְּנוּמָה slumber.
תעב III §65b.
תָּעָה stray 74.
תעע Pilpel mock *73.
תֹּף 26.
תִּפְאֶרֶת 36g.
תְּפִלָּה prayer.
תָּפַשׂ seize.
תִּקְוָה hope.
תְּשׁוּקָה desire.

V. Exercises for Translation into Hebrew.

1. **Article § 17 (Ges. 35, Dav. 11). A.** [1]The righteous (man); the wicked (man); the father; this time; [5]that man; the dust; this great tumult; the sword; the Jebusite; [10]the blind (man); the ox; the dry land (2); the Amorite; [14]the people (2).

B. Complete the pointing of: [1]הִעִבְרִים, הֶחֳדָשִׁים, הָעַמִּים, [5]חַי, הָרָמָה, הִירְדֵּן[P], הַלְּבָנוֹן[P], הַצִּיר, [10]הַחֲכָמִים, הַהָרִים, הַעִוְרִים, הֶחֳרָבוֹת, הָאָרֶץ, [15]הָעֵת הַהִיא, הֶעָרִים, חֵץ, הַחֲמוֹר, הַחֶרֶב, [20]הָאֲרַמִּי.

2. **Waw copulativum §§ 11 g. h. 46 (G 104, 2. D 15). A.** [1]The head and the foot; the great and terrible God (אֵל); David and Solomon; Joseph and Benjamin; [5]Reuben and Juda; Jacob and Esau; Sodom and Gomorrah; hunger and sickness; man and God (§10c.).

B. Complete the pointing of: [1]יִשְׂרָאֵל וַאֲמַלֵּק, דָּוִד וִיהוֹנָתָן, אַבְרָהָם וֶאֱלִיעֶזֶר, וַאֲנִי, [5]וַאדֹנָי, שֹׁמְרוֹן וִירוּשָׁלַם, מֹשֶׁה וּמִרְיָם, חַגַּי וּזְכַרְיָהוּ וּמַלְאָכִי, [10]עֲדָה וְצִלָּה, אֵלִיָּהוּ וֶאֱלִישָׁע, וַאֲנִי.

3. **בְּ, כְּ, לְ §§ 11 g. h. 45 (G 103, 2. D 14).** [1]To David and to Solomon; in Jerusalem and in Samaria;

in Edom; to a sickness; [5]to Chananiah; to the Lord; in safety; [8]like God. B. To wisdom; [10]as the people (2); to the Amorite; to the sin (2); in the house; like the king. [15]A father (am) I to the poor (man). [16]Thus (this *f. sg.*) did Joshua do to Jericho and to Ai (with Article!).

C. Complete the pointing of: לַחֲנוֹךְ[1], לֵאלֹהִים, כְּאֶפְרָיִם[P],
[5]בֵּאלֹהִים. ׀ וּכְמִי־בָשָׂה ׀, בָּאדֹנִי, לָמָה אָמַר, לָמָה יָצָא, כִּיהוֹנָתָן,
[10].— ׀ D. With article: בַּשָּׁנָה הַזֹּאת, בַּיּוֹם[12], לִירוּשָׁלַיִם, לָנֶצַח,
הַהוּא, לָרָשָׁע[15], הֶחֳרָבוֹת, כָּעִיר[16].

4. מִן §§ 10 g. 44 (G 103, 2. D 14). [1]He went out of the city. He went up out of Egypt. He took of the blood. From Jerusalem. [5]From the Lord. From Assyria unto Egypt. Greater (is) he than (§82b) Reuben. [8]Better (art) thou than Saul.

5. **Nouns with unchangeable Vowels** § 22 (G 91, 4. D 17. 19). [1]The flock of Abraham; Joseph's cup; the voice of Jahweh; the spirit of God; [5]thy (*m.*) heroes; their (*m.*) heroes; thy (*f.*) gods, your (*f.*) ass; his flock; [10]our strength; thy (*f.*) dead (*m. sg.*); thine (*m. p.*) ass; my city; [14]his pilgrimage.

[15]Near (is) the day of Jahweh. Where (are) the idols of Samaria? Holy (is) Jahweh our God. Not as our rock (is) their rock. This Philistine (has been) a man of war from his youth. [20]These witnesses (are) lying witnesses. [21]Merciful (is) our God.— ׀ B. [1]The

prayer of the upright (man); his daughter-in-law; our booths; your (*m.*) burnt-offering;⁵ thy (*f.p.*) burnt-offerings; their (*m.*) wickedness; my paths; your laws; my daughter-in-law; ¹⁰their (*m.*) booths. My praise (art) thou. Behold, the fear of Jahweh, it (*f.*) (is) wisdom. ¹³Good (is) the law of Jahweh.— C. Perf. Qal (§54). ¹Fallen are the heroes. They have buried their (*m.*) dead. Jahweh heard the voice of Hagar. Judah conquered Gaza and its (Hebr. *f.*) border. ⁵I have hearkened unto (בְּ) your voice. They took their horses and their asses and went out of the land of Egypt. Ye have not kept the law of Jahweh. Thou (*f.*) hast not buried thy dead. I have taken pleasure in thy law. ¹⁰Ye have killed our witnesses. ¹¹Thou, (O) Jahweh, hast preserved my life.

6. **Masculines with changeable Vowel in the Penult** §23 (G 93 IV *a*. D 18). A. ¹My princes; the belly of the serpent; our prophets; my lord; ⁵our lord; our lords; her place; your places; his harvest; ¹⁰the (he-) asses of Abraham and his she-asses; his saints; our harvest; from our sin; from his right-hand and from his left; ¹⁵the sins of the Amorite.— B. ¹Your prophets (are) lying prophets. Where (are) thy (*f.*) prophets? Thy (*f.*) tongue (is) a lying tongue. Jahweh is near unto his saints. ⁵Manasse slew the prophets of Jahweh. ⁶He has gone out from his place.

7. Masculines with changeable Vowel in last Syllable

§ 24 (G 93 III *a. b.* D 18. 30). ¹Thy judgments; my food; their (*m.*) palaces; our messenger; ⁵your (*m.*) number; my stars; his weight; your (*m.*) judgments; his palaces.— ¹⁰Behold, Hagar (is) in thy (*f.*) hand. Great (is) the number of the stars of heaven. For Gibeon is a great city, greater than (§82*b*) Ai. Thy (*f.*) memory (is) dead. My rock and my redeemer (is) Jahweh. ¹⁵Behold, (here is) the fire and the wood for (*gen.*) the burnt-offering; but (ו) where (is) the ox? ¹⁵The voice (is) the voice of Jacob; but (ו) the hands (are) the hands of Esau. These (§16*a*) (are) the names of David's heroes. ¹⁸Great in (*st. c.*) might (is) Jahweh.— B. ¹God created (§86*e*) the sun and the moon and the stars. The king sent his messengers but (וַ) they did not find the prophet. The glory of Jahweh hath filled this house. David did not stretch forth his hand against (בְּ) Saul, the anointed of Jahweh. ⁵Our enemies have fled. Ye have pursued your enemies. Your hands are full of (*acc.* § 83 *b*) blood. They shed their blood like water. Jahweh hath given Israel into the hand of his enemies. ¹⁰He made an altar of (*gen.*) brass. Jehu burnt the sanctuaries of Baal with (בְּ with Article §17*f*1) fire. ¹²The enemies' messengers have drawn near.

8. **Masculines with two changeable Vowels** § 25 (G 93 II *a—e*. D 18). A. ¹The court of the tabernacle; her word; my beard; his son-in-law; ⁵thy booty (*p.*); your (*f.*) hire; in thy courts; the elders of the people; our hire; ¹⁰your flesh; Jacob's thigh.— ¹²This (is) David's booty. Jahweh (is) far from the wicked. A reproach (are) we to our neighbours. ¹⁵Pleasant (are) the words of the prophet. Thy (*f.*) redeemer, the Lord of Hosts (is) his name (§ 86 *e* α). Better (is he that is) longsuffering than a hero. ¹⁸Dry (faded, are) all the trees of this wood.— ‖ B. ¹The wisdom of his wise men has come to nought. Moses did according to (כְּ) the word of Jahweh. The cloud of Jahweh descended on the tabernacle. His heart was not perfect with (עִם) Jahweh his God, like the heart of David. ⁵Thus said Moses: I (am) slow of speech and of a slow tongue (render: heavy of mouth (*gen.*) and heavy of tongue). Our God hath no (לֹא) pleasure in the wicked. (There) has not fallen to the ground (§ 20 *c* α) one word of the words of Jahweh. ⁸Thou hast not remembered their lies.

9. **Masculines of one Syllable with the final Consonant doubled** § 26 (G 93 I *l,m,n*. D 43). A. ¹Their (*m.*) oppressors; in his shadow; your mothers; your end; ⁵our heart; your teeth; the times; the shadow of the cloud. His teeth (are) the teeth of a lion. ¹⁰Jahweh

is my strength and my shield. Sinners (are) ye all.
A word in (בְּ) its season, how good (it is)! ¹³Those
mountains (are) smaller than Lebanon.— ‖ B. Qal.
¹Jahweh hath chosen (with בְּ) the people of Israel out
of all peoples. The oppressors of Jerusalem have fled.
Thou hast clothed-thyself (with) strength and glory.
Ye have buried your mother. ⁵Jahweh hath sent forth
his sharp arrows (Hebr. his arrows the sharp ones).
Sell your camels. Jahweh hath poured out his fierce
anger upon Egypt. The whole people heard the words
of the king. They will burn every house. ¹⁰ The
number of their oppressors will be great.

10. **Masculine Segholate Forms from strong Stems**
§ 28 (G 93 I *a—f*. D 29. 35 ff.). I. A. ¹My way; your
ways; thy kings; your (*m.*) dogs; ⁵my dog; our soul;
your (*f.*) souls; the children of the Hebrews; his horn;
¹⁰our door; the horns of the ox; your swords; thy (*f.*)
stone; thy(*f.*) grave; ¹⁵his knees.— ‖ ¹⁶Your servants
(are) we. His horns (are) the horns of a wild-ox.
Jahweh (is) our righteousness. Righteous (is) Jahweh
in all his ways. ²⁰Better (is) his favour than (82*b*)
life. The heavens (are) the throne of Jahweh and the
earth is his footstool (render: the stool of his feet).
²²Thy word (is) a lamp unto (לְ) my feet.— ‖ B. (Niph.,
Pi., Pu.) ¹The bow is broken. Seek ye the way to
(*genet.* § 21*f*) the city. Shut thy door. Thy horn is full

of (*acc.* §83*b*) oil. ⁵I will remember thy favour. He did not give of his bread to the poor. We have sought our dog. Broken is my heart within me (see vocabulary). He walked in the way of the kings of Israel. ¹⁰Jahweh will break-in-pieces (Pi.) the cedars of Lebanon. My vows will I pay to Jahweh. ¹²Jahweh will keep the feet of the godly.

II. ¹His seed; their (*m.*) wounds; your transgression; thy (*f. p.*) boys; ⁵your boys; his master; ⁷my anger.

III. ¹His staff; my staves; the names of the tribes of Israel; thy portion. ⁵In the law of Jahweh (is) my delight. My help (is) in the name of Jahweh. ⁷Jahweh (is) our portion.

IV. A. ¹Our ransom; our ear; our ears; thy spear; ⁵her work; their works; thy threshing-floor; his holiness; ⁹your tent.— B. ¹Ye have broken our spears. We have broken your spears. They have slept in their tents. ⁴I will speak these words in their ears.

11. **Masculine Segholate Forms from ע״י and ע״ו** § 29 (G 93 I *g. h. i.* D 41). ¹Thine (*f.*) eye; her eyes; my wine; your wine; ⁵the rams of Bashan; our venison. ⁷He stood in their midst.

12. **Masculine Segholate Forms from ל״ה** § 30 (G 93 I *k.* D 45). ¹Our captives; his affliction. Better is my fruit than (82*b*) silver and [than] gold.

13. **Nouns with two full Vowels from ל"ה** § 31 (G 93 IV b. II f. III c. D 45). A. ¹Our afflicted ones; the innocent (pl.) among (genet.) my people; a false (שָׁוְא gen.) vision; our deeds: ⁵his work (deed); David's seers; his face; ⁸our faces.— ⁹Greater (are) my works than (82b) your works. ¹⁰Jahweh (is) my shepherd. Where (are) my shepherds and thy shepherds? ¹²Jahweh, the work of thy hands (are) we all.— ||
B. ¹David sought the face of Jahweh. Joshua fell upon his face before the ark of Jahweh. His field will be sold. Jahweh will remember the afflicted of his people. ⁵Shed not (אַל § 41, 3) innocent blood.

14. **Feminines with one changeable Vowel** § 33 (G 95 II c. D 17. 18. 29). A. ¹My year; the years of the famine; thy (f.) counsel; your counsel; ⁵your abomination; your kingdoms; ⁷his thoughts.—
B. ¹The counsel of the elders of Israel has come to nought.

15. **Feminines with two changeable Vowels** § 34 (G 95 II a. b. D 18). A. ¹My vengeance; your vengeance; our myriads; your (f.) cry; ⁵thy (f.) blessing; the father's blessing; the blessings of Jahweh; the sighs of the afflicted; your sighs; ¹⁰our cry; ¹¹your cry.— B. ¹Jahweh heard the sighs of the afflicted of his people. The Egyptians sold all their land to Pharaoh.

16. Feminines of Segholate Forms from strong Stems

§ 35 (G 95 I *a. b. c.* D 17. 18). A. [1]Your queen; the garments of the poor; our garments; thy maiden; [5]the maidens of the city; my maid; my maids; thy joy; joys; [10]their (*m.*) meal-offering; the meal-offerings; your (*f.*) fruit; her reproach; [14]his foreskin.—
B. [1]God hath no pleasure in your burnt-offerings and in your meal-offerings. They will mourn upon their ruins.

17. Feminine Segholate Forms § 36 (G 95 III. D 29).

[1]My cloak; the land of our birth; their (*m.*) wages; the queens' signet-rings; [5]thy (*f.*) sin; [6]her ornament.

18. Feminines in ûth and îth § 37.

A. [1]Your captivity; the Hebrew virgins (*adj.* after *subst.*). Thy kingdom (is) an everlasting kingdom.— B. [1]Jahweh knew the imaginations of thy heart. Keep the commandments of Jahweh and his testimonies.

19. Nouns of peculiar Formation § 38 (G 96. D page 198).

I. [1]Your father; his fathers; thy (*f.*) brother; their (*m.*) brother; [5]thy (*f.*) brothers; the sister of Moses; thy (*f.*) sister; my husband; your men; [10]my men (*p.*); her maid; your maid; thy (*f.*) maids; your house; [15]his houses; thy (*f.*) son; your son; his daughter; my daughters; [20]his sons; [21] our daughter.

II. ¹My day; your day; my days; in the days of Joshua; ⁵his vessels; your vessels; his waters; his heavens; since (מִן) the days of Moses; ¹⁰their (m.) city; their cities; our head; your heads; thy mouth; ¹⁵our mouth. Behold, to Jahweh thy God (belong) heaven (w. art.) and the heaven of heavens. Better (is) one day in the house of Jahweh than (82b) many days in the palaces of the wicked. ¹⁸I (am) not better than my fathers.

20. **Numerals** § 39 (G 97. 98. 120. D 48). ¹5 kings; 5 cubits; her 5 maidens; the 5 (c.) kings; ⁵the 5 (abs.) righteous; 10 boys; 7 oxen; 7 cows; 7 (c.) days; ¹⁰the 7 (c.) days; his 7 (c.) sons; 5 trees; 9 cubits; 9 months; ¹⁵8 years; 8 sons; 8 (c.) days; 10 times. 17 years; ²⁰12 princes; 19 men; 13 oxen; his 11 children; 15 years; ²⁵18 years; 14 shekels. 25 years; 87 years; 25 (20+5) cubits; ³⁰75 years (70 yrs.+ 5 yrs.). ⁞ 500; 700; ³³207 years (7 yrs.+ 200 yrs.).

³⁴In the 17th year of (בְּ) Jehoshaphat; on the 27th (20+7 or 7+20) of (לְ) the month; on the 17th day of (לְ) the month. In the 5th year of (לְ) Joram; in the 5th year of (לְ) king Rehoboam; ³⁹in the 10th month.

21. **Particles with suffixes** §§ 40. 43. 44. 45 (G 100. 103. D 49). A. ¹With me (3), between them (2); like her; upon thee (f.); ⁵behind thee; instead of her; instead of them (3); to them; them (2); ¹⁰round about

you; to her; unto me; from me; [14] from you.— [15] The Lord of Hosts (is) with us. I (am) a stranger among you. Ye (are) witnesses against yourselves (בְּ *w*. 2 *pl. suff.*). The spirit of Jahweh (is) upon him. [19] Who (is) wise as thou?— B. [1] Jahweh hath not dealt with us according to (כְּ) our sins. Jahweh hath given this land to you and to your sons after you. According to your ways will I judge you. Cast from (מֵעַל) you all your transgressions. [5] Jahweh will judge between me and [between] you. I will pour out my fierce anger upon you. Solomon will be king in my stead. He pursued after them. While he yet talked (*part.*) with them, behold (Hebr. and behold *c. part.*) the messenger came down to him. [10] She said unto me: Where is Jahweh, thy (*f.*) God? Behold, they are coming out (*part.*) to you. They stood the whole day before me. Jahweh your God, who goeth (*part.*) before you, he will fight for (לְ) you. They have fled before thee. [15] We fled before you. He destroyed them from off (מֵעַל) the face of the earth. He has parted from me. Your oppressors will I remove (far) from you. Abraham bought the cave from (מֵאֵת) Ephron. [20] Joseph took Simeon from them. [21] Jahweh took Amos from (מֵאַחֲרֵי) the flock.

22. **Negative Particles** § 41 (G 152). [1] Thou shalt not (לֹא *c. impf.*) steal. Do not steal. Destroy not.

Remember not the days of your affliction. ⁵Gather (together) your heroes that your city be not captured. Pray to Jahweh, that sin may not have dominion over you. (There is) no God beside thee. (There is) no peace, Jahweh hath said, for the wicked. We are seeking (*part.*) water, but (וְ) there is none. ¹⁰If there is an answer, speak; but (וְ) if not, hearken unto me. They do not know (*part.*) what is due to (מִשְׁפַּט with *gen.*) the God of the land. Thus said Pharaoh: I will not give (*part.*) you straw. If thou savest not thy soul this night (§ 17 *a*), to-morrow thou (art) a dead man (render: son of death). ¹⁴Ye do not keep (*part.*) my commandments.

23. **Interrogative Particles** § 42 (G 100. 153. D 49). ¹What aileth thee (Hebr. what to thee), Hagar? Is (יֵשׁ) Jahweh in our midst or not? (Are) thy days as the days of a (frail) man (אֱנוֹשׁ), or thy years as the days of (strong) man (גֶּבֶר)? (Art) thou better than Balak? ⁵Spy out the people, whether they (be) strong or weak, whether they (be) few or many. ⁶Spy out the land, whether there are trees (*sg.*) in it or not.

24. **Perfect Qal** § 54 (G 44. D 20. 22). ¹She has reigned; ye have reigned; thou (*f.*) hast watched; they have watched; ⁵we have sold; I remembered; ye (*f.*) have remembered; ye lay down; she has shut (*p.*); ¹⁰we have followed. — ¹¹She is heavy (*p.*); ye

have drawn near; they have drawn near; thou art old; ¹⁵thou (*f.*) wert able; thou (*m.*) wert small; ¹⁷we have become great.

25. Infinitive and Imperative Qal §§ 55. 56 (G 45. 46. D 21. 22. 23). ¹To remember; to bury; in judging; from burying; ⁵to count. — Break (*s.*); break (*pl. f.*); judge ye; bury (*f.*); ¹⁰pray remember.— | ¹¹Remember the mercies of Jahweh. Put on your (*f.*) garments. Gather stones. They have gone to gather in the field. ¹⁵The trees said to the olive: Be thou, we pray, king over us.

26. Imperfect and Participle Qal §§ 57. 58 (G 47. 50. D 21. 22. 23). ¹I shall judge; we shall judge; they (*f.*) will steal; thou (*f.*) wilt watch; ⁵she will sell; they (*f.*) will sell; thou wilt reign; they will pour out; I shall shut; ¹⁰ye will remember; ye will watch (*p.*); thou wilt remember (*p.*). — We will lie down; thou shalt draw near; ¹⁵they shall draw near (*p.*); they (*f.*) shall clothe themselves; we will lie down (*p.*). — Watching; watching (*f.*); ²⁰burying (*f.*); shut; shut (*f.*); buried (*f.*); ²⁴watched (*f.*). — ²⁵Jerusalem (*f.*) will no longer remember the days of her affliction. Remember not the sins of my youth. To Jahweh your God must (*impf.*) ye cleave (*p.*). Thou shalt cleave to thy husband. We will make a covenant. ³⁰I will make a covenant with (אֶת־) thee. I will gather all Israel unto (אֶל) my Lord. ³²Jahweh shall reign for ever.

27. Niph'al [Niqtal] § 59 (G 51. D 25). A. ¹They have taken heed; ye have been sold; she has been sold (p.); thou (f.) hast taken heed; ⁵I hid myself; Ye have gone to law; they have been burned; I have gone to law with (אֶת־) you.—To take heed; ¹⁰(those who were) sold; (those (f.) who were) burnt.—Hide yourselves; take heed (f. s.).—We will hide ourselves; thou (f.) wilt hide thyself; ¹⁵they (f.) will be burnt; ye will be sold (p.); ye (f.) will be sold; I shall take heed; ¹⁹I will take heed.— B. ¹Behold, for (בְּ) your sins were ye sold. The wicked will be cut off from the midst of (מִתּוֹךְ) the land. The city was captured. Thy (f.) dead shall not be buried. ⁵Thy kingdom shall be destroyed. ⁶I will go to law with (אֶת־) you before Jahweh.

28. Pi'ēl, Pu'al [Qittēl Quttal] § 60 (G 52. D 26). A. ¹Thou hast sanctified; they have sanctified; ye (f.) have spoken; she has spoken (p.).—⁵To seek; teach (pl. m.); teach (s. f. p.); speak (pl. f.).—Ye will teach; ¹⁰thou (f.) wilt teach; ye (f.) will teach; we will teach; teachers; the seekers.—¹⁵She was stolen. They were buried; thou (f.) wast born; they will be gathered; ye (f.) will be buried. ²⁰Thou (f.) wilt

lie.— B. ¹The heavens recount (*part.*) the glory of God. Ye have sanctified the Sabbath-day. They sought the face of Jahweh. Honour thy father and thy mother (*p.*). ⁵Those that honour me (*part.*), I will honour. I will seek my father's asses. She will gather in the field. Ye should not lie to your king. Moses sanctified the people. ¹⁰Jahweh will teach the humble His way. Recount to me, I pray you (נָא), the former mercies of Jahweh (Hebr.: the mercies of J., the former). I will teach transgressors thy ways. I will praise thy name. ¹⁴They (*f.*) will praise the name of Jahweh.

29. **Hiph'il, Hoph'al [Hiqṭil, Hoqṭal]** § 61 (G 53. D 27). A. ¹I have separated; we have separated; they have destroyed; thou hast destroyed; ⁵she has cast; thou (*f.*) hast cast; ye have cast.—To cast; separate; ¹⁰separate (*pl. f.*); cast (*pl.*).—I will cast; we will corrupt; let him separate; ¹⁵they (*f.*) will separate; thou (*f.*) wilt corrupt; Ye will cast.—Casting; casting (*f.*).—²⁰Ye have been cast; ²¹thou (*f.*) wilt be cast.— B. ¹Thou hast hid thy face from (מִן) the wicked. How long wilt thou hide thy face? Hide not thy face from thy people. Thou hast not attended to (לְ) my commandments. ⁵Attend to the word of my mouth. Thou hast cast my word behind thee. They each (אִישׁ) cast away his staff. Cast thy sorrow upon

Jahweh. ⁹Jahweh will separate between the righteous and [between] the wicked.

30. **Hithpaʾēl [Hithqaṭṭēl]** § 62 (G 54. D 27). ¹I have walked; ye have walked; they have walked (*p.*); we hid ourselves; ⁵thou hast taken heed.—To hide one's self; they that hide themselves (*part.*); they that walk.—They will walk; ¹⁰Ye will take heed; we will hide ourselves. | ¹²Ye prayed unto me, but (וְ) I did not hearken to your cry.

31. **Waw Consecutivum** § 64 (G 49. D 60) ¹And they pursued their enemies and captured the city and burnt it with (בְּ; article § 17 *f* 1) fire. ²And Abraham prayed to God. Thou wilt capture the city and burn it with fire. And they buried him in the city of David, and his son reigned in his stead. ⁵I will remember my word and will send my messenger before (לְפָנֶיךָ) thee. We will rise early in the morning and sell Joseph. Verily (§ 63 *d*) ye ought to keep (*impf.*) the commandments of Jahweh and teach them (to) your children. Write these words on the two tables and teach them (unto) the children of Israel. Get thee up early in the morning, and take thy stand before Pharaoh and (then) thou shalt say to him: Let the people of Jahweh go. ¹⁰Then Moses hid his face; for he was afraid. Then Pharaoh hardened (made heavy) his heart. ¹²Behold, I (§ 40 *d*) will rain (*part.*) bread

F*

for you from heaven, and (ו *cons.*) the people shall go out and shall gather a day's portion every day (Hebr. the word of a day in its day).

32. **Relative Clauses** § 87 (G 123. 155). ¹David and the men that (were) with him fled before Saul. They put to death all the women that (were) in the city. The spies told the woman all that Jahweh had done (*perf.*) to Pharaoh. The land which I am giving (*part.*) you (is) like the garden of Eden. ⁵The word which thou hast spoken (is) good. I will destroy all flesh, in which (is) the breath of life. The place, where he had pitched his tent. Holy (is) the place whereon thou standest (*part.*). ⁹They have gone to (אֶל־) the land, from which (where) they went out.

33. **Guttural Verbs** § 65 (G 63—65. D 34. 36. 37). A. I. ¹Ye have driven out; drive ye out; they (*f.*) will drive out; and he drove out; ⁵thou wilt bless; they will be put to death; thou (*f.*) wilt be forsaken; we shall be forsaken; to be forsaken.—¹⁰Ye have made haste; he will make haste; thou hast been comforted; ¹³we shall be comforted.

II. ¹Fleeing; to hear; to cause to swear; thou wilt cause to hear. ⁵send; flee (*pl. f.*); we shall hear; they (*f.*) will hear; and she opened; ¹⁰thou (*f.*) wilt sow (*p.*); he will be heard; and we swore. They will covet; thou wilt spare; ¹⁵I shall cross over; we shall cross over; we will cross over; thou (f.) wilt serve; they will serve; ²⁰they' (f.) will serve; we shall love; thou wilt be wise; I have brought over; ²⁴and thou wilt cause to serve.

III. ¹Ye (f.) have served; to serve; washers; thou (f.) wilt wash; ⁵she has washed; thou (f.) wilt be proved; and they were amazed; and they placed; and ye caused to serve; ¹⁰I shall place; we will send over. ‖ Wash (sg. f.); bless (sg. f.); and they blest; ¹⁵she has blest: a sower (f.); ¹⁷thou (f.) hast taken.

B. ¹Thou wilt shave thy head. He refused to let the people go. Jahweh hath redeemed Jacob and will glorify himself in Israel. They have destroyed my vineyard. ⁵He went up to destroy the city. Choose ye this (Article § 17 a) day whom (§ 83 e) ye will serve. Then (וַ cons.) the people made haste (pl. § 86 c a) and crossed the Jordan. Make haste (sg. f.), (and) slay the calf. Thou shalt not covet thy neighbour's house. ¹⁰Ye have not coveted your neighbours' wives. Thou (f.) hast not forgotten the words of thy prophets. Even (גַּם) a fool, if (part.) he keep silence, is esteemed (impf.) § 47 d) a wise man. Thy land thou hast destroyed, thy people thou hast put to death. We were esteemed as (כְּ) the cattle (in the stalls). ¹⁵Ye have devised evil against (עַל) me. They will devise evil against me. I will spare you, for ye did spare me. Comfort ye,

comfort ye my people. Ye forsook Jahweh; therefore
(ו cons.) did he forsake you. ²⁰Jahweh (is) my shepherd;
I shall not want.

34. Verbs פ״א §66 (G 68. D 35). ¹Thou wilt speak;
then I spoke; thou (f.) wilt eat; they will eat (p.);
⁵I shall eat; then ye did eat; and ye ate. Then spake
Jahweh to (ל) the prophet, saying: Because this people
has refused (render: has not been willing) to hearken
to my voice, I will send (Pi.) against (ב) them the
(wild) beast of the field, and the lions shall tear and
devour your flocks (sg.) and your herds (sg.) ⁹The
she-asses will perish in the wilderness.

35. Verbs פ״י § 67 (G 66. D 33). A. ¹Thou (f.)
wilt fall; they have fallen; and they (f.) fell; they
told; ⁵and I told; to let fall; ye have saved; and she
saved; he will be saved; ¹⁰he shall look; one who
looks (part.); we shall plant; they will touch; thou
(f.) wilt remove (§ 6ƒ3). ¹⁵And ye have taken; they
will take; take thou (f.); then thou (f.) didst take;
we will take. | ²⁰Ye (f.) have given; thou (f.) wilt
give; then she gave; we will give (p.); ²⁴thy giving
(inf.).— B. ¹And (ו cons.) he sent his servant to
take a wife for Isaac. I will give thy flesh to the
birds of heaven. I have given the land into his hand.
The word of Jahweh will not fall to the ground
(§ 20 c a). ⁵Tell me, I pray thee (נא), the words of the

seer. Give now (הָ) thy heart to the God of thy fathers. Take off thy shoes from (off) thy feet; for this place (is) holy.

36. **Verbs** פ״וי § 68 (G 69. D 39). A. ¹She will be born; we shall be rebuked; rebuke (*sg. f.*) | They have begotten; ⁵then they begat; ye were brought down; thou wilt be brought down. | Thou wilt sleep; they will sleep; ¹⁰thou (*f.*) wilt be weary. | She will go down; they will dwell (*p.*); know thou; thou (*f.*) hast known; ¹⁵ye will know (*p.*); and ye knew; thou (*f.*) wilt go (*p.*); ¹⁸they that go (*part.*).— ‖ B. ¹And (then) the kings took counsel. With (אֶת־) those that take counsel (is) wisdom. Let my soul be precious in thine eyes! After these things he took a wife and (§ 64) begat sons and daughters. ⁵He heard the sound (voice) of the rain from afar; and he brought down his flock from the mountain in haste (§ 84*e*). Let thy servant, I pray thee, know these things. ⁷Know ye that I (am) God.

37. **Verbs** פ״וי § 69 (G 70. D 39). ¹She will be good; thou hast done well; we shall do well; they will suck (*p.*); ⁵thou (*f.*) hast given suck; she will give suck; she was dry (*p.*); they will be dry; they have dried (*trans.*).— ‖ ¹⁰The grass in the field has become dry. And (then) the king's hand dried up. And all their herbage will I dry up. Moses heard the

word of Aaron, and (§ 64) it was good in his eyes. ¹⁴If thou wilt hearken to my voice, then (ו cons.) will Jahweh do thee good and thou wilt remember thy handmaid.

38. **Verbs** פ״יצ § 70 (G 71. D 39). ¹I have kindled a fire in the houses of the gods of Egypt. And (then) they set the city on (בָּ, Article § 17f 1) fire. Her gates were set on fire. And Jahweh formed out of the ground every beast of the field. ⁵Every beast of the field was formed out of the ground. Take your stand, that (§ 46d, e) I may plead with you. Jahweh cleft the sea and (§ 64) set the waters like a (Art.) wall. Ye stand (render: are set) to-day before Jahweh your God. I will pour out my spirit upon thy seed. ¹⁰And he poured the oil upon his head.

39. **Verbs** ע״י § 71 (G 72. D 40). A. ¹We have lifted up; thou wilt fly; flying; thou hast fled; ⁵she has returned; ye have returned; return (pl.); we will return; to return; ¹⁰let him return; and (ו cons.) he returned; thou wilt be circumcised; ye have circumcised; we will circumcise; ¹⁵she is dead; ye are dead; thou (f.) wilt kill; and they killed; they were killed; ²⁰they will be killed (p.); thou hast lifted up; they (f.) will die; then was I exalted (high); and I lifted up; ²⁵ye have scattered.— B. ¹In thee did our fathers trust and they were not put to shame. Then I knew that I should not be put to shame. Get thee

(*Dat. com.*—לְ w. suff.) up. Return ye (*Dat. com.*) to your tents. ⁵Be thou exalted, (O) Jahweh, through thy might! And now will my head be exalted above mine enemies. Righteousness exalteth (*Polēl impf.*) a nation. I lifted up my voice. Then Moses lifted up his hand. ¹⁰Jahweh my God, let, I pray thee, the soul of this boy return within him (עַל־קִרְבּוֹ)! Lift up thy voice like a (Art.) trumpet. Mine eyes were enlightened (shone). Arise (*f.*), shine; for thy light is come. Lightnings lighted up the sea. ¹⁵Make, now (§52*c*), thy face to shine upon thy servant. And he rested [on] the seventh day. ¹⁷They refused to return.

40. **Verbs** ע״ו § 72 (G 73. D 40). ¹Ye will set; set thou (*f.*); thou wilt lodge; and we lodged; ⁵ye have been glad; he will be glad.—Let my heart rejoice. And the daughters of Judah rejoiced. Be ye glad and rejoice; for behold I (*suff.*) am about to create (*part.* §47*i* β) Jerusalem and her people for joy, and (ן *cons.*) I will rejoice over (בְּ) Jerusalem and be glad in my people. ¹⁰Then David perceived that the child was dead. ¹¹Get understanding (understand), and thereafter (אַחַר) we will talk.

41. **Verbs** ע״ע § 73 (G 67. D 42). A. ¹We have praised: and he praised; and thou (*f.*) didst praise; they have spoiled their spoilers; ⁵he rolled the stone; thou wilt

curse; ye will spoil; he will be merciful and he was merciful. |¦ ¹⁰Ye were merciful; thou hast done wickedly.— B. ¹In Jahweh will my soul glory. Let not (the § 17 g 2) wise man glory in his wisdom, and let not (the) rich man glory in his riches. They will glory in the Holy (One) of Israel. I will praise Jahweh while I live (render: in my life). ⁵And they praised her beauty. And Joshua said: Compass (go round) the city; and they compassed the city. Swifter (lighter) than eagles (Art. § 17 f) are his horses. I am despised (light) in thine eyes. Ended are the words of Job. ¹⁰They wandered in the wilderness, till (c. inf.) the whole generation was consumed. Men (coll.: sg. c. Art.) began to be numerous. Numerous are (oxytone) our transgressions. Hushai has gone to bring to nought the counsel of Ahithophel. And (וָ cons.) God brought their counsel to nought. ¹⁵I will not break my covenant with you. They have broken thy law. Be not (אַל) dismayed; for Jahweh thy God (is) with thee. Let my pursuers be put to shame, but let not me be put to shame (אַל c. cohort.); let them be dismayed, but let not me be dismayed. And (וָ cons.) this word was evil in the eyes of Saul. ²⁰And Moses said: Lord, why (§ 45 e 6) hast thou done evil to this people? Since (מֵאָז) I went unto Pharaoh, to speak in thy name, he hath done evil to this people. They did evil more than (§ 82 b β) their fathers. My brethren, do not wickedly. Depart from me, ye evil-doers (*part.* V). And (ו֗ *cons.*) they were in distress. ²⁵Hide not thy face from thy servant; for I am in distress; make haste to hearken (Hebr.: make haste, hearken § 84*f*) unto my voice.

42. **Verbs** ה״ל § 74 (G 75. D 44. 45). A. I. ¹He will see; he will show; thou wilt finish; we shall be seen; ⁵they (*f.*) will build; ye (*f.*) will finish; give ye (*f.*) to drink; thou wilt answer; I shall answer. ¹⁰Build thou; I was finished; thou wert built; we were built; we have built; ¹⁵ye (*f.*) have answered; ¹⁶ye have watered.— II. ¹He has seen; he was seen; to build; to go up; ⁵to finish; to weep; she wept; she has finished; ⁹she has watered.— III. ¹They have wept; weep thou (*f.*); weep ye; they finished; ⁵give thou (*f.*) to drink; thou (*f.*) wilt finish; ye will finish; ye will build; they were built; ¹⁰answer ye; bring ye up; ¹²they will be seen.— IV. ¹And she drank; and he wept; and thou didst despise; and she saw; ⁵and he saw; do not (אל § 41,3) answer (*sg.*); and he finished; and she watered the camels; and she ordered; ¹⁰let him do; we will hear and answer; thou didst fall down; and she fell down; and they fell down; ¹⁵thou (*f.*) wilt fall down; ¹⁶one who falls down (*part.*).— B. ¹Arise, go up to Ai (*acc. p.*); see,

I have given into thy hand the king of Ai and his people. See (*f.*), thy son (is) alive. Ye have done according to all that Moses commanded you. All they will be glad, that (*part. st. c.* § 21*g*) take refuge in thee. ⁵What seest (*part.*) thou? See, a little cloud, like a man's hand (כַּף), is coming up (*part.*) from the sea. What are ye doing (*part.*)? We are building (*part.*) the wall. The city (is) large and the people (are) few (small *sg.*) in the midst of it, and there are no (אֵין § 41, 2) built houses. ¹⁰And David said: I am come to buy the threshing-floor from (מֵעִם) thee, to build an altar to Jahweh. Thou wilt build a house but thou wilt not dwell in it. They (*pron.*) will build, but I will pull down. The city has been built. The cities of Judah will be built. ¹⁵She was in the field, till (עַד *c. inf.*) the harvest was finished. We have been consumed by thine anger. The eyes of the wicked will fail (render: be consumed). I have consumed my strength. In the third month they began, and by (בְּ) the seventh month they had finished. ²⁰She finished watering (§ 84 *b. d*) the camels. And he finished his business. Ye shall do according to the word of Jahweh; see, I have commanded you. And Moses commanded the people saying: keep the whole commandment which I give unto you (render: wh. I command you, *c.* 2 *acc.*) this (*art.* § 17 *a*) day.

Command (*sg. apoc.*) the children of Israel, that (ו) they cast out every leper from the camp. ²⁵ Command ye the people, saying: Get up early in the morning and (ִ *cons.*) cross over the river. Command (*sg.*) the priests to (ו) come up out of the Jordan. And Joshua commanded the priests, saying: Come up out of the Jordan. Let us arise and go up to (*acc.*) Beth-El. ²⁹ Do (*pl.*) not (אַל־) offer unto me burnt-offerings.

43. **Verbs ל"א** § 75 (G 74. D 38). ¹He has sinned; she will sin; he was created; thou hast sinned; ⁵ye have sinned; ye have defiled; thou hast defiled thyself; we have filled.— ‖ And Jahweh said: I will blot out (§ 74 *v*) man (*coll., w. art.*), whom I have created from off (מֵעַל) the face of the ground. ¹⁰ In the place where (§ 87 *h*) thou (*f.*) wert created will I judge thee. My soul has sought but I have not found. Ye have not found my riddle. I shall not find among (בְּ) you a single wise man. Ye will seek but ye will not find. ¹⁵ I have been found (*Ni.*) of (לְ) you. In that day, the sins (חַטֹּאת) of Judah shall not be found; for I will forgive them. Jacob have I loved, but Esau have I hated. Thou shalt not (לֹא *c. impf.*) hate thy brother. ¹⁹ I hate (*impf.* § 47 *c. d.*) them that hate thee, (O) Jahweh (Hebr.: thy haters—*part. Pi.*).

44. **Doubly and trebly weak Verbs** § 76 (G 76).
A. ¹He will assuredly (63 *d*) become (followed by לְ)

a great nation. And (וֹ *cons.*) there was again war between David and [between] the Philistines. And he drank of the wine and lived. Thou hast stretched forth thy hand. [5]They have perverted judgment. Do not ye pervert judgment. Then they smote the Philistines. She proved Solomon by riddles. The kings will not leave the wicked unpunished. [10]I have prophesied, but (וֹ) ye have not inclined your heart unto Jahweh. And (then) they lifted up their eyes. And she lifted up her voice again (§ 84*b*). We will praise the name of Jahweh. Praise ye Jahweh (לְ); for (he is) kind. [15]They confessed. He instructed. They will instruct. And (וֹ *cons.*) I brought you to (אֶל־) the land of Canaan. Go thou unto (אֶל־) Pharaoh. [20]As I was with Moses, (so) will I be with thee. Bring forth (*f.*) the men that came (*part.*) unto (אֶל־) thee, who are come to (לְ) thy house. Thee hath Jahweh, thy God, chosen, to be to him [for לְ] a peculiar people. I feared the people, and (וֹ *cons.*) hearkened to their voice. This (is) the woman and this her son, whom Elisha brought to life. [25]Stretch forth thy hand. I have brought you forth out of Egypt with a strong hand and with an outstretched arm. Then Moses stretched forth his hand. Ye have not inclined your ear. Incline thine ear and hear. [30]And they perverted the judgment of the orphans. Wherefore, then (לָמָּה § 42*g*), did we go out of Egypt? And (ו *cons.*) Jephthah came to his house, and behold his daughter went forth (*part.*) to meet him. And (then) Moses lifted up his rod, and smote the rock twice (*du.*); and there came forth much water and the congregation drank. ³⁵Thou shalt not (*impf.*) take (תִשָּׂא) the name of Jahweh in vain (Hebr.: for falsehood); for Jahweh will not let him go unpunished that taketh his name in vain.

45. **For Repetition.** ¹Declare unto us what shall happen (*f. pl.*, § 18*a*), that (§ 46 *d.e.*) we may know that ye (are) gods. Build houses and dwell (therein), and plant gardens and eat the fruit thereof (*suff.*); take (to yourselves) wives and beget sons and daughters, and take wives for your sons, and give your daughters to husbands, that (§ 46) they may bear sons and daughters; and there do ye increase (*imper.*). Call ye with (בְּ) a loud voice; perhaps he is asleep (*part.*) and will wake up. ⁴He will say to those that (are) in darkness: go forth.

46. **Comparison** § 82 (G 119. D 47). ¹Better (were it) for us to serve Egypt than to die in the wilderness. I have understanding (see Vocab.) above (more than § 82*b* β) all my teachers. ³Behold, the hand of Jahweh is not too short for him (cf. § 82*b* α) to save, nor (and not) is his ear too heavy for him to hear.

47. **Verbs with the Accusative** § 83 (G 138. 139). ¹Their houses are full of swords and spears. They have filled (*Qal*) the land with violence. He has filled (*Pi.*) them with wisdom. He that tills (*part.*) his land will be satisfied with bread. ⁵Her poor will I satisfy with bread. She clothed Jacob with the clothes of Esau. I will serve Jahweh with all my heart. I shall answer him. ⁹Answer (*sg.*) a fool according to his folly.

48. **Subject and Predicate** § 86 (G 146. 147). ¹The people answered him not a word. The people went up out of the Jordan. Thy (*f.*) oppressors shall be taken captive, and (ו *cons.*) all flesh shall know that I am Jahweh thy redeemer. ⁴There died Saul and his son Jonathan.

49. **Conditional Sentences** § 88 (G 155, 2). ¹And he said unto her: if thou wilt go with me, then (ו *cons.*) I will go; but (ו) if thou wilt not go, I will not go. If thou wilt indeed (§ 63 *d*) give this people into (ב) my hand, then (ו *cons.*) I will utterly destroy their cities. (O) Lord of Hosts, if thou wilt indeed look on (ב) the affliction of thy handmaid, and (ו *cons.*) wilt give unto thy handmaid a man-child (Hebr.: seed of men), then (ו *cons.*) will I give him to Jahweh all the days of his life. We will send messengers to all the cities of Israel, and if no one

deliver us (*part.*). then (ו *cons.*) will we go out to thee.—⁵If thou, indeed, returnest in peace, Jahweh hath not spoken by (בְּ) me. If it (be) good in thine eyes to come with me to Babylon, come.—Should (כִּי) ye say to me: We trust in Jahweh our God, (is it) not he, whose altars Hezekiah has removed? And what could I do (*impf.*) should God arise? ⁹Shouldest thou buy a Hebrew slave, he shall serve (*impf.*) six years, and in the seventh he shall go [forth] free (לַחָפְשִׁי).

50. **Sentences expressing a Wish** § 89 (G 136). ¹Thy mercy, (O) Jahweh, be upon us! Let not thine anger be hot! May Reuben live and not die! Let my soul die with (the) Philistines! ⁵Let thine anger be turned away (render: turn back)! Let thy hand be high above thine oppressors! Let not thy voice be heard in the street! I should like (נא) to go into the field (*acc.*). I would fain hear what Jahweh will say. ¹⁰The Lord judge between me and [between] thee, and look (thereon) and plead my cause! And now let thy servant, I pray thee, remain (Heb.: sit) instead of the lad a bondman to my lord, and let the lad go up with his brethren! And the prophet said: Amen! the Lord do (§ 74 *u a*) so, the Lord bring to pass the things (Hebr.: thy words) which thou hast prophesied! Let us not perish, we pray thee! O that I might

die (§ d)!— ¹⁵Thy blood (be) on thine (own) head! Blessed (be) ye of (לְ—cf. G 14, 19) Jahweh. Cursed (be) the man before Jahweh, who shall rise up and (ו cons.) (re-)build this city! ¹⁸Cursed (be) the day, in which I was born (Pu.)!

51. **Sentences expressing an Oath § 90 (G 155, 2f).** ¹And Moses on that day swore, saying: Verily this land shall be to thee for an inheritance and to thy sons for ever. And I made the people swear by God: Verily ye shall not give your daughters unto their sons, nor (וְאִם) shall ye take of their daughters for your sons or (and) for yourselves. And Elijah said: As the Lord of Hosts liveth before whom I stand, I will show myself to (נִרְאָה אֶל־) him this day. And the king swore: As the Lord liveth who made us this soul, I will not put Jeremiah to death. ⁵And Uriah said: As thou livest, and as thy soul liveth, I will not do this thing (word).

52. **Waw Copulativum used to introduce Subordinate Sentences § 46 B (G 155, 1). I. Circumstantial clauses.** ¹And they came unto the house (acc.) while he lay upon his bed. And the angel of Jahweh came again unto the woman, as she sat in the field.— Say not to thy neighbour: "Go and come again, and to-morrow I will give", while thou hast it (rend: there is) by thee. Thy (f.) prophets say (part.) thus: "Peace,

peace", while there is no peace. ⁵I have called but (and) no one has hearkened unto my voice. They burned the city with fire, and there was no deliverer; for it (was) far from Sidon.

II. **Purpose Clauses.** ¹Pray (*sg.*) for me that my hand may be restored (rend: return) to me. We will call [to] the maid, that we may ask her [mouth]. Stand (*pl.*) that I may hear. I will give him my daughter, that she may be [for לְ] a snare unto him.

III. **Clauses giving Ground or Reason.** ¹The stranger shalt thou not oppress (לֹא *c. impf.*); for ye (*pron.*) know the heart (soul) of the stranger, since (כִּי) ye were strangers in the land of Egypt.

ENGLISH-HEBREW VOCABULARY.*)

Aaron אַהֲרֹן.
able, be יָכֹל 68g. 84d.
abomination תּוֹעֵבָה 33.
above (in comparisons) מִן 82b.
Abraham אַבְרָהָם.
according to כְּ.
afar (from) מֵרָחוֹק.
afflicted עָנִי 31a.
affliction עֳנִי 30.
afraid, be יָרֵא 76g.
after אַחַר, אַחֲרֵי 43b.
again עוֹד, suff. 40f.; also by (הוֹסִיף (יָסַף 84a.b.
against עַל־ 43a.
Ahaz אָחָז.
Ai עַי (c. artic.).
alive חַי 26, make a. הֶחֱיָה 76c.
all כֹּל 26 (כֻּלָּנוּ).
also גַּם.
altar מִזְבֵּחַ 24e, pl. וֹת.
amazed be נִבְהַל.
amen אָמֵן.

among, amongst עִם 43d; cf. midst.
Amorite אֱמֹרִי.
Amos עָמוֹס.
angel מַלְאָךְ 24b.
anger אַף 26, זַעַם 28; fierce (hot) anger חָרוֹן 23, אַף ׳חֲ.
anointed, the מָשִׁיחַ 23b.
answer, to עָנָה 74, acc. pers. 83e.
answer (subst.) מַעֲנֶה.
arise קוּם 71.
ark (of covenant) אָרוֹן.
arm זְרוֹעַ f., pl. וֹת.
around סָבִיב 43b.
as (prep.) כְּ; (conj.) כַּאֲשֶׁר.
ask שָׁאַל (ē) 65e.
asleep, be יָשֵׁן 68d; (adj.) יָשֵׁן 25f.
ass (he-) חֲמוֹר; she-a. אָתוֹן 23, pl. וֹת.
assuredly, v. verily.
Assyria אַשּׁוּר.
attend הִקְשִׁיב, to לְ.

*) The Arabic numbers refer to the sections of the Grammar (in some cases merely serving to indicate the rule for the inflexion of the word to which they are appended); the Roman numbers accompanying verbs denote the voices (conjugations).

ENGLISH-HEBREW VOCABULARY.

Baal בַּעַל c. art. 28.
Babylon בָּבֶל.
bad רַע 26.
Balak בָּלָק.
Bashan בָּשָׁן.
be הָיָה 76 b. There is, was &c. יֵשׁ 40 e; there is, was not, אַיִן 41, 2.
bear יָלַד 68; pass. II, IV.
beard זָקָן 25.
beautify פָּאַר 65.
beauty יֳפִי 30 c.
because יַעַן כִּי, כִּי.
become הָיָה לְ 76 b.
bed מִטָּה.
before לִפְנֵי (e. g. stand), מִפְּנֵי (e. g. fear).
beget יָלַד 68, genly. V.
begin חָלַל V, 73.
behind אַחֲרֵי, אַחַר 43 b.
behold הִנֵּה 40 d, הֵן.
belly בֶּטֶן 23.
Benjamin בִּנְיָמִין.
beside, besides זוּלַת (st. con. with suff.).
Bethel בֵּית־אֵל.
better טוֹב מִן 82 b.
bird עוֹף collect.
birth מוֹלֶדֶת 33.
bless בָּרַךְ 65 b. r.
blessing בְּרָכָה 34 d.
blind עִוֵּר 24 d, Art. הַ.
blood דָּם 24 c.; b. (shed) דָּמִים.
blot out מָחָה 74.
bondman עֶבֶד 28.
booth סֻכָּה 22.

booty שָׁלָל 25.
border (territory) גְּבוּל.
bow קֶשֶׁת f. 28, pl. וֹת.
boy נַעַר 28 i.
brass נְחֹשֶׁת f. 36 b.
bread לֶחֶם 28 i.
break שָׁבַר; (a covenant) פָּרַר V 73 k; b. in pieces שִׁבֵּר I, III.
breath נְשָׁמָה 34.
bring בּוֹא V 76 h; b. down יָרַד V. 68 f; b. forth, b. out יָצָא V. 76 g; b. up עָלָה V. 74.
brother אָח 38.
build בָּנָה 74.
burn (trans.) שָׂרַף.
burnt-offering עֹלָה.
bury קָבַר.
business מְלָאכָה 36 g.
but, genly. וְ.
buy קָנָה 74.
by 1.=agent after Pass. Vb. לְ, מִן; 2.=instrument, per בְּ; 3.=chez (Ex. 52) אֵת.

calf עֵגֶל 28 l.
call קָרָא 75.
camel גָּמָל 26 d.
camp מַחֲנֶה 31.
can יָכֹל 68 g. 84 d.
Canaan כְּנַעַן.
captive, take שָׁבָה 74.
captives coll. שְׁבִי 30.
captivity גָּלוּת f. 37 a.
capture (city) לָכַד.
cast, c. away הִשְׁלִיךְ; c. out שִׁלַּח 65.

cattle בְּהֵמָה 34d; בָּקָר 25.
cause רִיב, see: plead.
cedar אֶרֶז m. 28.
child יֶלֶד 28; pl. genly. בָּנִים.
choose בָּחַר; transit. with בְּ.
circumcise מוּל 71.
city עִיר f. 38.
cleave בָּקַע 65 I, III; c. to דָּבַק בְּ(ē).
cloak אַדֶּרֶת 36.
clothe one's self לָבֵשׁ, c. some one V, 83f.
cloud עָנָן m. 25; עָב f. (Ex. 42).
come בּוֹא 76h; c. back שׁוּב 71; c. down יָרַד 68f.; c. forth, out יָצָא 76g; c. up. עָלָה.
comfort נחם III, 67; Pass. IV.
command צִוָּה 74, acc. pers.
command, commandment מִצְוָה 22.
compass (circumire, circumdare) סָבַב 73.
congregation עֵדָה 28a.
consume (one's strength &c.) כָּלָה 74. be consumed כָּלָה 74.
corrupt הִשְׁחִית.
counsel עֵצָה 33; take c. יָעַץ II 68d.
count סָפַר.
court חָצֵר 25d.
covenant בְּרִית, make a c. בּ' כָּרַת.
covet חָמַד acc.
cow פָּרָה 22.
create בָּרָא 75.
cross, c. over עָבַר 65.
cubit אַמָּה.
cup כּוֹס.

curse אָרַר, קִלֵּל 73.
cut off חִכְרִית; pass. נִכְרַת.
Daniel דָּנִיֵּאל.
darkness חֹשֶׁךְ 28.
daughter בַּת 38.
daughter-in-law כַּלָּה.
David דָּוִד.
day יוֹם 38.
dead מֵת.
death מָוֶת 29c.; put to d. מוּת V, 71 i. u; הָרַג.
declare נגד V, 67.
deed מַעֲשֶׂה 31, פֹּעַל 28.
defile, v. pollute.
delight חָפֵץ 28; take del. in חָפֵץ בְּ 65h.
deliver נִצֵּל; מִלֵּט V, 67.
depart סוּר 71x.
despise בָּזָה 74; be despised קַל (קלל) 73.
destroy (break in pieces) שָׁבַר I, III; (of a city, country &c.) הִשְׁחִית 65b; (of persons) הִשְׁמִיד, הִכְרִית; d. utterly (=devoveo) הֶחֱרִים 65p.
devise חָשַׁב.
devour אָכַל 66a.
die מוּת 71 i.u.
dismayed, be חַת (חתת) 73f.o.
distress, be in: impers. צַר (צרר) 73o. Folld. by לְ w. suff.
divide הִבְדִּיל.
do עָשָׂה 74.
dog כֶּלֶב 28.
dominion, have מָשַׁל, over בְּ.
door דֶּלֶת 28.

drink שָׁתָה 74, 77; give to d. שִׁקָּה V, 74, 77.
drive out גֵּרֵשׁ 65b. 64l.
dry יָבֵשׁ 25f; be, become d. יָבֵשׁ 69a; to dry up, dry (trans.) V.
dry land חָרָבָה, יַבָּשָׁה.
due, (what is d. to one) מִשְׁפָּט (Ex. 22).
dust עָפָר 25.
dwell יָשַׁב 68f.

each (adj.) כֹּל 26; (pron. opp. to other) אִישׁ.
ear אֹזֶן f. 28.
early, v. rise.
earth אֶרֶץ f. 28, Art. 17d.
eat אָכַל 66a.
Eden עֵדֶן.
Edom אֱדוֹם.
Egypt מִצְרַיִם.
Egyptian מִצְרִי, pl. מִצְרִים.
elder זָקֵן 25.
Elijah אֵלִיָּהוּ.
Elishah אֱלִישָׁע.
end קֵץ 26.
enemy אֹיֵב 24d.
enlightened, be: v. shine.
Esau עֵשָׂו.
esteem (æstimare) חָשַׁב.
eternity עוֹלָם 24.
ever, for e. לְעוֹלָם.
everlasting: render by genetive of עוֹלָם; an e. king מֶלֶךְ עוֹלָם.
every כֹּל 26.
evil (subst.) רָעָה 22; be e. רַע (רעע) 73; do e. V.

exalt רוֹמֵם 71 Pōlel; be exalted רוֹם.
except, v. beside.
eye עַיִן f. 29.

face פָּנִים 31a.
fall נָפַל 67; f. down (in adoration προσκυνεῖν) שָׁחָה VII, 74we.
false: render by genet. of שָׁוְא, a f. witness עֵד שָׁוְא.
falsehood שָׁוְא 29c; שֶׁקֶר 28.
famine, v. hunger.
far רָחוֹק 23; be f. רָחַק.
father אָב 38.
favour חֶסֶד 28.
fear (verb) יָרֵא 76g; (subst.) יִרְאָה 35.
feast, festival מוֹעֵד 24e.
few מְעַט.
field שָׂדֶה 31b.
fierce, v. anger.
fight נִלְחַם.
fill, fulfil מָלֵא 75 I, genly. III; f. with sthg. acc. 83b.
find מָצָא 75.
finish כָּלָה, pass. IV; be finished כָּלָה 74, תַּם (תמם) 73m.
fire אֵשׁ 26.
flee בָּרַח 65e, נוּס 71.
flesh בָּשָׂר 25.
flock צֹאן.
fly עוּף Pōlēl 71.
food מַאֲכָל 24.
fool כְּסִיל.
foot רֶגֶל f. 28.
footstool הֲדֹם רַגְלַיִם.
for (conj.) כִּי; (prep.) לְ; (=pro) בְּעַד

D.E.F
G.H.I.J.K.
M.N.O.P.Q.
S.T
U.V.W.
X.Y.Z.

foreskin עָרְלָה 35.
forget שָׁכַח 65.
forgive סָלַח 65.
form, to יָצַר 70.
former רִאשׁוֹן.
forsake עָזַב 65.
frail, f. man אֱנוֹשׁ.
from מִן 44.
fruit פְּרִי m. 30c.
fugitive פָּלִיט.
fulfil, v. fill.
full, be מָלֵא 75, acc. 83b.

garden גַּן 26.
garment בֶּגֶד 28r.
gate שַׁעַר 28.
gather לָקַט I, III; Pass. IV; g.
  together קָבַץ.
Gaza עַזָּה f.
get up, v. rise.
Gibeon גִּבְעוֹן.
give נָתַן 67i.
glad, be שָׂמֵחַ (ē), in, בְּ; שׂוּשׂ 72.
glorify פָּאַר 65; g. one's self VII.
glory כָּבוֹד 23; (verb) הִתְהַלֵּל
  seq. בְּ.
go הָלַךְ 68i, 64h; g. down יָרַד
  68f; g. forth, out יָצָא 76g;
  g. round סָבַב 73; g. up עָלָה 74.
/ go, let (send away) שִׁלַּח.
God אֱלֹהִים (with preff. v. 10c 4);
  אֵל.
godly חָסִיד 29.
gold זָהָב 25.
Gomorrha עֲמֹרָה.
good טוֹב; be g. יָטַב 69; do g. V.

grass חָצִיר 23.
grave קֶבֶר 28, c. suff. 'קִבְ.
great גָּדוֹל 23; be, become g.
  גָּדַל (ē).
ground אֲדָמָה 34b.

Hagar הָגָר.
Hananiah חֲנַנְיָה.
hand יָד 24c.
handmaid שִׁפְחָה 35, אָמָה 38.
happen קָרָה 74.
harden (heart) כָּבֵד V.
harvest קָצִיר 23.
haste, in: render by מִהַר III.
  folld. by finite Vb. w. ׳, acc.
  to § 84e.
hate שָׂנֵא 75.
head רֹאשׁ 38.
hear שָׁמַע; make to h. V.
hearken שָׁמַע, h. unto sthg. אֶל־,
  h. unto one's voice בְּקוֹל ׳שׁ.
heart לֵבָב 25c, לֵב 26.
heaven שָׁמַיִם 38.
heavy כָּבֵד 25h.
Hebrew עִבְרִי, עִבְרִית f.
heed, take שָׁמַר II, VII.
herbage עֵשֶׂב 28.
herd בָּקָר 25, coll.
hero גִּבּוֹר.
Hezekiah חִזְקִיָּהוּ.
hide הִסְתִּיר, h. one's self סתר
  II, VII.
high, be רוּם 71.
hire שָׂכַר 25, מַשְׂכֹּרֶת 36.
holiness קֹדֶשׁ m. 28.
holy קָדוֹשׁ 23; be h. קָדַשׁ.

ENGLISH-HEBREW VOCABULARY. 105*

honour (*Vb.*) כִּבֵּד; (*Subst.*) כָּבוֹד 23.
horn קֶרֶן 28.
horse סוּס.
host צָבָא 25; Lord of Hosts יַהְוֶה צְבָאוֹת.
hot, be חָרָה 74.
house בַּיִת 38.
how כָּה 16*f.*
humble עָנִי 25.
hunger רָעָב 25.
husband אִישׁ 38.
Hushai חוּשַׁי.

idol אֱלִיל.
if אִם, כִּי, ἐάν.
imagination (thought) מַחְשָׁבֶת 37*b*.
in, into בְּ 45.
incline (ear, heart) נטה V, 76*d*.
increase רָבָה 74.
indeed: render by *inf. abs.* of accompg. Verb, *v.* §63*d*.
inheritance נַחֲלָה.
innocent נָקִי 31*a*.
instruct ירה V, 76*f*.
Israel יִשְׂרָאֵל.

Jacob יַעֲקֹב.
Jahweh יהוה 9*b*.
Jebusite יְבוּסִי.
Jehoshaphat יְהוֹשָׁפָט.
Jehu יֵהוּא.
Jephthah יִפְתָּח.
Jeremiah יִרְמְיָהוּ.
Jericho יְרִיחוֹ.

Jerusalem יְרוּשָׁלַיִם 9*b*.
Job אִיּוֹב.
Jonathan יְהוֹנָתָן.
Joram יוֹרָם.
Jordan יַרְדֵּן *c. artic.*
Joseph יוֹסֵף.
Joshua יְהוֹשֻׁעַ.
joy שִׂמְחָה 35; מָשׂוֹשׂ 23 (Ex. 40).
Judah יְהוּדָה.
judge שָׁפַט.
judgement מִשְׁפָּט 24.
just צַדִּיק.

keep שָׁמַר; k. one's self II.
kill הָרַג, מות V, 71 *i. u.*
kind טוֹב.
kindle יצת V, 70.
king מֶלֶךְ 28.
kingdom מַמְלָכָה 33*b*, מַלְכוּת 37*a*.
knee בֶּרֶךְ 28.
know יָדַע 68*f*.

lad נַעַר 28*i*.
lamp נֵר.
land (country) אֶרֶץ f. 28, artic. 17*d*; (for cultivation) אֲדָמָה 34*b*.
large גָּדוֹל 23.
law, go to נִשְׁפַּט, with אֶת־.
leper מְצֹרָע.
lest פֶּן 41, 4.
lie (*subst.*) כָּזָב 25, שֶׁקֶר 28; (*vb.*) כזב.
lie, l. down שָׁכַב impf., *a*.
life חַיִּים.
lift up רום V, 71; (the voice, eye) נָשָׂא 76*e*.

light, be קַל (קלל) 73.
light up אוֹר V, 71.
lightning בָּרָק 25.
like כְּ.
lion אֲרִי, אַרְיֵה 30
little קָטֹן 26d.
live חָיָה 76c. As the Lord liveth
  חַי יהוה 90b.
lodge לִין 72.
long, how 1.? עַד אָנָה, עַד מָתַי.
longer, no 1. לֹא ... עוֹד.
longsuffering אֶרֶךְ אַפַּיִם 25h.
look נבט V, 67; רָאָה 74.
lord אָדוֹן 23, בַּעַל 28. The Lord
  (Jahweh) יהוה 9b; אֲדֹנָי,
  preff. 10c.
loud (voice) גָּדוֹל.
lying: render by a circumlocution with gen. of שֶׁקֶר. Cf. false.

maid, maiden נַעֲרָה 35.
make עָשָׂה 74; (a covenant) כָּרַת.
man אִישׁ 38, אָדָם; (mankind) אָדָם.
Manasseh מְנַשֶּׁה.
many רַב pl. 26; be, become m.
  רָב (רבב) 73.
master בַּעַל 28.
meal-offering מִנְחָה 35.
meet, to לִקְרַאת.
memory זִכָּרוֹן 23d.
merciful חַנּוּן; be m. חָנַן 73, acc. pers.
mercy חֶסֶד 28.
messenger מַלְאָךְ 24b.

midst תָּוֶךְ 29c; from the m. of
  מִתּוֹךְ seq. gen.; in our m.
  בְּקִרְבֵּנוּ.
might עֹז; בֹּחַ 26c.
month חֹדֶשׁ 28.
moon יָרֵחַ.
morning בֹּקֶר 28.
Moses מֹשֶׁה.
mother אֵם 26.
mountain הַר 26. Artic. 26cε.
mourn סָפַד.
mouth פֶּה 38.
myriad רְבָבָה 34.

name שֵׁם 24f. pl. ות.
near קָרוֹב 23; draw n. קָרַב.
neighbour שָׁכֵן 25f; (companion)
  רֵעַ. Cf.: one.
night לַיְלָה m.
no (adj.) לֹא ... כֹּל.
no one, none, nobody אֵין c. genet.
  (part.) 41, 2.
not לֹא; in prohibitions אַל 41, 3.
nought, come to (perish) אָבַד
  66a; bring to n. (one's counsel) פרר V, 73.
now עַתָּה.
number מִסְפָּר 24.
numerous, v. many.

of מִן 44; (bef. agent=by) לְ.
offer (sacrifice) עָלָה V, 74.
oil שֶׁמֶן.
old זָקֵן 25; be, become o. זָקֵן.
olive זַיִת 29a.
on עַל 43a; בְּ.

one (single) אֶחָד 39a; (each)
one to the other אִישׁ אֶל־רֵעֵהוּ.
open פָּתַח 65.
oppress לָחַץ 65e.
oppressor, enemy צַר 26c.
ornament תִּפְאֶרֶת f. 36g.
orphan יָתוֹם 23.
other (adj.) אַחֵר; (pron.) see: one.
out, out of מִן 44.
outstretched, part. pass. of נָטָה 76d.
over עַל 43a.
ox (young) פַּר 29cε.

palace הֵיכָל 24.
part חֵלֶק 28l.
part (separate) הִבְדִּיל; (intrans.) נִפְרַד.
pass, come to (of events foretold) בּוֹא 76h; bring to p. בּוֹא V.
path נָתִיב 23, נְתִיבָה 22.
pay שָׁלַם.
peace שָׁלוֹם 23.
peculiar: a p. people עַם סְגֻלָּה.
people עַם 26cε λαός; גּוֹי 19b ἔθνος.
perceive בִּין 72.
perfect שָׁלֵם 25f.
perhaps אוּלַי.
perish אָבַד 66a.
pervert (judgement) נטה V, 76.
Pharaoh פַּרְעֹה.
Philistine פְּלִשְׁתִּי, pl. תִּים; genly. without Artic.
pilgrimage מְגֻרִים.

pitch (tent) נָטָה 76d.
place (subst.) מָקוֹם 23, pl. וֹת; (vb.) הֶעֱמִיד.
plant נָטַע 67 e.f.
plead one's cause רִיב רִיב פּ׳ 72.
pleasure חֵפֶץ 28; take p. חָפֵץ 65h, in בְּ.
pollute טִמֵּא 75; p. one's self II, VII.
poor אֶבְיוֹן.
portion חֵלֶק 28l.
possession, property סְגֻלָּה. Cf.: peculiar.
pour, p. out שָׁפַךְ 70.
praise (vb.) הִלֵּל; pass. IV; (subst.) תְּהִלָּה.
pray הִתְפַּלֵּל, to אֶל, for בְּעַד; I pray thee, you (doch) נָא.
prayer תְּפִלָּה.
precious, be יָקַר 68e.
preserve שָׁמַר.
priest כֹּהֵן 24.
prince נָשִׂיא 23a.
prophesy נבא II, 76e.
prophet נָבִיא 23b.
prove בָּחַן.
pull down הָרַס.
pursue, רָדַף; p. after אַחֲרֵי ר׳.
pursuer רֹדֵף part.

queen מַלְכָּה 35a.

rain (subst.) מָטָר 25; (vb. trans.) הִמְטִיר.
ram אַיִל 28.
ransom כֹּפֶר 28.

rebuke הֹכִיחַ V; pass. II, 68.
recount סִפֵּר.
redeem גָּאַל 65e.
redeemer גֹּאֵל 24e.
refuge מַחֲסֶה 31; take r. חָסָה 75,
  in בְּ.
refuse מֵאֵן 65b.
regard (look) נָבַט V, 67.
regard (æstimare) חָשַׁב.
Rehoboam רְחַבְעָם.
reign מָלַךְ; V.
rejoice גִּיל 72.
rejoicing גִּילָה.
remember זָכַר.
remove (change one's dwelling
  place) נָסַע 67f; (put away)
  הֶחֱרִיק V; סוּר.
reproach חֶרְפָּה 35c.b.
rest נוּחַ 71.
return שׁוּב 71.
Reuben רְאוּבֵן.
rich עָשִׁיר 23.
riddle חִידָה 22.
right (hand, side) יָמִין 23.
righteous צַדִּיק.
righteousness צֶדֶק 28a; suff. צִ.
rise, r. up קוּם 71; rise early
  הִשְׁכִּים.
river נָהָר 25b.
rock צוּר.
rod שֵׁבֶט 28, מַטֶּה 31.
roll גָּלַל 73.
ruins חָרְבוֹת f. 35a.
rule מָשַׁל, over בְּ.

Sabbath שַׁבָּת f. S.-day יוֹם חַשּׁ׳.

safety, in לְבֶטַח.
saints חָסִיד 23; קָדוֹשׁ 23 pl.
Samaria שֹׁמְרוֹן.
Samson שִׁמְשׁוֹן.
sanctuary מִקְדָּשׁ 24a.
satisfied, be שָׂבַע (ē) c. acc.;
satisfy V.
Saul שָׁאוּל.
save יָשַׁע V, 68; נָצַל V, 67; מִלַּט.
say אָמַר 66. Saying, לֵאמֹר 10c.
scatter פּוּץ V, 71.
sea יָם 26.
season מוֹעֵד 24e; עֵת 26.
see רָאָה 74.
seed זֶרַע 28.
seek בִּקֵּשׁ 60b.
seer חֹזֶה, רֹאֶה 31.
sell מָכַר; pass. II.
send, s. forth שָׁלַח 65, I, III; s.
  over עָבַר 65 V.
separate הִבְדִּיל.
serpent נָחָשׁ.
servant נַעַר 28i, עֶבֶד 28.
serve עָבַד acc. pers. 83e.
set (place) שִׂים 72; הִצִּיב 70; s.
  on fire יָצַת V, 70.
shadow צֵל 26.
shame בֹּשֶׁת f.; be put to s. בּוֹשׁ
  71i, 77.
sharp שָׁנוּן 23.
shave (head) גִּלָּה 65.
shed שָׁפַךְ.
shekel שֶׁקֶל 28.
shepherd רֹעֶה 31a.
shield מָגֵן 26 (‿ unchangeable).
shine אוֹר 71i; make to s. V.

ENGLISH-HEBREW VOCABULARY. 109*

shoe נַעַל 28.
short, be קָצַר.
show רָאָה 74 V.
shut סָגַר.
sickness חֳלִי 30c.
Sidon צִידוֹן.
sigh אֲנָחָה 34.
signet-ring טַבַּעַת 36c.
silence, keep הֶחֱרִישׁ.
silver כֶּסֶף 28r.
sin עָוֹן m. 23c, חַטָּאת 36e.
sin, to חָטָא 75, against לְ.
since (prep.) מִן; (conj.) מֵאָז.
single (one) אֶחָד.
sinners חַטָּאִים.
sister אָחוֹת 38.
sit יָשַׁב 68f.
slave עֶבֶד 28.
slay הָרַג; (for sacrifice) שָׁחַט 65.
sleep יָשֵׁן 68d.
small קָטֹן 26d; be s. קָטֹן.
smite נָכָה V, 76d.
snare מוֹקֵשׁ 24.
Sodom סְדֹם.
Solomon שְׁלֹמֹה.
son בֵּן 38.
son-in-law חָתָן 25.
sorrow יָגוֹן 23.
soul נֶפֶשׁ f. 28, pl. וֹת.
sow זָרַע 65.
spare חָמַל 65, seq. עַל pers.
speak דִּבֶּר, אָמַר 66.
spear רֹמַח 28.
spirit רוּחַ f. pl. וֹת.
spoil בָּזַז 73.
spy מְרַגֵּל 24.

spy, spy out רִגֵּל.
staff מַשֶּׁה 31; שֵׁבֶט 28.
stand עָמַד 65, נִצַּב 70; take one's s. הִתְיַצֵּב.
star כּוֹכָב 24.
stead, instead תַּחַת 43b.
steal גָּנַב; pass. IV.
still עוֹד, suff. 40f.
stone אֶבֶן f. 28.
stool, v. foot.
stranger גֵּר.
straw תֶּבֶן.
strength עֹז 26c.
stretch forth (the hand) שָׁלַח; נָטָה 76d (esp. of superior to inferior).
strong חָזָק 25.
suck יָנַק 69a; give s. V.
sun שֶׁמֶשׁ m. and f. 28.
swear נִשְׁבַּע, by בְּ; make, cause to s. V.
swift קַל (קלל) 73.
sword חֶרֶב 28.

tabernacle מִשְׁכָּן m. 24.
table, tablet (for writing) לוּחַ m. pl. וֹת.
take לָקַח 67h; t. off (shoe &c.) נָשַׁל 67f.
talk דִּבֶּר.
teach לִמֵּד; teacher, part.
tear (of beast of prey) טָרַף.
tell (inform) נָגַד V, 67; (relate) סִפֵּר.
tent אֹהֶל 28.
terrible נוֹרָא.

testimony (law) עֵדוּת f. 37a.
than (compar.) מִן 82b.
that (adj.) הַהוּא 17c; (conj.) כִּי;
that ... not אֵין 41, 4.
then: in Exx. often used for
  'and' to suggest employment
  of ו consec.
there יֵשׁ; there is, was: see 'be'.
thigh יָרֵךְ 25e.
things (events) הַדְּבָרִים.
this זֶה 16a.
thought מַחֲשָׁבָה 33.
threshing floor גֹּרֶן 28p.
throne כִּסֵּא 34d.
thus כֹּה.
till (prep.) עַד.
till, to עָבַד.
time פַּעַם 26;(=Germ.mal, Fr.fois)
  פַּעַם f. 28. Twice, two times
  פַּעֲמַיִם.
to-day הַיּוֹם 17a.
to-morrow מָחָר.
tongue לָשׁוֹן f. 23.
tooth שֵׁן 26.
touch נָגַע 67 e.f.
transgression פֶּשַׁע 28.
transgressor פֹּשֵׁעַ 24e.
tree עֵץ 24 f. (also coll.)
tribe שֵׁבֶט 28.
trumpet שׁוֹפָר m. 24, pl. ות.
trust בָּטַח 65, in בְּ.
tumult הָמוֹן 23.
turn back שׁוּב 71.
twice, v. time.

under תַּחַת 43b.

understand בִּין 72; have, get
  understanding בִּין; הִשְׂכִּיל
  (Ex. 46).
unpunished, leave נקה III;
  remain u. II, 76d.
unto לְ 45, אֶל־ 43a; (usque ad)
  עַד 43a.
upon עַל־ 43a.
upright יָשָׁר 25.
Uriah אוּרִיָּה.

vain, in לַשָּׁוְא (Ex. 44).
vengeance נְקָמָה 34.
venison צַיִד 29.
verily: render by Inf. Abs. bef.
  finite Verb, 63d.
vessel כְּלִי 38.
vineyard כֶּרֶם 28.
virgin בְּתוּלָה 22.
vision מַחֲזֶה 31.
voice קוֹל m.
vow נָדַר, נֶדֶר, c. suff. יְ 28m.

wages, v. hire.
wake up יקץ 69a, 77.
walk הִתְהַלֵּךְ 22.
wall חוֹמָה.
wander נוּעַ 71.
want, to חָסֵר 65h, c. Acc. 83b.
war מִלְחָמָה 36g;man ofw.אִישׁ מ׳.
wash רָחַץ 65.
watch שָׁמַר.
water, waters מַיִם 38.
water, to (give to drink) שׁקה
  V, 74, 77.
way דֶּרֶךְ 28.

ENGLISH-HEBREW VOCABULARY. 111*

weak רָפֶה 31b.
weary one's self, be weary יָגַע 68d.
weep בָּכָה 74.
weight מִשְׁקָל 24.
well, do יָטַב 69 V.
what? מָה 16e, f. 45e6.
where שָׁם...אֲשֶׁר; where? אַיֵּה, suff. 42f.
wherefore, why לָמָה 45e6.
whether (in an indirect question) הֲ 42a; whether ... or הֲ...אִם... 42d.
who, which אֲשֶׁר 87.
who? מִי 16e.
whole כֹּל 26.
wicked רָשָׁע 25, רַע 26.
wickedness, do wickedly, v. evil.
wild ox רְאֵם.
wilderness מִדְבָּר 24.
willing, be אָבָה 66a, seq. לְ c. Inf. 84d.

wine יַיִן 29.
wise, on this: v. saying.
wise (man) חָכָם 25; be w. חָכַם 65.
witness עֵד 22.
with עִם 43d, אֵת 43c.
within (prep.) קֶרֶב w. suffs., within me בְּקִרְבִּי. Cf.: midst.
wood עֵץ 24f, pl. pieces of wood; (forest) יַעַר 28.
word דָּבָר 25; אֹמֶר 28o.
work פֹּעַל, מַעֲשֶׂה 28.
wound פֶּצַע 28; suff. 'פ.
write כָּתַב.

Year שָׁנָה f. 33, pl. ־ים.
youth נְעוּרִים 22.

Zion צִיּוֹן f.

APPENDIX.

Explanatory Notes on Gen. 1—3.

I. 1. רֵאשִׁית f. beginning. ‖ 2. הָיְתָה 74l. ‖ תֹּהוּ 30d wasteness, waste. ‖ בֹּהוּ emptiness, וָ 46a4. ‖ תְּהוֹם tumult of waters, the deep. רחף III hover (of bird hovering over its young Deut. 32,11). ‖ 3. וַיֹּאמֶר 66a3. ‖ יְהִי 76b. ‖ 4. וַיַּרְא 74q3. ‖ 5. לָאוֹר 17e. ‖ קָרָא 13a8. 6. בְּתוֹךְ 29c. ‖ וִיהִי 11g2. ‖ לְבִים 45/β. ‖ 7. וַיַּעַשׂ 74oε. ‖ בְּעַל לְ above. ‖ 9. יִקָּווּ 74m. ‖ וְתֵרָאֶה 74ua. Serê under ת s. 65b1. ‖ 10. יַמִּים pl. not numerical but to indicate extent: "expanse of sea", "ocean". יַבָּשָׁה the dry land (terra firma).
11. דֶּשֶׁא verdure, grass; דָּשָׁא become green, spring up, V causat. ‖ זרע V produce seed; זָרֵעַ 65d. ‖ עֹשֶׂה 74g3. ‖ אֲשֶׁר זַרְעוֹ בוֹ 87a. ‖ עַל־הָאָרֶץ to be joined with תִּדְשֵׁא הָאָרֶץ. ‖ 12. וַתּוֹצֵא 76g. לְבִינֵהוּ 22iβ. ‖ 14. לְאֹתֹת וְהָיוּ 86f. ‖ וְהָיוּ Wāw cons. 64c. ‖ בְצָדְרִים fixed, stated times, seasons. ‖ יָמִים 38. ‖ 15. לְהָאִיר 71.
16. שְׁנֵי 39b. ‖ הַגְּדֹלִים 17h. ‖ הַגָּדֹל 82c. ‖ קָטֹן small. ‖ 17. וַיִּתֵּן 67i, posuit. ‖ וּלְהַבְדִּיל (ed. Baer) 5d. ‖ 20. יִשְׁרְצוּ to move in a mass, swarm. שֶׁרֶץ swarm, mass (esp. of the lower forms of animal life), acc. 83b. ‖ עוֹף coll. birds. ‖ יְעוֹפֵף 71b.
21. תַּנִּין sea-monster, whale, κῆτος. ‖ חַיָּה, fem. of חַי. ‖ אֲשֶׁר 87e (acc. depending on שָׁרְצוּ 83b). ‖ לְמִינֵהֶם 22k3. ‖ כָּנָף עוֹף winged birds. ‖ 22. וַיְבָרֶךְ 65b1. 64lβ. ‖ לֵאמֹר 65o. ‖ פְּרוּ 74m. ‖ רְבוּ 74oγ. ‖ 24. תּוֹצֵא 76g. ‖ וְרֶמֶשׂ 46a4. ‖ וְחַיְתוֹ 20cβ.
26. נַעֲשֶׂה 74v. ‖ וְיִרְדּוּ 74m. ‖ וּבְכָל, after this word חַיַּת appears to have dropped out. ‖ 27. זָכָר mas, masculus. ‖ נְקֵבָה female, oppos. זָכָר. ‖ 28. וְכִבְשֻׁהָ 79iγ. ‖ 29. נָתַתִּי 67i; perf. 47b. ‖ אֲשֶׁר־בּוֹ 87b. ‖ זֹרֵעַ 28g. ‖ אָכְלָה food. ‖ 30. After חַיַּת הָאָרֶץ supply נָתַתִּי. 31. הַשִּׁשִּׁי Article sometimes with the adj. only (e. g. 41, 26) esp. with ordinal numbers.

II. 1. וַיְכֻלּוּ 64f. 74m. ‖ 2. וַיְכַל 74s. ‖ אֲשֶׁר עָשָׂה 87e. ‖ שָׁבַת rest. ‖ 3. לַעֲשׂוֹת 74k, לְ 45eβ. בָּרָא לַעֲשׂוֹת, union of two verbs to

APPENDIX. 113*

express a single idea (§84): wh. he had made as Creator, cf. Ewald
§ 285a. ‖ 4. תּוֹלְדֹת (only plur. constr.) generations; hence family
history, history. ‖ אֵרֶץ וְשָׁמַיִם acc., depending on עֲשׂוֹת. ‖ 5. שִׂיחַ
plant. ‖ טֶרֶם יִהְיֶה "was not yet". טֶרֶם is usually joined with the
Impf. (47c), even where the reference is to the past, since it contains
in itself the idea of incompleteness: 19, 4. 24, 45; in the same way
בְּטֶרֶם 37, 18. ‖ לַעֲבֹד 65n.

6. אֵד mist. ‖ יַעֲלֶה 74gα, p. Addend. to 47c. The Impf. is also
employed to denote such events as happen frequently, and to indicate "use and wont", or continually recurring actions: G 29, 2
הִשְׁקוּ "they were wont to water"; hence, too, when the reference
is to lasting events in the sphere of the past: וְאֵד יַעֲלֶה "but a mist
went up continually"; G 2, 10 יַשְׁקֶה. ‖ 7. וַיִּיצֶר 70. ‖ עָפָר. The
material of which anyth. is made appears usually in the Acc.: cf.
1 Kgs. 18, 32. ‖ וַיִּפַּח 67. ‖ 8. וַיְהִי 67. ‖ אָדָם n. pr. ‖ בְּקֶדֶם litly.:
"from the East", i. e. Eastwards, in the E. (cf. Fr. s'approcher de
qn.). ‖ וַיַּשֵּׂם 72. ‖ 9. וַיַּצְמַח 65sβ. ‖ נֶחְמָד 65k. ‖ עֵץ הַחַיִּים 17g. ‖ דַּעַת
68f. ‖ יָצָא acc. 55b note. ‖ יָרַד 46a4. ‖ 10. לְהַשְׁקוֹת 74k. ‖ יִפָּרֵד
s. to v. 6. ‖ יִהְיֶה Wāw cons. ‖ רָאשִׁים 38, "beginnings" (viz: of
streams).

11. הַסֹּבֵב predicate. ‖ שֵׁנִי and חֲוִילָה nomm. pr.; so v. 13
בּוּשׁ, עֵירוֹן; v. 14 חִדֶּקֶל Tigris, אַשּׁוּר Assyria, פְּרָת Euphrates. ‖ אֲשֶׁר־שָׁם
87b. ‖ 12. זָהָב 5d. ‖ הַהִוא 9b. ‖ בְּדֹלַח Bdellium (an aromatic resin-
ous substance). ‖ שֹׁהַם Onyx?, Beryll?. ‖ 14. קִדְמַת (only st. c.) in
front of, before. ‖ הִוא הִיא 85c*. ‖ 15. וַיִּקַּח 67h. ‖ וַיַּנִּחֵהוּ 71y. ‖
לְעָבְדָהּ 55e; suffix. objecti 78a; גַּן here fem.

16. וַיְצַו 74s. ‖ אָכֹל 63d. ‖ תֹּאכֵל 66a2. ‖ 17. בְּיוֹם 44b. ‖ אָכְלְךָ
55e. 65o. ‖ מוֹת (71i). 63d. ‖ 18. הֱיוֹת 76b. ‖ וְהָיָה 28k. ‖ 19. וַיִּצֶר 70. ‖
וַיָּבֵא 76h. ‖ לִרְאוֹת 74k. ‖ שְׁמוֹ 24f. ‖ בָּא עַד 13bδ.

21. וַיַּפֵּל 67a. ‖ תַּרְדֵּמָה deep sleep. ‖ וַיִּישָׁן 68d. ‖ בְּצַלְעֹתָיו 25i. ‖
תַּחְתֶּנָּה 43b. ‖ 22. וַיִּבֶן 740γ. ‖ וַיְבִאֶהָ 76h; suff. 79f 2. ‖ 23. הַפַּעַם
17a. ‖ לָקֳחָה (ed. Baer), קַח 60b. ‖ 24. עַל־כֵּן for this reason, therefore. ‖ וְהָיוּ וְדָבַק Wāw cons. ‖ בְּאִשְׁתּוֹ 38. ‖ 25. עֲרוּמִּים 26d. ‖ יִתְבֹּשָׁשׁוּ
77 (₇ 62dγ).

III. 1. עָרוּם בֵּן 82bα; ע wise, cunning. ‖ אַף really; הַאַף=אַף
42h. ‖ 2. אֲבָל Ipf.=we may 47c. ‖ 3. תְּמֻתוּן 67. ‖ תְּבָרוּן 71i; יֶן

114*

53a.b. ‖ 4. לֹא־מוּת 63d. ‖ 5. יֹדֵעַ 65eβ. ‖ יִפָּקְחוּ 64c. ‖ יִהְיִיתֶם 76b. ‖ כֵּאלֹהִים 10c4.

6. וַתֵּרֶא 74oô. ‖ תַּאֲוָה desire; here concrete: something to be desired. ‖ לְעֵינַיִם 17e. ‖ נֶחְמָד part. II of חָמַד (65k) desirable, pleasant. ‖ וַתִּתֵּן 67i. ‖ 7. וַיֵּדְעוּ 68f. ‖ הָפַר sew together. ‖ עָלֶה 31c. ‖ וַיַּעֲשׂוּ 74m.p. ‖ לָהֶם sibi 79b. ‖ חֲגֹרָה girdle, apron. ‖ 8. לְרוּחַ הַיּוֹם about the cool of the day=towards evening; לְ cf. G 8,11. 17,21. ‖ וַיִּתְחַבֵּא sing. 86i. ‖ עֵץ collect. ‖ 9. אַיֶּכָּה 42f; suff. הַ= 22ia. ‖ 10. וָאִירָא 76g. ‖ אָנֹכִי 14g. ‖ וָאֵחָבֵא 65b1.

11. הִגִּיד 67a. ‖ אֲתָּה 14c.h. ‖ הֲבֶן 42a. ‖ בִּמְּנִי... אֲשֶׁר 87a. ‖ צִוִּיתִיךָ 74eβ. ‖ לְבִלְתִּי 41,5. ‖ אָכַל 65o. ‖ 12. נָתְתָה 67i. ‖ עִמָּדִי 43d. ‖ 13. מַה־זֹּאת 42g. ‖ עָבִיתָ 74ea. ‖ הִשִּׁיאַנִי 76e; ánī 79e. ‖ 14. כִּי־ because. ‖ מִכָּל־; כִּן here particularises: of all the beasts thou art the one on which the curse falls. ‖ תֵּלֵךְ 68i. ‖ יְמֵי 38. ‖ 15. אֵיבָה enmity. ‖ אָשִׁית 72d. ‖ יְשׁוּפְךָ 71. ‖ יְשׁוּפֵךְ רֹאשׁ 83i. ‖ תְּשׁוּפֶנּוּ 80a.

16. הִרְבָּה 74wô. ‖ אַרְבֶּה 74ga. ‖ הֵרוֹן ἄπ. λεγ. conception. תֵּלְדִי 68f. ‖ 17. בַּעֲבוּר on account of, for (thy) sake. ‖ תֹּאכֲלֶנָּה 80a; בְּ: when followed by ג demonstr. with suff. the ב of אֲבָל receives Chaṭēph-Pathach instead of Šʷwâ. ‖ 18. דַרְדַּר thorns. ‖ הִצְמִיחַ, Subj. the earth. ‖ לְךָ 45c. ‖ וְאָכַלְתָּ Wāw cons. 64c. ‖ 19. זֵעָה sweat. תֹּאכַל 13a8. ‖ שׁוּבְךָ 71. ‖ אַתָּה 14c. ‖ 20. חַוָּה i. e. Life.

21. כָּתְנוֹת 36f. ‖ עוֹר skin. ‖ וַיַּלְבִּשֵׁם 79e. ‖ 22. כְּאַחַד 21g. ‖ לָדַעַת 45fa. ‖ וְלָקַח Wāw cons. 64c. ‖ וָחַי 76c; ; 46a4. ‖ 23. שָׁם here: drive out. ‖ אֲשֶׁר... מִשָּׁם 87a. ‖ 24. וַיְגָרֶשׁ 64lβ. 65b1. ‖ מִקֶּדֶם see on G 2, 8. ‖ לַהַט flame. ‖ הֶפֶךְ VII to turn in every direction. ‖ לִשְׁמֹר 55d. ‖ דֶּרֶךְ עֵץ הַחַיִּים 21f.

Explanatory Notes on Pss. 1—3.

I. 1. On the Perfects v. 1 (הָלַךְ &c.), the Impf. (וְהָגָה) v. 2 s. 47d. ‖ בַּעֲצַת s. עֵצָה. ‖ רְשָׁעִים without artic. 17g2. ‖ חַטָּאִים pl. tant. sinners. ‖ מוֹשַׁב consessus. ‖ 2. כִּי אִם but (after a negative). ‖ חָגָה meditate. ‖ וְלַיְלָה 46a4. ‖ 3. וְהָיָה Wāw cons. 64a. ‖ שָׁתַל (poet.) plant. ‖ נָבֵל wither, impf. יִבֹּל. ‖ 4. מֹץ chaff. ‖ נָדַף, 67, scatter, רוּחַ 80a. ‖ 6. תֹּאבֵד 66a.

APPENDIX.   115*

II. 1. רָגַשׁ raise a tumult, rage. ‖ רִיק vanity. ‖ 2. יִתְיַצְּבוּ still depending on לִבּה. ‖ רוֹזֵן only in poetry: prince. ‖ נְסַדוּ 68c; יָסַד to found, II here: crowd together, assemble. ‖ יַחַד together. ‖ 3. נָתַק break off, III break in pieces. ‖ מוֹסְרִים, מוֹסֵרוֹת (pl. tant.) vincula; suff. 22kα. ‖ עֲבֹת cord. ‖ 4. שָׂחַק laugh. ‖ לָעַג mock, לְ pers. ‖ לָמוֹ 45c. ‖ 5. אָז then. ‖ אֲלֵימוֹ 43a. ‖ חָרוֹן wrath, fierce anger. ‖ יְבַהֲלֵמוֹ 79c. ‖ 6. נָסַךְ here: establish, install (cf. יָצַק 70). ‖ הַר־קָדְשִׁי "My holy mt." When the adj. is periphrastically expressed by the genet. of the corresponding subst. the possessive pron. (*suff. nom.*) is appended to the latter; cf. Isa. 2, 20.

7. אֶל־ concerning, *de*, cf. ψ 69, 27. ‖ אֵחָז 14c. ‖ הַיּוֹם 17a. ‖ יְלִדְתִּךָ, i to be explained acc. to 11f1. ‖ 8. וְאֶתְּנָה 67i. ‖ אֶפֶס prop. cessation, hence: end. ‖ 9. רָעַע, impf. תָּרֹעֵם, 73 break, dash in pieces. בַּרְזֶל iron. ‖ נָפַץ I and III dash in pieces, shiver. ‖ 10. מְלָכִים Vocative. ‖ הִוָּסְרוּ 68; יָסַר II tolerative: let one's self be admonished, 49c. ‖ 11. אֲרֶץ 83e. ‖ רְעָדָה trembling. ‖ 12. נַשְּׁקוּ־בַר prob.: act with sincerity, uprightly; cf. G 41, 40. יַעְלְזוּ יְשָׁרִים Others: kiss ye the son (בַּר Aram.=son, Prov. 31, 2). ‖ דֶּרֶךְ acc. of nearer definition. 'ד=fortune, fate. ‖ בָּעַר to burn (*trans*. and *intrans.*); also, as here, kindle (*intr.*). ‖ כִּמְעַט *c. impf.* to indicate something that might easily happen. ‖ חוֹסֵי בוֹ 21g.

III. 1. לְדָוִד belonging to him=composed by him (לְ *auctoris*). ‖ 2. רַבּוּ 73g. ‖ קָמִים 71. ‖ 3. לְנַפְשִׁי; לְ in regard to, concerning, *de*, G 20, 13; cf. אֶל־ ψ 2,7. ‖ ה, יְשׁוּעָתָה accus. ending, now meaningless as in לַיְלָה 20c. ‖ בֵּאלֹהִים 10c4. ‖ סֶלָה a musical term, perhaps: forte. ‖ 4. בְּעַד, *suff.* בַּעֲדִי &c., round about. ‖ מֵרִים 71n. ‖ 5. קוֹלִי *acc. instr.* ‖ אֶקְרָא I call, 47d. ‖ וַיַּעֲנֵנִי and he answers (83e), hears me. Wāw cons. characterises the hearing as the *result* of the prayer. ‖ מֵהַר 44aγ. ‖ 6. יָאִישָׁנָה 64i. ‖ הֱקִיצוֹתִי 77; הֵקִיץ 71o. ‖ יִסְמְכֵנִי impf., because the reason is a permanent one. ‖ 7. אִירָא 76g. ‖ רְבָבוֹת 5d. ‖ שָׁתוּ 72d. ‖ שִׁית here without obj.=take up a position, "have arrayed themselves". ‖ 8. קוּמָה 71e3. ‖ הוֹשִׁיעֵנִי 68. ‖ הִכִּיתָ 76d. ‖ לֶחִי 83i. ‖ שִׁבַּרְתָּ 60f. ‖ 9. לַיהוָה 9b. ‖ בִּרְכָתֶךָ, supply תְּהִי or תָּבֹא, cf. 89e.

p. = pausal form.

Printed by W. Drugulin, Leipzig.

H. Reuther, Publisher, Berlin S.W.

ARABIC GRAMMAR
WITH
PARADIGMS,
LITERATURE, CHRESTOMATHY AND GLOSSARY
BY
D^R. A. SOCIN,
PROFESSOR IN THE UNIVERSITY OF TUBINGEN.
8o. XVI. 294 p. cloth 7 s. 6 d.

Opinions and Reviews.

The *need of a brief handbook for elementary instruction in Arabic has long been felt in England,* since the vast amount of matter contained in Prof. Wright's excellent grammar is apt to frighten rather than to encourage a beginner in this difficult branch of linguistic studies.

Dr. Socin of Tübingen, *therefore, deserves the sincere thanks of all engaged in Arabic tuition in this country for having recast into a new and more acceptable form the* late Prof. Petermann's "Brevis linguae arabicae grammatica" which forms the 4th part of the well-known series of introductory oriental grammars styled "Porta linguarum orientalium."

— — *Quite a novel feature is the addition of a series of well-chosen English sentences for translation into Arabic,* which *will be welcome to Indian Civil Service candidates* at least as a stepping-stone to Arabic composition on a larger scale. The general outlines of the grammar *have been preserved*, but the *hand of a judicious reviser is visible almost on every page* — — room has been made for a short chapter on syntax, which gives, in the narrow space of 22 pages *a clear and intelligible account of Arabic tenses, the governement of verb and noun, and simple and compound sentences.*

This will no doubt be highly appreciated by the student, and assist him in mastering the contents of such standard grammars as Wright's, Caspari's or De Sacy's.   Athenaeum March 19. 86.

The **Grammar** is *very definite and perspicuous in its statements*, and *nicely accurate, containing only what is necessary for a beginner, with scarcely any repetitions,* though well supplied with illustrative examples. — — The **bibliography** is *well*

London: WILLIAMS & NORGATE, 14 Henrietta Street, Covent Garden.
New York: B. WESTERMANN & Co., 383 Broadway.

H. Reuther, Publisher, Berlin S.W.

selected. The **chrestomathy** is *well arranged* for a beginner, and the **glossary** *is likewise well done.* — The *excellence of this work* is *that when it is mastered*, which is easy to a faithful student, the *foundation is laid for rapid* and *secure advance* to *proficiency in Arabic.* Prof. Socin has a speaking acquaintance with the language, and has avoided the minor inaccuracies that frequently beset the closet-scholar. Independent June, 25. 1885.

Hebrew Grammar

with Reading book, Exercises, Literature and Vocabularies

by

Hermann L. Strack, D. D., Ph. D.

Professor of Theology in Berlin.

HEBREW GRAMMAR	GRAMMAIRE HÉBRAÏQUE
WITH	AVEC
EXERCISES LITERATURE AND VOCABULARY	PARADIGMES, EXERCICES DE LECTURE, CHRESTOMATHIE ET INDICE BIBLIOGRAPHIQUE
by	par
Hermann L. Strack.	Herm. L. Strack.
Translated from the German by Arch^{d.} R. S. Kennedy.	Traduit de l'allemand par Ant. F. Baumgartner.
Second enlarged edition.	Edition revue et augmentée par l'auteur.
8. XVI. 264 p. cloth 5 *s.*	8o. XII. 250 p. sewed 3,6 *d.*

Opinions and Reviews.

Le Muséon, Janvier 1886: La grammaire hébraïque de Mr. Strack, spécialement dans la seconde édition, mérite d'*être qualifiée d'excellente;* elle donne ce qu'un livre de classe doit fournir pour mériter cette qualification ... C'est surtout dans l'exposé du verbe que l'auteur témoigne d'une *connaissance magistrale* et d'une *méthode scientifique,* unie à un système pratique excellent ...

Rev. Prof. *Aiken* (Princeton) in: *The Presbyterian Review*, July 1886. *This little book will be found useful even by advanced Hebrew scholars.*

The American 1886, No. 290: It is yet *the best Hebrew Grammar* for teaching purposes which has thus far appeared.

London: WILLIAMS & NORGATE, 14 Henrietta Street, Covent Garden.
New York: B. WESTERMANN & Co. 383 Broadway.

H. Reuther, Publisher, Berlin S.W.

The Guardian 1886, Aug. 25: A work which has a high reputation in Germany. It is *"the result of many years' experience"* in practical teaching.

Rev. Prof. *Kirkpatrick* (Cambridge) in: *The Expositor*, June 1886: Prof. Strack's name is a guarantee of accurate and careful work.

Rev. *Ch. H. H. Wright* (Dublin) in: *Irish Ecclesiastical Gazette*, July 1886: A *most valuable synopsis* of Hebrew Grammar... *The syntax is peculiarly satisfactory*.

Prof. *Will. Harper* (Yale College) in: *Hebraica*, January 1886: In this work, Dr. Strack has given an indication of the Hebrew learning for which he is so well known, not only in Europe, but also in America. But more than this, he has indicated his ability as a practical teacher. *The book is fresh, vigourous, scientific.*

Dr. *Landauer* (Strasbourg) in: *Deutsche Litteraturzeitung* 1886, No. 13, „Hier erkennt man in jedem Paragraphen, dass man es mit einem tüchtig geschulten Hebraisten zu thun hat, und es wäre im Interesse der Theologie-Studierenden lebhaft zu wünschen, *dass das Buch auf den Gymnasien allgemein angeführt würde.*"

Prof. *S. R. Driver* (Oxford) in: *The Academy*, Dec. 1883 [1re édit.]: The work is an *eminently practical* one and bears traces throughout of the independent labour, which has been bestowed upon it.

Prof. *Kautzsch* (Tübingen) in: *Theologische Literaturzeitung 1884*, No. 2: „Überall gibt sich gründliche Vertrautheit mit dem Stoff und *reichliche pädagogische Erfahrung* kund."

Prof. *A. Kolbe* in: *Theologisches Literaturblatt 1883*, No. 38: „Schon der Name des Verfassers lässt etwas Gediegenes erwarten, zumal wissenschaftliche Selbständigkeit, ausgebreitete Gelehrsamkeit und praktische Erfahrung sich bei ihm in glücklichster Weise vereinigen. Dieser Erwartung entspricht die vorliegende Leistung."

Paradigms to the Hebrew Grammar by HERM. L. STRACK. 8º. 22 p. 6d.

LITTERATURA SYRIACA
without the
Syriac Grammar
by
DR. EBERH. NESTLE.
8º. IV. 66 p. M. 2.—.

London: WILLIAMS & NORGATE, 14 Henrietta Street, Covent Garden.
New York: B. WESTERMANN & Co., 383 Broadway.

H. Reuther, Publisher Berlin S.W.

Just issued:
SYRIAC GRAMMAR
with
Bibliography, Chrestomathy and Glossary
by
Dr. Eberhard Nestle.

Translated from the *second* German edition
by
Arch[d.] R. S. Kennedy, B. D.

8º. XVI. 267 p. cloth 8 s. 6 d.

It is an admirable little work, the best probably for beginners, as it contains a short but complete grammar, a reading specimen with analysis, a survey of Syriac literature, a Chrestomathy consisting of the first four chapters of Genesis, and a Glossary containing all the words occurring in the Chrestomathy, and explaining all the diffcult forms.

Trübner's Record.

L'éditeur »a refait la grammaire de fond en comble et il l'a mise au courant des travaux qui ont paru sur ce sujet depuis 1881. Elle comprend non seulement les éléments nécessaires à l'étude de la langue, mais aussi un résumé de l'histoire de la grammaire syriaque. La syntaxe, exclue de la première édition, occupe quelques pages, etc. etc.« *R. Duval.*

Dass Nestle's Grammatik *praktisch* ist, beweist der Umstand, dass eine Neuauflage nöthig geworden ist. Sie wird sich in dem neuen Gewande noch grösserer Gunst zu erfreuen haben. *Prof. Fried. Baethgen.*

London: WILLIAMS & NORGATE, 14 Henrietta Street, Covent Garden.
New York: B. WESTERMANN & Co., 383 Broadway.

H. Reuther, Verlagsbuchhandlung in Berlin S.W.

Keilinschriftliche Bibliothek:

Sammlung
von
assyrischen und babylonischen Texten
in
Umschrift und Übersetzung.

In Verbindung mit
Dr. L. Abel, Dr. C. Bezold, Dr. P. Jensen,
Dr. F. E. Peiser, Dr. H. Winckler
herausgegeben
von
Eberhard Schrader.

Das vorstehende Unternehmen ist dazu bestimmt, die seit einer Reihe von Jahren im Bereiche des alten Assyrien und Babylonien gemachten Inschriftenfunde in einer chronologisch und zugleich sachlich geordneten Sammlung in ihren wichtigsten Repräsentanten zu vereinigen und in transcribirtem Text mit gegenüber stehender deutscher Übersetzung vorzulegen Wird die Wiedergabe des transcribirten Originaltextes den Anforderungen strenger Wissenschaft Genüge zu leisten bestrebt sein, so wird die beigefügte wortgetreue Übersetzung die für die Geschichte so hochwichtigen Inschriftenfunde auch den nicht assyrologisch vorgebildeten Lesern, in erster Linie Historikern und Theologen, aber auch Juristen und Alterthumsfreunden im weitesten Sinne des Worts zugänglich zu machen suchen. Durch sorgfältige literarische Nachweise und die Beifügung sachlicher und sprachlicher Erläuterungen in knappester Form ist für die Orientirung des Lesers auf dem betreffenden Gebiete in entsprechender Weise gesorgt. Bezüglich der bei Auswahl, Transcription und Übersetzung im Einzelnen befolgten Grundsätze verweisen wir auf das Vorwort. Das Zusammenwirken einer Reihe von fachmännischen Gelehrten, an deren Spitze **Prof. Dr. Eberh. Schrader** in Berlin steht, dürfte dem Werke eine dauernde Bedeutung sichern.

Der erschienene I. Band (XVI, 218 S. gr. 8. Mit 1 Karte M. 9.—) umfasst die historischen Texte des alt-assyrischen Reichs nebst chronologischen Beigaben. Band II der keilinschriftlichen Bibliothek, welcher zum Herbst 1889 erscheinen wird, bringt in Umschrift und Übersetzung, sowie mit den nötigen einleitenden Bemerkungen und sonstigen Erläuterungen versehen, ausgewählte

Inschriften:
Tiglath-Pileser's II. (III.);
Sargon's II.;
Sanherib's;
Asarhaddon's;
Asurbanipal's; ferner
Inschriften aus der Zeit der Ausgänge des assyrischen Reichs;
Die babylonische Chronik betr. die Zeit seit dem Regierungsantritte Tiglath-Pileser's II. (III.);
Den babylonischen Regenten-Kanon;
Den Kanon des Ptolemäus;
dazu: **eine historische Karte des neu-assyrischen Reichs von 745 v. Chr. bis zum Falle Ninivehs.**

Die ganze Sammlung ist auf vier, in jährlichen Zwischenräumen erscheinende Bände im Umfange von je ca. 15 Bogen bemessen, jedem Bande historischen Inhalts wird eine erläuternde Karte von Prof. H. Kiepert beigegeben sein. Der Preis eines jeden Bandes wird M. 9.— nicht übersteigen.

Indem wir zur Subscription auf die

Keilinschriftliche Bibliothek

hiermit ergebenst einladen, bemerken wir, dass jede solide Buchhandlung in der Lage ist, den erschienenen I. Band auf Verlangen zur Einsicht vorzulegen.

Berlin, Ostern 1889.

H. Reuther's Verlagsbuchhandlung.

London: WILLIAMS & NORGATE, 14 Henrietta Str., Covent Garden.
New York: B. WESTERMANN & Co. 383 Broadway.

www.ingramcontent.com/pod-product-compliance
Lightning Source LLC
Chambersburg PA
CBHW032100220426
43664CB00008B/1078